The Paternity of Abraham Lincoln;

THE PATERNITY OF
ABRAHAM LINCOLN

WILLIAM E. BARTON

THE PATERNITY OF ABRAHAM LINCOLN

WAS HE THE SON OF THOMAS LINCOLN?

AN ESSAY ON
THE CHASTITY OF NANCY HANKS

BY

WILLIAM E. BARTON
AUTHOR OF " THE SOUL OF ABRAHAM LINCOLN," ETC.

NEW YORK
GEORGE H. DORAN COMPANY

THIS BOOK IS DEDICATED
TO THOSE WHO HONOR ABRAHAM LINCOLN
AND DESIRE TO KNOW THE TRUTH

PREFACE

A LARGE portion of this volume was written before the author realized that it had begun. In the preparation of his former book, *The Soul of Abraham Lincoln,* the author undertook a painstaking study of Lincoln's successive environments, which involved, incidentally, inquiry into his heredity. This latter aspect was of secondary interest, nor was the author greatly interested at the beginning in the various theories which he encountered as to Lincoln's paternity. While he made careful notes of all material which came to him in his researches, he had no occasion to utilize any of the subject matter in his preparation of the other volume, nor did he expect to write this one.

As he proceeded, however, he was surprised to find a number of intelligent collectors of Lincoln books and students of his history who believed that Abraham Lincoln was not the son of Thomas Lincoln. He also found that while Mrs Hitchcock had done enthusiastic work with reference to the paternity of Nancy Hanks, and several people had entered the lists as champions of her chastity, no one so far as he could learn had compiled the various theories adverse to Thomas Lincoln's paternity of Abraham and subjected them to a critical examination.

Moreover, the author found himself at length compelled to ask of himself the question, What if these reports are true? And he pursued his investigations with an open mind, and, as he hopes and believes, in accordance with the true spirit of historical inquiry.

The author had frequent occasion to visit the county of Lincoln's birth and other portions of Kentucky in quest of material for his previous book, and he made careful inquiry on the ground, by personal interview, supplemented by extended correspondence with all persons there and elsewhere who seemed at all likely to be able to give him any information favorable or unfavorable to the view which he personally was disposed to accept.

All this material was reduced to writing as it accumulated, and carefully preserved with the large quantity of Lincoln matter which was assembled in the course of an industrious study of the whole life of Lincoln; for, in addition to the book already published entitled *The Soul of Abraham Lincoln,* and the present monograph, the author hopes and expects to issue a work more strictly biographical and containing a character study of America's great commoner and liberator.

By the time the author had arrived at a definite, and as it appears to him, a final, opinion regarding the paternity of Lincoln, it became evident that he had in his possession material for a book, and that no such book was already in existence.

The author has endeavored to trace every rumor and report relating to the birth of Abraham Lincoln, to assemble all the available evidence in favor of it and against it, to judge each one of these reports upon its own merits, and to render what, he believes, is a judgment from which there can be no successful appeal.

From the time it became evident to his own mind that he must write a book on this subject, the author determined to make it unnecessary for any one else ever to do so; and he sincerely believes that in this he has succeeded. It appears to him quite certain that no previous writer has made anything approaching a thorough investigation of this subject, though many have treated it more or less confidently.

There exists in some quarters an impression that the stories concerning the birth of Abraham Lincoln which were once widely current were completely disposed of by the discovery of the marriage bond and the minister's return of marriage of Thomas Lincoln and Nancy Hanks. The discovery of that document was important, as this book will show; but it is probably true that those stories were never so widely current as they are today. They have passed the acute stage of curious gossip, and have their respectable place in literature and oratory. At least one man is even now busy in the preparation of a book intended to prove that Abraham Lincoln was not the son of Thomas Lincoln, and there may be ten men at work on books, more or less conclusive, intended to prove that he was. The English biographies of Lincoln, now appearing in considerable number, including Charnwood's, and the Encyclopedia Britannica, give serious attention to these reports; and American authors do not feel at liberty to publish their books without somewhere intimating that they are at least familiar with these stories. Beside books formally devoted to the study of Lincoln, a very large number of other volumes are issued in which some reference to Lincoln occurs, and many of these make more or less direct allusion to these reports. Colonel Watterson's interesting autobiography, " Marse Henry," devotes a half dozen pages to " that calumny " and to the like report concerning Andrew Johnson.

As for oratory, the temptation is far too great for the average speaker to resist, and it offers an attractive field to orators who are beyond the average. In Chicago, on Lincoln's Birthday in 1920, the Sons of the American Revolution listened to an able address by a distinguished lawyer, himself the author of a valuable book on Abraham Lincoln, a considerable part of which address was devoted to the statement and refutation of these stories; but he did not succeed in refuting them. That address the author of this volume heard; it was a notable address, but in this portion it failed completely. The old Presiding Elder in the Methodist Church gave wise advice to a young minister who was much given to superficial refutations of the arguments of infidelity,—" Never raise the devil unless you are sure you can lay him."

At the same hour and in the same city where the address referred to in the preceding paragraph was delivered, another distinguished lawyer, a man of high character and large ability, was delivering an address on " The Lineage of Lincoln " at a patriotic gathering held in Memorial Hall in the Chicago Public Library. It was an address that displayed great industry of the painstaking sort which characterizes the work of this eminent attorney and has won him wide repute at the bar, but it was inconclusive   He did not know all the facts which he needed to know.

What happened in Chicago probably occurred on the same day in other cities; such addresses are to be numbered by the hundred if not by the thousand.   They are delivered with the best of intentions, but their zeal is not always according to knowledge, and they serve to disseminate yet more widely the stories which they inconclusively oppose.

We are not at liberty, therefore, to treat the subject of the paternity of Abraham Lincoln as one that may safely be dismissed with silent contempt.   If any one knows the truth about this matter, he ought to tell it.

The present author believes that he knows the truth about the paternity of Abraham Lincoln   His investigation has involved no little travel and research   He believes that the truth ought to be known, and that the truth is better than either falsehood or uncertainty.   That is why he has decided to pursue to the end the rather unwelcome task which grew out of his previous study, and which this book completes.   And he does not expect to refer to it in any subsequent book about Abraham Lincoln; nor does he apprehend that such reference will be necessary.

This volume may be considered as a footnote to the author's book, *The Soul of Abraham Lincoln*, and a suppressed preface to the *Life of Lincoln* which he hopes to publish at some future date.   In that volume he does not now intend to make any extended reference to the material in this book, but its conclusion will be assumed.

The author believes that he has gathered all important material bearing upon the question of Abraham Lincoln's paternity, and this volume contains all the material which a diligent search has brought to his knowledge bearing upon that subject.   Pursuing these investigations with an open mind, he has reached for himself a definite conclusion, which together with the evidence upon which it rests, he submits herewith in confidence that on the more important aspects of the question there remains henceforth not very much more to be said.

As compared with my previous book on Lincoln, the

preparation of this work has called for comparatively little use of books. My obligations for such books as I have used, and some measure of my indebtedness to correspondents, is indicatèd in the text; but I shall not be able to acknowledge in full my debt to those who have made researches for me. I venture to name some of those to whom my obligation is largest.

Among libraries and librarians, I owe much to Miss Caroline M. McIlvaine, and the Library of the Chicago Historical Society; to Mrs. Jessie Palmer Weber and Miss Georgia L. Osborne, and the Library of the Illinois State Historical Society at Springfield; to Mr. A. P. C. Griffin, Chief Assistant Librarian, and the Library of Congress in Washington; to Mr. J. H. Tuttle and the Library of the Massachusetts Historical Society; to Miss Euphemia B Corwin and Mrs. Florence Ridgway of the Library of Berea College, Kentucky; to Mrs. Charles F. Norton and the Library of Transylvania University of Lexington, Kentucky, and to Miss Helen Bagley and the Oak Park Public Library.

For assistance in correspondence and research I name among those who have helped me most:

Mr. O. M. Mather, Mr. L. B. Handley, Judge Richard W. Creal, Mr. Charles F. Creal, Mr. Robert Enlow and Rev. Louis A. Warren, all of Hodgenville, Kentucky; Mr. G. H. Geiger of Anderson, South Carolina; Hon. James H. Cathey of Sylva, North Carolina; Mr. D. J. Knotts of Swansea, South Carolina; Mr. L. S. Pence of Lebanon, Kentucky; Mr. George Holbert of Elizabethtown, Kentucky; Mr. Jesse W. Weik of Greencastle, Indiana; Hon. Clinton L. Conkling, Hon. Hardin W. Masters, Hon. G. W. Murray and Mr. H. E. Barker of Springfield, Illinois; Mr. Hugh McLellan of Champlain, New York, Mr. Truman H. Bartlett of Boston; Hon. Daniel Fish of Minneapolis; Mr. Arthur E. Morgan of Dayton, Ohio; Mr. Judd Stewart of New York City; Mr. F. H. Meserve of New York City; Mr. Oliver R. Barrett of Chicago; Mr. Charles F. Gunther, deceased, of Chicago; Mr. Joseph Polin of Springfield, Kentucky; and Mr O. H. Oldroyd of Washington. Mr. Stewart died as this book was nearing press.

This is far from being a complete list. Some additional names will appear in the text. As for the others, I can only say that I have endeavored to secure information from every one from whom it seemed possible to obtain any, and I thank all who assisted me.

The author is not unaware that it is easy for writers to overestimate the importance of their own writings, and to attach undue weight to their conclusions. Nevertheless, he wishes to affirm that in the preparation of this book he has reached a complete and final answer to the many questions which were forced upon him at the beginning and at different stages of its preparation. He is sending this volume to the press with the profound conviction that it contains the truth, and the whole truth, and that its conclusions are irrefutable

W. E. B.

First Church Study,
  Oak Park, Illinois,
    August, 1920

CONTENTS

PART I: THE NATURE AND IMPORTANCE OF THE INQUIRY

PART I: THE NATURE AND IMPORTANCE OF THE INQUIRY

CHAPTER I

THE SEVEN SIRES OF ABRAHAM LINCOLN

WHEN, in 1860, Abraham Lincoln became a candidate for the Presidency of the United States, but little was known of him in his own nation and in the world, and less concerning his antecedents. The biographical sketches which he furnished to Jesse W. Fell in 1859 or 1860 and somewhat later to John Locke Scripps, exhibited marked reserve on the subject of his family history, especially on his mother's side. In these sketches furnished by Lincoln himself, the Lincoln line was indicated for several generations, from Berks County, Pennsylvania, through Virginia to Kentucky, whence in his own childhood his father had migrated in 1816 into Southern Indiana, and in 1830, the year of Abraham's majority, into Illinois.

The meagerness of the information did not escape comment at the time, and vague and nebulous rumors were current in the campaign of 1860 that Abraham Lincoln had little occasion for pride in his birth. In 1864, the campaign was waged with great bitterness, the Copperhead press stopping at nothing that would belittle him, and the rumors became more widely extended. So far as the writer is aware, however, these did not emerge into print. The writer has seen a considerable body of hostile political literature, much of it issued by the Society for the Diffusion of Political Knowledge, of which Prof. S. F. B. Morse, inventor of the telegraph, was President, and while Lincoln is mercilessly criticized, lampooned and caricatured, the writer has not seen in print any direct charge that Abraham Lincoln was illegitimate, or that his mother

17

was illegitimate, that was published during either of the
two campaigns in which Lincoln was running for the Presidency. That the rumors were in circulation by 1864, is, however, certain.

The gravamen of these rumors, and the definite charges
subsequently printed in various forms, is two-fold. The first
of these is that his mother, Nancy Hanks, was a bastard.
Her mother, Lucy Hanks, it is alleged, being at that time
unmarried, bore her, in Virginia, in 1783. Subsequently
Lucy Hanks married Henry Sparrow, and the illegitimate
daughter of Lucy was, by the Hanks family, called Nancy
Sparrow. But that, it is affirmed, was not her name. Her
father, so it is alleged, and so her son Abraham Lincoln is
alleged to have believed, was a Virginia planter of good
family, through whom Nancy inherited qualities which distinguished her as superior to her own family, qualities which
she transmitted to her son, Abraham, and which largely made
him the great man whom he afterward became.

The other rumor, which has become a definite allegation,
printed in several forms, is that Abraham Lincoln was an
illegitimate child; that his mother, Nancy Hanks, either before or subsequent to her marriage with Thomas Lincoln, if
indeed she was married to him, became the mother of a son
whose father was other than Thomas Lincoln.

In some forms this rumor alleges that she was pregnant
when Thomas Lincoln married her; in others that the child
was already born, but an infant; in others that he was " old
enough to run around," and that " he sat between Thomas
and Nancy when they went away to be married." In others
the implication is that he was begotten in adultery, Lincoln
and his wife having been married, and she proving unfaithful
to her marriage vows.

The name of Abraham Lincoln's father is variously given
by those who hold to the truth of this rumor. He is alleged
to have been a grandson of Chief-Justice John Marshall, or a
son of John C. Calhoun; and several other names, noted in
Kentucky and the older states to the east of it, are men-

tioned each with more or less confidence as that of his father.

Certain family names that were current in the immediate vicinity of his birth have also been mentioned, among them that of Abraham Enlow, Inlow or Enloe. According to a very widespread rumor, current in various forms in several sections of the South, Lincoln received his name of Abraham from his real father, Abraham Enlow, Enloe or Inlow, and his surname from his putative father, Thomas Lincoln, who either than was or later became the husband of Nancy Hanks, the mother of the future President.

With the first of these two questions the present book has no concern. Mrs. Caroline Hanks Hitchcock published in 1899 her little book entitled " Nancy Hanks," and she and Miss Ida M. Tarbell in their researches obtained information which satisfied them that Nancy Hanks was of legitimate birth. The large work of Lea and Hutchinson, while following primarily the Lincoln line in England, practically confines its American research concerning the immediate progenitors of Lincoln to the work already done by Mrs. Hitchcock, and accepts her conclusions apparently without independent investigation of the maternal line of Abraham Lincoln's ancestry.

The present writer has no occasion to traverse this ground. It is not the field of his chief interest, nor, so far as he can judge, is it the more important half of the inquiry. We should be glad to know that Abraham Lincoln's grandmothers and great-grandmothers were virtuous to all generations; but we know that few families can go back many generations without finding the bar sinister somewhere upon the family escutcheon; and every man or woman who boasts of descent from William the Conqueror confesses with more or less of pride to that condition of his own family register. Each receding generation divides by two the feeling of moral obliquity, and each quarter century of remoteness lessens the feeling of disgrace If Nancy Hanks was born in lawful wedlock, the fact is of interest; but it is nothing like as important as it is to find whether she herself was a virtuous woman, and her son, the President of the United States, the legitimate son of her husband, whose name Abraham Lincoln bore.

This book, therefore, confines itself wholly to the question of the paternity of Abraham Lincoln.

" Regarding the paternity of Lincoln a great many surmises and a still larger amount of unwritten or, at least, unpublished history have drifted into the currents of western lore and journalism. A number of such traditions are extant in Kentucky and other localities."

So wrote William H. Herndon in 1889 in the first volume of the first edition of his much discussed *Life of Lincoln.* He added that his associate, Mr. Jesse W. Weik, had devoted much time to investigating one of these traditions, which he outlined, and which we shall have occasion to consider in detail. This paragraph is interesting for many reasons. Among others, it shows that on Herndon's first investigation there was more than one story. There are several now. The author of this present volume has made diligent search, and has tabulated all the rumors and definite charges which he has been able to secure. Some of them are too vague to be certainly identified, but even these will be alluded to, with whatever is to be said for and against them. The chief stories permit of grouping under seven definite heads, and they charge that Abraham Lincoln was not the son of Thomas Lincoln, but was the son of another man, who is named with evidence, in some cases more and in other cases less circumstantial, intended to show that some man other than Thomas Lincoln was Abraham Lincoln's father.

The author has catalogued these allegations. The seven men, other than Thomas Lincoln, who are credited with the paternity of Abraham Lincoln, and whose claims to that honor we shall consider at length, are the following:

1. Abraham Enlow, a farmer, of Hardin County, Kentucky.
2. George Brownfield, a farmer, of Hardin County, Kentucky.

3. Abraham Inlow, a miller, of Bourbon County, Kentucky.
4. Andrew, an alleged foster son of Chief-Justice John Marshall.
5. Abraham Enloe, of Swain County, North Carolina.
6. John C. Calhoun, of South Carolina.
7. Martin D. Hardin, of Kentucky.

It would have been possible to increase the number beyond seven, but several stories that at first appeared to be distinct resolved themselves into separate forms of the same story. These several forms will all be considered either in the presentation of the evidence or in its analysis. We will also consider one or two of these stories that had more or less vogue for a time and then disappeared. This book undertakes to be complete, so far as the author's information and research have enabled him to gather material, and he thinks that he has discerned and here recorded all that is of any value, and some beside. But he has kept the number of Lincoln's alleged fathers down to seven, in addition to Thomas Lincoln, who also is to be considered.

> "Seven cities strove for Homer dead,
> Through which the living Homer begged his bread"

Seven men are now adduced as the alleged fathers of Abraham Lincoln, few if any of whom, if living in 1860, would have voted for him. But that does not settle the question of his paternity. It only illustrates the complexity of the task which he assumes who undertakes to trace these rumors and discover what truth, if any, lies at their root.

CHAPTER II

IS SUCH AN INQUIRY WORTH WHILE?

THE reader of the foregoing chapter will be quite certain to ask himself at this point, Is any such inquiry worth while? What does it matter, anyway? Why not let all such rumors alone?

Let him be assured that the author has asked himself the same questions and many others. The answers that have come to him are, first, that it does matter, and that the truth is better than any form of falsehood, and very much better than so many kinds of falsehood that one cannot be sure which of them to choose.

But a more important answer is that we are not permitted to choose whether these rumors shall die out or not. They persist. They were in active circulation before the death of Lincoln, and troubled him; and they have to be reckoned with by every serious student of the life of Lincoln. It is better, so the author has come to believe, that these be dragged into the open, and met on their merits. If Abraham Lincoln was not the son of Thomas Lincoln, it is time the world knew whose son he was. If he was the son of Thomas Lincoln, those who deny that fact should be refuted.

Abraham Lincoln had his own homely phrase for investigations of this character. He used it more than once, and always effectively. In 1864 a story was industriously circulated, for which General George B. McClellan must have been in some measure personally responsible, that Lincoln, visiting the field of Antietam just after the battle, caused himself to be amused by the singing of vulgar songs within sight and hearing of the burial of the dead. This story was published in New York papers, and, while grossly untrue, had in it just enough of truth to make it difficult to refute.[1] Lincoln's associate in this affair, and the man who actually sang, though not while the burials were in progress,

> " I've wandered to the village, Tom,
> I've sat beneath the tree,
> Upon the school-house playground,
> That sheltered you and me ",—

was Colonel Ward Hill Lamon, who, when the story appeared in New York papers, wished to rush into print with a hot denial. Lincoln read Lamon's proposed communication, and doubted the wisdom of publishing it. Instead he wrote, in the third person, an account of the event, which, however, he later decided not to print. It was published in fac-simile many years afterwards Lincoln, declining the well-meant but too belligerent offices of Lamon, said:

" No, Hill. Leave this to me. Every man must skin his own skunk."

Abraham Lincoln would gladly have skinned for himself the unpleasant story of his paternity if it had been possible for him to do so; and beyond a doubt would have done it in the third person, a method he employed in other delicate matters. But this was a matter which Lincoln was unable to confront and settle. He knew of these stories, and how much he believed of them we shall presently undertake to learn; but he lacked the facts necessary to their settlement. Indeed, his own futile efforts to learn something more of his ancestry had something to do with the origin of some of the rumors, and warned him to desist. This was a skunk he would gladly have skinned if he could, and he would have been profoundly grateful to any man who could have nailed its pelt to the barn-door, and scrubbed his hands with a gourd

---

[1] While General McClellan was not named as the author, still it is impossible to relieve him from a share in the moral responsibility for this story He was present when the incident occurred, and was displeased with what happened, and when the reports were published he did not deny or modify them, though he was named as a witness This fact, and also the fact that his candidate for Vice-President, Hon George H Pendleton, advertised his campaign speeches in a pamphlet in which Lincoln was proclaimed " the Rebel Candidate," illustrate the amenities of that campaign

of soft soap at the spring before returning to receive the reward of his valuable labor.

But it is a fair question now, and one which the author has earnestly asked of himself, whether at this day the skin is worth the removing, and whether it would not be better to bury the carcase as it is.

On this matter the author has come to a definite answer in his own mind. If he could bury the matter just as it is, he would. But it cannot be done. Every biographer of Lincoln finds the unburied and unskinned skunk in his path. Some authors walk around it, visibly holding their noses. Others take a contemptuous kick at it, and pass on, but leave the odor behind their well-meant allusion. Each of them disclaims responsibility for the actual skinning.

Miss Ida M Tarbell has thus written of the several stories of Lincoln's illegitimacy:

Among the many wrongs of history—and they are legion —there is none in our American chapter at least which is graver than that which has been done to the parents, and particularly the mother, of Abraham Lincoln. Of course, I refer to the tradition that Lincoln was born of that class known in the South as " poor whites," that his father was not Thomas Lincoln, as his biographers insist on declaring, but a rich and cultured planter of another State than Kentucky, and that his mother not only gave a fatherless boy to the world, but herself was a nameless child. The tradition has always lacked particularity. For instance, there has been large difference of opinion about the planter who fathered Abraham, who he was and where he came from. One story calls him Enloe, another Calhoun, another Hardin, and several States claim him. Only five years ago [in 1899] a book was published in North Carolina to prove that Lincoln's father was a resident of that State. The bulk of the testimony offered in this instance came from men and women who had been born long after Abraham Lincoln, had never seen him, and never heard the tale they repeated until long after his election to the Presidency. Of the truth of these statements as to Lincoln's origin no proof has ever been produced. There were rumors, diligently spread in the first place by those who for political reasons were glad to belittle a political opponent. They grew with telling, and curiously enough, two of Lincoln's best friends helped perpetuate them—Messrs. Lamon and Herndon—both of whom wrote lives of the President which are of great interest and value. But neither of these men was a student, and they did not take the trouble to look for the records of Mr. Lincoln's birth. They accepted rumors and enlarged upon them. Indeed, it was not until perhaps twenty-five years ago that the matter was taken up seriously and an investigation begun. This has been going on at intervals ever since, and I venture to say that few persons born in a pioneer community, as Lincoln was, and as early as 1809, have their lineage as clearly established as that of Abraham Lincoln It takes, indeed, a most amazing credulity for any one to believe the stories I have alluded to after having looked at the records of his family. Lincoln himself, backed by the record in the Lincoln family Bible, is the first authority for the time and place of his birth, as well as the name of his father and mother. The father, Thomas Lincoln, far from being a "poor white," was the son of a prosperous Kentucky pioneer, a man of honorable and well-established lineage, who had come from Virginia as a friend of Daniel Boone, and had there bought large tracts of land, and begun to grow up with the country, where he was killed by the Indians. He left a large family. By the law of Kentucky the estate went mainly to the eldest son, and the youngest, Thomas Lincoln, was left to shift for himself. This younger son was married at Beechland, Kentucky, to a young woman of a family well known in the vicinity, Nancy Hanks. There is no doubt whatever about the time and the place of their marriage All the legal documents [2] required in Kentucky at that period for a marriage are in existence. Not only have we the bond and the certificate, but the marriage is duly entered in a list of marriage returns made by Jesse Head, one of the best

---

[2] This is not quite correct The license has not been found, nor, in my opinion, has the marriage certificate In expressing the judgment that the marriage certificate of Thomas and Nancy Lincoln has not been found, but only the signed return of the minister, and the marriage bond, I do not forget that what purports to be the original marriage certificate is in a private collection and that a fac-simile of it has been published in one of the Lives of Lincoln. I have not seen the so-called original; but any one who wishes may compare the fac-simile with the

known early Methodist ministers of Kentucky. It is now to be seen in the records of Washington County, Kentucky. There is even in existence a very full and amusing account of the wedding and the fan-fare [infare] which followed by a guest who was present and who for years after was accustomed to visit Thomas and Nancy. This guest, Christopher Columbus Graham, a unique and perfectly trustworthy man, a prominent citizen of Louisville, died only a few years ago.

But while these documents dispose effectually of the question of the parentage of Lincoln, they do not, of course, clear up the shadow which hangs over the parentage of his mother.

The remainder of the interesting little brochure is devoted to the ancestry of Nancy Hanks, which does not belong to the present inquiry.

This well written argument, printed in 1907 in a little booklet by the Lincoln Farm Association, and used in various other publications, appeared to me, when I first read it, to be eminently satisfactory, and I had no inclination to pursue the subject farther. I already believed that Thomas Lincoln was the father of Abraham Lincoln, and had no temptation to meddle with any other opinion, and was glad that Miss Tarbell in so simple a fashion had disposed of the whole subject without effort which I had no desire to put forth.

But, while I still admire the manner in which Miss Tarbell swept up the whole affair into a dustpan and threw it out of doors, I am forced to the opinion that that is not the best way to treat the matter. Either it should be ignored altogether, or the issue should be squarely met: and it is not possible for a thoughtful student to ignore it; if it had been possible, I should not be writing this book.

genuine records of Jesse Head. How such a document, if in existence, and presumably preserved in the Lincoln family, could have been concealed from President Lincoln, and produced after it ceased to have important value as evidence, but when it had undeniable commercial value, I do not undertake to explain. I am confident, however, that the author of the volume in which it first appeared had no share in the imposture, but was imposed upon.

In the first place, one may not dispose of Lamon and Herndon by saying that while they wrote Lives of Lincoln of great value, "neither of these men was a student, and they did not take the trouble to look for the records of Lincoln's birth. They accepted rumors, and enlarged upon them."

In his own erratic way, Herndon certainly was a student, and a very diligent one. In a matter which interested him, as this one did profoundly, he was industrious and discriminating, and followed his clues unremittingly. He did "take trouble to look up the records of Lincoln's birth," and it was with no little trouble that he found them. And Lamon, or whoever wrote Lamon's book, though he wrote in most ungracious spirit and in great unwisdom, was no fool, nor did he lack the qualities of a student

But the thing that most troubled me when I discovered it was that, whatever Herndon believed about the parentage of Lincoln, *he knew all that Miss Tarbell knew.* The testimony of Lincoln, as given in his autobiography, and the record in the family Bible, were before Herndon when he wrote, and he reproduced the record in the family Bible in fac-simile in his book. He even knew the place and date of the marriage of Thomas and Nancy Lincoln, and told of it in his first edition, and that is where Miss Tarbell probably learned of it. He said, in 1889:

In only two instances did Mr. Lincoln over his own hand leave any record of his history or family descent. One of these was the modest bit of autobiography furnished to Jesse W. Fell in 1859, in which, after stating that his parents were born in Virginia, of "undistinguished or second families," he makes the brief mention of his mother, saying that she came "of a family of the name of Hanks." The other record was the register of marriages, births and deaths, which he made in his father's Bible. The latter now lies before me. That portion of the page which probably contained the record of the marriage of his parents, Thomas Lincoln and Nancy Hanks, has been lost; but fortunately the records of Washington County, Kentucky, and the certificate of the minister who performed the marriage,—the Rev. Jesse Head—fix the fact and date of the latter on the 12th day of June, 1806. On the 10th day of February in the following year a daughter, Sarah, was born, and two years later, on the 12th of February, the subject of these memoirs came into the world. —*Herndon's Lincoln, First Edition, Volume I, pp. 4, 5.*

It is impossible to refute Herndon by the production of evidence with which he was entirely familiar, but which was outweighed (if it was so outweighed) in his mind by more than counterbalancing evidence.

Not only so, but Lamon conceded the fact of the marriage, and fixed the approximate date, although up to the time he wrote (1872) and for some years afterward, diligent search had failed to discover the marriage bond and the return of Jesse Head.

Some time in the year 1806 he [Thomas Lincoln] married Nancy Hanks. . . . It is admitted by all the old residents of the place that they were honestly married, but precisely when or how no one can tell. Diligent and thorough searches by the most competent persons have failed to discover any trace of the fact in the public records of Hardin and the adjoining counties. The license and the minister's return in the case of Lincoln and Sarah Johnston, his second wife, were easily found in the place where the law requires them to be; but of Nancy Hanks's marriage there exists no evidence but that of mutual acknowledgement and cohabitation —LAMON's *Life of Lincoln, p.* 10.

Whatever the opinions of Lamon and Herndon, and we shall examine them in detail, and whatever their faults in other particulars, these are as true and fair statements as could have been made when Lamon's book was issued in 1872 or Herndon's in 1889

When I discovered this fact, I saw that Herndon could not be confuted in the manner that had been so easily assumed; and that those persons who conceded all that Miss Tarbell claimed, but who still believed Abraham Lincoln illegitimate, must either be met by other arguments, or their claim admitted.

Furthermore, I continually discovered other matters which compelled attention; and they are hereinafter set forth, and in due course analyzed and given what appears to me their true value as evidence.

I have read with keen enjoyment and some profit Colonel Henry Watterson's breezy autobiography, "Marse Henry." He devoted a portion of one chapter to Andrew Johnson, and to the rumor that he was an illegitimate child. He quotes a letter received by him from Hon. Josephus Daniels, declaring this story to be false, and saying:

My own information is, for I have made some investigation of it, that the story about Andrew Johnson's having a father other than the husband of his mother is as wanting in foundation as the story about Abraham Lincoln. You did a great service in running that down and exposing it, and I trust before you publish your book you will be able to do a like service in repudiating the unjust, idle gossip with reference to Andrew Johnson.—"*Marse Henry,*" Vol. I, p. 158.

Colonel Watterson says, among other things, of the Lincoln story:

There used to be a story about Raleigh, North Carolina, where Andrew Johnson was born, that he was the natural son of William Ruffin, an eminent jurist in the earlier years of the nineteenth century. It was analogous to the story that Lincoln was the natural son of various paternities from time to time assigned him I had my share in running that calumny to cover. It was a lie out of whole cloth, with nothing whatever to support or excuse it. I reached the bottom of it to discover proof of its baselessness abundant and conclusive —"*Marse Henry,*" Vol. I, p. 155.

I had known that Colonel Watterson in some address or editorial had referred to this matter, but had no knowledge of any such thorough inquiry on his part as this seemed to imply. I had read his eloquent lecture on Abraham Lincoln, and a re-reading of it confirmed the recollection that it contained nothing on this subject. I therefore wrote to the Colonel, asking him to furnish me his material on this subject, as it was one in which I was deeply interested. I received a courteous reply from him, accompanied by a note from his secretary, who had made diligent search among the Colonel's papers, and could not find it. Colonel Watterson said, however, that what he had written on the subject was somewhere in the files of the *Courier-Journal,* though his secretary had not found it, and that the facts on which his article was based were those given by Miss Tarbell.

The article has been found. It is an address by Colonel Watterson, delivered November 8, 1911, on the occasion of his presentation of the Speed statue of Abraham Lincoln to Kentucky and the nation, and it is printed in the current issue of the *Courier-Journal.* The portion of the address which deals with this subject quotes in full the Christopher Columbus Graham affidavit, which, it appears from this article, was reduced to writing and sworn to by Mr. Graham at the request of Colonel Watterson. Omitting the affidavit, which will appear in another place, the statement of Colonel Watterson is as follows:

Let me speak, with some particularity and the authority of fact, tardily but conclusively ascertained, touching the . . . maternity of Abraham Lincoln. Few passages in history have been so greatly misrepresented and misconceived. Some confusion was made by his own mistake as to the marriage of his father and mother, which had not been celebrated in Hardin County, but in Washington County, Kentucky, the absence of any marriage papers in the old court house at Elizabethtown, the county seat of Hardin County, leading to the notion that there had never been any marriage at all. It is easy to conceive that such a discrepancy might give occasion for any amount and all sorts of partisan falsification, the distorted stories winning popular belief among the credulous and inflamed. Lincoln himself died without surely knowing that he was born in an honest wedlock and came from an ancestry upon both sides of which he had no reason to be ashamed. For a long time a cloud hung over the name of Nancy Hanks, the mother of Abraham Lincoln. Persistent and intelligent research has brought about a vindication in every way complete. It has been clearly established that as the ward of a decent family she lived a happy and industrious girl until she was twenty-three years of age, when Thomas Lincoln, who had learned his trade in the shop of one of her uncles, married her, June 12, 1806. The entire record is in existence and intact. The marriage bond to the amount of £50 was duly recorded seven[3] days before the wedding, which was solemnized as became the well-to-do folks in those days. The uncle and aunt gave an "infare," to which the neighboring countryside was invited. Dr. Christopher Columbus Graham, one of the most highly respected of Kentucky, before his death, in 1885, wrote at my request his remembrances of that festival and testified to it before a notary public in the ninety-sixth year of his age.

This is well said, and spoken like a gentleman, which Marse Henry is and always was; but it certainly cannot be called going to the bottom of the matter. It is evident that his sources of information were the personal testimony of Dr. Graham, and the researches of Miss Tarbell and Mrs. Hitchcock, which essentially were nothing more than the placing of a new emphasis upon the discovery of the marriage return, which Herndon had long before proclaimed.

Let us understand clearly that while the discovery of the marriage return and bond is a fact of very great importance, and a complete answer to some forms of the story we are discussing, it is of no value in meeting the charge that Thomas Lincoln, for a consideration, married a woman of bad character, already pregnant by another man, the paternity of whose child he assumed, and further, that the marriage bond, with or without the affidavit of Dr. Christopher Columbus Graham in his one-hundredth year, is no answer to the charge that Nancy Hanks, after her marriage, entertained men other than her husband, and by one of them became the father of Abraham Lincoln; on account of which,

---

[3] This is an unimportant error. The bond was dated June 10, and the marriage was performed June 12, 1806.

and of her husband's ferocious fight with him, the Lincolns left Kentucky.

This story should either be let alone, or it should be met resolutely, and the truth ascertained.

The author of this volume has corresponded with a number of people who have, to their complete satisfaction, refuted the stories that Lincoln was illegitimate, but who, when asked for their evidence, have nothing more than they have learned from Miss Tarbell and Mrs. Hitchcock. These two excellent ladies did service, but they did not go to the bottom of the matter.

In my judgment, nothing but harm can come from a superficial treatment of this subject, and every attempt thus far to treat it is superficial.

The more carefully one scrutinizes the manner in which the biographers of Lincoln have handled this matter, the more evident it becomes that they leave much to be desired. A considerable number of writers make plain reference to these stories, showing that they know of them, and dismiss them with some show of indignation that any such stories should have been circulated, but give no reason why, having been circulated, they should now not be believed. They resent the publicity, but do not disprove the charges. They manifest displeasure that the stories are in circulation, but do nothing except to increase a little the extent of the publiciy.

One may glance into almost any recent Life of Lincoln and wish that its author had said more or else said less.

Morse, whose book is of real value, but who writes without much knowledge of social life in backwoods districts, and with little warmth or sympathy, exhibits disgust for the whole Hanks family; he tells of some cases of illegitimacy in that family and hints that there were others, and leaves the reader in doubt of Morse's own opinion, save only that he evidently has a pained and impatient feeling of disillusionment concerning the entire background of Lincoln's infancy and youth.

Nicolay and Hay give a somber and vague description of the condition of the home of Thomas Lincoln, and say that not even to his closest friends did Abraham Lincoln talk about the conditions of that home.

Chapman, in his *Latest Light on Lincoln,* excoriates every man who has had a share in the publication of these rumors, and thus effectually publishes them a little more widely, without giving any facts that tend toward their refutation.

Among English books the situation is evidently one of perplexity. The authors do not know what to say. Apparently they feel that there is some truth in these rumors; certainly they do not feel that they have any call to rush in and refute them, for which fact, at least, we have reason to thank them. Binns, an early English biographer of Lincoln, tells the whole story as Herndon told it, and expresses the feeble hope that the situation was not quite so bad as that would appear to imply. Lord Charnwood, by far the ablest of Lincoln's English biographers, gives these stories recognition, but leaves the reader in doubt as to his own opinion.

No English biographer can be expected to investigate these rumors independently; and no American biographer has done it thoroughly.

The method which has come to be common among biographers of Lincoln is to give some general intimation that the author is aware of these stories, and dismiss them without discussion. Referring again to Lincoln's figure of speech, their method has been virtually to produce a scrap of skunk-skin and hint that there is more where that came from, but that it is just as well to let it alone.

The present author proposes rather that the unpleasant situation be faced, and the skin, if it is worth removing, be nailed securely to the barn-door; and if it is not of value, that the skunk receive decent and permanent burial.

It is time for vague rumor and undenied gossip to be brought to bar, and the truth discovered, if at this date it is possible to discover the truth.

There is good reason why some one should face this question with courage enough to learn and publish the whole truth. Enough has been said, and will continue to be said, to make it certain that these stories will not die down of themselves, and whoever refers to them but piques the curiosity of his hearers or readers with a desire to know just what it is that is being referred to and otherwise concealed.

If Thomas Lincoln was not the father of Abraham Lincoln, less harm will come at this day from admitting it than from slurring over a truth which is everywhere recognized as an extant rumor which no one has quite courage to face. If, on the other hand, he was the legitimate son of Thomas and Nancy Lincoln, it is high time that the skinning of the skunk, bit by bit, should cease, and the animal be given permanent interment.

If it be asked again, Has not the question been settled by the discovery of the marriage return of Thomas and Nancy Lincoln? the answer is that that does indeed settle some of the stories, and settle them forever; but it does not settle them all. Indeed, it does not settle the oldest, the most widely disseminated, or the most unpleasant of them.

This inquiry, therefore, is not one for the frivolous, nor is it to be pursued in a manner that will afford delight to scandal mongers. It is the serious facing of the questions which every student of the life of Lincoln knows must sometime be faced. And the author is not without hope and confidence that he is facing them with promise of a definite and permanent result.

This inquiry has need to be made both as a footnote to all extant biographies of Lincoln, and as a source of material for all future biographers, as well as a contribution to historical knowledge.

CHAPTER III

THE SOIL IN WHICH THESE STORIES GREW

CHANGING the graphic but not wholly pleasant figure of speech in the preceding chapter, it is well to ask, Out of what soil did these various rumors, reports and charges grow? What was their general background, the situation which made it easy for them to originate, and which has lent to them a degree of plausibility?

First, we reckon with the fact that Lincoln himself displayed "significant reserve" in matters of his family relationship. He furnished to his biographers very scanty material, passed lightly over the maternal side of his genealogy, and gave to John Locke Scripps in confidence some information which he did not desire to have published and which Scripps never published. Lincoln himself must be accounted the first and in some respects the most important witness against himself in this particular. If he could have displayed unquestioned descent from two of the "first families" of Virginia, it is hardly possible that these stories would have gained circulation. That he was sensitive on this subject is beyond question. Herndon relates that when some one undertook to establish a relationship with him he replied curtly, "You are mistaken about my mother." [1]

In the next place, we must remember that Lincoln made vain effort to discover the record of his parents' marriage, and that Herndon in 1865 extended that effort. The fact that search was made in several counties and no record found could not be kept secret. Not till many years afterward, about 1878, was the record found by W. F. Booker, clerk of the Washington County Court. This was much too late to stop the rumors, which had a long start; and for that matter

[1] This was in his letter to Samuel Haycraft in 1860. Reference to it is made elsewhere in this volume.

35

there were some of them which this discovery did not answer.

We have to remember, also, as a contributory cause, the low social scale of the Hanks family in Kentucky. Although careful search has shown that this family had many worthy representatives, it was not one of the first families, even in the backwoods of Kentucky. Herndon, in a private letter, says that the record of this family from 1790 to 1910 shows that the Hankses "must have been about the lowest people on earth." This is an extravagant statement, but the Hanks family was not one of the high-grade families. In it illegitimacy was not unknown.

It is also to be remembered that Sarah Bush Lincoln appears to have been very reticent in the information which she furnished to Herndon when, in 1865, he visited her and questioned her about the Hanks family. In the judgment of the author, a good deal too much has been read into this reticence. She was proud to think of Abe as her own boy, and to remember that she had done more for him than Nancy Hanks ever did; and she was herself of better family than the Hankses. Some of the stories related of her reticence to Herndon appear to be without foundation, and Herndon sometimes read meanings into such incidents which the incidents did not warrant. Nevertheless, the truth remains that when Herndon interrogated Sarah Bush Lincoln concerning the personality of Nancy Hanks Lincoln, she seemed to him to show more than a second wife's natural reserve touching her predecessor.

It is also to be remembered that Thomas Lincoln was not a very tall man, like Abraham, but a close-knit, solidly built man, who in mind and body was unlike to Abraham.

It is further alleged, and that on apparently good authority, that Thomas Lincoln habitually treated Abraham with "great barbarity," and Dennis Hanks tells us that Thomas knocked him off the fence for answering a civil question that was asked of him by a passing traveler.

It is further alleged that Abraham had no love for his father; that he did not visit him when his father was dying;

that he suspected the old man's veracity; and that he neglected his grave. It is remembered that he wrote to Thomas Lincoln that if he were to visit him the visit would perhaps be more painful than pleasant to both of them; and this has been held to mean that the reason was that each of the two men knew that Thomas was not Abraham's father.

To this is added the fact of Lincoln's habitual sadness, which, it is alleged, must have had behind it some deep and sad secret such as this.

It is also remembered that William H. Herndon, Lincoln's partner for many years, in the first edition of his book, seemed to imply that Lincoln was illegitimate, and even in his expurgated edition said that he had his origin "in the nameless bog where the foot of history leaves no track." It is alleged that because of its plain intimation that Lincoln was illegitimate, Herndon's first edition was suppressed, as earlier had been that of Lincoln's other intimate associate, Colonel Ward Hill Lamon.

The foregoing, and perhaps more of the same sort, stands at the background of all these rumors and gives to them color and some measure of apparent reasonableness. Particular charges are augmented and reinforced in the light of their apparent correlation with this general body of tradition. More or less, these come into the direct evidence; but whether they do or not, they are the soil in which particular rumors or charges are rooted. We shall consider these in detail, but it is well to have this general background in mind.

CHAPTER IV

WHAT DID LINCOLN THINK ABOUT IT?

THAT Lincoln looked back upon the conditions of his youth and home surroundings with painful realization of their privation is undoubted. He said to Scripps, his first biographer, that neither Scripps nor any one else could make anything of his life beyond what was contained in a single line of Gray's *Elegy*,—

"The short and simple annals of the poor."

"The chief difficulty I had to encounter," wrote Mr. Scripps to Mr Herndon, "was to induce him to communicate the homely facts and incidents of his early life. He seemed to be painfully impressed with the extreme poverty of his early surroundings, the utter absence of all romantic or heroic elements; and I know that he thought poorly of the idea of attempting a biographical sketch for campaign purposes. . . . Mr. Lincoln communicated some facts to me about his ancestry which he did not wish published, and which I have never spoken of or alluded to before."

What these supposed facts were, Mr. Scripps never revealed to Herndon, and probably not to any one else. It is evident from this that Lincoln believed some thing or things concerning his own ancestry which he did not wish to have published and about which he felt sensitive.

One of these things would appear to have been the matter of the paternity of his mother. Another would appear to have been a question concerning the marriage of his father and his mother.

What Lincoln thought of the ancestry of his mother is told by Herndon, no doubt substantially as Lincoln had told it to him. Whether Herndon ought to have published it is open to question, but there is no reason to dispute the essential

38

truth of his report of his conversation with Lincoln. Whether Lincoln himself was correctly informed, or whether indeed he had any definite information beyond his lack of knowledge of certain facts, some of which are now known, is, of course, another question.

"On the subject of his ancestry and origin," writes Mr. Herndon in his much discussed passage in the first chapter of the first edition of his book, " I only remember one time when Mr. Lincoln ever referred to it. It was about 1850, when he and I were driving in his one-horse buggy to the court in Menard County, Illinois. The suit we were going to try was one in which we were likely, either directly or collaterally, to touch upon the subject of hereditary traits. During the ride he spoke, for the first time in my hearing, of his mother, dwelling on her characteristics, and mentioning or enumerating what qualities he inherited from her He said, among other things, that she was the illegitimate daughter of Lucy Hanks and a well-bred Virginia farmer or planter; and he argued that from this last source came his power of analysis, his logic, his mental activity, his ambition, and all the qualities that distinguished him from the other members and descendants of the Hanks family. His theory in discussing this matter of hereditary traits had been that, for certain reasons, illegitimate children are oftentimes sturdier and brighter than those born in lawful wedlock; and in his case, he believed that his better nature and finer qualities came from this broad-minded, unknown Virginian. The revelation—painful as it was—called up the recollection of his mother, and, as the buggy jolted over the road, he added ruefully, ' God bless my mother; all that I am or ever hope to be I owe to her; ' and immediately lapsed into silence. Our interchange of ideas ceased, and we rode on for some time without exchanging a word. He was sad and absorbed. Burying himself in thought, and musing no doubt over the disclosure he had just made, he drew round him a barrier which I feared to penetrate. His words and melancholy tone made a deep impression on me. It was an experience I can never forget — *Herndon's Lincoln,* Vol. I, pp. 3-4

This tells us what Abraham Lincoln thought, about 1850, of his mother's parentage. What Lincoln thought about his own paternity is less certain. We shall presently discover what Herndon thought, but he never set forth a claim that Lincoln told him anything about his own misgivings, if he had any, concerning his own legitimacy. We do know, however, that Lincoln had caused the records of Hardin County to be searched for a record of the marriage of Thomas and Nancy Lincoln, and that the record was not found. Lincoln lived and died without knowing that this marriage was duly recorded in another county. What Lincoln knew is probably about what Lamon and Herndon knew in 1872 when Lamon's biography was published:

Some time in the year 1806 he [Thomas Lincoln] married Nancy Hanks. It was in the shop of her uncle, Joseph Hanks, at Elizabethtown, that he had essayed to learn his trade. We have no record of the courtship, and any one can readily imagine the numberless occasions that would bring together the niece and the apprentice. It is true that Nancy did not live with her uncle, but the Hankses were all very clannish, and she was doubtless a welcome and frequent guest at his house. It is admitted by all the old residents of the place that they were honestly married, but precisely when or how no one can tell. Diligent and thorough searches by the most competent persons have failed to discover any trace of the fact in the public records of Hardin and the adjoining counties. The license and the minister's return in the case of Lincoln and Sarah Johnston, his second wife, were easily found in the place where the law required them to be; but of Nancy Hanks's marriage there exists no evidence but that of mutual acknowledgment and cohabitation —LAMON. *Life of Lincoln,* p. 10.

As every one knows, the record of marriage has been found, and is beyond question. But Lincoln did not know that it existed, and it was doubtless a matter of considerable mental unrest for him.

CHAPTER V

WHAT DID LAMON THINK ABOUT IT?

In his *Life of Abraham Lincoln, from His Birth to His Inauguration as President,* published in 1872, by Ward Hill Lamon,[1] local law partner of Lincoln, at Danville, and Marshall of the District of Columbia, the opening paragraph reads:

Abraham Lincoln was born on the 12th day of February, 1809. His father's name was Thomas Lincoln, and his mother's maiden name was Nancy Hanks. At the time of his birth they are supposed to have been married about three years. Although there appears to have been but very little sympathy or affection between Thomas and Abraham Lincoln, they were nevertheless connected by ties and associations which make the previous history of Thomas and his family a necessary part of any reasonably full biography of the great man who immortalized the name by wearing it.

The implications of this paragraph are unmistakable, nor were they misunderstood by the readers of the volume from the beginning. Although Thomas Lincoln was said to be the father of Abraham, it was intended to be implied that he was Abraham's putative father, and that the name Lincoln did not belong to Abraham.

It would not be easy to account for the attitude of Lamon's *Life of Lincoln* on the hypothesis that Lamon was its sole

---

[1] In *Harper's Weekly* for July 11, 1911 (p. 6), and in *Lincoln and Herndon,* by Joseph Fort Newton, William H Herndon charges that the real author of Lamon's book was not Lamon, but that Chauncey F. Black (died 1904), son of Lamon's law partner after the war, and member of Buchanan's Cabinet before the war, was hired by Lamon to do a better piece of writing than Lamon himself could have done He charges that while Lamon was less true to Lincoln than he ought to have been, the real animus of the book was that of Black rather than Lamon. But Lamon doubtless believed what Black believed on this matter.

author. Lamon was Lincoln's friend of many years, his local partner, his intimate companion. He held for Lincoln genuine affection and respect. But Lamon's own character was not such as to make him capable of appreciating the best that was in Lincoln, and his familiarity did not breed the highest type of reference. Chauncey F. Black, Lamon's literary associate, was not a friend of Lincoln, though his father was Lamon's partner after the war. Black was personally and politically hostile to Lincoln and held his memory in small respect. The tone, therefore, of the book which bears Lamon's name varies with respect to Lincoln, sometimes speaking of him in terms of praise, at others thinly veiling hostility and scorn. With respect to "Old Tom Lincoln" and all his tribe, Black felt no restraint and Lamon no compunction. The tone of the book is cynical and contemptuous.

Not only does Lamon's biography treat the character of Thomas Lincoln with little respect, and it takes pains to give the impression that Abraham had neither respect nor affection for him, and that there always existed between Thomas and Abraham a lack of such sympathy as ought to exist between father and son. Lamon says:

Thomas seems to have been the only member of the family who was not entirely respectable. He was idle, thriftless, poor, a hunter and a rover. . . . In religion he was nothing at times, and a number of denominations by turns—a Freewill Baptist in Kentucky, a Presbyterian in Indiana, and a Disciple—vulgarly called Campbellite—in Illinois. In this latter communion he seems to have died. In politics he was Democrat—a Jackson Democrat.[2] (pp. 8, 9.)

Thomas Lincoln was not tall and thin, like Abraham, but comparatively short and stout, standing about five feet ten in his shoes. His hair was dark and coarse, his complexion brown, his face round and full, his eyes gray, his nose full and prominent. He weighed at different times from one hundred and seventy to one hundred and ninety-six. He was built so "tight and compact" that Dennis Hanks de-

[2] In *The Soul of Abraham Lincoln*, I have shown the mistake about Thomas Lincoln's religion.

clares he never could find the points of separation between his ribs, though he felt for them often. (p. 8.)

The contrast between this solidly and compactly built man and his extraordinarily long and loosely built son, or supposed son, is recorded not without intent by Lamon, though no comment is made upon it.

In 1828, Abe had become very tired of his home. He was now nineteen years of age, and becoming daily more restive under the restraints of servitude which bound him. . . . Poor Abe! Old Tom still had a claim upon him. . . . He must wait a few weary months before he would be of age, and could say he was his own man, and go his own way. Old Tom was a hard taskmaster. (p. 70.)

Lamon quotes Colonel Chapman, who married a daughter of Dennis Hanks, as saying that Thomas habitually treated Abraham with great barbarity, and Dennis himself as saying that he had seen Tom knock Abe off a fence for giving a civil answer to a passing traveler. His references to Thomas are habitually lacking in any tone of respect, and when, at the age of twenty-one, Abraham leaves home, the biographer says:

It is with great pleasure that we dismiss Tom Lincoln, with his family and fortunes, from further consideration in these pages. (p. 75.)

He inserts a letter of Abraham to his father in which Abraham appears to have believed that Thomas was lying to him. He is not much moved by Lincoln's letter written when his father was dying, giving him pious advice, but being too busy to visit him. He tells of Lincoln's visit to his relatives in February, 1861, after his election to the Presidency:

Thence they went to the spot where old Tom Lincoln was buried. The grave was unmarked and utterly neglected. Mr. Lincoln said he "wanted to have it inclosed and a suitable tombstone erected" He told Colonel Chapman to go to a "marble-dealer," ascertain the cost of the work pro-

posed, and write him in full. He would then send Dennis
Hanks the money and an inscription for the stone; and Dennis would do the rest. Colonel Chapman performed his part
of the business; but Mr. Lincoln noticed it no further; and
the grave remains in the same condition to this day [1872].
(p. 463.)

Lamon's references to "Old Tom Lincoln" are ungracious, and his allusions to Nancy Hanks are anything but
courteous:

Nancy Hanks was the daughter of Lucy Hanks. Her
mother was one of four sisters,—Lucy, Betsy, Polly and
Nancy. Betsy married Thomas Sparrow; Polly married
Jesse Friend, and Nancy, Levi Hall. Lucy became the wife
of Henry Sparrow, and the mother of eight children. Nancy,
the younger, was sent to live with her uncle and aunt, Thomas
and Betsy Sparrow. Nancy, another of the four sisters, was
the mother of Dennis F Hanks, whose name will be frequently met with in the course of this history. He also was
brought up, or permitted to come up, in the family of Thomas
Sparrow, where Nancy found a shelter.
    Little Nancy became so completely identified with Thomas
and Betsy Sparrow that many supposed her to have been their
child. They reared her to womanhood, followed her to Indiana, dwelt under the same roof, died of the same disease,
at nearly the same time, and were buried close beside her.
They were the only parents she ever knew; and she must
have called them by names appropriate to that relationship,
for several persons who saw them die, and carried them to
their graves, believe to this day that they were her father
and mother. Dennis Hanks persists even now in the assertion that her name was Sparrow, not Hanks; but Dennis was
pitiably weak on the cross-examination; and we shall have to
accept the testimony of Mr. Lincoln himself, and some dozens
of other persons, to the contrary.—LAMON: *Life of Lincoln,*
p 12

He notes that the family Bible, in which Abraham made
out the record, in his own handwriting, "has not a word
about the Hankses or the Sparrows."

He says that on the subject of his father and his mother, Abraham "never spoke without great reluctance, and significant reserve." (p. 17.)

He records that John Locke Scripps affirmed,—

"Mr. Lincoln communicated some facts to me about his ancestry which he did not wish published, and which I have never spoken of or alluded to before. I do not think, however, that Dennis Hanks, if he knows anything about these matters, would be very likely to say anything about them." (p. 18.)

He tells that Rev. David Elkin, in his funeral sermon over the grave of Nancy Hanks, "either volunteered, or was employed, to preach a sermon, which should commemorate the many virtues and pass in silence the few frailties of the poor woman who slept in the forest." (p. 28.)

He affirms that when Lincoln spoke in praise of his mother, it was not Nancy Hanks, but Sarah Bush whom he had in mind. He leaves the reader in no manner of doubt that Lincoln had no occasion to be proud of his own mother, whose frailty in the matter that resulted in his birth was a matter to be forgiven in view of his being a better man than Thomas Lincoln could have begotten. While this is nowhere affirmed in this blunt language, it is the evident belief of Lamon, and is the impression left and intended to be left by the perusal of the book.

Lamon thus describes Nancy Hanks:

Nancy Hanks, who accepted the honor which Sarah Bush declined, was a slender, symmetrical woman of medium stature, with dark hair, with regular features, and soft, sparkling, hazel eyes. Tenderly bred, she might have been beautiful; but hard labor and hard usage bent her handsome form, and imparted an unnatural coarseness to her features long before the period of her death. Toward the close, her life and her face were equally sad; and the latter habitually wore the woeful expression which afterward distinguished the countenance of her son in repose.

By her family, her understanding was considered something wonderful. John Hanks spoke reverently of her "high and intellectual forehead," which he considered but the proper seat of faculties like hers. Compared with the mental poverty of her husband and relatives, her accomplishments were certainly very great; for it is related by them with pride that she could actually read and write. The possession of these arts placed her far above her associates, and after a little time even Tom began to meditate upon the importance of acquiring them. He set to work, accordingly, in real earnest, having a competent mistress so near at hand; and with much effort she taught him what letters composed his name, and how to put them together in a stiff and clumsy fashion. Henceforth he signed no more by making his mark; but it is nowhere stated that he ever learned to write anything else, or to read either written or printed letters. (p. 11.)

On all these matters, Lamon's authority for his facts was Herndon, who vigorously, and truthfully, denied having written any part of Lamon's book, affirming that Black " wrote quite every word of it," but who sold to Lamon for $2,000, copies of all his manuscripts, and furnished data which Lamon, or Black, used.

Lamon does not assume responsibility for the story that Abraham Lincoln's father was Abraham Enlow, but he takes pains to make light of Dennis Hanks' refutation of it:

In the gallery of family portraits painted by Dennis, every face looks down upon us with the serenity of innocence and virtue. There is no spot on the fame of any one of them. No family could have a more vigorous or chivalrous defender than he, or one who repelled with greater scorn any rumor to their discredit. That Enlow story! Dennis almost scorned to confute it; but when he did get at it, he settled it by a magnanimous exercise of inventive genius. He knew this " Abe Enlow " well, he said, and he had been dead precisely fifty-five years (pp. 47, 48).[3]

Lamon takes pains to bring in the name of Enlow, however, in an unexplained fight with Thomas Lincoln, whose attendant

---

[3] If Dennis gave this testimony in 1865, Abraham Enlow had been dead not precisely fifty-five years, but only four years. He died in 1861.

ınd unrecorded circumstances he declares afforded one of the
·easons why the family was willing to leave Kentucky and
migrate to Indiana:

It has pleased some of Mr. Lincoln's biographers to repre-
.ent this removal of his father as a flight from the taint of
.lavery. Nothing could be farther from the truth. . . . He
.vas gaining neither riches nor credit; and being a wanderer
)y natural inclination, began to long for a change. His de-
:ision, however, was hastened by certain troubles which culminated in a desperate combat between him and one Abraham
Enlow. They fought like savages; but Lincoln obtained a
.ignal and permanent advantage by biting off the nose of his
ıntagonist, so that he went bereft all the days of his life, and
)ublished his audacity and its punishment wherever he showed
ıis face. But the affray, and the fame of it, made Lincoln
more than ever anxious to escape from Kentucky (p. 16).

It is usually the vanquished, not the victor, who feels the
lisgrace of living in the place where he has had a fight. The
eader is compelled to ask, and Lamon—or Black—intended
hat he should ask, what injury roused the usually good
ıatured Tom Lincoln to such fury, and why the fame of his
.uccessful battle should have driven him from the scene of his
)rowess.

The answer to all these questions is that Lamon, or Black,
ıpparently intended to leave the impression that Abraham
Înlow was the father of Abraham Lincoln, and that Thomas
Lincoln knew it, and that Abraham Lincoln knew or at least
.uspected it.

Ward Hill Lamon had great reason to love Abraham
Lincoln. They were long and intimately associated in Illinois,
vhere Lamon's habits were in many respects very different
`rom those of Lincoln. Lincoln made Lamon marshal of the
)istrict of Columbia for the sake of having him close at hand,
ınd kept him there in spite of the almost imperative demand
)f Congress for his removal. Lamon professed to the end
)f his life to have been Lincoln's true friend; and his daughter,
)orothy Lamon Teillard, has made that claim for her father

in two editions of his *Recollections of Lincoln* (a very different book from his biography of Lincoln) and in a magazine article of her own. But if ever a man had reason to pray to be delivered from his friends, Lincoln had such reason with respect to certain matters which related to the parentage and virtue of his mother.

CHAPTER VI

WHAT DID HERNDON THINK ABOUT IT?

What Mr. Herndon thought has usually been inferred from the passage already quoted in which he relates what Lincoln said to him about his mother. Herndon certainly believed that Nancy Hanks was of illegitimate birth: did he also believe that she was the mother of an illegitimate son? Most readers of his book, including his biographer, Dr. Joseph Fort Newton, answer unhesitatingly in the affirmative. That, it must be confessed, is a natural inference.

In his preface, Herndon prepares his readers for " ghastly exposures," and says that Lincoln rose from a lower depth than any other great man; although some great men have risen from very low down in the social and ancestral scale. He says:

Some persons will doubtless object to the narration of certain facts which appear here for the first time, and which they contend should have been consigned to the tomb. Their pretense is that no good can come from such ghastly exposures. To such over-sensitive souls, if any such exist, my answer is that these facts are indispensable to a full knowledge of Mr. Lincoln in all the walks of life. . . .

In determining Lincoln's title to greatness we must not only keep in mind the times in which he lived, but we must, to a certain extent, measure him with other men. Many of our great men and our statesmen, it is true, have been self-made, rising gradually through struggles to the topmost round of the ladder; but Lincoln rose from a lower depth than any of them —from a stagnant, putrid pool, like the gas which, set on fire by its own energy and self-combustible nature, rises in jets, blazing, clear and bright. I should be remiss in my duty if I did not throw the light on this part of the picture. . .
" God's naked truth " as Carlyle puts it, can never injure the fame of Abraham Lincoln —*Herndon's Lincoln*, ix, x.

Herndon recorded that Mr. Weik had spent much time in investigating traditions regarding Lincoln's paternity, particularly one current in Bourbon County, Kentucky, " that Thomas Lincoln, for a consideration from one Abraham Inlow, a miller there, assumed the paternity of the infant child of a poor girl named Nancy Hanks; and after marriage, removed with her to Washington or Hardin County, where the son, who was named Abraham, after his real, and Lincoln, after his putative father, was born " (p. 6). Against this tradition, he cites " the well established fact that the first-born child of the real Nancy Lincoln was not a boy, but a girl; and that the marriage did not take place in Bourbon but in Washington County."

He tells the camp-meeting story to show the uproarious and somewhat affectionate manner in which the Hanks girls took their religion, and his references to the Hanks family are not respectful, though they lack the open contempt which Lamon displays for both the Hankses and " old Tom Lincoln." His allusion to the funeral of Nancy Hanks Lincoln, and to Parson Elkin's passing in silence the " few shortcomings and frailties " of the poor woman, is suggestive, though not conclusive.

On the whole, it is not surprising that readers of the first edition of Herndon's book generally believed that Herndon believed that Abraham Lincoln was not the son of Thomas Lincoln, and that those who read the later edition were left in doubt.

There is a manuscript of Herndon's, which has never seen the light of publicity, in which he goes farther into this matter. It is not a letter, but a little treatise with a caption. For what purpose he prepared it I am not quite sure. He loaned it to a correspondent, permitting him to keep it until he called for it, and he never called for it. I shall presently quote it in full, and with it will close this chapter.

The little tract which I am about to quote is a remarkable document. It is written on four pages, letter size, and for many years was in private hands. It is now in an important collection, in a fire-proof building, but is not shown to the

curious, and I am informed by its custodian that it has never
been copied except by myself. It is safe from destruction,
either by fire or caprice, and scholars will find it as they have
occasion.

In this document, Dennis Hanks is directly addressed, but
the tract was not intended as a letter to Dennis. Herndon is
answering to himself the rebuke which the Hanks family will,
as he believes, visit upon him, if he publishes the statement that
Abraham Lincoln's mother's name was Hanks and not Sparrow. Herndon believed that Dennis knew that Nancy was
illegitimate, as Dennis himself was, and probably believed
also that Dennis thought Abraham illegitimate; but that Dennis
was shrewd and sly and willing to lie about a matter which
Abraham Lincoln, sharing the same belief concerning his
mother, met with silence, because Abraham Lincoln was too
honest to lie like Dennis.

Readers of Herndon's book have been left in doubt of his
own opinion as to the illegitimacy of Nancy Hanks herself:
but they have not always been sure just what he intended to
imply as to Abraham Lincoln's own paternity. On that subject his book is purposely somewhat vague. Herndon had some
of the shrewdness of Dennis. This little tract leaves no room
for question that at the time of its composition, Herndon was
inclined to believe not only that Nancy Hanks was illegitimate
but that she gave birth to an illegitimate son, whose name was
Abraham and whose proper surname was not Lincoln.

This little tract has appended to it a footnote in Herndon's own handwriting, saying, " These notes were made about
20 August, 1887, at Greencastle, Ind., when I was writing the
Life of Lincoln, or helping to do so." I believe this footnote
to be erroneous. I have compared this document with the
notes which Herndon made at Greencastle, and he used a
wholly different kind of paper and ink. This little tract is
much older than his Greencastle papers, and the note was made
afterward. This was a document which he had previously
prepared, and which he probably took with him to Greencastle, and loaned it to a correspondent with other matter
which he prepared there. In supplying the date, he made

the mistake of thinking that he had written it there. Such mistakes Herndon sometimes made.

I think he prepared this little tract between 1866 and 1871. I think it was in existence when Lamon wrote his book. A comparison of the language of this tract with Lamon's reference to the zeal of Dennis for the reputation of the Hanks family, will, I think, convince the critical student that Lamon had this before him, or at least that Herndon had by 1871 formulated his own ideas in essentially this form. It was probably written not many months after the date of the letter of Dennis, February, 1866 The ink, paper and handwriting, when compared with the Greencastle manuscript, show clearly that it is several years older than those.

Whether this was Herndon's final opinion, we shall learn toward the end of this book. It certainly was in his mind when he furnished his material to Lamon.

NANCY HANKS

By William H. Herndon

Dennis Hanks and all the other Hankses, their cousins and relatives, call Nancy *Hanks,* Nancy *Sparrow.* Lucy Hanks was her mother. Lucy, the mother of Nancy, married Henry Sparrow. Nancy Hanks was taken and raised by Thomas and Betsy Sparrow. Why did not her mother, Lucy Sparrow, keep and raise her own daughter? Did Henry Sparrow object to the mother, his wife, keeping and raising her own daughter?

Dennis Hanks says to me, this, substantially, (to be quoted word for word) in a letter written by him to me dated Feb. 1866·

" Don't call her Nancy Hanks, because that would make her *base-born."*

Very well, Dennis, shrewd, sly Dennis! It is a universal custom, habit and practical rule of all English-speaking people, including the American, as a matter of course, to call all illegitimate children after and from the *mother's* name and not the *father's* name, because of the cruel fiction of the law that such children are supposed to be the children of no one—a rather rash presumption, I willingly admit.

If Henry Sparrow had been the father of Nancy Hanks, then she ought by law and justice be called *Nancy Sparrow,* but, unfortunately, Henry Sparrow, the husband of her mother, was not her father.

Nancy Hanks was born before her mother was married to Henry Sparrow. How is this, Dennis?

Abraham Lincoln, always honest and truthful, says substantially under his own hand in a short life of himself written at Springfield, Illinois, to be a kind of campaign biography of '60, this:

"My mother's name is Nancy Hanks"; or, to put it exactly, Lincoln says, in that short biography of himself written to Fell, "My mother, who died in my infancy, was of a family of the name of Hanks."

Why did he not say, if such was the truth, that she was of the family of the Sparrows?

Simply because she was not of the Sparrow family. Lincoln knew her origin, but kept it to himself in that Fell biography.

I guess I can state what Lincoln himself states in that matter; and if to call her Hanks is to make her base-born, charge her son with the offense!

Dennis, sly, shrewd Dennis, wishes to cover up the truth, smother up the sad fact, if it be such. Lincoln boldly and truthfully speaks out.

And now the question comes, Who was the father of Nancy Hanks, Lincoln's mother?

Lucy Hanks, her mother, was never married to any Hanks, so far as I can find out, nor to any other person before or after she married Henry Sparrow, or before she had Nancy. When Nancy Hanks was born, who was Lucy Hanks' husband? This is quite a pertinent question. What did Lincoln say to Scripps, his campaign biographer?

No one need for this matter rely on what I say or have said, that Lincoln told me his mother was illegitimate. He told me that his mother was an illegitimate child of a Virginia planter or large farmer. However, the record tells its own story, and speaks for itself; and had not the record spoken out, it is more than probable that I should have kept the secret forever, though I was not forbidden to reveal the fact after Lincoln's death.

I never uttered this to mortal man directly or indirectly till after the death of Lincoln.

And now again, who was the father of Nancy Hanks, the mother of the President of the United States?

Will some gentleman, some lady, kindly tell me?

The father of Nancy Hanks is no other than a Virginia planter, large farmer, of the highest and best blood of Virginia, and it is just here that Nancy got her good, rich blood, tinged with genius.

Mr. Lincoln told me that she was a genius, and that he got his mind from her.

Nancy Hanks Lincoln was a woman of very fine cast of mind, an excellent heart, quick in sympathy, a natural lady, a good neighbor, a firm friend. Good cheer and hilarity generally accompanied her; and had she been raised at all [well] she must have flourished anywhere: but as it was, she was rude and rough, breaking, and having difficulty, through all forms, conditions and customs, habits, etiquettes of society. She could not be held to forms and methods of things. And yet she was a fine woman, naturally.

It is quite probable that a knowledge of her origin had made her defiant and desperate. She was very sensitive, and sometimes gloomy. Who will tell me the amount and influence of her feelings in this matter, caused by her origin? Let the world forgive her, and bless her, is my constant prayer.

Lincoln often thought of committing suicide. Why?

Did the knowledge of his mother's origin, or his own, press the thought of suicide upon him?

Who will weigh the force of such an idea as illegitimacy on man or woman, especially when that man or woman is very sensitive, such as Lincoln was? God help such people!

CHAPTER VII

THE COLEMAN PAMPHLET

ABOUT the end of the nineteenth century appeared a pamphlet entitled, *The Evidence that Abraham Lincoln Was Not Born in Lawful Wedlock, Or, The Sad Story of Nancy Hanks.* It was badly printed, with many typographical errors, but was rather well written. It was signed "Wm. M. C., Dallas, Texas." It contained sixteen pages, and was marked to sell for twenty-five cents. It did not sell as well as had been expected, and the author disposed of his remainder to a New York dealer. Some correspondence was had between them, which the dealer kept for some years, and subsequently sought for at the request of the present writer. It could not be found, however, and all that the dealer remembered was that the author of the pamphlet, William M. Coleman, seemed to him an "unreconstructed Rebel," with much prejudice against Lincoln; but he writes me that his recollection is too misty for him to be confident of anything further.

The Seventh Volume of *Who's Who in America* contains a sketch of Coleman, but the sketch dropped out of succeeding volumes, and the Library of Congress has been unable to locate him for me. He probably died in Washington about 1912. I have only one other of his pamphlets—a vehement attack on the Pilgrim Fathers, called by him, "The First Yankees."

All indirection was ended by the Coleman publication. He did not leave anything to be inferred. In his booklet, a spade was called a spade. The large sale which he expected did not occur, but his outspoken declaration cleared the air of all uncertainty. He made no original investigation, but he made it impossible for any one to read the books from which he quoted without remembering what construction had thus been placed upon them.

55

Coleman's pamphlet did not really add anything to what had already been printed by Lamon and Herndon, except that it assembled under one caption what they had said in various places, and by skillful arrangement put the worst possible face upon it. That, however, was probably what might have been expected. The conclusions which Coleman deduced from the Lamon and Herndon material were warranted by what those two had published.

The following pages contain the essential parts of the Coleman argument. The last pages of his booklet are devoted to a synopsis of the Cathey book which we shall examine later. Apparently Coleman had written his own booklet without knowing of Cathey and his theory, but he learned of it before his pamphlet was printed, and included a review of it without attempting to harmonize its theory with his own. As we shall come to the Cathey book in due time, we may omit those portions, as also the preface and the rather labored introduction which occupy the first few pages of Coleman's booklet.

FROM THE COLEMAN PAMPHLET

It is agreed on all sides that Mr. Lincoln knew but little, and cared still less, about his family history, and that he sedulously avoided any reference to it. It is certain that he is mistaken, if he is correctly quoted, when he said that both his parents were born in Virginia.

The name of his reputed father, was Thomas Linkhorn, or Linkern, (for it is found spelled both ways). It was first changed by Mr. Lincoln himself to "Lincoln," and it may be added by way of parenthesis, that, taken in connection with other facts in this history, this change of name may not be without its significance. Why should he bear the name "Linkhorn," if that person was not his father? Then, again, the simplicity of his character will not allow us to suppose that he refused the name of his own father and assumed a loftier sounding one from petty vanity.

Wherever Nancy Hanks may have come from, it is beyond doubt, that the father of Thomas—for whom some writers have forged the Christian name of Abraham—migrated from Virginia to Kentucky, and that Thomas was born in the last named state.

Widespread traditions exist that the son of Nancy Hanks was not a legitimate child.

Writing upon this subject Mr. Herndon says:

"Regarding the paternity of Mr. Lincoln, a great many surmises and a still larger amount of unwritten, or at least unpublished, history has drifted into the currents of Western lore and journalism.

"A number of such traditions are extant in Kentucky and *other localities.* Mr. Weik has spent a considerable time in investigating the truth of a report current in Bourbon county, Kentucky, that Thomas Lincoln, for a consideration from one Abraham Enlow, a miller there, assumed the paternity of the infant child of a poor girl, named Nancy Hanks; and after marriage removed with her to Hardin county." Mr. Herndon adds that a gentleman of Mt. Sterling, Kentucky, who had been judge, and afterwards was an editor, published a paper in support of this contention.

The allegations and arguments of this paper are not given further than to say that the paper alleged a resemblance between Inlow (Enlow) and Mr. Lincoln in facial and physical features, in extraordinary stature and length of limb.

Herndon's reply, however, is feeble. He says the Bible record shows that Abraham was the second child.

In reply to Mr. Herndon it is to be remarked, that this Bible record, made by Abraham Lincoln, contained no entry of the birth or marriage of his mother; and in regard to Abraham being the second child, it must be borne in mind that the entries were made by Mr. Lincoln himself long years after the events recorded, and admitting for a moment, that he was illegitimate, and that he knew it, it was a pious act in him to cover his mother's shame as far as in his power to do so, by making his sister older than himself in the Bible record.

There is also an account given by Lamon of a collision between Thomas Linkhorn and Abraham Enlow, or Inlow, which has its significance. Mr. Lamon says: "They fought like savages; but Lincoln (Linkhorn) obtained a signal and permanent advantage by biting off Enlow's nose." "*This* affray and the fame of it," continues Lamon, "made Lincoln (Linkhorn) more anxious than ever to escape from Kentucky." We are left to form our own conjecture about the origin of the quarrel; no cause is assigned But is not this desperate affray a powerful corroboration of the tradition that an illicit relation existed, or was supposed by Linkhorn to have existed, between Nancy Hanks and Enlow; and may we not presume that the fight was about her? And was not the increased desire of Linkhorn to get away from Kentucky owing to the fact that he felt himself disgraced by the publicity given to the scandal by his fight with Enlow? Is this an unreasonable supposition? Does it not, on the contrary, serve to fill out, explain, bring into harmony, and strengthen the other traditions relating to President Lincoln's birth?

Linkhorn did not remove from Kentucky to fly from slavery and locate in a free state where toil was honorable, as narrated by the romancers; for he was no toiler; but, from all accounts, an ignorant, shiftless vagabond. Besides, there was not at that time, fifty slaves in the county; his more fortunate relatives were slave owners, and there is no reason in supposing that he differed in opinion from other men of his class, of Southern birth. This story of his desire to escape from a land of slavery is of a piece with those fictions which describe the Linkhorn tumble-down shanty, fourteen feet square in an Elizabethtown valley, where the inmates lived in squalid poverty, as a frugal Christian home; the father a gallant frontiersman and the mother a Roman matron of the wilderness. One estimable New England lady, not satisfied with tracing the blood of the Hanks to the Saxon Kings of England, carries it back to the Egyptian dynasties, because in the old Egyptian language she says there is a word, " and " (Hank) meaning soul!

Nancy Hanks is described as being a beautiful girl, with pleasing manners, slender and symmetrical form, and above the ordinary height; a brunette with dark hair and soft hazel eyes, and a high intellectual forehead. It is further remarked of her that she always wore a marked melancholy expression which fixed itself upon the memory of everyone who knew or saw her. It would be interesting to know if she was possessed of this melancholy disposition before her marriage, and if so, when or how it originated.

The reticence of Mr. Lincoln about his mother has been alluded to. Mr. Lamon says: " While he seldom if ever spoke of his own mother, he loved to dwell on the beautiful character of Sally Bush."

Young Abraham Lincoln was ten years old when his mother died. The dearest and sweetest memories and associations which remain of a mother in after years are those which are fixed within the first ten years of life. Mr. Lincoln's nature was deeply affectionate. Why, then, this strange silence in regard to his own mother and the lavishing of all his affections on his stepmother, Sally Bush? Mr. Lincoln aspired to position in social as well as political life; and it may well be that a knowledge of his mother's frailty and his own origin (probably told him by his stepmother) cast upon him that pall of melancholy which shadowed all his life.

In the autobiography which Mr. Lincoln gave to Fell, he disposes of his mother in three lines, giving her Christian or maiden name, and saying she came of a family of the name of Hanks.

Sally Bush first brought sunshine into young Lincoln's life. She was a kind, good, and noble woman; devotedly attached to her step-son, and he no less devoted to her. He always spoke of her in after life as his "saintly mother," his "angel mother;" and yet, she did one thing which is utterly inconsistent with her character unless an explanation can be given. She changed the name of the girl, who had been named Nancy, after her mother, to Sarah. Unaccounted for, this was a mean and contemptible act. Why should not the child be permitted to bear her mother's name? If Sally Bush had some good reason to obliterate from the child's mind, as far as possible, all recollections of her mother, then her conduct is in keeping with her character; otherwise it is not. Her singular silence, too, in all that related to Nancy Hanks when Mr. Herndon visited and interviewed her after the assassination of President Lincoln is an additional ground for the belief that she held the key to the secret.

Mr. Herndon says: "There was something about his (Lincoln's) origin, that he never cared to dwell on"

After his nomination for the presidency, Mr. J L. Scripps, of the Chicago *Tribune*, went to Mr Lincoln and asked for material for a history of his life. Mr. Lincoln replied that it was folly to attempt to make anything out of his early years. Soon after the death of Mr. Lincoln, Scripps wrote to Mr.

Herndon as follows: "He (Mr. Lincoln) communicated some facts to me concerning his ancestry which he did not wish to be published then, and which I have never spoken of or alluded to before."

What these facts were, Mr. Scripps did not tell even to Mr. Herndon, who had been Mr. Lincoln's most intimate friend, and who was then collecting material for his biography.

How is the silence of Mr. Scripps under the circumstances to be accounted for? On one ground only, the communications must have been of such a nature that an honorable man could not use them without permission. Mr. Lincoln was dead, and Mr. Scripps died without revealing them. Was this the secret?

The treatment of young Lincoln by his mother's husband requires explanation. Cruelty is not a trait of such indolent, happy-go-lucky, contented tramps as Thomas Linkhorn is represented to have been. Col. Chapman, who knew as much about the family as any one outside of its circle, and who had possession of the Bible containing the records, is quoted by Mr. Lamon, as saying: "Abe's father habitually treated him with great barbarity." Can his treatment of the boy be connected with his "savage fight" with Abraham Enlow and a knowledge that the boy was not his child?

There is abundant evidence that the Hanks were low and ignorant people. Mr. Herndon quotes from a manuscript of Mr. J. B. Helms in which it is said: "The Hanks girls were great at camp-meeting." Mr. Helms then proceeded to relate a scene of which he was an eye witness at Elizabethtown, and in which one of the young ladies of the Hanks family figured conspicuously. He writes:

"I remember one camp-meeting in 1806. A general shout was about to commence. Preparations were being made. A young lady invited me to stand on a bench where we could see all over the altar. To the right, a strong athletic young man, about twenty-five years old, was being put in trim for the occasion, which was done by divesting him of all apparel except shirt and pants. On the left, a young lady was being put in tune in much the same manner, so that her clothes would not be in the way, and so that when her combs flew out, her hair would go into graceful braids. She, too, was young, not more than twenty. The performance commenced about the same time by the young man on the right, and the young lady on the left. Slowly and gracefully they worked their way towards the center, singing, shouting, and hugging and kissing (generally their own sex) approaching each other nearer and nearer. The center of the altar was reached, and the two closed with their arms around each other, the man singing and shouting at the top of his voice:

> " ' I have my Jesus in my arms,
> Sweet as honey, strong as bacon hams.' "

"Just at this moment, the young lady holding my arm whispered, ' They are to be married next week; her name is Hanks.' "

Mr. Herndon says he did not learn whether the lady performer was the President's mother or not. " The fact that Nancy Hanks did marry that year," gives color, he thinks, to the belief that it was she. He does not think, however, that her hugging partner was Thomas, because such a deed required an enthusiasm and a dash beyond the capacity of that inert individual.

There was undoubtedly irregular blood in some of the Hanks women. Mr. Herndon says he has the written statement of Dennis Hanks, the son of an aunt of the President's mother, that he came into the world by nature's back door.

We give in Mr. Herndon's own words what Mr. Lincoln told him about his mother. Mr. Herndon says (Chapter I, page 3):

" It was about 1850, when he and I were driving in his one-horse buggy to the court in Menard county, Illinois. The suit we were going to try was one in which we were likely, either directly or collaterally, to touch upon the subject of hereditary traits. During the ride he spoke for the first time in my hearing of his mother, dwelling on her characteristics, and mentioning or enumerating what qualities he inherited from her. He said among other things that she was the illegitimate daughter of Lucy Hanks, and a well-bred Virginia farmer or planter; and he argued that from this last source came his power of analysis, his logic, his mental activity, his ambition and all the qualities that distinguished him from the other members and descendants of the Hanks family. His theory in discussing the matter of hereditary traits had been,

*that for certain reasons illegitimate children are oftentimes
sturdier and brighter than those born in lawful wedlock;* and
in his case he believed that his better nature and finer qualities
came from this broad-minded unknown Virginian"

Mr. Herndon continues: " The revelation—painful as it
was—called up recollections of his mother, and, as the buggy
jolted over the road, he added ruefully, ' God bless my mother;
all that I am, or ever hope to be, I owe to her,' and immediately lapsed into silence.

" Our interchange of ideas ceased, and we rode for some
time without exchanging a word. He was sad and absorbed.
Burying himself in thought, and musing, no doubt, over the
disclosure he had just made, he drew round him a barrier
which I feared to penetrate. His words and melancholy tone
made a deep impression on me. It was an experience I can
never forget."

This is one of the "rare occasions" when Mr. Lincoln
made mention of his mother. His exclamation of pity for
her is suggestive of what was going on in his mind. His
melancholy silence is even more so His mother's mother had
sinned, and his own mother sinned in like manner, and did he
know it?

PART II: THE STORIES AND THE EVI-
DENCE IN SUPPORT OF THEM

PART II: THE STORIES AND THE EVIDENCE IN SUPPORT OF THEM

CHAPTER VIII

ABRAHAM ENLOW OF HARDIN COUNTY, KENTUCKY

WHAT I have attempted thus far might be considered a literary and chronological introduction to the subject under consideration. I have endeavored to trace the history of these reports as they appeared in book or pamphlet form down to the beginning of the year 1909, the centenary of the birth of Abraham Lincoln. Concerning two books that appeared in that year we shall have much to say later: but the Coleman pamphlet may be considered as a summation of the situation as it existed before the appearance of the flood of Lincoln literature which the centenary evoked. Of oral tradition and newspaper report we shall have something also to say, and in due order.

We are now at a stage in our inquiry where it will be convenient to consider the several stories separately: for, as Herndon implied, more than one story was current by 1889: and by 1909 the various forms in which the legitimacy of Lincoln was attacked, admitted of classification.

The foregoing chapters present a background for these stories and for their subsequent analysis. I now propose to present in successive chapters the evidence for each one of these in turn.

It has not been wholly easy to organize this material, and to present it as I have desired to do. Even the order in which these names should be considered has given rise to some difficulty; for in some respects the order in which it seems best to introduce them is not the most satisfactory order for their later consideration. But the method which I have chosen will,

I trust, be found to have this merit, that it presents each theory candidly and fairly.

I begin the presentation with the version of the story which has long been, and still is, current in the county where Abraham Lincoln was born, and which has been related to me repeatedly there on successive visits, with substantial uniformity as to its essential features.

The form in which this story is related in and about Hodgenville is that the father of Abraham Lincoln was Abraham Enlow, who lived in that part of Hardin County which is now La Rue, and whose home was near to that of the Lincolns after their removal from Elizabethtown and their settlement upon their own farm where Abraham Lincoln was born.

There is no question that Thomas and Nancy Lincoln were married when they came to Nolin Creek, and to the vicinity of Hodgen's Mill. And that fact gives this story the more ugly form. For, if Abraham Enlow of Hodgenville was the father of Abraham Lincoln, it was not a case in which an inexperienced girl was betrayed, but one in which a woman two years married and already the mother of one child, proved faithless to her husband and committed adultery with another man.

That, according to this story in its developed form, was why Thomas Lincoln and Abraham Enlow had their terrible fight, in which Lincoln is alleged to have bitten off Enlow's nose.

This is virtually all there is of the story. There are no details that tell how it happened. The Enlows were neighbors, and people of property, and there was apparent opportunity for what is alleged to have occurred. The Enlows were tall people like Abraham Lincoln, and are alleged to have resembled him more than did Thomas Lincoln.

On this account, so it is said by Lamon, Thomas Lincoln left Kentucky, and the implication is that the removal occurred because people knew that the fight Thomas had had with Enlow was on account of his wife Nancy.

The Enlows still live in that part of the country. The author has a map of La Rue County marking every creek, road and farm-house, and giving the name of every resident   The name of Enlow still is common there, and all of those who bear it are descendants of Abraham Enlow.   The people of that name are reputable people.   Their names appear, and in honorable relations, in the La Rue County papers   Originally the family were Baptists; but some branches of it are now affiliated with the Southern Methodists   The men are Democrats and during the war the sympathies of this family were with the South.   I have had personal interviews with several of them, and considerable correspondence with one, a grandson of Abraham Enlow.

In this and the following chapters I follow the local spelling of particular names   Some names occur which are differently spelled in different parts of the South   Hence we shall find an Abraham Enlow, an Abraham Inlow and an Abraham Enloe   The variant spellings are given with intent.   As we take up the first of them, Abraham Enlow of Hardin County, it may be noted here, as it will appear later, that this is the present orthography of the name in that locality   But Abraham Enlow's father spelled it Enlaws, and Abraham Enlow himself, to the end of his life, spelled it Enlows.   He was the son of Isom Enlaws, an early settler in Hardin County, and he himself was born, lived and died there.

This book must contain much about Abraham Enlow.   The prominence of his name in these stories has necessitated on the part of the author of this book a diligent effort to learn all that can possibly be learned about the man.   His grave has been visited, and the inscription on his tombstone copied.   His will has been found in the early records of the county where he lived, and a certified copy made.   His home has been located, and the paths, which now are roads, that led from it to the home of Thomas Lincoln and to the several points of interest in this chronicle, have been measured upon the county map.   This book will not end until it has given to Abraham Enlow a permanent record   He will be found a character not lacking in interest, and he has a legitimate place in this narrative.

For our present purpose it is enough to know that there was such a man, one of the old residents of Hardin County, and of that part of it which afterward became La Rue. There is nothing that we require to know about him which will not be discovered and duly attested before this chronicle ends.

CHAPTER IX

GEORGE BROWNFIELD

THE Brownfield story can be told very briefly, but it is important. It is found only in the vicinity of Hodgenville.

When Thomas and Nancy Lincoln and little Sarah moved from Elizabethtown into that part of Hardin County which is now La Rue, in late May or early June of 1808, they did not immediately go to their own farm. The summer of 1808 was spent on the farm of George Brownfield, where Thomas Lincoln lived as a tenant, and worked as a hired laborer, partly on the farm and partly as a carpenter.

George Brownfield, and not Abraham Enlow, so this story goes, was the father of Abraham Lincoln. The Lincolns had as yet no known dealings with Enlow, and may not even have met him, not having as yet removed to the Enlow neighborhood.

George Brownfield had sons, who were tall men like Lincoln, one of them, David, was a very tall man, with unusually long arms He bore, so it is said, a striking physical resemblance to Abraham Lincoln. None of the Enlows looked so much like Lincoln as did David Brownfield.

That is the Brownfield story, and the whole of it We shall comment upon it later. It now takes its place in the list as one of the stories told and still believed by some people concerning the birth of Abraham Lincoln.

George Brownfield, like Isom, the father of Abraham Enlow, was an early pioneer to Hardin County, arriving there about 1794, and his descendants are numerous in and about Hodgenville. They bear a good reputation. Their ancestor, George, was born in 1773, and died near Hodgenville in 1851. He was 36 years of age when Abraham Lincoln was born. He was a man of property, and Thomas Lincoln was in his employ when he first moved from Elizabethtown Mr. L. B.

Handley, attorney for the Lincoln Farm Association, informs me that in connection with his work for that association he made careful investigation, and assured himself that Thomas Lincoln lived on the Brownfield farm on his first removal from Elizabethtown, and was living there in the summer and autumn of 1808. He does not, however, credit the report that Brownfield was Abraham Lincoln's father.

George Brownfield is buried in the old South Fork buryingground, one of the oldest in La Rue County. It is located five miles south of Hodgenville, two and one-half miles beyond the Lincoln Farm. His tombstone bears this record:

" George Brownfield, Born October 23, 1773,
Died May 2, 1851."

The spot on the Brownfield farm where the Lincoln cabin stood is known as the "plum-orchard." It was a natural growth of wild crab-apple trees. I caused it to be identified, and photographed, as I suppose for the first time. It takes its place in the rather long list of residences of Thomas and Nancy Lincoln, and thus has a legitimate claim upon the interest of any lover of Lincoln. But for the purpose of this narrative, it is of very much greater importance than any other one spot with which we have to do. The world is interested, and properly so, in the place where Abraham Lincoln was born; but for the purposes of this inquiry the place of primary importance is that in which Thomas and Nancy Lincoln were living nine or ten months previous to his birth.

The house that stood in the "plum-orchard" is no longer standing, and the odor of the wild crab-apple blossoms is only a memory, but is fragrant as it was on the day in early summer in the year 1808 when Nancy Lincoln discovered in herself the premonitions of maternity. In May or early June of 1808 Thomas and Nancy Lincoln left the little court-house town of Elizabethtown, and took up their residence in a pole cabin in the "plum-orchard" on the farm of George Brownfield. Late in the autumn, after the crop was gathered, they removed to their own home, where in the following February

Abraham Lincoln was born. But the cabin where he was born was not that in which his unborn life began. He was conceived either in Elizabethtown or in the cabin among the apple-blossoms. We shall recur to this subject, and to the probable time, in a later chapter.

CHAPTER X

ABRAHAM INLOW OF BOURBON COUNTY, KENTUCKY

WE come now to what is perhaps the most widespread of all the stories concerning the alleged illegitimate birth of Lincoln. It is, that Abraham Lincoln was the son of a poor girl, Nancy Hanks, and of Abraham Inlow, a miller, who lived on the border between Bourbon and Clark Counties, Kentucky. The child was born, and was old enough to run around, so this story goes, when the father, Abraham Inlow, paid five hundred dollars, and a wagon and team, to Thomas Lincoln, in consideration of which, Thomas Lincoln drove away with Nancy Hanks and the child. They rode away in the wagon, with the child sitting between them, and Thomas and Nancy were married in some county to the west of Bourbon. The child was already named Abraham after his father, and he took the name of Lincoln from his mother's marriage with Thomas Lincoln.

This story has had wide currency among the members of the Kentucky bar, and is or was related in the neighborhood, of Clark and Bourbon Counties, always or nearly always with the information that the child Abe sat between Tom and Nancy when they drove away from Bourbon County to their future home.

The man who did most to make this story widely known was Hon. Belvard January Peters, of Mount Sterling, Kentucky, a classmate of Jefferson Davis at Transylvania University, and for many years a judge and some time Chief Justice of the Appellate Court of Kentucky He was a prominent member of the Disciples Church, and a man of probity, eminent in the annals of the Kentucky bar and bench. A sketch of his life is found in a book entitled *The Bench and Bar of Kentucky,* where his honorable record may be found.

His statement appears in the form of an affidavit, in part as follows:

"I was graduated from Transylvania University, Kentucky, in 1825. I read law with John Boyle, Chief Justice of Kentucky; obtained license to practice law in 1827. My legal and professional career has extended over a period of over sixty years. In all that time I have never heard, among my legal friends (and I have known nearly all the lawyers, old and young, in the State) the fact of Abraham Lincoln's illegitimacy disputed."

This story has been told and retold to successive generations of judges and lawyers until it has come very widely to be credited. In one of its forms it declares that Jesse Head, when a resident of Harrodsburg, Kentucky, told an eminent but unnamed lawyer that Abraham Lincoln was born and old enough to be running around at the time when he married Thomas Lincoln to Nancy Hanks.

Judge Peters wrote this story for the local papers in his home town, and toward the end of his life he took occasion to make oath to his belief in the truth of this story.

This is the story to which Herndon refers, in his statement that Mr. Weik spent much time in its investigation. I have talked this matter over fully with Mr. Weik, and in the proper place will relate what he has told to me concerning it.

I have made diligent effort, also, to learn whether in Mount Sterling, where Judge Peters lived, or in Clark or Bourbon Counties, there is any additional information on this subject. All essential knowledge of this matter appears to be compassed in the general statement, fully and concisely embodied in the affidavit of Judge Peters, that the story has long been current and widely believed as it has here been stated. No documentary proofs are submitted, other than a group of affidavits by people of mature years, and some of them of good standing, to the effect that they have long heard this story, and that it is believed by many people in the counties named, and in other parts of the State of Kentucky. The high reputation of Judge Peters, both for ability and veracity, and his complete confidence in the story, are, after all, the chief reasons to be alleged in favor of it.

CHAPTER XI

ABRAHAM ENLOE OF NORTH CAROLINA

THE story that Abraham Lincoln was the son of Nancy Hanks and of a man named Abraham Enloe of North Carolina, circulated for some years in Swain County, at the extreme western end of North Carolina, and became more widely current as Northern tourists to Asheville and vicinity penetrated in increasing numbers into that general region. These visitors were informed that they were not far from the home of the parents of Abraham Lincoln, and in due time pilgrimages were made to interview the alleged relatives of the President who were still living there. President Lincoln's so-called half-brother, Wesley Enloe, became a man of some note, and from time to time was interviewed by newspaper reporters and others. He and his family were photographed and measured, and their supposed resemblances to Abraham Lincoln were duly recorded. If at first the family shrank from this publicity, the reluctance of its members in time was overcome; and memory at first yielding nothing to the point, gradually grew pliant till it substantiated in all important particulars the story that came to be accepted in that region, by certain of the inhabitants and visitors, as the true history of the origin of Abraham Lincoln.

In the early nineties, allusions began to appear in print, and on September 17, 1893, the Charlotte *Observer*, printed, what is, so far as I am aware, the first full statement of the North Carolina story. It was signed "Student of History," and the author was alleged to have been "a worthy member of an illustrious North Carolina family."

The essential portions of this article follow:

A few years since, probably in 1889, the writer of this communication was informed by Dr. A. W. Miller that he heard n Western North Carolina that there was a tradition in Swain county that Abraham Lincoln was born in that county. That his father's name was Abram Enloe, and the name of his mother was Nancy Hanks. That the house in which he was born was at that time occupied by Wesley Enloe, a son of Abram Enloe, and, ergo, the half-brother of the great president.

In 1890, being in Webster, Jackson County, I met a gentleman who was county surveyor of Jackson, who gave me the story related by Dr. Miller, and added facts in the tradition. The story as related to the doctor was, that Nancy Hanks and Abram were carried to Kentucky by a mule-drover who was in the habit of stopping at Abram Enloe's, at the foot of the Smoky mountains, about 1804. The surveyor's information was that Felix Walker, the congressional representative—the author of the famous expression " speaking for Buncombe "—in order to do his constituent " Abram " a good turn, carried Hagar and Ishmael to Hardin county, Kentucky. He stated also that two citizens, Davis by name, lodged one night at his friend's house and stated that they lived in Illinois, and had emigrated to that State from Rutherford county, N. C. These gentlemen state that Abraham Lincoln was acquainted with them, and on learning they were from Rutherford county, told them his mother had frequently told him she had lived in that county. These gentlemen informed their host (Dr. Egerton of Hendersonville, I think) that Abram Lincoln was one of the big men of the great west, from which they had hailed. This incident happened about 1858.

The following week the writer was in Bryson City.

Dr. Miller was under the impression that Wesley Enloe was a facsimile of Abraham Lincoln, or certain members of the Enloe family were very similar in features to him. The Jackson surveyor had excited my curiosity, and, having a day off, I lost no time, and was soon on my route up the Tuckaseegee bound for the Abram Enloe homestead, just fourteen miles from Bryson City. The road was rocky, and my driver was of the silent kind, so I gave my attention to the shaping of my interview on what loomed up to me as a very difficult subject to handle. A silence of five miles was suddenly interrupted by the driver's inquiry as to my business with Mr.

Wesley Enloe. I replied promptly, " I am going up principally to look at him." This answer left me to my own reflections and the scenery of the Ocona Lufta, a branch of the Tucka-seegee, which is beautiful beyond description. The native Indian sunned himself along the roadside, or paddled his smooth canoe under the overhanging Rhododendron. Suddenly the driver, overburdened with curiosity, at the ninth milestone, interrupted me with the question, "Would I mind telling what I wanted to look at Wesley Enloe for?" "Not at all; I have heard he resembles Abram Lincoln, and that he is his half-brother." The driver then became satisfied and talkative. He stated he had heard the story frequently, and was a relative of the Enloe family himself.

Passing Yellow Hill, the Indian school supported by the government, a down-grade of three or four miles brought us to a beautiful, rich valley farm, the present home of Wesley, and the old Abraham Enloe homestead. The house was not unlike many of the old houses in North Carolina—one story, the roof sloping down over the piazza, with the company-room opening on the porch. Mr. Enloe and his wife were seated in front, a picture of undisturbed contentment and rural happiness. The driver carried his team to the barn, and Mrs. Enloe retired to look after the dinner.

Mr. Enloe was about six feet, two or three inches tall, and, to my great disappointment, bald-headed; his right shoulder a little lower than his left; when standing, just slightly stooped forward. Our conversation took a varied turn—the force bill, the Alliance, crops, walnut rails, etc. I inquired finally if he had a picture of himself before he lost his hair. His daughter Julia, about nineteen years old, was summoned and brought a basketful of photographs. My attention was taken at once by the striking resemblance between Julia and Abraham Lincoln. The picture with a full head of hair failed to satisfy me of a striking face resemblance between Wesley Enloe and Abraham Lincoln. The photograph was taken the year Lincoln was killed, in Waynesville, to which place Mr. Enloe had carried a drove of beef-cattle the summer of 1865.

Mr. Enloe stated that he had never heard his father's name mentioned in his family in connection with Abraham Lincoln. He said: " I was the youngest of a family of sixteen. Such might have been the fact, but of course the older ones would ot be apt to talk to me on a subject like that to which you llude. About 1871, say ten years ago, I learned and heard ıe story read from an Asheville paper for the first time."

The subject was dropped until four, when I started for ome. I remarked, after thanking him for his hospitality, that was perhaps the only man who had ever called just to look t him. The old man was without his coat, with wool hat, arrow brim. He replied pleasantly: " Now that you have een me, what do you think?" My reply was that I must onfess that I was disappointed, but that now seeing him with ıis hat on, with his hands crossed behind him (a favorite osture with Mr. Lincoln), taking in the whole six feet, three ır four inches, there was a resemblance which I had no doubt vas greater twenty-five years past. The resemblance in the ase of Miss Julia is striking.

The old gentleman then related the following incident: ' Two months past, in Dillsboro, in my daughter's parlor (she narried in that town) is a map picture of President Lincoln. She said to me, ' Look at that picture. Did you ever see a ietter picture of my brother Frank?' Frank is my son and ̇ have alway heard he was much like my brother Scroup, who vas said to be very like his father Abraham Enloe. I favor ny mother's people. In size I am like the Enloes."

I failed to find Frank Enloe at home. At Dillsboro, having ı draft to cash, I was informed by the hotel-keeper that William Enloe would cash it. On going into the store filled with customers, I recognized William Enloe by his resemblance ̇o Mr. Lincoln.

On my return east, arriving at Asheville at 3 P.M., I had lismissed the subject from my mind, but resolved to see Colonel Davidson, the father of our late attorney-general. I found him at home, willing to talk. And now, Mr. Editor, here is Colonel Davidson's story as your correspondent re-members it:

" Abram Enloe lived in Rutherford county. He had in his family a girl named Nancy Hanks, about ten or twelve years of age. He moved from Rutherford to Buncombe and settled on a branch of the Ocona, in what was afterwards Haywood, and what is now Swain county. At the end of eight years he moved to the house at the foot of the Smoky mountain, the place above described as the present home of Wesley Enloe.

"Soon after Abram moved, his own daughter, Nancy Enloe, against his wishes, ran away and married a Kentucky gentleman named Thompson, from Hardin county in that State

"In the meantime during the absence of Mrs. Nancy Enloe Thompson in Kentucky, at the home of Abram Enloe a son was born to Nancy Hanks, then about twenty or twenty-one years of age. The relations between Mrs. Enloe and her husband became, as a matter of course, unpleasant.

"There is a lady now living," says Colonel Davidson, "who, as a girl, was visiting Abram Enloe. This lady says that Nancy Enloe Thompson, having become reconciled with her parents, had returned from Kentucky to North Carolina. They were to start to Kentucky again in a few days, and she remembered hearing a neighbor say, 'I am glad Nancy Hanks and her boy are going to Kentucky with Mrs. Thompson. Mrs. Enloe will be happy again.'

"I married into the Enloe family myself. I settled Abram Enloe's estate, and have frequently heard this tradition during my life, and have no doubt of its truth."

He added the following story, which is significant:

"I am a lawyer. I was seated in my office, since the war and soon after its close. A gentleman called, introduced himself as Thompson and stated he learned that I was the man who settled Abram Enloe's estate; that he was a son of Nancy Enloe Thompson. He stated, among other things, that he was a Democrat, and had been an Indian agent during the Lincoln administration.

"I asked," said Col Davidson, "how Lincoln, who was a Republican, appointed him, a Democrat, an Indian agent?"

Thompson replied that Lincoln was under some great obligation to his (Thompson's) mother, and expressed a desire to aid her, if possible, in some substantial way. She finally consented that he might do something for her son, and this is the way I got my appointment.

I have written this at your request, Mr. Editor, hoping that you will open your columns to Col. Davidson and others, so that we may follow the clues these people may furnish, and thus see if there is any truth in this interesting North Carolina tradition.

STUDENT OF HISTORY.

In 1899, Hon. James H. Cathey, State Senator from a district in Western North Carolina, published a volume of 185 pages entitled *Truth Is Stranger than Fiction,* in which he told this story at length. The edition was soon sold out, and he issued a new and enlarged edition under the title, *The Genesis of Lincoln.*

This is the fullest statement in print of the argument against the legitimacy of Lincoln, and it brings to its support the largest body of recorded testimony. Mr. Cathey sincerely believed what he wrote, and he signed his own name and gave the names of the people who furnished him the information. The substance of his argument is thus set forth in the opening pages of his book:

It is the historical teaching that Abraham Lincoln was virtually "without ancestors, fellows, or successors." Whether this is a delusion it does not concern us to argue. He came into the world, and the world understood him not.

It is, therefore, the sole purpose of this little book to present a tradition tending to prove that this wonderful man was not without ancestors. His mother was Nancy Hanks If he was the son of a worthy sire the world is entitled to know who that sire was; when, where and how he lived; whence he came and what his characteristics.

For ninety years, or thereabout, from the time it is said Abraham Lincoln was begotten or born, as the case was, and the breeze occurred in the Enloe home, there has subsisted among the honest people at the center of authority a lively tradition that Abraham, the head of the Enloe family, was Lincoln's father by Nancy Hanks, who occupied the position of servant-girl in the Enloe household

So confident and persistent have the keepers of this old testimony to the origin of Abraham Lincoln been, when plied with interrogatories, that they knew what they were talking about, that there was no opening for superstition, and the most one who was inclined to be skeptical could do was to wonder and say nothing.

One might hug his incredulity by imagining that the people who fathered the strange accounts of Nancy Hanks and Abraham Enloe and a child, and the wonderful story of the striking personal likeness of Abraham Lincoln and Wesley Enloe, are illiterate, fanatical folk who have conjured up a fragmentary fable, how and for what they know not; but this incredulity is all cleared away, like fog before the sunbeams, when one learns that the custodians of the " Lincoln tradition " are numbered by the scores and hundreds of the first people—men and women—of Western North Carolina.

Ladies as well as gentlemen, not only of the immediate section, but also of distant States, visiting at Asheville and other places of resort in our mountains, finding a thread of the tradition, they pulled until their curiosity, at least, becoming excited, they visited Wesley Enloe, the alleged half-brother of Abraham Lincoln, in his hospitable mountain home, were filled with amazement, and went away convinced that the tradition was wrought in cords that could not easily be broken.

People who were familiar with Mr. Lincoln's history, or who knew him personally, were struck with the strange physical resemblance on first sight, and then watched a series of impersonations of Lincoln, as they studied the features and noted the varying postures of the person of Wesley Enloe.

The remarkable tradition, with its flesh and blood corroboration, was from time to time engaged to be written up by journalists, lawyers and clergymen of culture and standing, but nothing more than a hasty, desultory newspaper article was the result. The people over a very limited area of population were being made conversant with the valuable tradition, and its worthy repositors were, one by one, stepping from the earthly stage. It was plainly apparent that in a very few years the old generation would be gone, and a truth of American history, by sheer neglect, would be forever lost.

We felt our incapacity to undertake so responsible a task. We were conscious of the delicacy of the undertaking, but the implicit, unquestioned faith which we had in the truthfulness of the tradition gave us a courage which shrank not from the most formidable-looking anti-traditional hobgoblin.

Thus emboldened we set to work to gather the odds and ends of our folk-history. We resolved at the outset that we would interrogate none but the most trustworthy—people who were in the best position to give a reason for the faith that was in them, together with the story of the relatives of the distinguished subject of our memoir. This we have, in every instance, done. In 1895 the writer conceived the idea of writing a newspaper or magazine article for the simple purpose of making known the tradition to the public generally, hoping thereby to attract the attention of the enterprising journalist, and after that the enduring chronicler; but private concerns interfered, and our purpose was frustrated for the time. Luckily, however, we then obtained the statements of some very aged gentlemen whose testimony will herein appear, and which is of the most important character, who have since died.

With this statement of his reasons, which the author of this volume is confident are truthfully stated, Mr. Cathey proceeded to set forth in detail the tradition which he had heard in the State of his nativity, the publication of his two books, or two editions of the same book with changed title and added matter in the second issue, stimulated greatly the interest of biographers of Lincoln and tourists to the region about Asheville. He said:

The following tradition is more than ninety years old. Its center of authority is Swain and neighboring counties of Western North Carolina:

Some time in the early years of the century, variously given 1803, 1805, 1806, and 1808, there was living in the family of Abraham Enloe of Ocona Lufta, N. C., a young woman whose name was Nancy Hanks. This young woman remained in the household, faring as one of the family until, it becoming apparent that she was in a state of increase, and there appearing signs of the approach of domestic infelicity, she was quietly removed, at the instance of Abraham Enloe, to Kentucky.

This is the most commonly accepted version of the event.

Another pretty current construction of the story is that when Abraham Enloe emigrated from Rutherford county, there came with his family a servant-girl whose name was Nancy Hanks, and who, after a time, gave birth to a boy child which so much resembled the legitimate heirs of Abraham

Enloe, that their mother warmly objected to the presence of so unpleasant a reminder, and the embarrassed husband had the young child and its mother spirited to Kentucky.   These are the two universally accepted versions of the one thoroughly accredited fact.

The tradition subsists on four salient and perfectly conversant points:

First.—That in the early years of the century a young woman took up her abode at Abraham Enloe's, in the capacity of hired girl, whose name was Nancy Hanks.

Second.—That this same girl, Nancy Hanks, while living at Abraham Enloe's, become *enceinte;* or entangled in an embarrassment in which her illegitimate child was the unconscious instigator.

Third.—That the wife of Abraham Enloe, believing that her husband was the father of Nancy Hanks' child, and being unwilling to countenance what she conceived to be a reproach upon herself and children, demanded the disconnection of Nancy Hanks from her household.

Fourth.—That Abraham Enloe heeded the demand of his wife and forthwith effected the transportation of Nancy Hanks and her offspring to the State of Kentucky.

In support of this theory, Mr. Cathey gave a considerable number of statements made to him by old inhabitants of the county where Abraham Enloe lived, including Wesley Enloe, a son, and William A. Enloe, a grandson, of Abraham Enloe. In order to set before the reader the whole body of tradition as it was gathered by Mr. Cathey, the following, which are his strongest testimonials, are given entire, together with his own introductory notes concerning the character of his witnesses:

PHILIP DILLS

Mr. Dills was born in Rutherford county, N. C., January 10, 1808. His father emigrated to the mountains of Western North Carolina almost contemporaneously with Abraham Enloe. Although Mr. Dills was four years old when Jackson whipped Pakenham at New Orleans, he is nimble both in body and mind. He describes the removal of the Cherokees west of the Mississippi; tells of the elections when Clay and Jackson were rivals—of casting his first vote for the latter; recalls the personal appearance of John C. Calhoun, whom he saw and with whom he talked; the duel between Sam Carson and Dr Vance, and many other incidents of early days he distinctly remembers and recites with genuine gusto.

Mr. Dills is a citizen of Jackson county. His post-office is Dillsboro. He said:

" Although a generation younger and living some twenty-five miles from him, I knew Abraham Enloe personally and intimately. I lived on the road which he frequently traveled in his trips south, and he made my house a stopping-place. He was a large man, tall, with dark complexion, and coarse, black hair. He was a splendid looking man, and a man of fine sense His judgment was taken as a guide, and he was respected and looked up to in his time.

" I do not know when I first heard of his relation with Nancy Hanks, but it was many years before the civil war, and while I was a very young man The circumstance was related in my hearing by the generation older than myself, and I heard it talked over time and again later. I have no doubt that Abraham Enloe was the father of Abraham Lincoln."

WALKER BATTLE

Mr. Battle was born February 12, 1809, in Haywood county. His father was one of the three men who came to Ocona Lufta with Abraham Enloe. He was a highly respected citizen of Swain county. The following statement was received from him in 1895. He has since died. His son, Milton Battle, a reputable citizen, is familiar with his father's statement His post-office is Bryson City, N. C. Walker Battle said:

" My father was one of the first settlers of this country. He came here with Abraham Enloe. I have lived here my entire life, and I knew Abraham Enloe and his family almost as well as I knew my own.

" The incident occurred, of course, before my day, but I distinctly remember hearing my own family tell of the trouble between Abraham Enloe and Nancy Hanks when I was a boy. I recall, as if it were but yesterday, hearing them speak of

Nancy's removal to Kentucky and that she married there a fellow by the name of Lincoln; that Abraham Enloe had some kind of correspondence with the woman after he sent her to Kentucky—sent her something—and that he had to be very cautious to keep his wife from finding it out.

"There is no doubt as to Nancy Hanks having once lived in the family of Abe Enloe, and there is no doubt that she was the mother of a child by him.

"No, I never saw Nancy Hanks' name in print in my life, and never saw a sketch of Abraham Lincoln, or heard of him, until he became a candidate for the presidency in 1860."

WILLIAM H. CONLEY

Mr. Conley was born about the year 1812, in Haywood county. He lived the greater part of his life within fifteen miles of Abraham Enloe's. He was a man of intelligence and perfect veracity. The following statement, the original of which is in the writer's possession, was obtained from him in 1895. He has since died.

Mr. Conley said:

"My father, James Conley, was the first white man to settle on the creek in this (Swain) county, which bears his name. Abraham Enloe was one of the first to settle on Ocona Lufta. Enloe and my father were warm friends. I knew Abe Enloe myself well. He was an impressive looking man. On first sight you were compelled to think that there was something extraordinary in him, and when you became acquainted with him your first impression was confirmed. He was far above the average man in mind.

"As to the tradition: I remember when I was a lad, on one occasion some of the women of the settlement were at my father's house, and in conversation with my mother they had a great deal to say about some trouble that had once occurred between Abe Enloe and a girl they called Nancy Hanks, who had at some time staid at Enloe's. I heard nothing more, as I now remember, about the matter, until the year before the war, the news came that Abraham Lincoln had been nominated for the presidency, when it was the common understanding among the older people that Lincoln was the son of Abe Enloe by Nancy Hanks.

" Not one of them had ever seen, up to that time, a written account of Lincoln.   There is no doubt that Nancy Hanks lived at Abraham Enloe's.   She became pregnant while there by Abraham Enloe, and to quell a family disturbance Enloe had her moved to Kentucky, just as my father and mother, and others, have time and again related in my hearing.

" I have no doubt that Abe Enloe was the father of Abraham Lincoln."

CAPTAIN EP. EVERETT

Captain Everett was born April 4, 1830, in Davy Crockett's native county, Tennessee.   He came to what was then Jackson, now Swain county, in the late fifties, and has since lived in twelve miles of the Abe Enloe homestead.   He was captain of Company E, Third Tennessee.   He served through the entire war, showing conspicuous courage at First Manassas. He helped to organize the county of Swain, in 1871.   He was a member of the Constitutional Convention of 1875, that amended the Constitution of the State.   He has been magistrate, mayor of the town of Bryson City, and sheriff of the county.   He is well known throughout the State as one of her best and brainiest citizens.   He said:

" In time of the war, in conversation with various old and reliable citizens of this section, I learned that Abe Lincoln's mother, Nancy Hanks, once lived in the family of Abe Enloe and was sent from there to Kentucky, to be delivered of a child.   The cause of her removal to Kentucky was a threatened row between Abe Enloe and old Mrs. Enloe, his wife.   The people in this county—all the old people with whom I talked—were familiar with the girl as *Nancy Hanks*.   This subject was not only the common country rumor, but I saw it similarly rehearsed in the local newspapers of the time.   I have no doubt of its truth."

CAPTAIN JAMES W. TERRELL

Captain Terrell was born in Rutherford county, S. C., the last day of the year 1829.   At the age of sixteen he came to Haywood, where he lived with his grandfather, Wm. D. Kirkpatrick, until 1852, when he joined himself in business with Col. Wm. H. Thomas, a man of great shrewdness and enterprise.   In 1854 he was made disbursing agent to the North Carolina Cherokees.   In 1862 he enlisted in the Confederate service as lieutenant in a company of Cherokee Indians. Later he was promoted. Since the war he has merchandised and been a railroad contractor. He has represented his county in the legislature and filled other offices of trust and honor. He is recognized throughout Western North Carolina as a most excellent and useful citizen. He said:

"Having personally had some hints from the Enloes, of Jackson and Swain, with whom I am intimately acquainted, my attention was seriously drawn to the subject by an article which appeared in *Bledsoe's Review,* in which the writer gives an account of a difficulty between Mr. Lincoln's reputed father and a man named Enloe.

"I then began to inquire into the matter and had no difficulty in arriving at the following indisputable facts, for which I am indebted to the following old people: The late Dr. John Mingus, son-in-law to Abraham Enloe; his widow Mrs. Polly Mingus, daughter of Abraham Enloe (lately deceased), and their son Abram Mingus, who still lives; also to the late William Farley and the late Hon. William H. Thomas, besides many other very old people, all of whom, I believe, are now dead.

"1st. Some time about the beginning of the present century, a young orphan girl was employed in the family of Abram Enloe, then of Rutherford county, N. C. Her position in the family was nearly that of member, she being an orphan with no relatives that she knew. *Her name was undoubtedly Nancy Hanks.* Abram Enloe moved about the year 1805 from Rutherford, stopping first for a short while on Soco Creek, but eventually settled on the Ocona Lufta, where his son, Wesley M. Enloe, now resides, then Buncombe, after Haywood, later Jackson and now Swain county.

"2d. Some time after settling on the Ocona Lufta Miss Hanks became *enceinte,* and a family breeze resulted and Nancy Hanks was sent to Kentucky.

"3rd. She was accompanied to Kentucky by or through the instrumentality of Hon. Felix Walker, then a member of Congress from the 'Buncombe district.'

"There is no doubt of the truth of these statements. They were all of them well known to a generation just passed away, and with many of whom I was well and intimately acquainted. The following I give as it came to me:

" A probable reason for sending the girl Nancy Hanks to Kentucky was that at that time some of the Enloe kindred were living there. I was informed that a report reached here that she was married soon after reaching Kentucky.

" Mrs. Abram Enloe's maiden name was Egerton, and she was a native of Rutherford county some years ago, meeting with Dr. Egerton, of Hendersonville, and finding that he was a relative of Mrs. Enloe, our conversation drifted toward the Enloe family, and he imparted to me the following:

" Some time in the early fifties two young men of Ruther-ford county moved to Illinois and settled in or near Spring-field. One of them, whose name was Davis, became intimately acquainted with Mr. Lincoln. In the fall of 1860, just before the presidential election, Mr. Davis and his friend paid a visit back to Rutherford and spent a night with Dr. Egerton. Of course the presidential candidates would be discussed. Mr. Davis told Dr. Egerton that in a private and confidential talk which he had with Mr. Lincoln the latter told him that he was of Southern extraction, that his right name was, or ought to have been, Enloe, but that he had always gone by the name of his *stepfather.*

" Mr. Enloe's Christian name was Abram, and if Mr. Lincoln was his son he was not unlikely named for him.

" About the time of the famous contest between Lincoln and Stephan A. Douglass, Hon. Wm. H. Seward franked to me a speech of Mr. Lincoln's, made in that campaign, entitled: ' Speech of Hon. *Abram* Lincoln.' He himself invariably signed his name ' A. Lincoln.'

" To my mind, taking into consideration the unquestioned fact that Nancy Hanks was an inmate of Abram Enloe's family, that while there she became pregnant, that she went to Kentucky and there married an obscure man named Lincoln, the story is highly probable indeed, and when fortified with the wonderful likeness between Wesley H. Enloe, legitimate son of Abram Enloe, and Mr. Lincoln, I cannot resist the conviction that they are sons of the same sire. A photo of either might be passed on the family of the other as their genuine head."

HON. WM. A. DILLS

Mr. Dills is a native of Jackson county, N. C., and resides in the thriving little town which was named in his honor—

Dillsboro. He is an intelligent, progressive citizen. His people have honored him with place and power. He has represented his county in the lower house of the legislature. He said:

"My information with regard to the subject, so far as this country is concerned, is traditional, as the events named occurred long before I was born.

"Several years ago, while I was teaching school in the State of Missouri, I read a sketch of the life of Abraham Lincoln, which ran as follows: 'Abraham Lincoln was born in the State of Kentucky, of a woman whose name was Nancy Savage or Nancy Hanks. His father is supposed to have been a man by the name of Enloe. When the boy was eight years old his mother married an old man by the name of Lincoln, whose profession was rail-splitting. Soon after the marriage he took a large contract of splitting rails in the State of Illinois, where he took the boy and his mother, and the boy assumed the name of Lincoln' The above is a verbatim quotation of the sketch that far.

"On my return from Missouri I took occasion to investigate the old tradition to my own satisfaction. I found that Nancy Hanks once lived with Abraham Enloe, in the county of Buncombe (now Swain), and while there became involved with Enloe; a child was imminent, if it had not been born, and Nancy Hanks was conveyed to Kentucky.

"The public may read in Wesley M Enloe, son of Abraham Enloe, a walking epistle of Abraham Lincoln. If there is any reliance to be placed in tradition of the strongest class they are half-brothers. I have not the shadow of a doubt the tradition is true.

"For further information, I refer you to Col. Allen T. Davidson, of Asheville"

JOSEPH A. COLLINS

Mr Collins is fifty-six years of age and resides in the town of Clyde, in Haywood county. He served three years of the war between the States as a private, after which he was promoted to the second lieutenancy of his company, in which capacity he continued until the surrender. He has been in the mercantile business for twenty-five years, ten years of which he was a traveling salesman. He is now proprietor of a hardware store in his home town.   He is well known over the entire western part of the State as a gentleman of the most unquestionable integrity.   He said:

"The first I knew of any tradition being connected with Abraham Lincoln's origin on his father's side was in 1867 At that time I was in Texas, and while there I made the acquaintance of Judge Gilmore, an old gentleman who lived three miles from Fort Worth.

"He told me he knew Nancy Hanks before she was married, and that she then had a child she called Abraham   'While the child was yet small,' said Judge Gilmore, 'she married a man by the name of Lincoln, a whisky distiller.   'Lincoln,' he said, 'was a very poor man, and they lived in a small log house'

"'After Nancy Hanks was married to the man Lincoln,' said Gilmore, 'the boy was known by the name of Abraham Lincoln.   He said that Abraham's mother, when the boy was about eight years old, died'

"Judge Gilmore said he himself was five or six years older than Abraham Lincoln; that he knew him well; attended the same school with him.   He said Lincoln was a bright boy and learned very rapidly; was the best boy to work he had ever known.

"He said he knew Lincoln until he was almost grown, when he, Gilmore, moved to Texas.   During his residence in Texas he was elected judge of the county court.   He was an intelligent, responsible man.

"Years ago I was traveling for a house in Knoxville.   On Turkey creek, in Buncombe county, N C , I met an old gentleman whose name was Phillis Wells.   He told me that he knew Abraham Lincoln was the son of Abraham Enloe, who lived on Ocona Lufta.

"Wells said he was then ninety years of age.   When he was a young man he traveled over the country and sold tinware and bought furs, feathers, and ginseng for William Johnston, of Waynesville.   He said he often stopped with Abraham Enloe.   On one occasion he called to stay over night, as was his custom, when Abraham Enloe came out and went with him to the barn to put up his horse, and while there Enloe said:

"'My wife is mad; about to tear up the place; she has not spoken to me in two weeks, and I wanted to tell you about it before you went in the house.' Then, remarked Wells: ' I said what is the matter?' and Abraham Enloe replied: ' The trouble is about Nancy Hanks, a hired girl we have living with us.' Wells said he staid all night, and that Mrs Enloe did not speak to her husband while he was there. He said he saw Nancy Hanks there; that she was a good-looking girl, and seemed to be smart for business.

" Wells said before he got back there on his next trip that Abraham Enloe had sent Nancy Hanks to Jonathan's creek and hired a family there to take care of her; that later a child was born to Nancy Hanks, and she named him Abraham.

" Meantime the trouble in Abraham Enloe's family had not abated. As soon as Nancy Hanks was able to travel, Abraham Enloe hired a man to take her and her child out of the country, in order to restore quiet and peace at home. He said he sent her to some of his relatives near the State line between Tennessee and Kentucky. He said Nancy and the child were cared for by Enloe's relatives until she married a fellow by the name of Lincoln.

" I asked the old gentleman if he really believed Abraham Lincoln was the son of Abraham Enloe, and he replied: ' I know it, and if I did not know it I would not tell it.'

" I made special inquiry about the character of Wells, and every one said that he was an honest and truthful man and a good citizen "

H. J. BECK

Mr. Beck was born and reared and has all his life lived on Ocona Lufta. He was one of Abraham Enloe's neighbors, as was his father before him. He is now an octogenarian. He is well-to-do, intelligent and of upright character. He said:

" I have heard my father and mother often speak of the episode of Abraham Enloe and Nancy Hanks. They said Abraham Enloe moved from Rutherford county here, bringing with his family a hired girl named Nancy Hanks. Some time after they settled here Nancy Hanks was found to be with child, and Enloe procured Hon. Felix Walker to take her away. Walker was gone two or three weeks. If they told where he took her I do not now think of the place.

" As to Abraham Enloe, he was a very large man, weighing

between two and three hundred. He was justice of the peace. The first I remember of him, I was before him in trials. In these cases, of difference between neighbors, he was always for peace and compromise. If an amicable adjustment could not be effected he was firm and unyielding. He was an excellent business man."

CAPT. WM. A. ENLOE

Captain Enloe was born in Haywood (now Jackson) county, and is sixty-six years of age. He is a successful merchant and business man. He is a gentleman of superior sense, modesty, firmness and integrity. He was Captain of Company F, 29th N. C. Regiment, commanded by Robt. B. Vance, and served through the war. He has represented his county in the General Assembly. He is a grandson of Abraham Enloe. He said:

"There is a tradition come down through the family that Nancy Hanks, the mother of President Lincoln, once lived at my grandfather's, and while there became the mother of a child said to be my grandfather Abraham Enloe's.

"One Mr. Thompson married my aunt Nancy, daughter of Abraham Enloe, contrary to the will of my grandfather; to conceal the matter from my grandfather's knowledge, Thompson stole her away and went to Kentucky; on the trip they were married. Hearing of their marriage, my grandfather reflected and decided to invite them back home. On their return they were informed of the tumult in my grandfather's household because of Nancy Hanks, who had given birth to a child; and when my uncle and aunt, Thompson and wife, returned to their Kentucky home, they took with them Nancy Hanks and her child. This is the family story as near as I can reproduce it from memory.

"In 1861 I came home from Raleigh to recruit my company. On my return, while waiting for the stage in Asheville, I took dinner at what was then the Carolina House. The table was filled largely with officers going to and from their various commands. The topic of conversation seemed to be Abraham Lincoln. One of the gentlemen remarked that Lincoln was not the correct name of the President—that his name was Enloe and that his father lived in Western North

Carolina. I maintained the part of an interested listener, and no one suspected that my name was Enloe.

"After this, during the war, and while stationed in East Tennessee, I was handed a paper with nearly a column of what purported to be a sketch of Abraham Lincoln's early life in Kentucky—alleging that his father's name was Enloe, and that he (Lincoln) was born in Western North Carolina."

WESLEY M. ENLOE

Mr. Enloe was born 1811, in Haywood county, N. C., and is the ninth and only surviving son of Abraham Enloe. He resides on the same farm and in the same house in which his father lived when Nancy Hanks was banished from the household. He is a quiet, suave, intelligent gentleman of the old school, and a prosperous farmer. He said:

" I was born after the incident between father and Nancy Hanks. I have, however, a vivid recollection of hearing the name Nancy Hanks frequently mentioned in the family while I was a boy. No, I never heard my father mention it; he was always silent on the subject so far as I know.

"Nancy Hanks lived in my father's family. I have no doubt the cause of my father's sending her to Kentucky is the one generally alleged. The occurrence as understood by my generation and given to them by that of my father, I have no doubt is essentially true."

Mr. Cathey's Second Edition reprinted the first edition entire, and added more than a hundred pages of supplementary matter. This was largely a discussion of what had preceded, and a comparison of the theories of the different biographers of Lincoln. There is also considerable added correspondence with scattered members of the Enloe family, but no important addition to the story. Perhaps the most important part of appended matter is in the following pages:

Four things have combined to prevent the real life of Abraham Lincoln: blind hero-worship; aristocratic sentiment; false modesty and aversion to laborious research—four things Abraham Lincoln trampled under his feet as an elephant would trample the mire of the jungle.

Little wonder Abraham Lincoln's origin has been the subject of imagination and conjecture. In childhood and youth his place of abode a squalid camp in a howling wilderness; his meal an ashen crust; his bed a pile of leaves; his nominal guardian a shiftless and worthless wanderer; his intimate associates and putative relatives a gross, illiterate and superstitious rabble.

Little wonder that in some quarters Abraham Lincoln's fame has bordered upon deification. His all but miraculous burst from the wilderness into the nation's eye; his heroic and glorious life-achievement; his sudden passing at the assassin's hand, these, with the element of sadness which was the inseparable genius of his nature and culminating incident of his fortune, are the elements needful to magnify the subject beyond human proportion. Abraham Lincoln passed from the mountain top of earthly greatness into the vast unknown in a halo of heroism, mysticism and sorrow; and doubtless he shall continue for all time to come to draw from all mankind admiration, wonder and tears. In the glamor of this mingled mist and glare the huge proportion of one of the greatest and most human of men has been despoiled by the rude hand of the ignorant enthusiast. The great, refreshing spectacle has been bungled. The pity of it! As a result of the operation of these abnormal influences the entire life of Abraham Lincoln has suffered, but no chapter like that on his origin Here was something out of the ordinary—something unseen; but instead of allowing the light to shine into this grotto in a great life, fanatic biographers and other sinister and designing persons, have endeavored to magnify and involve the mystery for purposes of heathen worship, or have sought to come into possession of it that they might destroy it. The paternal origin of Abraham Lincoln: this is the secret Light, once deflected here and an hundred other nooks and corners in his personality, will light up and become plain and comprehensible.

To evade or conceal a cardinal fact relative to Abraham Lincoln is not only a moral wrong, but a reflection upon his character and a violation of his memory. The nature of his origin is primarily indispensable to an intelligent, not to say full, conception of his character. The correct source of his origin is, practically, universally accepted as a matter of doubt —an unsettled question—an unknown quantity—in his life.

If no trustworthy means were in existence or accessible for the removal of the doubt, for the settlement of the question, moral responsibility would not obtain and the mystery would continue. But, fortunately for posterity, there is in existence and available all the means necessary to a final, correct and satisfactory solution. Using the approved methods of the historian in collecting data, there is not a fact in the first twenty years of the life of Abraham Lincoln easier of establishment than that of his real paternal origin.

There could be but three ways of accounting for the being of Abraham Lincoln or any other man: First, that he was of natural legitimate origin; second, that he was of natural illegitimate origin; and third, that he was of miraculous origin. The first hypothesis has been taken for granted as true and passed without further thought by the casual layman and biographical novice. The second hypothesis or theory has been affirmed by tradition so well defined, closely connected and emphatic that the element of myth is entirely absent; by the two most intimate and distinguished personal biographers of Mr. Lincoln after the most laborious, exhaustive and conscientious research; and by an extensive, intelligent and authentic public consensus. The third hypothesis has been *whispered* by the few, and *voiced* by at least one reputable eulogist who said that "*Abraham Lincoln was without ancestors, fellows or successors.*" It is barely possible that some of Mr. Watterson's contemporaries should construe him literally, and that mankind generally a thousand years hence would do so, it is more than probable. Granted that the third hypothesis is unreasonable, the settlement of the question turns upon the weight of evidence between the first and second.

It is the office of these pages to submit testimony in support of the second theory—that Abraham Lincoln was of illegitimate origin, his father being Abraham Enloe, and not Thomas Lincoln or any one else.

In addition to the sound, sustained and perennial tradition of North Carolina, the author submits in this addenda extrinsic historical data and other cumulative evidence.

Before giving to the public the record of the paternity of Abraham Lincoln in the present enlarged form, we desire to say that the data bearing upon the subject is cumulative, and promises to continue to be for an indefinite time. There is other material now in sight, but inaccessible for the present, or at all, without the expenditure of much time and no little money.

This enlarged edition is the result of the acquisition of several years, and, when time and opportunity permits, facts that may come to light that are worth while, will be included in a subsequent edition. Now that this investigation has been begun it is our duty to accept, preserve and publish all the material, trustworthy facts bearing upon the subject

Two things, we contend, our research have disclosed beyond question: First, that Abraham Lincoln was illegitimate, and second, that his father was an Abraham Enloe.

Another thing is clear as a result of our research: That there has been a determined and systematic effort on the part of at least two of Mr. Lincoln's most intimate personal biographers to discover the truth of his paternal origin and publish the same to the world—these biographers were William H. Herndon, his law partner, and Ward H. Lamon.

Again, there is another fact that is, as a result of this investigation, equally as certain: That there has been a determined and systematic war of suppression and destruction against the publication and dissemination of the truth of Mr. Lincoln's real paternal origin by certain individuals

It was the original purpose of Mr. Wm. H. Herndon to write a rigidly truthful narrative of the life of Abraham Lincoln. How much this purpose was influenced or prevented is a matter that is familiar to persons now living.

Mr. Jesse W. Weik, of Greencastle, Indiana, toward the last in the preparation of his biography, became a collaborator with Mr. Herndon. In 1865 Mr. Herndon visited the scenes of Mr. Lincoln's birth and early years in Kentucky, as did Mr. Weik, later.

These personal visits to Kentucky were made with a view to ascertaining the *truth* pertaining to these early periods in the life of their hero. Mr. Herndon says that " Mr Weik spent considerable time investigating the truth of a report current in Bourbon county, Kentucky, that Thomas Lincoln from one Abraham Inlow, a miller there, assumed the paternity of the infant child of a poor girl named Nancy Hanks, and after marriage, moved with her to Washington or Hardin county, where the son, who was named Abraham, after his real, and

Lincoln after his putative father, was born." Mr. Herndon does not say that Mr. Weik after investigation, found the report to be untrue, but, instead, goes on at considerable length to substantiate the report.

See *suppressed* matter following.

This much may be found in the suppressed three-volume edition of Lincoln by Messrs. Herndon and Weik The question then recurs upon the fact as to whether there was an elaborate investigation of the illegitimate paternity of Mr. Lincoln, and if so, did they write down in their manuscript for posterity, the complete account of their findings. The facts are that Mr. Weik, because of influences brought to bear upon him, receded from his original position of independent recorder of truth and fact and destroyed the original manuscript.

Mr. Lamon bought from Mr. Herndon the use of his original manuscript, paying him three thousand dollars therefor.

But Mr Weik and those associated with him in their campaign of destruction, were careful to make way with every volume of Lamon they could lay hand on.

Through Weik's influence other valuable evidence gathered by Mr. Herndon at great expense was destroyed.

It will be noted that the facts touching Abraham Lincoln's illegitimate origin as first recorded by his intimate friend and law partner between whom and Mr. Lincoln, as Mr. Horace White assures us, there was never an unkind word or thought, are three editions removed from Mr. Herndon's original manuscript. The Lamon biography which we count as one edition, it having within its covers the original Herndon manuscript, the three-volume Life by Messrs. Herndon and Weik, and the two-volume edition by Messrs Herndon and Weik.

It is evident that the three-volume edition was suppressed because of the statements with regard to Mr. Lincoln's illegitimate paternity, for the reason that these are the identical statements expurgated in the last or two-volume edition of Herndon and Weik.

It is establishable that the collaborator of Mr. Herndon, who was the collector of this illegitimate-paternity data, was also the chief agent in the destruction of it. It is even more remarkable that the current expurgated edition in two volumes contains numerous hints of illegitimate paternity but in very subdued form.

These facts evidently show that the original findings of William H. Herndon and Jesse W. Weik, upon the question of Abraham Lincoln's paternity, were indubitable This being admitted the facts which were published in meager or subdued form would indicate the facts which were written or published in complete or elaborate form

And more, is it reasonable that two reputable citizens, cultured and refined gentlemen, the one the law-partner and life-long, intimate friend, and the other an ardent admirer, of a man among the greatest and most illustrious of the time, would, as his personal biographers, write down for the gaze of posterity a *rumor, a report* affecting so personal and vital a subject as that of his origin, and that, too, in defiance of the well-known canons of society?

In view of these facts the conclusion is inevitable, leaving the North Carolina tradition entirely out of the question, that Abraham Lincoln was the son of an Abraham Enloe by Nancy Hanks.

We shall not discuss the question of Mr. Lincoln's illegitimate paternity from the Lamon biography point of view further than to invite the reader's careful attention to the entire quotation on the subject, and particularly to the allusions to the relations existing between Thomas Lincoln and *Abraham* Enloe or Inlow, the name being spelled differently in different localities.

Mr. Lamon's opening paragraphs are significant. He says almost emphatically that Lincoln was of illegitimate paternity. He wrote in the major part from Mr. Herndon's manuscript, and it is evident that he *knew* that Abraham Lincoln was an illegitimate.   Subsequent references to the " Inlows," and to " Abraham Inlow," afford strong reason for the inference that he knew to a certainty the fact he had obliquely though unmistakably stated at the outset.

It were far better had Messrs. Herndon and Weik and Mr. Lamon written and published the plain, blunt facts. By recording a rumor, a vague report, these biographers lowered, vulgarized and jeopardized their office. If, as it is our opinion based upon thorough investigation, these biographers wrote down the true facts about Mr. Lincoln's origin, and these facts were afterward modified and accommodated by others to the end that they might be shadowed with doubt, and ultimately ignored by the student of Abraham Lincoln, the perpetrators misjudged mankind and threw a challenge in the teeth of the very incident they were designing to intercept. Somewhere in the deep of the heart of mankind there is a chamber sacred to the love of truth. The tallest and whitest heroes of history are the martyrs to the cause of truth.

Through Mr. John E. Burton, of Lake Geneva, Wisconsin, the author entered into an extended correspondence with Mr. Cathey. He proved to be a frank and gracious correspondent. His first letter was addressed to Mr. Burton, and was answered by the present author, in a series of questions to which the reply was delayed for some time, but which came at length and was very pleasant in its spirit and ready with all desired information. As the author will comment later upon these letters and upon Mr. Cathey's theory, his own letters, with a single exception, are omitted; but enough will be given from the pen of Mr. Cathey to show his full and mature judgment of the matter.

My letter to Mr. John E. Burton, after purchasing the Coleman pamphlet and the Cathey book which had previously belonged to him, called attention to the following facts:

1. That these two did not agree. One represents Abraham Enloe, the father of Lincoln, as resident in North Carolina, and the other Abraham Enlow as a neighbor of the Lincolns in La Rue County, Kentucky. According to one, Nancy was sent to Kentucky alone, leaving Enloe in North Carolina to adjust matters with his wife as best he could; according to the other he and Thomas Lincoln were both married and neighbors in Kentucky.

2. Thomas Lincoln and Nancy Hanks were certainly married in 1806. Abraham was born in 1809. The pregnancy of Nancy did not antedate her marriage. Moreover, the picture which Mr. Helm gave to Herndon of her public performance at camp-meeting (if it was indeed Nancy whom Mr. Helm describes) does not indicate that she was then visibly

advanced in pregnancy, yet this was just before her marriage. In a community like that she would not have been likely to publish her condition by such conspicuous performance. The theory that she was pregnant at the time when she was married fails to meet many important conditions.

3. If Enlow was Lincoln's father, the matter could hardly have been one of seduction before marriage; it must have been of adultery after marriage. The two books compel the assumption of radically different conditions.

Mr. Burton forwarded my letter to Mr. Cathey, who wrote to him under date of May 16, 1919:

LETTER OF JAMES H. CATHEY TO JOHN E. BURTON

SYLVA, N. C., May 16, 1919.

MY DEAR MR. BURTON:

I was surprised and delighted to get a letter in your bold and steady hand at the comfortable age of 72, once again.

I congratulate you on the vigor which this letter discloses of body and mind. I cannot see why you should not attain the coveted human limit of a hundred.

No, I cannot help your ministerial friend, however much on your own or his account I should wish to do so, if he cannot find the information desired in my last edition of *The Genesis of Lincoln*. This he says he has read. I refer to the enlarged edition, containing your admirable lecture on Mr Lincoln.

It was after I had published my book containing the North Carolina story that I ran across the local yarn with regard to the "Old Abe Enlow" of Kentucky and Nancy Hanks. There is no exact date mentioned by any witness in my book as to when Nancy Hanks lived in the North Carolina Abe Enloe's home, or when she became pregnant.

The Enloes of North Carolina had knowledge of the fact that branches of the family lived contemporaneously in Kentucky. There is no doubt about this. They intervisited occasionally as business or pleasure impelled them.

I do not pretend to speak with the force of an oracle or even to present indubitable facts in my story. I simply conserve a most interesting tradition custodianed by plain pioneers of veracity and integrity who deal not in dates or in the refinements of philosophy.

In fact I do not pretend to believe with the faith that would remove a mole-hill that Abe Enloe of Kentucky could not have been the father of Abraham Lincoln. There is no doubt about there having been a North Carolina Abe Enloe, and that this, the narrative which my book recounts, originated and gained currency in North Carolina or Kentucky about the beginning of the last century.

I am as certain as I am of anything not actually demonstrable that some Abraham Enloe was the father of Abraham Lincoln, and that that responsibility lay between the " miller " Abe of Kentucky and the farmer Abe of North Carolina. I shall not enter into any explanation as to how the story became mixed, but the fact of family relationship and the intercourse between the two families would easily afford a premise from which to proceed.

The very fact that Herndon's and Lamon's lives of Lincoln were suppressed by men of high standing and influence some years ago, and that expurgated parts of these " lives " were the paragraphs which referred to Lincoln's Enloe origin, is sufficient proof of the foundation on *fact* of these statements. Neither Col. Lamon nor Mr. Herndon would have recorded a lie about Lincoln's paternity, and these suppressors knew it.

The real truth is that Abraham Lincoln, among the great men of history has had more than his share of pure personal fiction. Lincoln, like all the very powerful leaders of men, possesses in the language of Chauncey Depew " a superabundance of common sense," with an eccentric turn of intellect susceptible of the strange combination of emotion, deep, tense and feeling, and humor. And yet, in keeping with another character of superlative force, he could be cold and implacable, should occasion arise.

His own cabinet never properly or justly appraised him until he was cold in death. Stanton looked upon him and treated him as though he had been a sort of grotesque heavyweight clown, a sort of wilful incumbrance upon his cabinet. Lincoln is the most difficult of all modern leaders to account for in the usual conventional way. I have studied him from every angle, and the only way I can account for him is, that from his conception to his death he was the child and instrument of a special Divine Providence.

To tell you the truth, it little matters to me or the average or common man, how he came into being. We know that he was our friend and brother, and that his life was *spent* for our welfare. We know he overruled egotism and ignorance in his own camp, for Union and Liberty.

If you are looking for a religious man in Lincoln, as the orthodox world accepts and interprets the term, you shall be disappointed. Lincoln was a religion unto himself. He personified the virtues of mankind. In early life he was skeptical; in his maturer years he was no churchman. It may have been that in his Presidential years, with the awful weight of responsibility upon him, and in the shadow which the death of his son cast upon his great soul, he became humble and trusting and worshipful of the Deity. It is certain that he always recognized the Almighty in his messages and state papers, and that he acknowledged his dependence, and that of the nation, upon His blessing and guidance.

No! To a person who has spent much time and pains upon the story of Lincoln, there is so much that bears the marks of sinister and objective tempering that one despairs of the facts, and would wipe out the whole blurred thing if he could, and leave the great man alone in his naked, human, soul-grandeur.

You, sir, are just 20 years my senior, but I venture you are in some respects the younger man. In my younger days I was fool enough to hurt myself by drink; and while I am a teetotalist I shall never entirely recover from the effects. I lost my father two years ago; my two sons went to the army, and my eldest daughter and youngest son died from influenza last winter.

I suffered the loss of my business and my home, and am reduced to poverty, yet I have not lost faith in God or my fellow man, and am hopeful of a better day. . . .

I shall never forget the peculiar circumstances under which we came to collaborate on the last edition of the Lincoln "Genesis," and shall always cultivate a rich plot in my heart for you. May your elderly years be extended, and your peace be perfect when you " put out to sea."

I am, Yours at your instant service,

Cordially,

JAMES H. CATHEY.

At this point I took up correspondence with Mr. Cathey, and I quote one of his letters here, and others in the latter part of the book:

LETTER OF HON JAMES H. CATHEY

SYLVA, N. C., Aug. 29, 1919.

REV. WM. E. BARTON,
    OAK PARK, ILL.
DEAR SIR:

I am frank to confess to pure negligence and procrastination in failing to answer your letter. This is a very ugly failing of mine I beg your pardon.

No, I did not construe your letter as antagonistic or provocative. I think I understand your attitude. For fear you might misconceive *my* attitude toward the subject of Mr. Lincoln's origin, I wish to say that I do not deem the subject of the very profoundest importance. I think, if possible, the truth should be known, and that Mr. Lincoln should be accounted for through the regular human channels. I am sure from my limited investigation there has been more of newspaper exaggeration and prevarication, fiction and blaring untruth written and spoken about Abraham Lincoln than any other great man in history.

Lincoln was not of divine origin, as was the Carpenter of Nazareth, and he did not spring from nothing, as he must surely have done if Tom Lincoln and Nancy Hanks were his real parents. Worshipful biographers and delirious orators like Robert G. Ingersoll and Marse Henry Watterson have invested his advent with a godlike glamour and his character and career with superhuman qualities of the myth of pagan deities. Some of these ascribe to Nancy Hanks the highest and noblest characteristics of intellect and soul. There is absolutely no base founded in fact for any such extravagance. Not a single one of Mr. Lincoln's deifiers have had the audacity to claim anything superior for Tom Lincoln We make no doubt that Lincoln's mother was a woman of good native sense and sensibility, but like many another of Eve's progeny of unfortunate environment

My attitude toward the North Carolina and Kentucky traditions is this·

I am as completely convinced as I could be of any fact not mathematically provable that an Abraham Enloe was the " accidental " father of Abraham Lincoln. I think Lincoln was a child of special providence. That his unconventional advent into the world is *one* of the *mysteries*. I think God, if you please, shaped him *from before* his conception for the work which he wrought and the identical destiny which he fulfilled. The Architect designed him in the mold of the mass of men and gave him a mind to perceive and a soul to feel. To these was added a personality of perfect poise which functioned like a healthy human organ to the cry of every creature. Lincoln was always human. Indeed, he was one of the two *greatest humans* in a thousand years of Anglo-Saxon history. The other was Robert Lee. Lee was the greatest spiritual commoner among aristocrats. Lincoln was the great inte'-lectual aristocrat among commoners. Both were virtuous as Socrates. Yes, Lincoln was the instrument of Providence. through and by human if extraordinary means. It seems that if you would read my little book, brother Barton, you would get my attitude toward the story itself. I simply wrote it to preserve an interesting tradition. I do not claim infallibiliy for the " recollections " or the main fact. I do claim that it is very extraordinary; the subsistence of their tradition since the early years of last century here and in Kentucky among two generations of people as honest, honorable, and truthful as any.

Of late I have become somewhat disgusted with the attempt of a South Carolinian to prove that John C Calhoun was Lincoln's father. If this sort of thing persists, I shall call in every book of mine unsold, burn the last remaining copy, and wash my hands of the whole business. I have never been too deeply impressed with the correctness of the morals involved in the dissemination of such a story I may be prudish or cowardly. If it is a lie that Lincoln was sired by old Tom Lincoln, ought the world to be enlightened or should it remain in blissful ignorance?

As to my own story:

I am like the great savior of the Union,—" The short and simple annals of the poor."

I am fifty-three years of age next December; a long, lank Appalachian mountaineer of Scotch-Irish ancestry, as the name Cathey implies. I was raised up on the farm by a rigorous-minded hard-working great-hearted father; received a very common school training. Have farmed, lumbered, clerked in store, got law-license; written a little and drank liquor betimes. My wife has raised a highly respected family of four boys and three girls, three of whom are dead. Drink and the devil have deprived me of a career, but I am happy to tell you that I have done with drink and the devil, and with the return of fair health, I have hope and purpose to cut some figure for the better yet.

I did not tell you that I have misrepresented my section of the Tar-Heel State in both houses of the General Assembly.

I would advise you to say nothing in your book on the religious side [1] of Lincoln about his illegitimate origin. If you doubt, give the public the benefit of your silence.

Pardon this presumption.

Yours very respectfully,

JAMES H. CATHEY.

P.S. I am due you and myself to say that I have been a semi-invalid since last October, but am improving. Write me again, and pardon my open-speaking, as this (frankness) is my trait. J. H. C.

---

[1] This letter was written when the author was preparing his *The Soul of Abraham Lincoln* for the press. He had no occasion in that volume to refer to these stories.

CHAPTER XII

THE HARDIN STORY

In a short essay by Miss Ida M. Tarbell on the parents of Abraham Lincoln, used in a brochure for the Lincoln Farm and also as the preface of one set of Lincoln's writings, several names are given of men who severally have been reputed as the father of Abraham Lincoln. Among the family names she gives that of Hardin. In the course of my investigation of this subject, I listened for any mention of that name, but for a long time I did not hear it. I made a few inquiries without result, and had come to question whether this name belonged in the list which I was compiling. At length, in Washington County, Kentucky, I learned the story. It was given to me by a lawyer, belonging to one of the old families, who, however, took pains to assure me that he did not himself credit it. He said, however, that so far as he had ever heard, this was the only form in which the story of Lincoln's illegitimacy had ever been current in that county; and I found that he was totally ignorant of such other forms of the story as I had occasion to mention to him.

The story in brief is this: That while Nancy Hanks was living in Washington County in the home of Richard Berry, Martin D. Hardin, afterward known as General Hardin, visited her on his way to Frankfort, he being at that time a member of the Kentucky Legislature, with the result that a child was born who was subsequently known as Abraham Lincoln. This is virtually all there is of the story, and any additional details are to be supplied from the records of the Hardin family.

The Hardin family is one of the oldest and most honorable in Kentucky. It first settled in Washington County in 1786 and its history in the state is nothing short of illustrious. The family is of Huguenot descent. After the massacre of St. Bartholomew three Huguenot brothers migrated from France to Canada. Finding the climate there too cold, one of them migrated to South Carolina and two to Virginia. About 1765 Martin Hardin, descended from one of the two Virginia brothers, removed from Fauquier County, Virginia, to George's Creek on the Monongahela River. His seven children, three sons and four daughters were born in Virginia between 1741 and 1760. All these removed to Kentucky and settled within a circuit of ten miles of the present site of Springfield

The eldest of these three sons was Colonel John Hardin, for whom Hardin County was named. He was born in Virginia October 1, 1753. He fought against the Indians in 1774 and was wounded. He fought bravely in the Revolution. In 1780 he located lands in Kentucky on his treasury warrants. In April, 1786, he removed with his wife and family to Nelson County, settling in that part which afterward became Washington County. He fought with George Rogers Clark. He had three sons and three daughters.

One of his sons, Martin D. Hardin, was born June 21, 1780, and died October 8, 1823. He married, 1808, Elizabeth, daughter of General Benjamin Logan. He studied law with Colonel George Nichols and practiced it at Richmond and Frankfort in that state He was Secretary of State of Kentucky under General Isaac Shelby, 1812-1816, and United States Senator, 1816-1817. He died in Frankfort, October 8, 1823, aged 43. He was the father of Colonel John J Hardin, M.C, of Illinois, who was killed at the battle of Buena Vista in Mexico, February 23, 1847.

General Martin D Hardin is the hero of whatever romance is associated with the name of Nancy Hanks in Washington County Those who told me of this story were careful to say that it never had any wide vogue in that county and now is never heard of In a subsequent chapter I shall have occasion to refer to it again.

CHAPTER XIII

CHIEF JUSTICE MARSHALL AND ANDREW

THE Enlow or Inlow story as related in Bourbon County, Kentucky, is the one most widely current in the State, and the one vouched for by the highest names that stand behind any of these stories. It is the one to which Mr. Jesse W. Weik gave most attention when investigating these rumors before the publication of Herndon's first edition.

In the same locality is found another story, which names Inlow, but assigns him a more honorable part; making him in a way the protector rather than the betrayer of Nancy, and a chief agent in securing for her a home and a husband and a name for her boy.

This story has a place in literature, having been written up in a thin volume which now lies before the author

In 1889, Mrs. Lucinda Joan (Rogers) Boyd published her book *The Sorrows of Nancy*. Its argument is:

1. That Nancy Hanks, the mother of Abraham Lincoln, was an illegitimate child, daughter of Lucy Hanks, Hornback or Sparrow, and a man named Marshall, son of Judge Marshall, of Virginia, Chief Justice of the United States. Nancy Hanks was born near Lynchburg, Virginia, in sight of the Blue Ridge mountains, and there her mother, Lucy Hanks, Hornback or Sparrow, lies buried. The father of Nancy Hanks, son of Hon. John Marshall, was killed "in border warfare."—BOYD, *The Sorrows of Nancy,* pp. 77-78

2. That Abraham Lincoln, son of Nancy Hanks, was born out of wedlock, near Thatcher's Mill, on or near the line that divides Clark from Bourbon County, Kentucky. "In the year 18—," Nancy was living "with other women" in a cabin near this mill, a place apparently open to all comers. Lincoln's father was Andrew ———, adopted son of John

Marshall. Andrew's father was an Englishman who perished in the same battle with young Marshall. In that "battle," therefore, Abraham Lincoln lost both his grandfathers, ——— Marshall, and the English father of Andrew ———.

In this narrative, "Inlow, the miller," is represented as having been intimate with the women of the cabin, but as not being the father of Abraham Inlow is represented as expostulating with Andrew and warning him not to desert Nancy, the mother of his child. Nancy was deserted, however, and Inlow was presumably the agent of Andrew, or else acted under some sense of consideration for the forlorn young woman, whom he also had assisted in the downward path. Although he himself was neither her betrayer nor the father of her child, he felt some responsibility for her shame, and appears to have been the man who secured a shiftless fellow, Thomas Lincoln, to marry her and assume the parentage of a son who sat between Thomas and Nancy as they rode away to be married.

On this theory the name of Abraham Lincoln's father is not given, and Inlow is shielded from direct responsibility for her condition. But the implication concerning her is that she was at this time a public prostitute; though the story which is written around these alleged facts holds her up to pity because of her love for her betrayer, and her hard fate in marrying a man who was her inferior.

Mrs. Lucinda Boyd set forth her theory in a statement in her preface:

I visited Washington, D.C., for the first time, about ten years ago. As I was approaching the Capitol, I came in sight of the statue of Chief-Justice Marshall, seated. There, thought I, as I looked at it, is the finest likeness of President Lincoln I have ever seen. I looked at it for some time from all points of view before I read the name After reading the inscription, a certain saying of my father's flashed across my mind, and I determined to learn the truth, *the whole truth,* concerning Abraham Lincoln's ancestry. I have done so—as the following affidavits will show.—*The Sorrows of Nancy,* pp. 6, 7.

The visit to Washington would appear to have been made about 1889; the book was issued in 1899.

The affidavits which make up the Appendix are several in number, and some of them will be cited in other relations. That portion of her own affidavit which embodies her father's testimony is immediately in point:

The affiant, L. Boyd, states that a few days after the assassination of President Lincoln, her father, the Rev. Samuel Rogers, born near Charlotte Court House, Va., in the year 1789, (a soldier in the War of 1812, and minister of the Christian Church in Kentucky and other states from the time or shortly after the time when Alexander Campbell founded the Disciples' Church, until 1877, when he died) said to her:

" The grandmother of Abraham Lincoln was called by the several names of Lucy Hanks, Hornback, or Sparrow. Nancy, Lincoln's mother, was the child of Lucy Hanks, Hornback or Sparrow, and a son of Judge John Marshall, of Virginia. Nancy Hanks, Hornback or Sparrow was born near Lynchburg, Va., and in sight of the Blue Ridge Mountains, and at the foot of them, her mother, Lucy, lies buried.

" Nancy's father—son of Judge Marshall—was killed in ' Border Warfare.'

" Lincoln's father was the adopted son (whether by law or not, I do not know,) of the same Judge Marshall, of Virginia, mentioned above, and was the son of an Englishman, who fought and was killed in the same battle in which the said Nancy's father perished. Abraham (afterward called Lincoln) was born near Thatcher's Mill, on or near the line that divides Clark County from Bourbon County, Kentucky, and was born out of wedlock. I have often seen the place where he was born."

Rev. Samuel Rogers is dead, as above stated, but in his life he knew Kentucky and Virginia well, and was among the first men who preached the new religion in those two states.— *The Sorrows of Nancy, Appendix.*

This statement, with other matter with which we are not immediately concerned, was sworn to by Mrs. Boyd, probably in Lexington, as it is witnessed by the clerk of the Fayette County Court, September 25, 1895.

It opens at least three interesting lines of inquiry,—

1. The identity of "Nancy Hanks, Hornback or Sparrow," and her mother, "Lucy Hanks, Hornback or Sparrow," with the mother and grandmother of the President.

2. The identity of the son of Chief Justice John Marshall who was the father of Nancy Hanks, and who was killed in "Border Warfare."

3. The identity of the "son of an Englishman who was killed in the same battle in which the son of Judge Marshall was killed," thus depriving Abraham Lincoln of both grandfathers at one swing of the scythe of Time. In the narrative which makes up the body of the book, and of which an outline follows, she names him "Andrew," but does not give his last name.

Between the Preface, in which she sets forth her thesis that Lincoln was the son of a protégé of Chief Justice Marshall, and his mother a daughter of one of Judge Marshall's sons, and the Appendix, in which she publishes the affidavits on which her theory rests, Mrs. Boyd tells in the form of a short story or novelette what she believes happened to Nancy Hanks. While she does not pretend to confine herself to historic facts in this part of her book, the novelette is her reconstruction of history, and claims to be in its essential statements historical.

The story begins in Virginia, at the foot of the Blue Ridge Mountains, in the latter part of the eighteenth century. In a cabin lives a young unmarried woman, Lucy, and her little daughter, Nancy, who has no right to a father's name. Near them lives an old Negro woman, Joult, whose stories of frontier life are interwoven, but form no vital part of the narrative.

In her girlhood, Nancy meets a boy named Andrew, who assists her at the burial of a dead bird, whose death sets Nancy to asking questions of immortality and the resurrection, when she might better, perhaps, have been strengthening her soul against the time when she should meet Andrew again.

There is an aged white woman, Old Nance, who visits the cabin, and who knows that the best blood in Virginia flows in the veins of little Nancy. Old Nance comes to celebrate the birthday of little Nancy, which Lucy keeps as a day of mourning. Lucy remembers her unwedded lover, and believes that had he not been killed in border warfare, he would have come back and married her. She still loves the dead man who gave her child life.

One day a grand gentleman in three cornered hat and gold knee-buckles[1] visits the neighborhood, and is struck by the appearance of little Nancy. He inquires whose child she is, and Lucy covers her face with her hands and does not tell him. But " the grand gentleman lost his self-control, and dashed the gourd " in which Lucy was giving him a drink, upon the rocky bridle path, and rode away. In answer to Nancy's question, " Who is that?" Old Nance, little Nancy's aunt, replies, " That is your grandfather, Judge Chief Justice M——."

Andrew is with the judge, and Nancy asks about him.

" He is the son of his adoption. He is the son of an Englishman, who came here and died, and Judge M—— made him his heir at law after his own son was killed on the frontier, some years ago."

Lucy did not live long after this incident. She died on the next Christmas, and was buried there in sight of the Blue Ridge. Slaves dug her grave and made her coffin, and no minister conducted a funeral service, but the dome of heaven was her mausoleum, and above her grave was whispered by the winds, " I am the resurrection and the life."

The next Spring the widowed robin, whose mate Nancy and Andrew had buried, came with a new mate, and Nancy prayed by her mother's grave.

The second part of the story is laid in Kentucky. " How old Nancy and little Nancy came to Kentucky, and with whom, is not known. Certain it is, however, that in the year 18—— they were living with other women in a cabin on the line that divides Clark County from Bourbon."

There, in time, Andrew appears: and Mrs. Boyd discourses on the negligence of the guardian angel, on the selfish

[1] Chief Justice Marshall was as negligent in his attire as was Abraham Lincoln. The gold knee-buckles are probably not historical.

way in which men love and of the tender and confiding and unprotected way in which the women love. In these respective ways Andrew loved Nancy and Nancy loved Andrew.

"Inlow the miller" is introduced, apparently to clear his name. He sits on a log with Andrew and whittles, and as they sit he warns Andrew that Nancy is young and loves him, and that he must not treat her as if she were a hardened sinner. But the lesson was lost upon Andrew.

"That man never lived, who, if he heard a girl loved him, and were convinced of the fact before he heard it from another, did not seek the girl and prove it again and again to the satisfaction of his own inordinate vanity." This is the not very flattering opinion of Mrs. Boyd, and Andrew is her instance in point.

One day Old Nance and Little Nancy visited Winchester, the county seat of Clark County. It was new and rough but had its own pride and fashion. There Nancy met face to face Andrew, with "a real lady" on his arm. Not only did he pass Nancy without speaking, but the "lady" asked Andrew, in Nancy's hearing, "What lovely barbarian is that?"

Nancy went back to the cabin with the other women, sick in body and mind, nor did she ever recover her cheerfulness.

Two years later a new lover appeared, and Nancy accepted his suit, pressed through Abraham Inlow. She consented to become the bride of Thomas Lincoln, and when the two went away together, there rode between them a little boy, the child of Nancy and Andrew.

Nancy did not live long. She died still kissing the hand that had smitten her and loving Andrew to the end. "Nancy died young, and her soul has long since confronted the soul of the man without whom Abraham Lincoln never would have been born."

Above her lonely grave in Indiana, Parson Elkin, whom Mrs. Boyd calls Robert, though other authorities call him David, read the words of Holy Scripture, "I am the resurrection and the life."

So ends the story, and then follow the affidavits which attest the principal facts alleged. We shall later inquire into the accuracy of this story.

CHAPTER XIV

JOHN C. CALHOUN

MOST of these traditions have given us instead of Thomas Lincoln male parents not greatly above him in mental caliber or in culture. But we have found certain stories which cannot thus be reproached. We end this list with one which ascribes the paternity of Abraham Lincoln to John C Calhoun, the noted South Carolina Senator and advocate of States Rights. Together with Henry Clay and Daniel Webster, he made up the famous triumvirate of the Senate, during the long discussions that preceded the Civil War.

This story appeared in four articles in *The State,* a leading newspaper of Columbia, South Carolina, by Mr. D. J. Knotts, a resident of that State.

With some difficulty the author secured access to these articles. Extra copies of the papers containing them were not available, and few if any of the great libraries had noticed or preserved them. They were obtained, however, after some search.[1] But the author will not quote them here, as a prolonged correspondence with the author led him to go over the ground more thoroughly than the articles had done; and the story can best be presented in his letters, which, after having been copied, were sent to him for revision, and were corrected by his hand:

LETTER FROM D. J. KNOTTS

Swansea, S C., Aug. 23, 1919.

DR. BARTON.

MY DEAR SIR: Your letter of inquiry with regard to President Lincoln dated Aug. 17 was received today. I will say, I continued my investigations very much beyond

---

[1] I am indebted to Mr. F. H. Meserve of New York for photostat reproductions of these articles; but as my own letters from Mr Knotts are much more complete, I use those instead of the articles in *The State*

what was reported in the four articles in *The State*. I examined by mail through clerks in the office of lands and wills in about 44 counties in about nine states, Illinois included. I found the Illinois and Indiana clerks very careful and prompt and exceedingly attentive. Some of the Virginia, North Carolina and Kentucky clerks were slow and indifferent. Most of the clerks were very communicative as to conveyances and wills. I always sent $1.00 as a spy-out, to see if there was anything of value; if so, I would send more and ask more; and that would furnish ground for more talk. In all I spent several hundred dollars.

The great war broke into my plan for a full pamphlet. I wrote an article of about four columns, and another of about 4 or 5 more for the paper, but the war occupied so much space they could not publish the contributions now.

Mr. John P. Arthur of North Carolina wrote a history of Western North Carolina about four years ago and gave space to about twenty pages as to my views and endorsed them fully. He had previously written some in a North Carolina paper claiming Abraham Enloe, a man near his home in North Carolina. A book had been written by Cathey of the same county as Enloe, who knew all the Enloe descendants and they all claim that, too.

A daughter of this Enloe, then quite old (she made her statement twenty-five years ago) stated that when she was 8 or 10 years old she could well remember a young Nancy Hanks and child in her father's home; and that an old negro woman that had belonged to this family would swear (she was nearly grown at the time) "that there was a young lady by the name of Hanks and baby in her master's home, and caused Old Mis' much trouble." From this they fully believed it when told that this girl was taken across into Tennessee. Their efforts failed to get any refuge for this Nancy Hanks how she got there, and finally resolved she was a hired girl in the Enloe home and came to this end. Enloe's eldest daughter, also a Nancy, carried her across into Tennessee, where she (Nancy Enloe) had married, and thus they provided this escape for this poor deceived girl. Nancy Enloe married John Thompson, recorded as owning land in Carter County, Tennessee. In 1809 she sold out, and with the Enloes moved west.

My own research is from Amelia County, Virginia, where William Hanks came from the Rappahannock country and raised a family of twelve children, and hence the great exodus of this family almost everywhere.

One of the girls married Abraham Lincoln's father, Thomas Lincoln, and moved to Kentucky.[1] Then Joseph settled in Nelson County, Kentucky. Two of the girls married Berrys and settled in Washington County, and also a single sister, Lucy, came to Washington County with them.

Now remember Lucy; she cuts a big figure in this play.

Luke, the youngest boy, James and John came to South Carolina. James and John shortly went on to Kentucky and Tennessee. Luke left a will which I found after hard searching giving 210 acres of land and all other property to his wife, Ann. Joseph in Kentucky died, leaving will and one horse to each of five boys and a heifer to each of three girls—eight children. Nancy, the youngest, got a heifer named "Pied" Nancy gave birth to Dennis Hanks, and then married. Here is the firm hold of Mrs. Hitchcock and Henry Watterson for Lincoln's mother.

I fortunately got hold of Mary Ellen Hanks, who married a Manon, and now lives in California. She is a daughter of John Hanks, Lincoln's associate, rail-splitter in Illinois, and grandson of Joseph and nephew of Nancy. Mrs. Manon writes fully and freely about matters. She says she was about 18 years old when Abraham was nominated; was in Springfield at the time; knew him, and also Dennis, who was her father's cousin. Lucy Hanks, of Washington County, was mother of Nancy, and then married Thomas Sparrow. Lucy was Thomas Lincoln's aunt, and one of four sisters in the county near Springfield, Kentucky (two Berrys and Mrs. Sparrow and Lucy). Thomas and Nancy had one child, Sarah, and their friends after Nancy's death tried to fix the records to date back the marriage, and failed signally. Richard Berry signs as Nancy's guardian the marriage bond of Thomas Lincoln and marries Thomas, and then Jesse Head poses as a Methodist minister and returns for marriage eighteen certificates[2] alleged to have been performed

[1] This paragraph stands as Mr Knotts wrote it and as it was approved by him in the revision, but I think he did not intend to say this exactly as it is said—W. E B.
[2] The number is sixteen—W. E B.

by him in about two years. The law requires an order from the clerk of the court before the issue of the bond or the performance of the marriage; these forgers were really ignorant of the law's requirements.

I wrote the great Methodist publishing house of Louisville to inquire if there was any Methodist minister of the name of Jesse Head in Kentucky from 1800 to 1820. They replied that they had no such man on their record, but that Dr. Gross Alexander, of Nashville, Editor of the *Methodist Review*, had all records and could answer fully. I appealed to him in the same words, without giving reasons, if any Jesse Head was a Methodist minister in Kentucky from 1800 to 1820. He answered emphatically, " No."

The clerk in Springfield, Kentucky, would answer no letter or give any information. I tried three lawyers and asked them to search the records and neither of them would answer. I hired a lady expert from Nelson County who had done my work there. She reported fully the bad condition of office, and said the clerk said he was a Democrat and he could not afford to hurt the feelings of Lincoln's friends; that the vote was too close. She gave inventories of the Lincolns' and Berrys' estates (all good, and owned several negroes).

I do not know when Luke's wife Ann came into Anderson County, North Carolina. But she kept for several years a tavern near her home at the famous cross roads called Craytonville. In 1807 John C. Calhoun passed there from his home and law office at Abbeville Court House. It was 21 miles to the tavern and 20 miles to Pendleton, the next Court House. It was in 1807 that John C. Calhoun commenced his practice at Abbeville, and in that year began his journeys which occasioned his visits to the tavern going and coming. The lawyers and judges were accustomed to stop at the tavern for dinner or over night. Here Calhoun met Nancy Hanks. She was born February 10, 1787, and was just about twenty years of age.

Well, to make a long story short, for it would take several pages to show the reality of this from his kindred and from hers, which I have beyond question, Abe Enloe, from North Carolina, was a horse-dealer and slave-trader also. Thomas Lincoln had come from his uncle, Isaac Lincoln's, home in

Carter County, Tennessee, to assist Enloe with his mules and slaves, and here Calhoun hired Lincoln for $500 to take this girl to the west with him. She was confined on the way at Enloe's home, and several weeks after crossed through into Tennessee. Enloe lived in what is now Swain County, North Carolina, on its western edge adjoining the mountains.

The Enloes surrendered their claim of kinship to Lincoln when they got this trail.

In 1816 Isaac Lincoln died, and in 1816 Thomas sold his little farm in Hardin County, Kentucky. He had never paid for his farm, and he started his westward trail. Nancy, poor girl, died in May, 1818, and was released from this unnatural confinement and entered into rest.

In 1834 Ann Hanks's estate was settled, and the disclosure shows twelve children, and one, Nancy, missing. I have searched the record closely and there are full returns of each, except Nancy.

Lincoln's life is a sad story, and, he said, made him a fatalist. He was a truly great figure in history, a plain, unpretending man, the opposite of Jeff Davis and Woodrow Wilson.

What Lincoln told his co-partner, Herndon, in 1850 about his lineage, and reported in his Life of Lincoln, was obnoxious to his many friends, and they recalled the entire publication, except about half a dozen copies, which they did not get: they expunged that matter completely in the new edition. W. C. Hinson, of Charlestown, S. C., who was a great admirer of the war President, and a wealthy producer of sea-island cotton, and who died about two years ago, struggled hard to obtain one of these copies, and finally succeeded in procuring one for about $300.[1] He kindly loaned it to me, and I compared it with the second edition, which I own, and it certainly is true. Mr. Herndon seemed to admire his great friend truly, and to be fair, but told the entire truth, good and bad, as he saw it.

Jeff Davis' record is really worse than Lincoln's. Thomas Lincoln and Joe Davis, Jeff's father, were both very trifling men. Joe's wife taught in the family of Simeon Christie, and is said to have been a very intelligent woman. Christie

[1] If Mr Hinson paid $300 for a first edition of Herndon, he paid an excessive price. It can be had for $50 —W. E. B.

was a slave lord, and a wealthy man. When things had gone too far with Mrs. Davis, Christie gave Joe Davis four slaves and some money, and sent him off to Kentucky, too. His family shifted further South, and got more under slave conditions; Thomas Lincoln went North and got under abolition ideas. These two men, Abraham Lincoln and Jefferson Davis, came to the front in the critical time of God's providence, each the right man. Davis' energy and independence served the negro in the end, for it drove the Confederacy to its ruin; and Lincoln's capacity to keep the Union mainmast up brought the war to an end with the nation unbroken. I am a real believer in God's sovereignty, and can see how He managed our Civil War. I see His hand, also, in this last great war.

Respectfully,

D. J. KNOTTS.

I asked Mr. Knotts so many questions suggested by this letter, he responded in a formal article, with a caption. Although it repeats some things which he had previously written, and states some things which appear in his later letters, it deserves to be printed entire; for it is the most complete exposition of the theory of which Mr. Knotts is the earnest protagonist, that John C. Calhoun was the father of Abraham Lincoln.

THE FATHER OF ABRAHAM LINCOLN

By D. J. KNOTTS

We have located the Hanks family, William and Joseph, in Nelson County, Kentucky, and the wives of the two Berrys, Mrs. Lincoln and Lucy, in Washington County. Abraham Hanks sold out and moved West. Thomas and his sister, Mrs. Draper, remained and died in Virginia. James and his wife, Nancy, and John, who owned real estate, are of record as selling out in Virginia. John is on record as being in two law suits by the court records. Both these brothers left Virginia. The Anderson tradition is that Luke, the youngest, and his three older brothers, came to South Carolina. John and James are especially mentioned as two of them and others by tradition, name a George or a Robert. They all went West and left Luke in South Carolina. In his own sons he calls his eldest son, Thomas, for his oldest brother in Kentucky. The next bears his own name Luke, then follow John, Robert and George, named for his other brothers. He calls his youngest daughter Nancy, the name of his brother James' wife.

In 1785, Benjamin Harris obtained among other grants in South Carolina one of two hundred and ten acres of land on Hen Coop Creek of Rocky River. On this place Luke Hanks lived and made a will on May 14, 1789, giving to "my beloved wife, Ann Hanks," all his property, real and personal, and appointing her and "my friend, John Hanie," as co-executors. In October afterwards it was properly probated from record by John Ewing Calhoun. The real estate and personal property were appraised in pounds, shillings and pence, the farm being valued at forty-two pounds, or $210, and the personal property at one hundred pounds, or $500 It included one mare and colt at $38.50; one bay filley, $20; two cows and calves, $18 50; one steer, $7 75, and one heifer, $5. Among the items was one feather bed and furniture, $38.50; another feather bed and furniture, $42. There were ten hogs valued at $17. This place was then in Pendleton County and the records in the clerk's office at Abbeville have been destroyed, except records of wills were saved. I cannot learn when or how Luke Hanks obtained ownership.

Nothing more is of record until 1833, by which time Anderson County was formed. A suit for division is of record in the clerk's office and it is there the heirs or children are named. The sons, Thomas, Luke, John, Robert and George, and the daughters, Lucinda Pruit, Scilla South and Elizabeth, who had married the co-executor, John Hanie. He was a widower, and three of his sons, Stephen, George and Anthony Hanie, had married three of the younger girls, Martha, Susan and Judith. Anthony had died and his widow, Judith, had married John Hall. In all there were eleven heirs when properly classified, but most of them were dead or living in other States and the illegal arrangement and citation made the process anullity. Valentine Davis and his wife, Jane, who was daughter of the eldest girl, Elizabeth, now dead, brought a suit properly by employing Peter Van Diver, a competent lawyer, and he properly arranged the entire heirship and notified in all fifty-six heirs of the estate. Twenty-seven of them were beyond the State. Amongst them appears a new heir to this humble estate, Nancy Hanks.

Nancy Hanks and the other twenty-six heirs who lived beyond the State were legally notified by a newspaper citation There was no personal property, the real estate alone being advertised and sold.

Mr. Geiger, of the law firm of Geiger & Wolfe, and myself searched carefully for the cost and result of sale and for the receipts. Of these which we knew to be in full, or the definite amount of the dead ancestor, we discovered by comparing with other receipts of known percentage of the estate that twelve shares of equal amount were necessary to balance properly the total and make possible a clear sale receipt. This showed that they first tried to settle with one share too few, and the appearance of a Nancy beyond the State explains fully the twelfth heir. Myself and my old friend and schoolmate, James F. Tribble, and Mr. Geiger, made search afterward and could find no receipt for this Nancy Hanks, either personally or by proxy. The poor girl had been resting in the little graveyard on Pigeon Creek, Indiana, since 1818, and it was 1834 before the estate was finally settled. Of course, living members of the family knew of the escape of Nancy; but really these men did not likely know the real trail of this exiled South Carolina girl, which has so bewildered her biographers.

The mystery remained till 1849, when James L. Orr was elected to Congress and chanced to meet Mr. Lincoln, who had previously served for two years, but was not re-elected for this Congress. Mr. Orr was afterward Governor of South Carolina and also judge. He died in 1872 in St. Petersburg, Russia, whither President Grant had sent him as Ambassador.

Judge Orr had made physiognomy a special study in his political life. On meeting with Mr. Lincoln in Washington, after the expiration of his term, possibly as a lawyer appearing before the Supreme Court, or as a political explorer for the future, Judge Orr informed him of his marked resemblance to the Hanks men, in Anderson County, South Carolina. Mr Lincoln replied, " We may be of kin, as my mother was a Nancy Hanks." On pursuing the matter, Judge Orr noticed Mr. Lincoln quietly but decidedly denied him the opportunity of any further inquiry, and he so informed the Hanks men on his return. From them he got the truth of the trouble which led to the flight of Nancy Hanks.

Judge Orr's father had succeeded Ann Hanks as tavern-keeper at Craytonville about five miles east of the historic two hundred and ten acres of land already referred to. This tavern was at the famous cross-roads, one leading from Abbeville by Craytonville on to Pendleton. It was eighteen miles to Craytonville and twenty miles farther to Pendleton. This was a regular resting place for the lawyers going either way. Here John C. Calhoun, the young lawyer from Abbeville, who had graduated from Yale and commenced his practice at Abbeville in 1807, met very often this orphaned country girl.

Who was Mrs Ann Hanks or when she died I have no information excepting that contained in these lists made in the suits and by the assistance of Mrs. Laura Hanks, who, in 1841, married Stephen Hanks, the grandson of this Ann Hanks, and Mrs. Jane Drake, a daughter of James Emerson, who was born in 1821 and raised in this Hanks settlement with whom I had two interviews; and also by the aid of Matthew E. Hanks, of Gum Log, Arkansas, who left here in 1846, when he was twenty-one, with whom I had an extended correspondence. These three knew mostly all of these Hanks heirs, and through their contact with these could tell of the others. All these could tell me very decidedly that about all members of the family whom they knew who were members of any church were Baptists. Mr. M. E. Hanks says that his father, George, joined no church, and he himself became a Methodist after he moved West. He could remember when he was a small boy of their damming a little branch on his father's place to provide a pool for the baptism of Elizabeth, his aunt Betty. In later years the Hanks family became divided between Baptists and Methodists.

I have already related that General Armistead Burt, who married a niece of John C. Calhoun, and served for a long time in Congress with Calhoun, told some young lawyers in great secrecy and in the privacy of his own home that young John C. Calhoun in his early life loved a handsome country girl named Nancy Hanks, and when things came to the worst he hired a man named Lincoln to take her away; and that this proved to be a very serious period in Calhoun's young life.

Mrs. Anna L. Byrd, whose first husband was Dr. W. C. Brown, of Belton, S. C., and who was younger brother to Governor Joe Brown, of Georgia, was before marriage a Dean, a highly respected family of intelligence, moral worth and refinement. She was herself a cultured, refined matron. She gave me before her death a statement that in 1856 she married Dr. Brown and shortly after her husband, in her presence, asked old man Johnny Hanks if these reports of Lincoln's being Calhoun's son had any base in truth, and that Mr. Hanks replied that they were true, saying "Nancy was my father's sister and I know whereof I speak." He said that when it was known that Nancy had sinned, she asked permission to stay until she conferred with her uncle, who lived as she said, as best I can remember, in Tennessee, that Calhoun was the cause of her trouble and that he had promised to give her $500 to take her away.

Mr. J. B Lewis also told me that he was for years secretary of the Masonic Lodge at Anderson, and while he was making out Judge Orr's Masonic credentials to go to St. Petersburg as Ambassador in 1872, he talked freely about this matter to his brethren in the hall, how he came to catch on to this, and that he had investigated to his full satisfaction. He said that Nancy went from South Carolina with horse-traders and that little Abe was born on the way and subsequently went on to Kentucky after a few weeks.

I had a lengthy correspondence with the Enlow family in western North Carolina in whose charge Nancy was placed by her friends here to convey her West. Abraham Enlow lived in western Buncombe County, in the part which is now Swain County, on Ocona Lufta River, right at its entrance through the Smoky Mountains. J. J. Enlow, a grandson of Abraham Enlow, says very flatly that the Enlows all know that in the early part of the nineteenth century a girl named Nancy Hanks was in their grandsire's home with a little baby, who afterwards became the President of the Republic, but they always considered that he was really Abraham Enlow's son. He told me these two facts, that his father's sister, Polly Mingus, was at this time quite small, but could relate the facts, not being old enough to comprehend the situation, but that "old Aunt Milly," who was nearly a grown negro girl at the time and raised by his father, had told his father and mother (Wesley Enloe and wife) she knew that young girl Nancy well and it gave old Miss " a heap of trouble," but Miss Nancy, who had run away and married John Thompson, carried her off when she came back to see old Master and Missis before she moved to the West, and Mr. Enloe says that Al. Davidson and others say that President Lincoln had appointed her son as agent in the Indian Mission, a paying and responsible office, as a reward for " his mother's kindness to my dear mother."

I was in Asheville, N. C., two years ago and spent a half-day in the clerk's office, and with Mr. J. S. Styles, a great grandson of Abraham Enlow. He frankly admitted that the presence of this girl in his grandsire's home was conceded by all the family and that they all looked on President Lincoln as a kinsman, but had never been able to ascertain how and from where he came. He said President Lincoln had appointed members of the family to two offices in Washington in 1861 and that he had attempted writing up the matter from this view, but that a year or so ago his house had burned and had destroyed all his data and proof. He said that beyond a doubt his great-grandsire employed Congressman Felix Walker to see and convey this girl and her infant son across into Tennessee; that there was no question concerning Mr. Walker, who represented the government in charge of the Cherokee Indian interest near his home. He placed Nancy in charge of a prominent Indian, named New, who took charge of this girl and his great aunt, Nancy Thompson, and conveyed them through the Pass in the mountains into Tennessee. Mr. Styles was a middle aged man and a successful lawyer at Asheville. He talks freely and without reserve about this matter. The records in Carter County show that John Thompson bought a hundred acres of land in 1801 and sold them in 1809, and disappears from the records. Abraham Enlow bought several tracts in Henderson County and sold out, and in 1808 bought the home in Swain.

Mr. John P Arthur, who wrote the *History of Western North Carolina* a few years ago, obtained for me the statement of two ladies whom he said were reliable, that they heard Miss Elvira Davidson, who married the son of this Congressman Felix Walker, say that she was visiting Mrs Walker before marriage and saw Enlow and Walker in a long conversation, and when Walker came in he told Mrs. Walker that Mr. Enlow was arranging with him " to carry that young woman and her baby across into Tennessee "; and that Mrs. Walker replied, " I do hope now that will bring peace to Mrs. Enlow's home." She said also that Enlow and Walker lived near each other and this Mrs. Elvira Walker died about forty years ago, an old woman, but she made this same statement to others before her death. She was a sister of Colonel A. F. Davidson, of Asheville, who was the lawyer that controlled the estate matters of Abraham Enlow in 1844, about the time that Colonel Van Duyver was straightening up the Ann Hanks estate in South Carolina. Mr. John P. Arthur vouches for the veracity of these two ladies who gave him this statement.

While in Asheville two years ago attending the Southern Baptist Convention, I searched the office for records. The estate had been settled I found in Heyward County, which had been cut from Buncombe County and included what is now Swain County. The clerk very kindly assisted me. We found a transcript of a portion of the estate sent up from Heyward to arrange with some heirs who lived in Buncombe still. In this transcript was a record of sixteen negroes divided by the widow, Mrs. Abe Enlow, amongst her children and one named Milly is in the list and described as " active, hearty and intelligent, but old." Also I find Nancy Enloe Thompson named among the heirs who had already gotten her share and that she was beyond the State,—a very strong corroboration of J. J. Enloe's statement. Mr. Enloe is a son of Wesley Enloe, who was born in 1808 and died about fifteen years ago. J. J. Enloe says he is fifty-five years old and has talked this over with his father and mother.

Mr. James H. Cathey, who lives near the old Enloe home in North Carolina, several years ago gathered a great amount of information from the older citizens of the surroundings and from the family. Their family tradition is an effort to prove that Abraham Lincoln was a son of Abe Enloe, as he was familiarly called, but Cathey cannot account for the presence of this girl there and furnished suppositious statements from others to the effect that she was there as a servant girl attending to the duties of the home and was thereby caught in this misfortune.

Isaac Lincoln owned several tracts of land across in Tennessee on Watauga River, from 1787 to 1815. This home was about three miles from Elizabethtown and now holds the remains of Isaac Lincoln and Mary Ward Lincoln, his wife. Their resting place is nicely marked by suitable tombstones. So Mrs. W. M. Vaught and James D. Jenkins both inform me. They have given me the epitaphs from both, and furnished me copy of wills of each from record. It is near Cumberland Gap through the mountains in Virginia and about fifty or sixty miles from Enloe's home in North Carolina.

It was here Thomas Lincoln had gone and awaited the arrival of this belated girl, who met him at Isaac Lincoln's farm. The details of her stay there and her removal into Kentucky and the time of her leaving Isaac Lincoln's home and the length of her stay in Kentucky before her leaving in 1816 for Pigeon Creek, Indiana, will ever remain the mystery and uncertainty in this wonderful tragedy in American history. From her leaving Kentucky in 1816 till her death in 1818, there is much less speculation, but only a few things are known beyond controversy and doubt. Much has been written without any foundation in fact or reality of those two years, prior to her death in 1818, with no minister to preach her funeral, until a Baptist minister named Elkin rode from Kentucky several months afterward and preached it.

This and Mr. Lincoln's statement to a prominent Baptist editor that " What I may be worth to the world is due to the influence of my dear Baptist mother," and what Mr. Herndon says in his life of Lincoln, that the influence of his Baptist mother in his early life made Lincoln a fatalist for life is about all the definite information we possess as to her religious faith and life. The Hanks family elsewhere than Luke's family are pedobaptist as far as can be learned, and Mrs. Manon sustains this statement of the Kentucky and Illinois branches.

Thomas Lincoln was a religious cosmopolite. He had no firm abiding faith and went from one denomination to another, and finally died a Campbellite. He seems to have had as little aim in life as in his religious faith.

The statement so often made that Thomas Lincoln worked for years at Elizabethtown, Kentucky, with a Joseph Hanks, a carpenter, who had brought up this girl Nancy Hanks, is all without any foundation. This Joseph Hanks died in Nelson County in 1783, leaving a will. There is no record of his ever owning any property in Hardin County. Mrs. Mary Ellen Manon, daughter of John Hanks, says the old Hanks home was out on the falls of Rough Creek, about fourteen miles from Bardstown, the county seat of Nelson.

I have gotten from Miss Barber, the librarian of the Carnegie Library at Atlanta, a true copy from the *Atlanta Constitution,* made for me September 5, 1915, of a letter of Abraham Lincoln of April 2, 1848, to a relative of his, David Lincoln, of Virginia, in answer to his of March 30, inquiring about the Lincoln family. He says he knows but little of the brothers of his grandfather, Abraham; speaks a good deal of Mordecai, Thomas Lincoln's oldest brother, and can tell a good deal of him and that he moved to Illinois, where he died. He says, " My father is still living in the seventy-first year of his age in Coles County, Illinois; I am in my fortieth year." He says, " Thomas, my father, has told me that my grandfather had four brothers, Isaac, Jacob, John and Thomas: is this correct? " He seems to know but little of them in the rest of the letter, except of Isaac, of whom he says, " I am quite sure that Isaac resided on the Watauga River near a point where Tennessee and Virginia join and that he has been dead more than twenty or perhaps thirty years, and that Thomas moved to Kentucky, where he died many years ago."

Now Isaac bought his home in that locality in 1787 and Thomas Lincoln was then not over eleven years old, but he was the one from whom Abraham seems to have gotten all his information of the Lincoln family and he appears clearly to have known the exact place of Isaac's residence and about when he died. Thomas Lincoln bought 238 acres of land in Hardin County in 1803 and sold in 1814. He possibly lived here till 1809 and went with Enloe, with Kentucky mules and horses, and met Nancy, whom he brought back with him. He never paid for this place and may have lived in Tennessee at Isaac Lincoln's when employed by Enloe to go into South Carolina. He moved on five or six miles from this place and then in 1816 left for Indiana. He moved often, was a wandering Arab. He and Nancy of Washington

County could have commenced life when he was twenty-one and given room for Sarah to have married Aaron Grigsby in 1816 and not 1826, as the biographers claim. When this Nancy died no one knows and where this Sarah lived while he was away after 1809 in Tennessee no one can tell. Likely she lived with her grandmother, Lucy Sparrow, or in the home of one of her three aunts. Her mother Nancy must have died shortly after 1806, or about that time, after spending these years with Thomas Lincoln. In 1806 it is claimed this forged marriage took place. It is very certain when he came off to South Carolina in 1809 he had made overtures to Miss Sarah Bush, whom he afterward married and brought to the situation in 1819, after Nancy's death. That is why I have struggled so hard with the clerk of Washington County and the three lawyers to ascertain definitely as to the date of the marriage and its record and why they all evade.

Mr. James D. Jenkins says Mrs. W. S. Tipton, now of Texas, and a very old lady and a near relative, had written him that she is a daughter of David Lincoln Stover and a great-niece of Mrs. Isaac Lincoln. She says that in early life she had seen a chimney on the side of Lynn Mountain where once stood a house, the foundations of which are still visible, and says her grandmother told her that Thomas and Nancy Lincoln once lived in that house and that they were very poor people. This was on the farm of his uncle, Isaac Lincoln.

Mrs. Tipton's grandfather went and lived with Isaac Lincoln and his wife after they lost their only son and child by drowning. Her relatives became the heirs by the will of Mrs. Isaac Lincoln at her death in 1834. She relates that it was said Thomas Lincoln was a very lazy, thriftless man and his uncle could not improve him. Her estate in 1815 possessed about thirty-eight negroes.

We have read much of Nancy Lincoln's bright intelligence and of her capacity to teach little Abe and Sarah, but the records show that the only place where her signature occurs is to a deed in Kentucky, where she joins Thomas Lincoln in the sale of the farm, and she signs with a cross mark. Her father, in 1789, in the certified copy of his will, also signs with a cross mark, and Joseph Hanks in Nelson County in his will in 1783 signed with a cross mark. But illiterate as she seems to have been she left an ineffaceable impression on the mind of her distinguished son; and has left the impression so far as collectable of being a woman of good, hard sense But she is justly accused of brooding over a sad situation too hard and too severe for endurance.

On Pigeon Creek, Indiana, the admirers of her son have erected a nice monument to her memory; but the life of her son and its results will ever be the greatest crown to that mother of whom he always spoke with a respect and reverence nigh akin to adoration

He was a child of destiny, if ever such a one existed. He had the peculiar traits to fit him for his arduous, irksome task, and no public servant in American history ever more earnestly or more unselfishly devoted himself to his task. Not till General Garfield could telegraph, " President Lincoln is killed, but, blessed be God, the Republic lives," did his eventful life come to its end and he to rest from his labors.

He was a man elevated from the common people, but it never misled him. Though sorely tried he was never cast down; though awfully beset by trials he never gave up, but met his duty with reverent energy.

After 1832 John C. Calhoun made slavery and not the tariff the real issue and his letters to distinguished Southern men showed that we could not unite the Southern people on the tariff, but that the slavery question must be pressed as the vital issue and the tariff and others as secondary or subsidiary. For twenty years this distinguished Carolinian was forging the issue which really brought on the collision of 1860 and became the chief factor and agency in the slave-lord dynasty in urging the crisis for which the hard life and early labors of his own son carried by fortune to the atmosphere of a different political region prepared him to be the Union's great friend. Thus it was that the influence of the father's life was largely nullified by that of his distinguished son.

When his part in the nation's great drama had been played and his performance came to its eventful end the admiration of friends and those who were once his foes now vie with each other in doing reverence to his memory. Before his nomination in 1860 he became fully convinced of his lineage and nativity.

Mr Herndon, his law partner, says he knows of many

an occasion of his receiving letters from his old reputed home asking about his life and those rumors of his legitimacy and that he always destroyed and never answered them.   Herndon says that these rumors became so common and scandalous that Mr. Lincoln received only six votes from La Rue County, which furnished 500 soldiers for the Union Army.   La Rue was cut from Hardin in 1840 and is a small county.   I have tried hard to get the vote that John C. Breckenridge and Stephen A. Douglas received for the Presidency at the same election, but the records there do not furnish me the information.   I tried Mr. Lever, Congressman, to try at Washington, D. C., for them and he states that he cannot get the information for me there and that he tried through the Congressman from that district in Kentucky to procure them.   After some effort he reported to Mr. Lever that the records were destroyed or lost and he could not get the vote of the three men for the Presidency in La Rue County in 1860.

Slavery, once a blessing, had come to be a severe curse.   It was a blessing to the negro savage who was taken from his haunts of brutality and idolatry and placed amongst the most advanced state of Christian civilization in the world.   He became Christianized and worth far more to himself and his race than if he had been left alone in his stolid heathenism in Africa.   In his new home he became a wonderful factor in our national development, in spite of all that has been said and is being said against the negro by Southern politicians. In his case the missionary custom was reversed, and by the cupidity and selfishness of his white master, North and South, the heathen was brought to the Gospel.   Great interest was taken in the moral and spiritual condition of the slave by the American master.   The white man believed it would redound to the comfort and elevation of the slave; but they forbade his educational advancement because they believed it would destroy the good of his moral elevation and endanger his usefulness as a servant, and even imperil his ownership and continued servitude.   Not many men who would invest hundreds and thousands of dollars in the slave trade would pay a single cent to send the Gospel to the Africans at home.   Our selfish aims and intentions were controlled by God to very beneficent ends and splendid results.   And while it occupied the time of our national Legislature for a long time, and while many men, North and South, were debating the slave question and slave rights, and Abolition, like all great issues, had to have an igniting to bring it forth. The papers and periodicals did much to this end, but when the time was ripe for the change, "Uncle Tom's Cabin" set the magazine on fire and our Civil War and its terrors were required to relieve the situation and bring a lasting quietus to this country. Wars are the greatest civilizers and reformers in the world. The four years' war did more to change and advance the American situation and political life than fifty years of campaigning and political speech-making and Congressional disputations could have done, and it was more perfectly enacted. The peculiar traits and superiority of the Anglo-Saxon are his capacity to revolutionize and make changes slowly without bloodshed; but the time had come in his progress when that method was too slow and God had to use a speedier means of change to meet these emergencies. God's forecast is always equal to the emergency.

The situation proved, all told, the greatest Protestant missionary effort of the world and he is the most completely Protestant of any race of men on earth, and in the South the Catholic efforts to catch him are a dismal failure,—even in New Orleans the Catholic negroes are not a corporal's guard. In 1860 one defense the Confederacy and propagators urged against Abolition was that the Catholic would catch him and teach him superstition and ruin him, and a second was the free negro would be lazy and produce no cotton and our chief industry would be destroyed, but the free negro has glutted the markets of the world and as a citizen has in war met every duty and as a soldier in Europe equally with his former masters successfully met the German—a failure of prophecy complete

Mr. Knotts wrote in pencil, and in some places his manuscript was not easy to read. I caused it to be copied as it was received, and sent each of the longer letters, and all of whose reading there was any doubt, to him for revision. He often made additions and wrote postscripts, sometimes as long as the original communication, and frequently of as great interest. His revision of the foregoing brought back with it this addition:

LETTER OF D. J. KNOTTS

SWANSEA, S. C., Aug. 30, 1919.

DR. BARTON:

DEAR SIR—Yours of 28th, inclosing typewritten copies of my letter at hand, and I am glad to make very important changes. I write, as you see, a bad hand, and in a hurry, and sometimes omit to express things fully.

John Hanks' daughter was Mrs. Mary Ellen Manon, and lives in California. She wrote me a dozen letters, I suspect, from first to last, on various features of the situation, trying to get at what I wanted. About two years ago or so she had been in hospital, but was then at home, and was thought better, from an operation. Her husband answered that. If she is dead, she had a cousin, Mrs. Jordan, living in same town who was Hanks who frequently united with her on some statement about which she was not certain. You may get yet one of the three.

I have no copies of the *State* paper, and the Editor says he has none and has had several pleas for copies.

I will give also statement of Mrs. W. M. Vaught, a great-niece of Mary Lincoln, Isaac's wife, of what her great aunt and others have told her of Thomas Lincoln's home on Isaac's farm. She says Thomas and Nancy lived on side of Lynn mountain, and that the old rock foundations of the house still are there on Isaac's old farm.

Mr. John Arthur lived in a little town near Asheville. His book was published by the Daughters of the American Revolution or Confederacy. He died last year.

I don't object to your quoting me at all, as I am fully convinced these facts are true.

I am busy for a day or two, but next week will answer you more fully as to your inquiries, especially as to the local information.

One from the husband of the niece of John C. Calhoun, and was in Congress with him many years (in the lower house) and a great lawyer, who died since the war. In 1866 he told some young law students of this affair in great secrecy in his home and sitting room, which I got accidentally. I wrote one of them and he declined, but owned my information was true, but refused to be quoted. I told Mr. Arthur of this, and he said he and this man went to law school to-gether, and he was a personal friend and he would make him tell.   Mr. Arthur states these facts in his book, but said his friend was a strong friend of the Calhouns and he did not care to offend them.

I have also a statement of John Hanks, a nephew of Nancy (son of Luke, her brother) to Dr. Brown, his fam-ily physician, brother of Governor Joe Brown, of Georgia, in presence of his (Brown's wife), who died four or five years ago.   She was very old and feeble and her daughter and eldest child, Mrs. A. C. Latimer, the widow of Hon. A. C. Latimer, a U. S. Senator from South Carolina, who died about ten years ago.   Also statement of Mr. Lewis, secretary of Ma-sonic Lodge in 1872, of what Judge Orr said to his Masonic brethren while he (Lewis) was making out Orr's Masonic credentials to go to St. Petersburg when President Grant had appointed him as Minister.   Judge Orr was a lawyer at the county seat, and knew all the older Hanks men.   His father succeeded Ann Hanks as tavern-keeper at Craytonville.   He was Congressman from South Carolina, and Speaker of the House before the war.   He saw Lincoln in Washington and told him of his resemblance to the Hanks family and Lincoln said, " Very likely of kin; my mother was a Nancy Hanks." But when pushed Judge Orr said he retired into silence and he could not venture further.   Judge Orr told it to Luke Hanks, Nancy's brother, and learned the real facts of the fate of his sister Nancy, " and, poor girl, we don't know what finally became of her," said Luke.

I will give you this and other soon.

Respectfully,

D. J. KNOTTS.   .

Mr. Knotts made plain in this extended correspondence that he was an admirer of Lincoln, and a firm believer in the soundness of his policies.   Though the son of a slave-holder, he looked back upon slavery with profound disapproval, and he is in politics a Republican, and, as it appeared, an opponent of the policies of President Wilson.   Indeed, his interest in current political questions as expressed in some of these letters, almost overshadowed that in their main theme.   Most of these discussions of current politics I have omitted, but here and there have permitted some of the briefer allusions to remain :

(September 1, 1919)

The Hanks home was about eight or nine miles from Bolton, South Carolina, where Dr. W C. Brown, a young physician, settled, and in 1856 was married to Miss Anna Dean, an intelligent, cultured Christian young lady, of one of the standard well-bred families of the county. Dr. Brown was a younger brother of Governor Joe Brown, later a U. S. Senator.

Judge Orr was from that county, and had met Lincoln in Washington, and noticed his likeness to Luke Hanks and others of the family, and attempted to discuss the matter with Lincoln Lincoln would only say that his mother was Nancy Hanks, and then retired into his shell, and Congressman Orr desisted He pursued the matter further at home, however, and his investigation disclosed the fact that the slave debater with Douglas was the son of an Anderson County girl, some of whose brothers and sisters were still living, and furnished the data to this congressman, Orr. This spread all around, and Mrs Byrd, Mrs. Brown's niece, told where she learned of what she knew. I asked her daughter, Mrs. A. C. Latimer, widow of a South Carolina senator, A C. Latimer, then recently deceased, to get her statement. She was very feeble, and in declining health. She, in substance, said :

"In 1856 I married Dr. W. C. Brown of Bolton Very shortly after my removal to my new home, ' Uncle Johnny Hanks,' a patron, came to Dr. Brown for medicine for some of his family. Dr. Brown in my presence asked him, was there any good ground for all this talk about Lincoln and Calhoun? The old gentleman replied very decidedly, ' I am sorry to tell you, Doctor, that there is. Nancy was my father's youngest sister and I know whereof I am talking. When the family found out that Nancy had sinned and gone astray, she asked to be allowed to stay till she could get away to her uncle's, as best I remember, in Tennessee; that Calhoun had promised her $500 to take her away where it would not hurt him. This uncle was a John Hanks, who came here with her father, and had moved out to Tennessee. Just at this time Thomas Lincoln appeared, with Enloe, as helper with horses, and solved the trouble. He became scapegoat for Calhoun's sins.'"

Mrs. Brown said that Mr. Hanks stood well as a reliable, truthful man. Hanks further said that young Calhoun often stopped as he passed through, and fished and hunted with the Hanks boys.

In 1849, James L. Orr was elected to Congress. Anderson was his home. The Hanks home was about eleven miles south of the County Seat. Orr knew all the Hanks men and girls and their husbands. Luke, the older brother, was a "court crier" for years, and Orr was a lawyer, and became Speaker of the National House of Representatives, before the War. He was afterwards Governor of South Carolina and Judge. In 1870, President Grant appointed him minister to Russia, and there he died in 1872. He was a great figure in Masonry. While the clerk of his lodge was making out his credentials to carry with him, he was talking freely of this tragedy, and comparing Lincoln's and Calhoun's portraits and discussing their likenesses. Mr. Lewis, the clerk, told me and wrote me of this matter very frankly, and told me what he had heard old men then dead, relate of the matter. Lewis said he was busy, but could remember a good deal of what Judge Orr said to his brother Masons in the hall. Orr related the meeting with Lincoln and its results, and he had traced the matter through the Hanks family, and was fully convinced that there could be no mistake about it whatever. Luke Hanks had two sons, Thomas and James; and Mr. Lewis and other Anderson men say they were living portraits of President Lincoln. The mole, so prominent on Mr. Lincoln's right cheek, had its counterpart in many of the older Hanks men Monroe Hanks, who is now doing business in Anderson, on side view is a splendid profile of the President. He promised me a side-view portrait for publication, but has not done so. He drove me around and assisted me much in getting a mass of lineage and history too large for this letter. I went to the old burying lot of long ago There are about 35 or 40 graves in it, all of the Hanks family. After about 1845 they removed their burying place to Ebenezer, a Methodist Church some two and one half miles from the old home.

In the southeast corner of the plat is the lonely resting place of Luke and Ann Hanks. Around this little grave plat in 1789, in May, trod a little country girl three years and three or four months old, whose wanderings have baffled the skill of historians and biographers alike, but the path and highway trodden by her distinguished son are in reach of every grateful American.

You may think it strange, but Lincoln has more and truer admirers here in this Southern country now than has either Jefferson Davis or John C. Calhoun.

I am the son of a slave lord and land baron in 1860, and who was a sincere and outspoken secessionist, and have no natural antipathy for the cause. But we see now that ruin would have resulted from Confederate success. I am a firm believer in God's sovereignty and control in national affairs. I feel confident the world's history shows that, but the rage now in the last war now seems to assume that man power and money can do anything. God's control seems but little recognized. In our Confederate cause it took draining, loss and drainage, to bring General Lee to Appomattox and the South to a real true conquest.

General Armistead Burt was a lawyer of great celebrity in upper South Carolina in 1860, and before the war. He married Calhoun's niece. He and his wife had considerable slave property. He greatly admired Calhoun as a man and his ideas of government. Just after the Civil War, under protection of coverture of his own home he confided in secrecy that in his early life Calhoun fell in love with a handsome, poor country girl, named Nancy Hanks When things came to the worst he hired a man named Lincoln to carry her away. He never intimated to them where Lincoln was from or how he got possession of this poor girl, or whatever became of her He lived in the town when Calhoun commenced the practice of law, and near here lived others of the Calhoun line They were well to do in slave property. John C. Calhoun became near the same time the father of an illegitimate child, who became during the war and after one of South Carolina's brightest stars in the legal fraternity. A brother of John C. Calhoun (older) became father of a boy by a girl in a very poor, common family in Abbeville (his county) and educated him, and gave him a start. He became a rampant secessionist in South Carolina and in Washington, was Governor, and then a national figure. He was George McDuffy.

It was in this General Burt's house that Jeff Davis spent his last night in South Carolina. In his house the Confederate Cabinet had its last sitting at night, and used the Great Seal of the Confederate Government for the last time, and no one can trace the seal from there. In his house General John C. Breckenridge began to dismiss the Southern Army from service by giving discharges to soldiers. He had two brigades with him, and he asked each general if his men could be relied on as a nucleus for a new army, and each replied: "No, their men were going home." He burst into tears and said he had done the best he could with his charge, and his mistakes, if any, were of the head and not the heart.

Mrs. Fanny Marshall, of this town, told me she was in this home that night to try and interest and care for this honorable body. She was a Calhoun, and second cousin of John C. Calhoun, and told me a great deal more of the inner life of the Calhouns—a very intelligent woman. She owned the land and house a few blocks from this, where the public meeting was held in 1860 to call a secession convention. Here were quite a number of distinguished South Carolinians, and around here was a good deal of slave-land aristocracy. With them it became very common for close kin to marry, "to keep the negroes in the family." That was getting to be one of the slavery curses, and also that of masters having slave wives, and in so many cases becoming common, of their sons having concubines among the better looking negro girls and then remaining single otherwise.

I spent two days there in Calhoun's home town looking up records. It was here I found Luke Hanks' will, dated May 3, 1789, and signed by making his mark   Joseph Hanks, in Nelson County, Kentucky, in 1783 (a brother) also made his mark. In 1816 in Hardin County, when Thomas Lincoln sold out, his wife, Nancy, signed with him, and made her mark. This was two years before the poor girl died.

After the death of the Nancy of Washington County, Thomas Lincoln courted and was engaged to a Miss Sarah Bush, of Hardin County, and so matters stood when he went with Abe Enloe to South Carolina to assist with his drove of Kentucky mules. This left Sally Bush destitute: but she married a Johnston, and when Nancy died this Sally Bush, or Mrs Johnston, was a widow with some children. Then Thomas Lincoln came back and married her. She was alive after the war when Mr. Herndon made such a failure in trying to get any information about Nancy, and says she would become angry and positively refuse to answer any inquiry about this poor, ill-fated girl.[4]

The Hanks family, in all the records of marriage, etc., seems to have been Pedo-Baptist in faith, except this family of Luke Hanks. They were all Baptists as far as any records show. There is positive evidence of the mother, Ann, and Luke and four sisters who died near the old home. Tom Lincoln was a religious cosmopolite, belonging to several churches at different times, and finally died a Campbellite. Luke and the girls here had membership in a Baptist church, and a Baptist, Elkin, rode a long distance several months after Nancy's death to preach her funeral. President Lincoln told a Baptist editor during the war his mother was a Baptist, and what good he was to the world was due to " my angel Baptist mother," as he reports her.

Mr. Herndon[5] says the early training of his Baptist mother made him a fatalist for life. This is, so far as I know, all I know of her denominational faith. She made a profound impression on his mind in the few years she had his control, and it is to his lasting honor he always spoke of her in almost a sacred manner.

President Lincoln's inclination to those periods of sadness and ennui is due to his Calhoun inheritance. Mr. Calhoun's biographers (one at least) report this and also some letters by a Presbyterian minister who married his sister, and with whom he stayed and went to school in boyhood for a while; and I believe his brother-in-law was his teacher. He wrote to the family he feared these periods of sadness and anguish might yet have a sad influence on his life, and told his home folks to encourage him to active outdoor exercise, such as hunting, fishing, etc. But most of his biographers do not like to report this fact, and generally omit it. Calhoun had a high power of analysis and discrimination,

[4] This is not an accurate report of Herndon's statement —W E B
[5] Herndon says that Lincoln's early Baptist environment made him a fatalist. He does not, in that connection, make direct reference to Lincoln's mother —W. E. B.

and these President Lincoln possessed in a high degree. Mr. Calhoun, though of a Presbyterian family, was accused of being dangerously infidel, like Thomas Jefferson. Mr. Calhoun greatly admired Jefferson, and Jefferson was a pronounced infidel, and a very immoral man. It was through his influence that a house of impure women was attached to the University of Virginia, and all under medical control. In all his early and middle life President Lincoln was strongly infidel. but the press and weight of the war seems to have about eliminated his infidelity, as his two greatest efforts show,—the Gettysburg address and the Second Inaugural. I was writing some articles for the press on the great men of history, Cyrus, Alexander, etc., showing how God controlled in the civil convulsions of men: and in one of them referred to Lincoln as coming to the top just as the world needed a great man, and dilated a little on his capacity and fitness and how he brought to a finale the long life of his distinguished father. Then I got into a hornet's nest. For a while after my reply not all was quiet in Warsaw.

I feel really that Lincoln passed out in a really beautiful evening. His mission was ended, and his big heart was not adapted to the convulsions which followed.

Lincoln could appoint a personal enemy to service, if he was suitable for the job. Jeff Davis never could do that. Like Mr. Wilson, he favored his friends, whether capable or not. Mr. Davis was painfully so. Being an Episcopalian, he strongly advanced that faith whenever possible in any appointment. He was continually flouting or snubbing some member of his Cabinet or Senate whom he feared or suspected was trying to succeed him. He was often in a sweat with some member of Richmond high society whose wife had criticised Davis' wife as being unsuited to lead in Richmond high life, but he had the energy and vim to carry out the views of his slave-lord creators, and to bring God's aims to their fruition, and running down the South's force and power to a nullity. What Davis aimed at failed, but God's aim bore fruit in providing the two most suitable men for the situation.

Mr. P. B. Christie, several years ago, ran a large store in Columbia, S. C, and I was frequently there, living only twenty-five miles south of it. I suggested to him one day right cautiously that I had heard that he and President Davis were half-brothers. He smiled right pleasantly and said, "Mr. Knotts, I am told by the best men and women in Edgefield, his county, that this is true; and really, I believe so myself. If you will go with me out to dinner I will show their pictures side by side."

I accepted, and really there is the rarest number of cases where a father and son more decidedly favor each other. He told me that often times men in his home had taken his father as a brother or near kinsman of Davis, and when told that he was his father, the next question generally was, What kin was he to President Davis?

How strange that both the principal actors should come from South Carolina, and from adjoining counties, and both sons of poor ladies by slave lords!

Lincoln's exportation placed him under different ideals.

In the record made by President Lincoln in his father's family Bible, he says, "Sarah, daughter of Thomas Lincoln, married Aaron Grigsby." Again, "Sarah, daughter of Thomas Lincoln, wife of Aaron Grigsby, died." He twice denies, thus, that she is Abraham's sister, and does not say in either case when she was born. I doubt if he knew. But being Nancy's daughter of Washington County might confuse with his kinship, and he leaves that part off. But in writing his own birth he says, "son of Thomas and Nancy Lincoln." He says also "Nancy Lincoln was born 1–87." The second figure is gone, and the third shows that it cannot be an "o," to make it 1807. Herndon says that he was recording his own mother's birth. A microscope shows it to be very much as above. Henry Watterson and others say this was the daughter Nancy, and that she and Sarah were the same. But Mr. Herndon says that Mrs. Lincoln, John and Dennis Hanks all deny positively that she was ever called anything but Sarah. Mrs Manon, daughter of John Hanks, does not say who Lincoln's mother was; seems a little confused; but does give all of Joseph Hanks' children, and the three girls and who two of them married, and says that Dennis was Nancy's son. She says about this, "I know that Dennis Hanks was father's first cousin." She says she knows the two older girls' husbands and says that neither of them was Lincoln's mother, and leaves the only alternative for Nancy as his mother.

In such a condensed statement I have to leave out a great deal that would make better connection. I cannot think of Lincoln as taking such huge responsibilities on his single shoulders as the League and Treaty. Wilson's course in Versailles and here will be a peculiar possession of Mr. Wilson. It seems to me to be one of the most erratic, insane productions in all diplomacy. Mr. Wilson seems to have no conception whatever of God's control in civic affairs. He seems to regard that a peculiar fitness of his and a field for man's greatness and research. To take this great question into his own custody is a vanity I do not think even Nebuchadnezzar exceeded.

I trust I have not wearied you.

Respectfully,

D. J. KNOTTS.

The correspondence of Mrs. Manon, daughter of old John Hanks, was one of the important features in Mr. Knotts' letters to me, and I endeavored to learn from him all that he had learned from her. As there were important gaps in the narrative, I wrote to Mrs. Manon and to her cousin; but I did not find them communicative. I infer from her letters to Mr. Knotts that she does not confirm the tradition of Mrs. Hitchcock, which fact I regret; for I should like to have that tradition confirmed by the Hanks family. I did not press the matter, however, because it had only an incidental interest and no real importance for this inquiry. Mrs. Manon says that her father, John Hanks, was a first cousin of Dennis. Nancy Hanks, the mother of Dennis and aunt of the President's mother, appears to have been John Hanks' first cousin.

LETTER OF D J. KNOTTS

September 3, 1919.

Mrs. Manon gives fully the names of all the Joseph Hanks' family (five sons and three girls), just as they are in his will, a copy of which I have from the records, giving one horse to each son, naming the horses, and one heifer to each of the girls, naming the heifers Nancy's was " Pied." Mrs. Manon tells whom each boy married, and whom the two older girls married. One married Jesse Friend, and the other I do not remember just now. Mrs. Manon was daughter of William's oldest son, who was executor of Joseph Hanks' will and eldest brother of Nancy. Mrs. Manon says she knows her father, John Hanks, was son of William, and gives names of all John's brothers and sisters. She says she knows positively that Dennis and her father were first cousins, and of course that means that one of the three girls was his mother. She says she knows that he was illegitimate. She knew him from girlhood, and was frequently in his home, even after he moved to Charlestown; that he was a splendid shoemaker and married one of Sarah Bush Johnston-Lincoln's daughters.

Mr. Herndon says Dennis told him that he was illegitimate and that his mother was a Nancy Hanks. Mr. Herndon also says that Dennis told him that Lincoln's mother was Nancy Sparrow, and that she was not a Hanks at all: that she was a daughter of Thomas and Lucy Sparrow.

I questioned Mrs. Manon, and she did not know who Nancy, her great-aunt, married, or what became of her, but she knows Dennis was illegitimate and her father's first cousin, and that his mother was Nancy. The Washington County Nancy was the one alleged to have been Lincoln's mother till Mrs. Hitchcock found the will of Joseph and his daughter Nancy, and she fully settled the matter without any further investigation.   D. J. KNOTT.

I endeavored to learn from Mr. Knotts something more of his correspondence with the daughter of John Hanks, and asked him to loan me his letters from her, which he kindly did. I endeavored to obtain information direct from her and her cousin who lives near her in California, but had no great success; nor do I think she knows much more than she told in her letters to Mr. Knotts. As her letters to him were written before she was quite as guarded as she later appears to have become, I desired to examine her letters to him; and he kindly sent them. Excerpts from them are found in the appendix; but they do not add much to what is contained elsewhere. Mr. Knotts relates in this letter how he lost some of her correspondence:

SWANSEA, S. C , Oct. 1, 1919.

DR. BARTON:

My DEAR SIR—Your letter received today.

The most of Mrs. Manon's letters were about the kin of John Hanks, her father, and Dennis Hanks, and most of them were about the Hanks family in Illinois, Joseph Hanks, and the Lincoln family in Illinois. She wrote two or more to me in answer to mine, about the Republican Convention of 1860, and what she saw. Amongst other things, she saw her father drive home with the two-horse load of rails selected from fences built of rails split by her father and Abraham Lincoln. She remembered well that her father walked into the Convention with three of them, which he and Governor Oglesby had selected, and that he sold the rest of them for $10 each as souvenirs to Lincoln's political friends. She gave me the names of several distinguished men who bought them, and she said she knew that there were persons in Illinois who had them, but she did not give their names to me.

In corresponding with clerks with regard to records, some of them made themselves very intimate, and wanted to know more of what I was doing; and one of them wrote to me that he had seen an old coat once worn by Lincoln, and it was badly tattered and very ragged.

I am very sorry of losing about a year ago many of Mrs. Manon's letters, and some also from Anderson County, and also those of the lady who examined the records in Springfield, Kentucky. I sincerely regret losing these.

It occurred in this way: One day I was writing and had many of these letters by me on the floor, and I was called to dinner. I carelessly left the door open, and many of the papers were blown into the fire. After dinner I went to the postoffice, and the girl who cleaned up my room in my absence thought them refused letters, and swept quite an amount into the fire. I can regain those from offices in Anderson and Abbeville, but Mrs. Caruthers, of Kentucky, is dead, and I really regret the loss of the examinations she made for me in the estates of the families of the Berrys and Lincolns. She made an exhaustive report of the records in the clerk's office at Springfield, Ky., showing the fraudulent returns of about eighteen couples alleged to have been married by Jesse Head, and the failure of the clerk's office to show anything until these returns. Amongst these papers also was an exhaustive examination of the records in Amelia County, Va., of the Hanks family there, their sales and suits, and of William Hanks' leaving.

I am also in hopes and expectations a pure, genuine Republican; have been so since the end of Cleveland's second term. Since then I have had no confidence in the capacity or cohesion of the Democratic party on any national issue. I have never had any confidence in Woodrow Wilson. He is so vain, silly and conceited that I have a contempt for him that I have never had for any public man of importance. He is an imaginative theorist and blatherskite, and I really fear is deceptive and selfish. He is a buffoon of the first degree. His trip west to drive the Senate was certainly an idiotic and bigoted stand for a President. He feels that he is the government.

[*The remainder of the letter relates to present-day politics, and to religion, and does not contain further reference to the papers relating to Lincoln.*]

I hope you are well and continue to be useful in the world's betterment.   Respectfully,

D. J. KNOTTS.

Mr. Knotts is a voluminous correspondent, an ardent Baptist, a strong believer in the overruling Providence of God in the life of America, and an admirer of Abraham Lincoln. I am indebted to him for a number of important letters which he loaned to me, as well as for information which enabled me to procure, after much search, Arthur's *History of Western North Carolina*. But I did not make much progress in my effort to secure a consistent report of the relations of Lincoln on the Hanks side, and finally abandoned it. Mr. Knotts continued to send me interesting items and some documents:

LETTER OF D. J. KNOTTS

SWANSEA, S. C., Nov. 12, 1919.

DR. W. E. BARTON:

DEAR SIR—A few days ago I sent you some of the collection of letters I had remaining and other records of value.

Mrs W. M. Vaught, of Elizabethtown, Tenn., had furnished me copies of Isaac Lincoln's will and his wife, Mary,—Mrs. Vaught is a great-niece of Mrs. Mary Lincoln, who was Mary Ward before her marriage. Mr. J. D. Jenkins, some of whose letters I sent you, is a great nephew of Mrs. Lincoln. A good deal of my correspondence with Mrs. Manon was about the family in Illinois and how descended. I was especially anxious to fix John Hanks and Dennis Hanks' kinship. She says she knows they were first cousins and that he was an illegitimate son of one of his grandfather, William Hanks' sister, but did not know which one, nor did not even know how many sisters and brothers her grandfather had till I sent her a copy of Joseph Hanks' will, naming his children. She had seen one of Watterson's pieces and cut it out and sent it to me, in which he made the daughter of Joseph Hanks Lincoln's mother, but as Mrs. Manon said, without any proof of her life or origin. Watterson said Joseph lived in Hardin County and was a carpenter. To this statement Mrs. Manon and her cousin, Mrs. Jordan, took issue and said that William Hanks' father was a shoemaker and so was Dennis Hanks. I spent, after writing to her, a good deal of time and money looking after the Hanks family in Illinois.

I was really interested in the matter, for my interest is in the real manhood and true greatness of Abraham Lincoln, and not for fault-finding or blemish-hunting. After 1832 Calhoun's life was embittered with the sadness and disappointed ambition in failing to grasp the Presidency. His life was ambitious and selfish, and then revengeful. He was not a national character, was entirely Southern and sectional in his political life and indulged in a bad spirit. I do not believe that American history produces Lincoln's equal as a purely, loyal, patriotic national character, entirely unselfish, but purely a friend to the Union and to the best way to preserve it. A plain, blunt, unpretending man, but honest and candid. I rode by Mr. McGee's home, who was an old man, about 85 years old, an intelligent man. He told me he married in 1851 James Emerson's youngest daughter and had lived within three or four miles of this Hanks family ever since. James Emerson was a magistrate and slave-lord, who died in 1865, an old man. Mr. McGee told me that Mr. Emerson had employed Luke Hanks for years as his court officer and constable and that he had an abiding faith in his integrity and honesty and said all his children had established that credit and all the older Hanks folks he had any transactions with appeared to be of this stamp and that the girls and women of the older Hanks family bore a fine name. He rode to the Ebenezer Graveyard and we looked around over the same. On Luke's tomb was this inscription, "God gave him an honest heart." Mr. McGee and Mrs. Drake, an older daughter of Squire Emerson, and a very intelligent old lady of 92 years, said she had known the Hanks men and women from her girlhood and it was for truth and honesty. I could give evidences of what these two intelligent old slave-holders told me of the Hanks character and both told me that you could not tell Thomas Hanks from Lincoln in two good photographs.

Keep the letters and book as long as you need them.

Respectfully,

D. J. Knotts.

The next letter deals mostly with other matters, but gives the name of the man who told Mr. Knotts of General Burt's information concerning J. C. Calhoun.

Swansea, S. C., March 12, 1920.

General M. L. Bonham, a former Attorney General of the state of South Carolina, was a classmate of John P. Arthur at law school of Washington and Lee University of Virginia. He lives at Anderson and practices law. He it was who heard General Burt in the secrecy of his home say to him and certain other young law students in 1867, I believe, about Calhoun's paternity of Lincoln. He refused myself and Mr. Arthur to disclose his name, possibly on account of his intimacy with the Calhoun family.

D. J Knotts.

While I did not pursue the questions arising out of the relations of the large and widely scattered Hanks family, I desired, and most earnestly, to be sure of the family of Luke and Ann Hanks, and especially to know about the daughter Nancy. This I had difficulty in accomplishing, and my inquiries addressed to the Clerk of the Anderson County Court brought answer that no such lists were to be found there. Later, I procured them, as will be stated in a subsequent chapter, and they are of very great importance. This last letter which I quote from Mr. Knotts bears on these records, to whose significance I shall later refer:

SWANSEA, March 15, 1920.

MY DEAR SIR:

The long list of the Hanks heirs is on record in Anderson, S. C., in the Clerk of Courts' office. The Hanks family tried to have a division and made a list of the children, and even sold the land under the division. The list they made out named only the real children or the husbands or wives. Of some of the dead ones they would say, " heirs of Susan Hanks," meaning children; and in the case of Charles Hanie by right of his wife, Elizabeth, making eleven in all, and the final showed twelve divisions.

The whole being illegal, Jane Davis and her husband Valentine Davis brought suit by employing a very proficient lawyer, Peter Van Diver. It is said he never appeared in the courthouse but was a splendid office lawyer. He brought suit as Jane Davis and her husband against this long list of heirs, all of record in the courthouse in Anderson In 1789 when Luke Hanks died this home was in Abbeville County, but in 1828 Anderson was cut off into a new county.

Mr John P. Arthur sought information in these matters, and I referred him to his classmate of Washington and Lee University, General M. L. Bonham. Somehow Mr. Bonham stopped with the first illegal division, and I told Mr Arthur to get Mr. Geiger who had assisted me; and he and General Bonham obtained what he wanted. Officers then were not so regular and precise as they are now and it requires a little caution in tracing estates. I have ascertained that the Virginia records are most regular, and next to these those of Illinois, of all the states I examined.

I think Lincoln's early life was full of infidelity, but I really believe the cares and trials of his life entirely eliminated this and he became a full believer in God. He was a man of spotless moral character.

D. J. KNOTTS.

PART III: A CRITICAL AND CONSTRUCTIVE ANALYSIS

PART III: A CRITICAL AND CONSTRUC-
TIVE ANALYSIS

CHAPTER XV

THE RULES OF EVIDENCE

IT will not be surprising if the reader finds himself at this point somewhat bewildered, and a trifle doubtful concerning the result of this inquiry We have gone to great labor, and soiled much white paper, and what have we but a confused collection of scandal, expressed in some instances in labored argument and in others in vague surmise and indistinct rumor How are we ever to emerge from a dismal swamp such as that in which we now find ourselves?

If the reader does not experience some such feeling as this, his emotions are quite different from those of the author, when he came at length to realize that in his pursuit of another aspect of Lincoln's life, he had mired his feet in this morass, from which his first attempts to escape got him in the deeper, and tangled him in thorns. It was a debatable question whether to turn back or to force his way through.

How are we ever to learn the truth about matters of this character ?

The ready answer is that we are to appeal to History.

But what is History, and how is it born or made, and what is its authority ? `

I trust the reader will not find wearisome a few pages of personal reminiscence, which may possibly have some illustrative value at this point.

I have always been interested in History It was a great day in the annals of my early education when to Reading, Writing, Arithmetic, Grammar and Geography, I was permitted to add a study of Quackenbos' History of the United

States. I devoured it with avidity. I did not stop with the assigned lesson, but kept myself out of mischief by reading the book when I was not required to do so. A year or two later, having advanced into a higher grade in our so-called High School, I was introduced to Barnes' School History of the United States. It comprised a narrative of events in large type, and a great wealth of footnotes containing historic incidents. This book I practically committed to memory, the text and especially the notes.

In those days school terms closed with public oral examinations The teacher as well as the school was under examination, and the teacher took pains that pupils called upon should be examined in those branches in which they were supposed to excel. I shone in History Asked any question in the book, I could start and very nearly recite the book backward or forward. The proud look of my teacher on these occasions still serves to comfort me when I recall some experiences in which, for reasons which I will not here narrate, the facial expression was less benign. In History I was not counted a failure. I thought I knew History.

In college I was introduced to Universal History. My record there was perhaps less brilliant but was rather better than moderately satisfactory to the instructors, and I never had any doubt about my grades in that department.

I entered upon my post-graduate study for my degree in Theology with what was supposed to be advanced credit in History. For that reason I took up in my first year those courses in Church History which were regularly shown in the catalogue as belonging to more mature students. I found this study much more exacting, and I will not pretend to any such record as I believed myself to have made in my earlier years, but I still thought well of my knowledge of History, and often said to myself that if I should ever become a college professor, that was one of the branches which I should feel competent to teach

In the middle of my Divinity course, I elected advanced work in Church History. Then I learned the Seminar method, at that time rather newly imported from European universities. We did not learn History from books of History, treating of particular periods and countries; we went to original sources, and were required to write chapters of History that were supposed to be original.

Then it was I discovered that I had never known History.

If up to that time I had been asked, What is History? I should have answered that History is the record of past events, as they have been duly accredited and set forth in reliable books. I knew, to be sure, that books disagreed, and that the student must compare historian with historian and make allowance for national prejudice and for other limitations.

But when I began to write histories of my own, I was appalled at the nature of the sources.

Out of what material do historians make the books in which History is recorded?

Largely out of other books.

But what was the material used by the authors of the earlier books?

They used, or endeavored to use, original sources.

What are original sources?

Original sources consist in such materials as these:

The verbal testimony of eye-witnesses when this can be obtained; if not, then testimony of those to whom events are related by eye-witnesses; oral traditions; newspapers, or clippings from newspapers giving information of current events; diaries; personal letters and family records

And this litter of uncertainty was what History was to be made of! We were given trunks full of this stromata and told to make History of it! Surely here was a demand that we produce a sweet-voiced whistle out of a pig's tail! This fragmentary and contradictory material, preserved in patches and often for quite other purposes, was what historians had to work with, knowing all the time that the really important material must often have perished and the unimportant and perhaps the misleading, preserved!

I had long bowed down to History. It was for me an idol with head of gold and breast of silver and thighs of brass.

Now I beheld it as having feet of iron mingled with mirey clay, and standing, not on the rock of certain established verity, but knee-deep in the perilous quicksand of tradition.

Who could ever hope to know anything? What was History, but what Voltaire called it, a lie which men agree to call truth? History, I said to myself, was Mystery.

But I found the case to be not quite so hopeless. I beheld, and since have had abundant occasion to discover, that many so-called historians merely mire themselves in the swamp of unverified tradition, and that, when they once succeed in getting their books printed, wiser people receive them as possessed of authority. But I also found that it is possible to attain, not complete certainty, which never belongs to things human, but sufficient probability to be accepted as trustworthy.

Some little study of law which I had pursued before entering the ministry, proved of value to me; and I employed, when from time to time I had occasion to pursue historical investigation, some of the principles which I learned under the rules of evidence.

First of all, we need to assure ourselves that we have secured the essential facts. I will not say *all* the facts, for we can never secure all the facts. Every fact is related to every other fact, and every story, if fully told, begins with the creation of the world. Out of the impossible total of facts, bearing directly or remotely upon our inquiry, which are really essential to our purpose? Are we sure that we have all such facts that can possibly be secured? Are we sure that among those facts which we are unable to secure there can be none which would materially alter the significance of those which we already have?

Now, it must be apparent to any one who knows books of History that very many of them were prepared by men and women who did not approach their task with any such view of the method which they were to pursue. They gathered a few facts and some traditions from apparently reliable sources, and built up their books almost wholly out of unverified material. They did no intelligent work of selection. They had no adequate theory of the working of cause and effect in History. They merely gathered so much of the shale of tradition and, heaping it into a book, proclaimed it to be solid historical rock. One who would buy the truth and sell it not has to pay the bookseller for the same old lies told over and over, often by men who do not know enough of History to know that they are lying. Let the most stupid of blunders find its way into type and it will be copied and affirmed by men much wiser than the original author of the blunder.

Our task, and the task of all serious historians, is,—

First, the assembling of the whole body of fact, so far as that is humanly possible.

Secondly, the sifting of these facts into those that are and those that are not relevant to our purpose.

Thirdly, the subjecting of the testimony to a merciless but sympathetic analysis, a keen and determined critical inspection, that will permit no error to masquerade as truth, and no irrelevant detail to throw us off the scent of the really important fact.

Finally, there must be a constructive genius. This is not easy to combine with the critical spirit. But it requires both of these to write History.

In the matter now before us, we have gone part way. We have painstakingly assembled our evidence, and so far as we can learn, we have in hand all the evidence that can be of material assistance to us. One side of that evidence has been presented. We are now to examine it in the true historic spirit, a spirit of careful analysis, a spirit of constructive expectation that we shall learn the truth. If we succeed, we may make it unnecessary for any one else to write books on this subject. We may actually make, what historians aspire to make, a contribution to the sum of human knowledge.

I should like at this point to ask the reader to agree with me that thus far, at least, the inquiry has been a fair and impartial one. It will be difficult to seem impartial after we take up the cross examination of these witnesses. Inevitably the author will disclose what will appear to be prejudices, and will seem to become a prosecuting attorney rather than a judge. Let us now pause for a moment, and reflect that thus far there has been no evidence of bias. The author has endeavored to obtain every fact, every report, every rumor, that had a bearing upon this question. He has expended more money for postage than he is likely to get back in profits on the book. He has traveled far to points remote and not all of them easy of access. He has interviewed or corresponded with every person whom he had reason to believe could give him any information, on either side of any of the questions which he has now been discussing. It will now become his duty to sift this evidence, and bring to it such critical skill as he may have learned, in order that the truth shall finally be discovered. Let the reader agree that thus far the evidence has been sought out with a considerable degree of industry, and in a spirit that has been at least willing to learn.

We now have before us, as fully as it has been possible to secure it, the evidence in its several forms that Abraham Lincoln was not the son of Thomas Lincoln. The author has assumed the responsibility, which he does not regard as a light one, of producing every allegation, including some that have never been in print before, against the chastity of Nancy Hanks. It is now in order to submit each one of these in turn, and then the group as a whole, to a critical analysis. We must inquire concerning each of these, where and when it originated; whether the persons who first made these statements and those through whom they were transmitted, were truthful, unbiased and competent; whether the stories were in circulation at the time or whether they became current later, and if so how much later; whether they are supported by sufficient evidence to outweigh the legal and moral presumption that stands in favor of the virtue of a woman who can no longer speak on her own behalf; and whether they corroborate or contradict each other.

The law of libel holds not only with regard to the good name of the living, but also with respect to that of the dead. It is as serious an offense against the civil law and against good morals to blacken the reputation of the dead as it is to assail the fair fame of the living. Nancy Hanks cannot be heard in her own defense, but she must not be condemned on idle hearsay. Those who defame her must come into court with clean hands, and must produce their evidence, and submit to cross examination and to contrary testimony.

The burden of proof is not upon Nancy Hanks, but upon those who declare that she was not virtuous. She is fully entitled, both in law and in good morals, to the presumption that she was a virtuous woman. She married at twenty-three and she lived with one man as his wife until her death. It is to be presumed that Thomas Lincoln knew what kind of woman he was marrying, and that she had so behaved before marriage that he could trust her, or believed that he could, and that after marriage she continued to conduct herself in such fashion that he continued to trust her. If that is not true, there must be sufficient evidence to establish her bad reputation, either before or after marriage. She is entitled to be considered innocent unless and until she is proved guilty.

It is not necessary that Thomas Lincoln shall produce witnesses to the act of procreation by which Abraham Lincoln came into being. That is not required of any man. If Thomas and Nancy Lincoln were living together as husband and wife at the time Abraham Lincoln was born, and sustaining in the sight of their neighbors relations that had the appearance of matrimony, their mutual consent and cohabitation is in itself satisfactory proof of the legitimacy of their offspring, unless there is overwhelming testimony to the contrary. If they had been living together for some time previous, and continued to live together for some years subsequent, to the birth of Abraham Lincoln, the presumption in favor of his being a legitimate child is greatly strengthened, and the evidence to overthrow that presumption must be strong and consistent.

Fornication and adultery are seldom proved by witnesses to the overt act; but neither of them is to be assumed except on the basis of such a volume of testimony as is sufficient to overthrow the presumption of chastity, and establish the fact of guilt beyond a reasonable doubt.

An important question will emerge as we proceed, and will several times confront us, and be fully considered at the close;

do these stories tend to confirm each other, or do they mutually weaken each other? Is their effect cumulative, or is it such as to indicate a vague mass of unfounded rumor?

We shall answer this question in its place. But one thing we should have in mind from the beginning; not all of these stories can be true. Indeed, when we look at them closely we discover that not more than one of them can be true. Out of the seven, six certainly are false. It is our clear duty to discover six false stories out of seven, and it is necessary that we find six that are false, if we establish one that is true.

Furthermore, if we find six that are false, that does not in any wise create a presumption that the seventh is true. The seventh must in its turn produce its evidence, submit to cross examination, and show that it is true beyond a reasonable doubt. Not only will the discovery of the six certainly false stories create no presumption that the seventh is true, but every element of plausibility that we discover in the six that we find to be false will serve to put us on our guard against the possibility of similar falsehoods that may take on the aspect of truth in the seventh.

Does this mean that we are determined to prove Nancy Hanks a virtuous woman?

No; but it means that she is entitled to be believed a virtuous woman unless clear proof can be adduced that she was not so. The judge upon the bench would so instruct the jury. She is entitled to every reasonable presumption in advance, and that presumption is to be strengthened by all the evidence which can be adduced in favor of her virtue. She does not have to prove it. The burden of proof is upon those who assail her character. They must prove their case.

With these reminders of the rules of evidence, we are now to take up one by one the several charges or reports that affect the paternity of Abraham Lincoln and the chastity of Nancy Hanks. And having examined them singly, we shall consider them as a whole.

CHAPTER XVI

ABRAHAM ENLOW OF HARDIN COUNTY, KENTUCKY

THE first of these stories which we are to examine is that which gained currency in the immediate neighborhood of Lincoln's birth, and which affirms that he was the son of his father's neighbor, Abraham Enlow.

There was such a man as Abraham Enlow. He lived in the neighborhood where Abraham Lincoln was born. His grandchildren and great grandchildren still are there.

It is not my intention in subsequent chapters to repeat in succession the stories that are found in Part II. The reader can turn back to them one by one and refresh his memory if he desires. In the case of this first story, however, it will be worth while to repeat it in the form in which it is easy to pick up in the vicinity of Hodgenville.

One has no need to go far into La Rue County to pick up gossip concerning the birth of Lincoln. Before I reached Hodgenville, on the occasion of my first visit, I had become fairly well acquainted upon the train, with a man who was born in Hodgenville and has lived there all his life. He furnished me much valuable information as to the people whom I might see. When we had talked of other matters, I asked him what he knew or had heard of Lincoln's parentage. He said:

"All I know about it is what all the old folks used to say, and they all said that the father of Lincoln was Abe Enlow. I never heard them give any reasons, or tell how they knew, but they all knew the story and believed it. There may have been some who did not, but all that I remember to have heard say anything about it took it for granted it was true.

"This county was Democratic, and sent its boys mostly to the Southern army. There was a time when Lincoln was not highly thought of here. People said he brought on the war, and he took away their niggers. But they think well of him now, and are proud that he was born here. I believe that if he had lived he would have colonized the niggers. If he had done that after freeing them, he would have been the greatest man this country ever produced.

"The old-time nigger was all right. He knew his place. But these niggers we have here now are no good. You can't hire one of them to make your garden. Once in a while there's an honest one, but most of them just steal.

"We think more of Lincoln now than we did just after the war. There was a good deal then to make people bitter, but that is nearly all gone. The farther we get from the war, the more people see that Lincoln was all right, and the best friend the South ever had

"But the old people did not think much of Lincoln, and you can't very well blame them. They used to talk about him, and they did not believe that he was Tom Lincoln's son. They do not talk much about it now as they used to do.

"There is a good deal of difference of opinion when they get to talking. Some say he was born in Elizabethtown, and some say that he was born somewhere else and moved here. But I do not believe either of those stories I believe he was born here, and that Abe Enlow was his father."

I give this story as it was given to me, without animus, by an intelligent man. It will stand as fairly typical of the stories which one may hear from the middle aged and elderly people of Hodgenville who believe the story.

But when these good and honest people are cross-questioned, the story weakens. When did the witnesses personally hear of this? They have heard of it all their lives. What was the first time they distinctly remember to have heard it? Who was it that told it on that occasion, and under what circumstances which fix the date?

Under questioning of this character the result is obtained that while certain of these people are sure that the "old folks" must have heard it long, long ago, no one living appears to recall having heard it until after the Civil War. Every attempt to fix an earlier date grows vague, and falls back on generalities. No one who was born, say in 1840, appears to be able to recall any definite event earlier than 1865 associated with the distinct memory of this story.

The author, having made a somewhat diligent inquiry, on the ground and through correspondence, is fully convinced that Hodgenville never entertained a suspicion of the legitimacy of Abraham Lincoln until the bitter days that came near the end of the Rebellion, and that then the rumor came from the outside.

In considering the truth or falsehood of these stories concerning the birth of Abraham Lincoln, it is important to ask, When did these stories originate, and on whose authority were they first promulgated?

This is a question to which no satisfactory answer appears hitherto to have been given. The author has made diligent inquiry in the vicinity of Hodgenville, and cannot learn that any hint or rumor reflecting upon the chastity of Nancy Hanks or the legitimate birth of Abraham Lincoln was current there in 1809, or during the period when the Lincolns resided there, nor for half a century after they had moved away.

There is no evidence known to the author that this rumor in any of its forms originated in the only place where, if true, it should have originated.

Critics of the meager biographical material furnished by Lincoln lifted their eyebrows a little in 1860, and by the time the Copperheads were doing their most evil work a full-fledged scandal was in circulation. But Hodgenville had never heard of it.

Not till Lincoln was a candidate the second time did a report reach Hodgenville in any way derogatory to the moral character of Nancy Hanks. Hodgenville did not make the discovery by any search of local records; this gossip filtered in from the outside world. Hodgenville had little pride in Lincoln during the war, and there were many people there who were not unwilling to believe the story.

The question about Lincoln's legitimacy was discussed at Elizabethtown before it made its way to La Rue County. The frequent convening of court in that county brought to town politicians who, in conversation with Samuel Haycraft, learned that he had been unable to locate the certificate of marriage of Thomas and Nancy Lincoln. This did not at first carry with it any necessity for the finding of another man, for it did not, in its first form, imply that Thomas Lincoln was not Abraham's father. Thomas and Nancy Lincoln were living together as husband and wife when their son Abraham was born, and the fact was not questioned in Hardin County, and has never been questioned there to this day. If they were not legally married, theirs was a common law marriage, and Thomas was still the father. No one needed to go to Hodgenville to learn anything about this, for the records were not there, but presumably in Elizabethtown if anywhere. Whatever gossip there was from 1860 to 1865 was wholly on the assumption that Thomas was still the father of Abraham.

Of this we have an interesting testimonial in Lamon's *Life of Lincoln:*

"It is admitted by all the old residents of the place that they were honestly married, but precisely when or how no one can tell" (p. 10).

This is on the basis of what Herndon learned in his visit to the spot in 1865; and it must not be forgotten. In 1865 the neighbors had not begun to mention Abraham Enlow or any other man to any extent that Herndon could learn through inquiry on the ground. The certificate had not been found, but all the neighbors believed they were married.

This is proof positive that no tradition had ever existed in the vicinity of her home and dating from the event that charged Nancy Hanks with being other than a virtuous woman. The statement of Herndon is in accord with all that I have later learned by the most diligent search; except that there began to be question whether there had been an actual marriage, though at this stage no question of Thomas Lincoln's paternity.

Furthermore, Nancy Hanks herself left no vestige of a memory of her own personality upon her neighbors in Elizabethtown, so far as could be discovered in 1860. She lived there with her husband from the summer of 1806 till the spring of 1808, but no one remembered her when in 1860 it became known that Abraham Lincoln, who was born in Hardin County, was nominated for the presidency.   Perhaps the two most prominent families in Elizabethtown were the Helms and the Haycrafts.   The Helms should have known something about the Lincolns, for Major General Ben Hardin Helm, later of the Confederate army, married a half sister of Mary Todd Lincoln and she is still living and has written to me; but when the Helm family began the process of remembering what they could recall about the Lincolns, *the stories which they furnished to Collins for his History of Kentucky went back* . *not to Nancy Hanks, but to Sarah Bush Johnston, whom, at the beginning, they supposed to have been the mother of Lincoln.*   The story as printed by Collins is edited to make her his step-mother, and it is a story of no importance in itself; but it shows two things first, that the memory of Nancy Hanks had completely faded from Elizabethtown; and secondly, that the little incident on which the story in Collins was based, never occurred   They were mistaken both as to the fact and the relationship.

When Samuel Haycraft wrote to Lincoln in an endeavor to establish a relationship, his knowledge was not of Nancy Hanks but of Sarah Johnston, whom in 1860 he supposed to have been the mother of Abraham Lincoln.

These facts are conclusive, and they do not stand alone, in their complete proof *that there was in Hardin and La Rue Counties in 1860 no memory of any charge against the chastity of Nancy Hanks.*

Reference should be made, however, to the story written out for Herndon in August, 1865, by J. B. Helm, which Herndon published in his *Life of Lincoln:*

The Hanks girls were great at camp-meetings.   I remember one in 1806.   I will give you a scene, and if you will then read the books written on the subject you may find some apology for the superstition that was said to be in Abe Lincoln's character.   It was at a camp-meeting, as before said, when a general shout was about to commence.   Preparations were being made; a young lady invited me to stand on a bench by her side where we could see all over the altar. To the right a strong, athletic young man, about twenty five years old, was being put in trim for the occasion, which was done by divesting him of all apparel except shirt and pants. On the left a young lady was being put in trim in much the same manner, so that her clothes would not be in the way, and so that, when her combs flew out, her hair would go in graceful braids. She, too, was young—not more than twenty, perhaps. The performance commenced about the same time by the young man on the right and the young lady on the left. Slowly and gracefully they worked their way to the center, singing, shouting, hugging, kissing, generally their own sex, until at last, nearer and nearer they came. The center of the altar was reached, and the two closed, with their arms around each other, the man singing and shouting at the top of his voice,

> " I have my Jesus in my arms,
>   Sweet as honey, strong as bacon ham."

Just at this moment the young lady holding to my arm whispered, " They are to be married next week. her name is Hanks." There were very few who did not believe this true religion, inspired by the Holy Spirit, and the man who did not believe it did well to keep it to himself. The Hankses were the finest singers and shouters in our country.

Concerning this incident Herndon adds:

Here my informant stops, and on account of his death several years ago I failed to learn whether this young lady shouter who figured in the foregoing scene was the President's mother or not. The fact that Nancy Hanks did marry in that year gives color to the belief that it was she. As to the probability of the young man being Thomas Lincoln it is difficult to say; such a performance as the one described must have required a little more emotion and enthusiasm than the tardy and inert carpenter was in the habit of manifesting.—*Herndon's Lincoln,* Vol. I, pp. 14-15.

I was not present, but I am willing to express an opinion which is based on a pretty intimate knowledge of social and religious life of the Kentucky hills, that if the young lady

in the above scene was Nancy Hanks, and she was to have
been married a week later, the young man was Thomas Lincoln.   Even in such incidents there were certain conventions
to be observed; as Mr. Helm notes the hugging and kissing,
though miscellaneous, was confined to persons of the same sex
in practically all cases (and for the exceptions if listed some
reason would appear for the exception) until these two met
who were known to be betrothed and about to be married.
The incident simply would not have occurred, with the approval and assistance of the large company, except on the
basis of some such general knowledge.

It would not be safe to assume that this couple consisted
of Thomas Lincoln and Nancy Hanks.   Thomas and Nancy
were both older than the couple described, and were probably
both in Washington County preparing for the wedding.   Moreover, if Mr. Helm is correct in his dates, it was certainly not
this couple; for farmers did not leave their corn-plowing for
camp-meetings the first of June   Camp-meetings were held
in the autumn.   If this occurred in 1806, Thomas and Nancy
were married and she was pregnant with little Sarah before the
camp-meeting season.

Mr. Helm was an old man when he told this story.   He had
to go back sixty years for the details of it, and sixty years
is a long time and plays havoc with details in an old man's
memory.   Perhaps he did not remember everything exactly as
it occurred.   Perhaps the young lady with whom he was present at the camp-meeting, and to whom if he made love he
probably did it less publicly, was mistaken as to the name of
the girl. Besides, there were other girls by the name of Hanks,
and others beside the Hanks girls who shouted and were
hugged at camp-meetings

But even if the young lady was correct, and Helm was accurate, and the girl was Nancy Hanks and the young man
Thomas Lincoln, the incident is to be judged in the light
of the customs of the time and the standards of propriety
then prevalent.   Assuming that the girl was Nancy, the young
man was Tom, or there would have been murder just after
the benediction   That noisy, ridiculous exhibition merely

showed that a couple betrothed and on the threshold of matrimony, sometimes mixed their religion and their love-making in proportions not in good taste. But that, I beg leave to assure any persons who like myself were not there, and who unlike myself have no knowledge of camp-meetings and other noisy religious demonstrations among people in the backwoods, does not even by inference or implication militate against the chastity of Nancy Hanks.

Personally, I deem the incident as containing no proof that Nancy Hanks was a participant in it; but if she was, whatever happened in the description was in broad daylight, in full view of a congregation, and was in accord with the ethical standards of the time.

A good many things occurred around the fringes of camp-meetings that ought not to have occurred. There was almost always a boot-legger with whisky. There were frequent fights. It was not at all infrequent for a crowd of toughs to attempt to break up the meeting, and for the preachers to show that they belonged to the church-militant. There were other evils which found opportunity for occurrence at various hiding places in the woods and which need not here be described. But the old-fashioned camp-meeting was an event of no little social and religious significance, and it did more good than harm.

I am not undertaking, however, to defend the old camp-meetings, none of which I ever organized or conducted, but in some of which I have participated as a preacher by invitation. I am saying, and wish to say it very plainly, that while such meetings were the scenes of demonstrations which I never enjoyed and do not defend, the things that happened out in the open, even if in as bad taste as those described by Mr. Helm, were not immoral. No couple who had come to camp-meeting for immoral purposes would have advertised the fact or set the whole camp to watching them by any such an exhibition. Nor would two persons known to be immoral have been permitted a leading place in such a demonstration.

If Nancy Hanks was publicly hugged at a camp-meeting a week before her marriage, as I think she was not, it was her own husband of a week later who hugged her. And that is a safe place to dismiss the matter.

The next discovery which I made upon a careful survey of the ground, and study of roads and distances and home-sites, was that in all probability Nancy Hanks Lincoln had never seen Abraham Enlow at the time of her conception.

Here I am greatly indebted to certain local attorneys, whose assistance I acknowledge. Hon. Richard W Creal, County Judge, who was born on the Lincoln Farm, Mr. O. M. Mather, local historian, great-grandson of several pioneers of Hodgenville, Mr. Charles F. Creal, partner of Mr. Mather and a descendant of the family that owned the Lincoln Farm, and Mr. L. B. Handley, attorney for the Lincoln Farm Association, gave me the fruits of their research and assisted me in further investigation.

When the Lincoln Farm Association was formed for the purchase of the birthplace of Abraham Lincoln, and which subsequently turned the birthplace and farm over to the United States Government, it became important to prove to the satisfaction of those who were to pay their money in the first place and of the Government afterward, that Abraham Lincoln was actually born there. Washington County set up a claim that he was born in that county, in the home of Richard Berry, and Washington County still insists that that claim is well founded. It became necessary to learn just when Thomas and Nancy Lincoln first occupied the Lincoln Farm on Nolin Creek. The investigation, as Mr. Handley informs me, and the others agree, clearly established that Thomas and Nancy Lincoln moved from Elizabethtown in the late spring or early summer of 1808, not to the farm aforesaid, but to the farm of George Brownfield, where they lived during that summer and fall in a cabin no longer standing but located in the orchard of wild crab-apples already described. That was where the life of Abraham Lincoln began, unless it had begun before the removal of his parents from Elizabethtown, though he was born in the cabin above the Rock Spring, on Nolin Creek, on what is now known as the Lincoln Farm.

When Abraham Lincoln was born, on the Rock Spring

farm, on Nolin Creek, two and one half miles south of the present town of Hodgenville, the Enlows lived some two miles distant, and were among the nearest neighbors of the Lincolns. But the date which immediately concerns us is not the date of Abraham's birth, but of his conception. Where were Thomas and Nancy Lincoln living at that time?

The normal period of gestation is ten lunar months, or two hundred eighty days Where were Thomas and Nancy Lincoln living on May 8, or about that date, in the year 1808?

They were not living on the farm where Abraham Lincoln was born ten lunar months later. We do not know that they had ever seen that farm or heard of it. Some authors have told us that Thomas Lincoln bought that farm in 1803, and had long been at work erecting a home there. The farm which came into his possession in 1803 was many miles from Rock Spring, and has no place in the life-story of Abraham Lincoln. We do not know that Thomas Lincoln had bought a farm at the time of his removal from Elizabethtown. So far as we know, he removed because he had employment offered him by George Brownfield; and while working there learned of a farm with a poor and unoccupied cabin and a good spring, where he would be permitted to squat with right of purchase if he found himself able to purchase it. That he built the cabin is unproved and improbable, and, for the purpose of this narrative, unimportant. He certainly was not living there in May of 1808; we have no slightest proof that he or Nancy had ever set foot upon the farm in May, 1808.

The precise date of removal from Elizabethtown must come up again. There are some interesting and important documents, hitherto unpublished, which help us to determine the approximate date. But for our present purpose, let it be made perfectly clear that Nancy Lincoln did not live in the Enlow neighborhood until several months after May 8, 1808.

She did not at this time wander very far away from home in quest of men She was caring for a baby daughter, Sarah, born February 10, 1807, and just fifteen months old when the unborn life of Abraham Lincoln began. In Elizabethtown, where she had spent the whole of her married life, the tongue of scandal never named her; and she was either just leaving Elizabethtown, or had just left it, when she became pregnant

He who will know the truth of this story should go to La Rue County, and travel the roads, and find where the blazed trees in 1808 marked bridle paths through the thick woods, and study the problem with the county map before him. He will find that when Thomas and Nancy Lincoln first came to live in that part of Hardin County which is now La Rue, no road to mill or meeting or to the county seat took Abraham Enlow past the Lincoln door. Ten months later, when the Lincolns were in their own home, he passed the house on his way to mill; but in May, 1808, there was nothing to call him to her door or her to his. Their homes lay eight miles apart, through dense forests, inhabited by bear and wolf and panther, and across deep streams.

Nancy Hanks Lincoln left no scandal behind her in Elizabethtown. If she was pregnant when she left, the fact was unknown, even to herself. If she became pregnant after her arrival in her new home, it was immediately after, and before she had time or opportunity to form acquaintance.

This, then, is my first reason for not believing that Abraham Lincoln was the son of Abraham Enlow, that in all human probability, *at the time the unborn life of Abraham Lincoln began, Nancy Hanks Lincoln had never seen Abraham Enlow.*

We meet then, the question, Why then did Thomas Lincoln and Abraham Enlow engage in that bitter fight in which Enlow lost his nose, and by reason of which, in good part, Thomas Lincoln decided to leave Kentucky? Lamon tells the story of that fight:

As time wore on, the infelicities of (Thomas) Lincoln's life in this neighborhood became insupportable He was gaining neither riches nor credit; and being a wanderer by natural inclination, began to long for a change His decision, however, was hastened by certain troubles which culminated in a desperate combat between him and one Abraham Enlow. They fought like savages, but Lincoln obtained a signal and permanent advantage by biting off the nose of his antagonist, so that he went bereft all the days of his life, and published his audacity and its punishment wherever he showed his face. But the affray, and the fame of it, made Lincoln more anxious than ever to escape from Kentucky. He resolved, therefore, to leave these scenes forever, and seek a roof-tree beyond the Ohio.—LAMON, *Life of Lincoln,* p. 16.

This fight, as thus recorded, is in its implications the worst feature of the whole story. No one who knows the Enlow story and reads this account can be in doubt what was the " audacity " of Abraham Enlow. Even as lethargic a man as Thomas Lincoln could be roused to desperation over a matter of that character.

So we do well to go to the bottom of the question about the fight in which Thomas Lincoln is alleged to have bitten off the nose of Abraham Enlow.

So far as is known, Thomas Lincoln never intimated to any one that his leaving Kentucky was related in any fashion to his alleged fight with Enlow. Conjecture only, and that long years and decades after the alleged affray and the departure, invented a relation between them. But if it be admitted that there was a connection, it is not difficult to imagine why it may have occurred. Family feeling in that region ran high, and the Enlow family was large, and related to most of the old families, while Lincoln was alone. If his fight with Enlow left the latter smarting under a visible and unpleasant disability which he could not be permitted to forget, there was reason to expect that sooner or later Thomas Lincoln would encounter more Enlows than he desired, and no one could predict the character of their revenge. It was a primitive region in which men fought with guns and knives as well as with fists and teeth. No matter what the original occasion of the fight; the thing now to expect was revenge for Abe Enlow's lost nose.

If this was the situation, Thomas Lincoln did well to gather his wife and his two small children and his meager supply of household goods, and float downstream to the Ohio River, and across into Indiana.

We meet, however, with this element of improbability in

the story. If this fight was an immediate cause of Thomas
Lincoln's migration from Kentucky, it occurred eight years
and more after the offense which it was supposed to avenge.
Thomas Lincoln may have been slow to wrath, but that was a
long time, even for him.

Furthermore, as one will discover who visits the region,   .
the removal of the Lincoln family to the Knob Creek farm
had effectually taken them out of the Enlow country. Muldraugh's Hill was a marked social barrier between the region
that faced toward Bardstown, Lebanon and Springfield toward
the east, and the country tributary to Elizabethtown on the
west. No longer did Thomas Lincoln send his grist to Hodgen's Mill or the Mather mill or the Kirkpatrick mill. He
was out of the neighborhood, removed by a goodly number
of miles, and by a very high ridge that formed a community
barrier from the associates of his former home. He still
went to court at Elizabethtown, and in the very last year of
his residence on Knob Creek was appointed Road Surveyor
in his district, but as for the rest, he had ceased to be resident
of the neighborhood when Abraham was born. For that matter, he removed from there, as I have some reason to believe,
much sooner than is commonly supposed.

But before we go to fatiguing lengths in our endeavor to
learn the occasion of the savage fight between Thomas Lincoln
and Abraham Enlow, let us ask the innocent question, Was
there any such fight?

The answer is, *There was no such fight.*

This discovery, I confess, surprised me. Lamon makes his
statement so unqualifiedly that I supposed of course he was
correct, and that Abraham Enlow went to his grave in 1861
having spent the last forty-five years of his life without the
nose that Thomas Lincoln had bitten off. I found that the
men in and about Hodgenville who know most about Lincoln
and most about Enlow had never heard of the fight. So far
as I know, there is no copy of Lamon's book in that county;
it is a scarce book, and La Rue County is not extravagant in its
book purchases. I asked lawyers, judges, county officials, and
men long resident, and not one of them had ever heard the

faintest rumor that Thomas Lincoln ever fought with any one, or that Abraham Enlow ever was a fighting man.

I inquired about his maimed nose; and men who knew him declare that he displayed no such deformity. I had to stop asking the question direct lest I start a new scandal, but I inquired in general terms, and what I learned was that, far from remembering the Lincolns with feelings of bitter resentment, Abraham Enlow was as proud to have been a neighbor of the Lincolns as so rock-ribbed a Democrat could possibly have been in the days of the Civil War. His reminiscences were few, but they were friendly. That he should have had any such fight as Lamon described is absurd. The best informed residents affirm that there is absolutely nothing on which such a lie can be based. The Enlows and Lincolns were on good terms so long as they lived in the same neighborhood, and parted with no unhappy memories.

The story has positively no local root. It cannot be grafted upon any event which bred a scandal at the time and caused the name of Nancy Lincoln to be spoken in derision by men and whispered innuendo by women.

Thomas and Nancy Lincoln had all the appearance of living together happily. They came to La Rue County honestly married, and lived in that county for several years. It is not known that they ever quarreled there or elsewhere. They had three children during those years, one of whom died, and the other two went with them as together they rode through the woods to their new home in Indiana Shiftless as Thomas Lincoln was, he is not known to have left any bad debts behind him, nor was he suspected of carrying away with him any of the property or any of the children of any other man.

In pursuing these inquiries in the vicinity of Hodgenville, the author came upon one dim and indistinct tradition which purported to have come down among the women of that neighborhood It was of the kindness of Thomas Lincoln to Nancy after her baby boy was born. When the story that Abraham Lincoln was the son of another man came to Hodgenville about the close of the Civil War, there were women living whose memory went back to that time, and who professed to recall that Thomas Lincoln was more kind to his wife at that time than husbands sometimes are.   His first child had been a daughter; and it seems that he and Nancy were hoping that the next one would be a son.   In the rude hut where she lay with her baby beside her, she lifted her wan face to her husband's with a tearful smile of satisfaction; she had given him a boy.   And the older women of the years just after the war, remembered that he was proud of the boy, and very tender toward Nancy.

But I found something very much more definite than this dim half-memory, and something fully in accord with it. I am able to present, on excellent authority, and with only one life between the statement and this record, the testimony of a woman who was a near neighbor of the Lincolns, a woman of about the age of Nancy Hanks Lincoln, and who was actually present at the birth of Abraham Lincoln.

This statement was made to me by Hon. Richard W. Creal, County Judge of La Rue County, in his office, and I made notes of it as he spoke.   After he had finished, I went across to the hotel and wrote it out within an hour   Subsequently I had it typewritten, and a copy mailed to Judge Creal in advance of my next visit to Hodgenville.   He then made one or two verbal emendations, and said:

" The report which you have made is entirely accurate, and you place great emphasis, and properly, upon the first-hand testimony of Margaret Walters.   But I use that incident as in a way representative of the testimony, positive and negative, of all the old people who lived neighbor to the Lincolns and were still living in 1864.   As I remember their conversation, the most convincing fact is their silence upon any aspect of the life of the Lincoln family that could have expressed or delicately concealed a scandal.   The outspoken word of Margaret Walters, which you value as the testimony of a woman actually present at the birth of Lincoln, stands to me rather as the testimony of the whole neighborhood. Boy though I was, I heard all the neighborhood talk.   Had there been any question about the Lincolns, it would have been heard by me at some time in a tone that a boy would not have failed to understand as at least mysterious or implying a question. There was no such expression And when the slander came first to this neighborhood, and in its first form without the name of any particular man attached, my father and his brother and Jack McDougal and all who had known Thomas Lincoln or known those who knew him, were outspoken in their refusal to credit it. To be sure, the rumor made headway. Those old people were few, and they did not live long, and the story did not die. But the people who had known the Lincolns did not help it to live. The people who would have known it if it was true did not know it even as a rumor, and when they heard it, they denied it. You have quoted me correctly as to Aunt Peggy Walters. I remember her well as she hobbled on her crutch down toward the Rock Spring when this matter was discussed by a group assembled there. But I do not think of it as if it had been her sole testimony. She knew the women of this neighborhood. She was a young married woman at the time and later was a frequent helper as a midwife. She was getting some of her early experience in this art when Abraham Lincoln was born. She was a woman of ability and character, and her word was perfectly good. Her memory was clear, and she knew the facts which she related. But what I have given you as from her stands out in my own mind rather as the united judgment of the people who had known the Lincolns and who talked about them that day at the spring, in what I am confident was the year 1864 "

I accept this statement of Judge Creal, as confirming the report which I am about to quote, and of strengthening it. I place great value on it as the first-hand testimony of a woman of unquestioned veracity, who was among the nearest neighbors of the Lincolns, and present at Abraham Lincoln's birth; and it gains in force in every aspect by his statement as given to me above, that the words of Margaret Walters [1] was virtually the word of the whole neighborhood.

[1] Margaret La Rue Walters was born December 11, 1789, and was the youngest daughter of John La Rue for whom La Rue County was

CONCERNING THE PATERNITY OF ABRAHAM LINCOLN
STATEMENT OF HON. R. W. CREAL

Judge of La Rue County Court, Hodgenville, La Rue County, Kentucky

I was born on the Lincoln farm. Richard Creal, my father, purchased it between 1825 and 1830. He was born in 1801. His birth occurred near the site of the present village of Buffalo. Population was very sparse at that time. Robert Hodgen was here, and had established Hodgen's Mill. There was another mill, the Mather mill some miles distant, and there was also the Kirkpatrick mill. These mills used small burr stones, driven by overshot wheels of local manufacture.

My father's brother knew Thomas Lincoln; my father did not, but knew his reputation. Thomas Lincoln was respected by his neighbors. He was a man of good mind and strong character, but had no advantages, and was diffident, reserved, quiet.

I grew up on the farm where Abraham Lincoln spent his first years, and was one of the heirs who sold it to A. W. Dennett.

I knew Margaret Walters, locally known as " Aunt Peggy," who assisted the midwife at the birth of Lincoln. She died at a great age, somewhere about 1864. She was on crutches the last time I saw her, shortly before her death. That interview occurred at the Lincoln Spring. She was an intelligent woman, who knew all the women of this region in the period of Lincoln's birth, and was in better position than most of them to know of their character and to hear any report affecting the reputation of any of them.

I was present on an occasion when she spoke of the paternity of Abraham Lincoln. It was not long before his death. I was born in 1853, and as this occurred in 1864, I was eleven or possibly twelve years of age.

I am not sure who introduced the subject. It may have

named. She was related to nearly all the original pioneers by birth or marriage. She married Conrad Walters, and became the mother of a large family, who intermarried with most of the prominent families of the county. She was married and twenty years of age when Lincoln was born, and her memory was clear until her death. She died October 26, 1864. Any one who is disposed to call her veracity in question would do well to keep away from La Rue County, or to go prepared to discuss the matter with a large number of tall and muscular men.

been Jack McDougal, whom I remember as present, but I think it was some one of a group of women who were there. Some one spoke of the rumor that Abraham Lincoln was not the son of Thomas Lincoln.

Aunt Peggy Walters denied it vigorously. She said, " Mrs. Lincoln was a fine woman." She affirmed that at that time she knew every woman who lived in this vicinity, knew their reputation, was on terms such that any such report concerning any of them was almost certain to come to her, and that she never heard during the lifetime of Mrs. Thomas Lincoln any charge or rumor affecting her moral character.

In my judgment this statement which I heard is entitled to very great weight. Mrs. Walters was an intelligent woman, and a woman of character and veracity. I am confident that if Mrs. Lincoln had borne during her lifetime any reputation of unfaithfulness to her marriage obligation, Mrs. Walters would certainly have heard of it, and would have been a good judge of its probable truthfulness. The fact that she not only did not believe it, but never heard it until nearly a half century after the Lincolns had removed from here, is, in my judgment, almost conclusive evidence that the story is untrue.

I cannot learn that the report had any existence in this county at the time that the Lincolns resided here, nor until Abraham Lincoln had risen to fame.

My father knew of these reports when they were current here, and so did my brother. Both of them knew the reputation of Thomas Lincoln, and neither of them credited the rumors.

The older people of this county knew nothing about these rumors until Mr. Lincoln wrote to Hardin County, of which La Rue was then a part, to obtain, if possible, a copy of the marriage record of his parents. He did not know, and no one here knew, that the record was not here but in Washington County.

When these reports gained currency here, many years ago, I made some effort to investigate the truth of them. I did not find any of the older people who believed them, nor any evidence that these rumors had originated here out of any circumstances that might properly have given rise to suspicion, nor that they were known here or anywhere at the time the events were alleged to have occurred. At the time of Abraham Lincoln's birth, all the neighbors believed him to be the son of Thomas Lincoln.

Thomas and Nancy Lincoln came here in 1806 as husband and wife, having been legally married, and the marriage is of record in the county where it occurred. They lived here in apparent domestic accord, and left here together, with their two children, both of them and the deceased child born in wedlock. No report was then in circulation that they were not happy together, and they continued to live together as husband and wife until the death of Nancy Hanks Lincoln. So far as any one knew then, or has any right to believe now, they were both faithful to each other until death separated them

I am only sorry that such rumors have ever been circulated I should not like to believe, and do not believe, that they originated here. I know of no one who is closer to the facts than I, and I cannot think that these things could have been true without my learning some evidence of the truth from some of the people of whom I have spoken.

In my judgment the rumors affecting the chastity of Nancy Hanks Lincoln are wholly without foundation, and are a cruel libel on the character of a virtuous woman.

RICHARD CREAL,
Judge of La Rue County Court.

I present herewith a sketch of the life of Abraham Enlow of Hardin, afterward La Rue, County, Kentucky.

Abraham Enlow was the son of Isom Enlaws, Enlows or Enlow, one of the pioneers of that part of Hardin County which is now La Rue. He was among the occupants of Phillips' Fort, which from about 1780 or 1781 to about 1790 gave shelter and protection from the Indians to the original inhabitants of the portion of Hardin County which now includes Hodgenville. Whether he was in the original group who built the fort, the author is not certain; but when the Indians had been driven away, and the occupants of the fort emerged and took up land, and erected homesteads outside the stockade, Isom Enlow was among them, and he located on a farm which has been continuously in possession of the Enlow family. It is one and one half miles from the present site of Hodgenville, and four miles, by the usual course of travel, from the Rock Spring Farm, where Abraham Lincoln later was born.

Isom Enlow came to Hardin County unmarried. He became the husband of Mary Brooks, the widow of John La Rue, for whom the county was later named. The marriage occurred in 1792.

John La Rue was born in Virginia, January 24, 1746, the son of Isaac La Rue, of Frederick County, Virginia, (died 1795) and died in January, 1792, in Hardin County, and in that part of the county later separated and named for him. His wife, Mary Brooks, was born May 3, 1766, being thus twenty years younger than her first husband.

John and Mary La Rue had four children. (1) Rebecca, born 1784, married George Helm. Their oldest child, John L. Helm, was born in 1802, and was Governor of Kentucky at his death in 1867; (2) Squire La Rue, named for Squire Boone, brother of Daniel Boone, and friend of John La Rue; (3) Phebe; (4) Margaret (" Peggy ") was born 1789, married September 11, 1804, Conrad Walters. Ben Hardin Helm, Confederate General who was killed in the Civil War, was a son of John L. Helm (son of Rebecca La Rue and George Helm). Ben Hardin Helm's wife, still living, was Emily Todd, a half sister of Mrs. Abraham Lincoln.

In the conditions which prevailed in pioneer society, widows were not permitted to weep long at the graves of their deceased husbands. Mary Brooks La Rue soon married Isom Enlow. Although the fact has no especial significance for this narrative, it may be of interest to record that she survived her second husband, and was married for the third time, to Thomas W. Rathbone. She died a few months after the erection of the new county, named for her first husband, and her will is the second will on record in that county, and was probated May 5, 1843, the earliest date of probate in La Rue County.

The will of John La Rue, which is on record in Nelson County, and was probated May 6, 1792, has more than the ordinary amount of formal piety in its introduction, and shows great concern for the education of his children. He left four children, ·the eldest of whom was eight years old.   He had much land and several negroes, one of whom, " a wench, Nancy," he left especially to his wife, to be her own.   Mary La Rue came therefore to the home of Isom Enlow cumbered by four children, but with a generous provision for their care —a provision which unfortunately was partially lost in the administration of the estate and in consequent litigation— and with Nancy the " wench " to assist in their care, and in the care of such further offspring as might come to her through her second marriage.

This provision was timely, for the first fruits of the second marriage was Abraham Enlow.   Mary Brooks-La Rue-Enlow-Rathbone continued to need all the help which the possession of Nancy afforded; for though she bore no children by her last marriage, by her first two marriages she became the mother of no small fraction of the population of La Rue County   When she died in 1843 she left 172 living descendants.   She lived almost to the time when persons now living could remember her, and her record is a good one   For the facts about her, and much beside, I am indebted to Hon. O. M. Mather of Hodgenville, whose careful preservation of historic data relating to his native county is of great service to me.

Isom Enlaws, the second husband of Mary Brooks La Rue, and the father of Abraham Enlaws, Enlows or Enlow, was a man of some prominence in his day.   He was Sheriff of Hardin County in 1810, and afterwards for some years a Justice of the Peace.   He died in July, 1816, leaving his widow and six children, two of whom were sons and four daughters.

Nancy was the only one of the slaves of John La Rue whom Mary Brooks La Rue continued to own after her marriage with Isom Enlaws.   The executors appear to have sold and squandered the rest, or eaten them up in law suits.   And she had a hard time keeping Nancy and her children from being taken by the executors under the will of Enlaws after the death of her second husband.   The reports of the Court of Appeals of Kentucky contain record of the attempt of her husband's executors to take them away from her by legal process, and of her stout and successful resistance. The case of *Enlaws' Executors vs. Mary Enlaws* is of interest. Therein it is set forth that,—

Mary Enlaws, in virtue of the will of her former husband, John La Rue, had an estate for life in the slave named Nancy, and being possessed thereof in 1792, married Isom Enlaws. After the marriage of Isom and Mary Enlaws, Nancy became the mother of other slaves. In July, 1816, Isom Enlaws departed this life, having previously made and published his will, which, after payment of his debts, contained the following clauses:

Item. My will is that my property, both real and personal, continue undivided until my youngest daughter, Malvina Enlaws, arrives at the age of twenty-one years, or until all my children are married. And upon either of those events, that said property be divided, share and share alike, between my said children, to wit,—Abraham Enlaws, Thomas Brooks Enlaws, Polly Enlaws, Lydia Enlaws, Betsy Enlaws and Malvina Enlaws, and their mother, my beloved wife, Mary Enlaws.

Item. In case my son, Abraham Enlaws, should prefer taking one hundred acres of land, to be stricken off to him by a line running parallel with my upper boundary line, and including the house in which he lives, in lieu of the equal undivided share in my landed property, as mentioned in the next preceding item, my will is that he be permitted to do so; and that he retain possession of the same as he how holds it.

Malvina, the youngest daughter, was eleven years old in May, 1819, and the executors would have to wait ten years, unless she died or married sooner, before they could obtain for the purposes of sale and division, the healthy and marketable children of Nancy. Malvina was living with her mother, and so were her older sisters, Polly and Betsy, but Lydia was married before her father died. Abraham, for a time after his father's death, came back and lived in his mother's home and managed the farm for her, and then accepted his option under his father's will, took his hundred acres of land, returned to his own home, which he had occupied before his father's death, and lived and died there.

The court held that although Nancy had been left to Mary La Rue as a life possession under the will of John La Rue, she became the property of Isom Enlaws the moment they were married, and that thereafter Mary had no estate in Nancy, except as she gained it through her second husband.

The court found, however, that while Mary had no right to Nancy under the will of her first husband, she had some right under the will of her second husband. The executors could not touch Nancy or her children until Malvina married or reached the age of twenty-one, and then Mary would share in the division with her children.

So Mary's troubles over the negro Nancy ceased, and so far as any one knows, this was the only Nancy who ever caused any trouble in that family.

Isom Enlaws did not own any other slaves at the time of his death in 1816, and Abraham Enlows did not own any slaves at the time of his death in 1861.

Whoever cares to read this decision in full will find it in 3, *Marshall, Kentucky Court of Appeals,* pages 228-230. It is interesting for several reasons, but its interest for us is in the background it affords us for the life of Abraham Enlaws, Enlows or Enlow

The village of Hodgenville is remote, but it is not wholly behind the times. In the Spring of 1920, when I made one of my visits to it, the local papers contained matter which showed that Hodgenville was fairly abreast of the rest of the world. The ministers were preaching on "The Inter-Church World Movement," and the boys in the Senior Class in the Hodgenville High School had organized an overalls brigade, just as they were doing in New York and Boston. Hodgenville has a little public library, named not for Andrew Carnegie, but for Abraham Lincoln.

This library contains the one known copy of a little book called *"Ministry of Faith."* Its sub-title is, *"The Ardent Ministry, Times, Anecdotes and Pulpit Selections of Rev.*

A. W. La Rue, A.M." The author was A. C. Graves, and the book was published in Louisville in 1865. For our purposes it is of interest because Rev. A. W. La Rue, who was graduated in 1842 with the first class in Georgetown College, was a grandson of John La Rue and Mary Brooks, who, after the death of her first husband, married Isom Enlaws, Enlows or Enlow, and became the mother of Abraham Enlow. This little book tells something about this good woman:

Mary Brooks, the wife of John La Rue, was of an old family of Virginia, and deserves from her peculiar character not to be overlooked in this chapter. From the marvellous strength of her faith and the great power of her ruling traits, one would not infer that her influence would be exhausted in a single generation. And who can measure the fearful responsibility of every mother when it is considered that her character is to be held up as a type for children's children, molding into the image of the Saviour, or forever paralyzing all aspirations for manliness and perfection of heart! Mrs. La Rue was a devoted Christian, and a prayerful reader of the Bible. Her judgment of the Scriptures was held in general respect, and knotty passages were frequently brought to her by preachers and others for her interpretation. She survived her husband many years, and lived to a ripe old age. At her death in 1843 her living generation numbered 172. Perhaps no generation in Kentucky has produced a larger number of worthy representatives in the pulpit, at the bar, in politics, medicine, and the other callings.

Many incidents and anecdotes are related of Mrs. La Rue, two of which may properly come in here to illustrate the might of that character whose weight still hangs upon her numerous progeny.

One occurred at old Nolin Church, while Rev. David Thurman (the father of our estimable brother, R. L. Thurman) was pastor. He was a man of strong logical mind, great decision and force of character, which led him to deal extensively in doctrine and discussion. He was a terrific Calvinist, and as a defender of our faith, the Baptists had not a more successful champion. One church-meeting day he rose under perceptible despondency over the low spiritual condition of the church. He was greatly discouraged with his pastoral prospects, and suggested that the church call another pastor. He sat down in a profound silence which continued some seconds. The stillness and embarrassment were soon broken by old Mrs. La Rue, who was the first to see through and solve a difficulty. She had been leaning forward all the while in a listening posture, never removing her eyes from the preacher. Straightening herself and pointing one finger at Elder Thurman, she said in a tone of confidence and feeling: " Brother Thurman, I'll tell you what the matter is—stop preaching John Calvin and James Arminius, and preach Jesus Christ." After a moment's pause, the preacher rose with streaming eyes, and repeated the words, " For I am determined not to know anything among you save Jesus Christ and Him crucified."

The sermon which followed was one of the most powerful and searching character. Perhaps old Nolin Creek never experienced a more thorough shock than was made among the dry bones by that discourse. A revival began with that day, in which there were one hundred additions to the church. Its influence spread from church to church until there were over a thousand conversions in that association, all following that one effort!

Upon her dying bed, Mrs. La Rue called her daughter and said, among her last words:

" From the hour of my conversion, now near sixty years since, I have prayed every day that God would raise up of my generation Baptist preachers."

She had watched her sons entering the pursuits of life one by one, and as yet her prayer was unanswered. From the time she first heard S. L. Helm, her grandson, the first of her generation to preach the gospel, she took courage at the answer of her life-time prayer. At the time of her death, A. W. La Rue, another grandson, was a young preacher of great promise, and she passed up from this world believing that God would still raise up others of her generation in answer to her prayer. From her descendants have sprung the following Baptist preachers: Rev. S. L. Helm, Rev. A. W. La Rue, deceased; Rev. Robert Enlows, Rev. John H. Yeaman, deceased, and Rev. W. Pope Yeaman, pastor of the First Baptist Church, Covington, Kentucky. The last two were brothers.—*Ministry of Faith*, pp. 18-21.

In that day, as this little book truthfully sets forth, educated ministers were rare among Kentucky Baptists, and not in very good favor; but this man sought and obtained a college education.

It is not with A. W. La Rue we are dealing, however, but with his half-uncle, Abraham Enlow. The long quotation shows the kind of mother he had, and the kind of home in which he was reared; and while her prayers that he might be a Baptist preacher were not answered in him, they were answered in his son, Rev. Robert Enlows.

Mary Brooks was born in Virginia, but she spent a part of her girlhood in Philadelphia, where she went to school. She learned, among other things, something of medicine, and in her mature years was widely sought as a nurse and midwife. Abraham Enlow had a capable mother.

Unlike some of the Enloes of North Carolina, the Enlows of La Rue County, Kentucky, refuse to slander their ancestor for the sake of cheap notoriety. I have the following statement from Robert Enlow, of Hodgenville, who has several times represented his county in the Kentucky Legislature:

STATEMENT OF ROBERT ENLOW

Made in Writing to William E. Barton, May 20, 1920

I do not think my grandfather, Abraham Enlow, was the father of Abraham Lincoln. I do not think he was that kind of man. From every inquiry I have made, I have found my grandfather to be a Christian of the highest character, a man who was a leader in Christian work, a man who was looked up to as an example for young men to follow.

I have heard of this report all my life, and since I have been in public life some, have heard much more. My great-grandmother, Mary Enlow, officiated at the birth of Lincoln. She was taken there by my grandfather, Abraham, on a horse. She usually had grandfather, who was then a boy, to accompany her on these trips. She gave Mrs. Lincoln what assistance the occasion required, and as the days passed, she sent many things to Mrs. Lincoln for her own and the child's comfort. Most of these things were sent either by my grandfather or a slave, all the time without a thought of pay, but from a heart of love.

Then, when this baby boy wanted a name, his mother gave him the name of Abraham, because of gratitude, and, as I believe, from no other reason, in recognition of the many acts of kindness shown by my great-grandfather's family The vision of the Christ life shown by Mary Enlow gave Mrs. Lincoln that conception of motherhood that enabled her so to train her son, that in after years he was heard to say, That all he had and all he hoped to be in this life he owed to his mother.

My father, and the whole family so far as I knew, did not believe the story that Abraham Enlow was the father of Abraham Lincoln. I think the story originated from malice toward slave-holders. You know there was such a feeling in the minds of people who did not own slaves or anything else. . . .

Yours for truth,

ROBERT ENLOW.

Not because we have need of further evidence, but because evidence is available and convincing, let us record one more important fact concerning Abraham Enlow. He died in 1861 and his grave is in the old Baptist Church-yard, near the church of which he was a member, and to whose erection he is said to have made the first subscription. There is a tombstone at his grave, and it gives the date of his birth as January 26, 1793. This would make him, at the time when Abraham Lincoln was begotten, not a man, but a boy of fifteen.

But may there not be a mistake in this old record? The people of that period were notoriously inexact in such matters, and except where there are contemporary court records, many inaccuracies occur. May not there be a mistake of ten or twenty years, so that the age of Abraham Enlow can be carried backward? For, if this record is correct, Abraham Enlow, at the time of the conception of Abraham Lincoln, was not simply at a highly improbable

distance from the Lincoln home, but was only a lad of
fifteen.

We are so accustomed to the commencement of the year
on January 1 it is difficult to realize how recently that date
has been established and definitely agreed upon. The custom
varied in different places. In England down to the time of
the Conquest, the year was reckoned in some places as beginning at Christmas, and in others on March 25. From the
Conquest to 1155 only it dated officially from January 1,
but that system was not popular, and from 1155 till 1751 it
was dated according to the Dionysian system from March 25.
In America the practice was not uniform, and we find frequent
instances of the March 25 date of beginning down to the end
of the 18th century. It is often necessary to indicate dates
falling between January 1 and March 25 by a double system, as February 1, 1764-5. Down to the opening years
of the nineteenth century, particularly in isolated and rural
communities, there were frequent datings according to the
Dionysian year. John La Rue died in January, 1792, as we
reckon time. Before the end of that year his widow married
Isom Enlaws; the true date of birth of Abraham Enlows or
Enlow would appear to have been January 26, 1793-4.

Yes, it is possible there is a mistake, but if so, it does
not make Abraham Enlow ten years older, but one year
younger. The local tradition gives the year of his birth,
not as 1793, but as 1794. John La Rue died in January,
1792. His widow married Isom Enlow, and Abraham Enlow was born, according to his tombstone, just one year
after the death of his mother's first husband. Although intervals between marriages were habitually short in frontier
communities, this seems an improbably brief interval, and
there is much reason to believe that the date of 1794 is correct. In that case, Abraham Enlow, at the time of the conception of Abraham Lincoln, was not even fifteen, but only
fourteen.

The confusion in the two accounts of the birthday of
Abraham Enlow is thus easily accounted for. It was the
time when " Old Style " dates were still in occasional use,

and threw the opening weeks of a year into the calendar of the preceding year. Abraham Enlow's birth as given on his tombstone is the Old Style date; and the date given by the family is the New Style date. His birth, according to our present reckoning, was January 26, 1794. He was born, not one year, but two, after the death of his mother's first husband.

At the time when Nancy Hanks Lincoln experienced the promise of the birth of a son, in May of 1808, Abraham Enlow was a chore-boy on his father's farm. He was in the beginnings of adolescence. The razor had never touched his face.

Abraham Enlow, whom ignorant and malicious gossip has made the father of Abraham Lincoln, was, at the time of Abraham Lincoln's birth, a beardless boy.

There remains nothing to be added.

I have done with the story that Abraham Lincoln was the illegitimate son of Abraham Enlow, of Hardin County, Kentucky. The other stories we shall consider one by one. But this one we shall have no occasion to examine further. We have considered every shred of evidence that I have been able to discover in support of it, and I am confident that I have discovered it all. We have given it a fair hearing, and have subjected it to a fair analysis. It fails at every possible point, and is conclusively contradicted and disproved. No right-minded man ought to refer to it in terms of possible credibility henceforth so long as the world shall stand. It is a blot on the memory of a plain, honest, religious man and upon the name of his descendants, and a libel upon the character of a woman, who, so far as this story is concerned, stands high above all reproach.

Let us consign this story to its place in the bottomless pit, and proceed with the next.

CHAPTER XVII

ABRAHAM ENLOW OF ELIZABETHTOWN

THIS book aspires toward completeness. Its purpose is to record every phase of the story, and each of the separate stories that affirm that Abraham Lincoln was not the son of Thomas Lincoln. I am thus constrained to consider briefly in this analysis two or three names that are not mentioned in the second part of the book. One of these is Abraham Enlow, a miller, of Elizabethtown, Kentucky. In the first draft of this manuscript I assigned him a chapter in the earlier portion of the book; but I removed from him that distinction for reasons which will presently appear; while, for the sake of completeness, I treat of him here. Like one of the heads of the beast in the Apocalypse, he "is of the seven, and is also an eighth." We shall spend no great space upon him, but will afford him all he requires.

Elizabethtown, where Thomas Lincoln and Nancy Hanks established their first home, is not without its local claim to an Abraham Enlow, who is alleged to have been the father of Abraham Lincoln. This report I give in the words of a letter from Mr. John E. Burton:

As to my belief regarding the birth of Abraham Lincoln, I believe that he was born *under* lawful wedlock. I was so interested in the Lincoln matters that when the Lincoln farm was sold in 1904 I went to Kentucky and spent several days in that vicinity. I took with me $3,500, which I judged to be sufficient, and I fully expected to buy the farm at the sheriff's sale. On this trip I left the railroad at Elizabethtown, and rode to Hodgenville in a buggy. On the way over the driver said to me that as I was so interested in Abe Lincoln, he presumed I knew who his father was. I said I had read several books on the subject, and knew the various opinions. He said, pointing to the large grist mill in the edge of Elizabethtown:

186

"Abe Lincoln's father used to own and run that very mill, and about everybody in Elizabethtown knows that Abe Enlow was Abe Lincoln's real father.   Yes, sir; we all like Abe Lincoln down here, and it is no fault of his that Abe Enlow got mixed up with the hired girl and paid Tom Lincoln to marry her and move over to Hodgenville."

Mr. Burton continued:

I found that almost every one in that part of the country when questioned had the secret.   I believe that Abraham Lincoln was the first child born to Thomas Lincoln and Nancy Hanks.   I do not believe there was a girl named Nancy or Sarah born to them before Abraham was born. Why I so believe is that Abraham's second mother, or stepmother, was named Sarah Bush.   I formerly owned her old hymn-book with her name written in it, Sarah Bush.   This woman had a daughter Sarah.   She and Abraham grew up as brother and sister.   That, in my opinion, is the occasion of the mix-up.

In my opinion, this story is true.   Lincoln himself knew the truth about it, and that was what made him habitually sad.   The dark and oppressive shadow which ever hung over him made him gloomy, and at times almost drove him to despair.   To interpret correctly the thousand and one odd and strange things that Lincoln did, these facts must be known in order to account for his doings.

I have written more than I meant to.   It is a subject which historians seem to fear.   They think the truth would injure Lincoln's fame and glory.   I do not.   I have only to recall Charles Martel, who saved the civilization of Europe from the Moors, and William of Normany, the Conqueror of England, to satisfy myself that children conceived out of wedlock are often of superior caliber.

Subsequent correspondence disclosed that Mr. Burton had made no comparison of the several Abraham Enlows, and was most moved by the apparent evidence in favor of the North Carolina Enloe.   He is quoted here not as showing his preference for this particular form of the story, but because he had opportunity to secure this form of it in the manner stated, and has written it as he heard it.

It interested me much to discover that this man, who
had studied Lincoln for so many years and had invested
large sums in books concerning him, held to the Enlow theory
in any of its forms. He holds, as I judge, to the theory in
general, rather than to any one form of it; but he has given
the best record I have of the Elizabethtown version.

This story is not entitled to any weight. It is an off-
shoot from the Hodgenville story, and has intermixed with
it so much of the Bourbon County story as makes its hero
a miller. The Lincolns bore a good reputation while they
lived in Elizabethtown. Thomas Lincoln had credit at the
stores, and paid his debts, and his wife was above suspicion.
An eminent judge in that town said to me.

"I regard every such story as a gross libel. Nothing
of the sort was ever heard in Elizabethtown while Thomas
Lincoln lived here, nor have I ever been able to trace it back
of the Civil War. My people were Southern in their sympathies, and so am I, and always have been: but this story
did not grow up here. It found credence here among certain
people, but it was imported. It has no basis of fact in this
county."

However, to go one step farther, I decided to learn
whether there ever was an Abraham Enlow, a miller, of
Elizabethtown. The mills of an early settlement are noted
institutions, and those of Elizabethtown are well known.
The large mill standing on the way to Hodgenville is noted
in the histories of the State, and long remained in the Haycraft family, one of the most prominent families of Elizabethtown. At my request the County Clerk searched the records of Hardin County with this result, that he can find no
Abraham Enlow as having owned a mill in that part of the
county. Furthermore, the Enlows lived where they originally settled, and, so far as he can discover, there was not an
Enlow in that part of the county which now is Hardin prior
to the birth of Abraham Lincoln.

The answer to the story about Abraham Enlow, the miller
of Elizabethtown, is that there was no such man.

CHAPTER XVIII

GEORGE BROWNFIELD

THE Brownfield story would not be entitled to a moment's notice but for one significant fact; it is one form of the local confession that the Enlow story is untenable.

As soon as the Enlow story began to be current in La Rue County, the people who knew where Thomas and Nancy Lincoln were living at the time of the conception of Abraham Lincoln, recognized the incredibility of the story. The unborn life of Abraham Lincoln began immediately before or immediately after the removal of his parents from Elizabethtown, and before Nancy had time to form acquaintances. Her conception occurred before their removal to their own home near the Enlows. As we have already seen, it is altogether likely that she had never seen the face of Abraham Enlow. The older inhabitants knew this fact. Under those circumstances, some other man had to be found to whom the paternity of Abraham Lincoln was a physical possibility. That man was George Brownfield; and, of course, Abraham Lincoln, being a tall man, was said to have looked much like the son of George Brownfield, who also was tall.

The story is the emptiest trash. But it is valuable; for it never would have come into existence if the local form of the Enlow story had not been recognized as impossible.

One of the prominent citizens of Hodgenville, a man active in political circles, and otherwise widely known, made an extended verbal statement which I summarize as follows:

"I have spent my life in La Rue County, and have been familiar from childhood with stories concerning the birth of Abraham Lincoln. I am a Democrat, and I had at the outset no natural disinclination to believe anything adverse to the reputation of Abraham Lincoln or the social standing of his family; for political interest and political hatred were very strong here in the days that followed the Civil War. I suppose I have had as much occasion as any other man living in this county to investigate the truth of these rumors. It became a part of my duty some years ago to look into them very carefully.

"I know only of the rumors that are or have been current in this locality. The others, more remote, I have never investigated; I do not think it worth while. Here, if anywhere, the irregularity occurred. Here, if anywhere, must the evidence be sought. I have had occasion to seek out and to weigh that evidence. I have no hesitation in saying that this story in all its local forms is unsupported by evidence, and in all those local forms but one is physically possible. The one possible exception is the Brownfield story. If Thomas and Nancy Lincoln came here from Elizabethtown as early as May, 1808, and she formed an adulterous association with the first man she met, then this story is barely possible, and that is all that can be said in its favor.

"But we do not know that she was here as early as May, 1808; the probabilities are that she and Thomas came about the first of June. And if she came as early as May, we have no evidence whatever that she then or ever was untrue to her husband. There is no vestige of a story current in the years of her life here that militates against her moral character. There is not the slightest reason to believe that any one suspected Brownfield until half a century had gone by. All that can be alleged in its favor is that it is not known to be physically impossible; and that is no evidence upon which to assail the character of a woman who has a right to be presumed virtuous, or of a man in good standing in the community.

"If any of these stories here locally current is true, this is the true one; for the others are impossible. This one is unsupported by any color of evidence, and is opposed to every inherent probability. It did not originate until the Enlow story had been weighed in the balance and found wanting. Then this grew out of the mere suggestion that it was not utterly impossible. The story is unworthy of credence.

"I began my investigation of these stories with no marked

disinclination to believe them. I am convinced that all of them that ever have been in circulation in Lincoln's home county are false; and as for the rest, I have only to say that it is incredible that any one of them should have been true. How could an event which certainly occurred here, if it occurred at all, leave no evidence of the fact in the place where it occurred, and become known to people in Virginia or North Carolina or South Carolina? The stories are all false; all impossible except the Brownfield story, and that might possibly have been true, but is false as are the others."

This makes a short chapter, but there is no reason why it should be longer. There is nothing more to be said about it.

CHAPTER XIX

ABRAHAM LINCOLN OF OHIO

In 1867 material on the life of Lincoln was still relatively scant. While Holland's *Life of Lincoln* and that of Barrett were based upon some original investigation, these had been issued as soon after Mr. Lincoln's death as the authors could well prepare them, and they depended upon the campaign biographies for most of their content with regard to Lincoln's early life. In that year the story gained currency that one reason for the departure of Thomas and Nancy Lincoln from Kentucky was the strong resemblance which existed between their son Abraham and a neighbor who was alleged to have been his father. It was further declared that between the time of their removal from Kentucky and their residence in Indiana the family lived for a time in a village in Ohio. This village was named, and the name could be mentioned here, and would be so mentioned if it were of any importance in this statement.

A noted Presbyterian minister in Lexington, Kentucky, became much interested in this matter, and learned that another minister, then editing a religious newspaper, had been a school teacher in that town in Ohio in the years when this boy, Abraham Lincoln, was supposed to have been resident there. The editor also was interested. He had seen Mr. Lincoln in 1860, and thought he recalled a resemblance to his pupil of former years. Furthermore, his computation disclosed the fact that President Lincoln's age was just about that of his old pupil. It further appeared that the father of this young Ohio Lincoln was named Thomas.

The correspondence resulting from these facts is still in existence, though not in possession of any of the original correspondents. I have communicated with the son of the editor, who writes to me:

192

"I am afraid I can give you no information in regard to the controversy of 1867. I have an indistinct recollection of the discussion and have looked over the files for 1867, but found nothing."

I have had access, however, to the original letters, in possession of another person, and have copied such portions as are important for this purpose. The owner of these letters has preserved them for possible use in case the story should rise again, and they are where they could be found if needed; but he does not desire that the letters or the place of their deposit should become public property.

These are the essential facts as brought out in these letters:

The man of whom I have spoken as the editor taught in a village in Ohio in 1827 a lad about nineteen, whose name he remembered as Abraham Linkhorn or Lincoln, and whose father was named Thomas. The President-elect in 1860 seemed to him to have the same figure and features. The story of the Ohio residence, with sufficient detail as to the relation of that residence to a prior one in Kentucky and a subsequent but very brief one in Indiana, appeared to support this impression.

The son of the editor has looked through the files of his father's paper for 1867, and finds no reference to these matters. Very properly so, for his father was not a man who would have been likely to publish a story of this kind until he had investigated the matter fully.

The results of his investigation lie before me in the handwriting of the father, the editor. His recollection of the name of the boy's father was correct; it was Thomas Lincoln. The son who went to school to him was born about 1809, and was a tall, raw-boned lad like the future President. Further, the family removed from Ohio, and settled in Indiana. Here, surely, was the basis of a plausible and scandalous story, for if the Ohio Lincoln was the President there was a scandal about his birth.

But at that point the stories diverge. Thomas Lincoln of Ohio had three sons, John, Thomas and Ananias. He had no son Abraham. The son whom the teacher, who later became the editor, taught in Ohio, and thought he recognized in the future President, was named John, and he died in 1840. There lies before me as I write a letter from the man for whom he was working and upon whose premises he died.

This discovery completely disposed of the report, and at the same time it illustrated how a considerable body of fact can be gathered in support of a theory that is utterly untrue, and how easily an honest man can be deceived in his own recollections of the appearance of a person whom he had known many years previous to the time of his making a statement.

For good reason, I prefer not to name any of the persons who participated in this correspondence; but I have copies of the letters, which I made with my own hand direct from the originals, and I have given herewith all the essential facts.

Furthermore, if the statements in this chapter should be called in question, the original letters can easily be located, and the statements in this chapter fully substantiated.

CHAPTER XX

ABRAHAM INLOW OF BOURBON COUNTY

OF all the forms of the story concerning Abraham Lincoln's paternity, I approach this one with the least patience. The reasons are, first, that the story itself is highly offensive, and, secondly, that it comes to us through the credulity of men who had been trained to sift evidence, and who ought to have known better. The story is that Thomas Lincoln, for a consideration, confidently named as five hundred dollars in money and a pair of horses and a wagon, married a woman named Hornback or Hanks, and assumed the paternity of her illegitimate child, who, according to some versions of the story, was not yet born, and according to others was able to run around, and to sit up between Thomas and Nancy as they drove away toward the more western portion of the State to begin their married life together. It partakes of the story told by Mrs. Boyd, but instead of attributing his birth to Judge Marshall's son, or adopted son, ascribes his paternity to one Abraham Inlow, a miller, who is alleged to have lived on the border between Clark and Bourbon Counties.

One of the first questions suggested by the story is, What did Thomas Lincoln do with the money? That amount of money would have made him a rich man on his arrival in Hardin County. He was not a drunkard nor a gambler, and while he was improvident, he was not a wastrel. What did he do with the money?

And what did he do with the horses and wagon? The tax collector was unable to find more than one horse, and almost every man had a horse to ride. If Thomas Lincoln secured any such sum we should find him with less difficulty on the tax returns, where I have found him in the counties of his residences, but not with two horses at any time while he resided in Kentucky, so far as tax returns have thus far been discovered.

The next fact which comes to our notice is that the name of the young woman, thus wronged by one man and married by another, was manifestly not Hanks but Hornback, a name not infrequent in Hardin and La Rue Counties. The more this story is followed upon the ground, the more it becomes apparent that the name Hanks was a later addition. One can discover the very bungling and unsuccessful attempt to accomplish what in the film-world is called a fade-out for the Hornback girl and the emergence in her place of Nancy Hanks.

We find in this story, as elsewhere, the alleged proof in the fact that relatives of the people supposed to have been involved in this situation have long arms, more or less, like those of Abraham Lincoln. One distinguished lawyer, related to the Inlows, shows his long arms as proof of his relationship to Abraham Lincoln. This proves that in several localities in Kentucky, Tennessee and the two Carolinas, there are men who have long arms, and it proves no more.

This story also affirms that an unnamed lawyer said to another unnamed lawyer that a Methodist preacher, unnamed but evidently Jesse Head, residing at Harrodsburg, told the lawyer who told the other lawyer, who told some one else, that when he married Thomas Lincoln and Nancy Hanks, the boy Abraham was old enough to run around the floor. And that is a lie. Jesse Head died in 1842, more than two decades before this story got into circulation.

Now we come to the irrefutable proof that this story is false, which is, that Thomas and Nancy Lincoln were married June 12, 1806, and that in February of the following year there was born to them a daughter named Sarah, who was their eldest child. Abraham was the second child, born two years and eight months after the marriage of his parents.

Nicolay and Hay in their record of the marriage of Thomas and Nancy Lincoln give correctly the date of June 12, 1806, and say:

" All previous accounts give the date of this marriage as

September 23rd. This error rose from a clerical blunder in the county record of marriages. The minister, the Rev. Jesse Head, in making his report, wrote the date before the names; the clerk, in copying it, lost the proper sequence of the entries, and gave to the Lincolns the date belonging to the next couple on the list." (*Vol. I,* p. 23)

Nicolay and Hay are mistaken Herndon gave the correct date in his first edition, and most authors have followed him. Moreover, the clerk of the Washington County Court usually copied it correctly, and that has been the record since followed. Nicolay and Hay were in error in supposing themselves to be the first who published this date correctly.

The date was incorrectly copied, however, in the first published article, and the wrong date has sometimes slipped into books, as, in the appendix of Miss Tarbell's *Life of Lincoln,* where she followed a date given to a Kentucky minister. But the correct date had been given years before by Herndon.

The Bourbon County story, though very widely current, is impossible. Busy as the devil is, it could hardly have originated at the time it obtained currency if the marriage return of Thomas Lincoln and Nancy Hanks had been found. The first male child of Nancy Hanks was not born before she married Thomas Lincoln, but was preceded by a daughter, born two years previously.

This daughter's name was certainly not Nancy. That myth comes plainly from the tear in the family record page of the Lincoln Bible. Her name was Sarah, and she was born at Elizabethtown, February 10, 1807, two full years before her brother Abraham. The story that when Thomas and Nancy rode away to be married the boy sat between them is opposed not only to all probability, but to certain fact.

The story is not without its own internal indications of its origin. The unfortunate girl who found a husband and went away with him and her child was not a Hanks, but a Hornback; and the evolution of some nearly forgotten Hornback girl into a Nancy Hanks is apparent on the face of the story. The Hornbacks still live in Hardin and La Rue Counties, and probably in adjacent counties.

The Hanks girls were known in Hardin County before the marriage of Nancy, as is plainly shown in the Helm story, told by Herndon. Nancy Hanks before her marriage to Thomas Lincoln was not living the life of a prostitute near Thatcher's Mills, but living around among her relatives, and possibly sometimes attending camp-meetings, and, so far as anybody knows, she was behaving herself like a virtuous young woman.

This story is one of the most discreditable to those who hold it, and it has very little to be said in its favor or in favor of those who so readily accepted it. It has formed a part of the gossip of lawyers in Kentucky for many years, but the evidence adduced in its favor, though with a Chief Justice of the Appellate Court as its sponsor, shows very little regard for the rules of evidence.

I count this story the more contemptible because the men who pieced together the bits and fragments of court-house and bar-room gossip of which it is composed, and who re-told it and enlarged it, were men who were accustomed to weighing evidence. Some of those who were chiefly responsible were men of ability and of character. They believed this story until it became almost a religion. Yet the story is sustained by no evidence which these lawyers would have accepted as proof in any case in court. They talked about it and rehearsed the gossip, and some of them finally swore to their belief in the truth of it; but when their affirmations are analyzed and the evidence in their favor is weighed, it is altogether less than vanity.

After a very thorough investigation of these matters, I had occasion to make inquiry as to certain details, and wrote to a friend of many years, who is a Kentucky editor and a member of the bar, and whose home is not far from the storm center of this particular story. He refused to assist me. He said of the men who circulated these stories, " They are liars, and scandal-mongers! "

Furthermore, he specified emphatically the kind of liars which he believed them to be.

I omit the adjective which he employed, but I find his declaration recurring to memory as I ponder the evidence and see what these men did with it. My editorial friend is a man who is rather accurate in his choice of adjectives. I cannot find it in my heart to contradict him.

CHAPTER XXI

THE HARDIN STORY

THE story that Abraham Lincoln was the son of Martin D. Hardin is not physically impossible. General Hardin was born in 1780 and was twenty-nine years old when Abraham Lincoln was born. The story that he visited Nancy Hanks when on his way to attend the Legislature in Frankfort, is manifestly incorrect, as he was never a member of the Legislature, nor had any member of the Hardin family been in the Kentucky Legislature up to that time; but he was a frequent visitor to Frankfort and perhaps at that time was a resident there. The story would have more approach to probability if it said that the incident occurred on his return to his home county on some visit from Frankfort.

But the story has not a shred of evidence in its favor, nor have I been informed of any reports concerning the life of Martin D. Hardin, which would make this probable. What makes it exceedingly improbable is: First, that in the very year of this supposed adventure, Martin D. Hardin was married and happily married to a beautiful and proud young woman, the daughter of General Benjamin Logan; and secondly, that at that time Nancy Hanks was married to Thomas Lincoln and living a long ride in the direction opposite to that which Martin D. Hardin had occasion to travel between his home in Washington County, his law practice in Richmond, or his political affairs in Frankfort. The story is opposed by every element of probability in the social and geographical situation, and it did not originate at the time, nor until seventy years afterward.

It was Ward Hill Lamon's *Life of Lincoln* that started whatever story became current in Washington County concerning the illegitimacy of Lincoln. This did not occur in 1872, when the book was published, nor until about six years afterward. So far as I can learn no one in Washington County bought or read the book then or afterward. All references to it that I have seen in print or manuscript indicate clearly that the persons who discussed it knew of it only by hearsay. Even in a little pamphlet, printed in the '80's by W. F. Booker, then County Clerk, and telling the story of the finding of the marriage certificate of Thomas and Nancy Lincoln, the evidence is plain that he had not seen the book. Knowledge of Lamon's book made its way into that region by way of the distillery at Athertonville. A man named Thompson, son of one of the then oldest inhabitants of Springfield, was a government officer at Athertonville, and there at the distillery heard discussions based upon the assertion that Lamon had written a book in which he charged or implied that Lincoln was an illegitimate child. Thompson brought this report to his father, Robert Mitchell Thompson, a highly respected citizen, then about sixty-eight years of age, who had known men that were present at the marriage of Thomas and Nancy Lincoln. He was sure that these reports grew out of the futile effort that had been made to discover the marriage record in Hardin County. Having definite knowledge that the marriage had not occurred in that County, but in Washington County, he reported the matter to William Frederick Booker, County Clerk. Mr. Booker is spoken of in Washington County in terms of highest praise He served as County Clerk for almost forty-four years, and after his first election never had opposition.

The county records were not indexed, nor were the old ones filed in any fashion which made it easy to examine them. The search proved to be long, and Mr. Booker gave himself to it in such time as he could spare from his official duties.

Meantime, the knowledge spread that Abraham Lincoln had been declared an illegitimate child, and there was some effort, amounting to nothing more than a conjecture, to determine who his father might have been. Washington County gave to him tentatively the best name it had.

It should be remembered that Washington County not only knew that Thomas and Nancy Lincoln were married in that County but believed and still believes that Abraham Lincoln was born there. If another father than Thomas Lincoln had to be found, Washington County was disposed to find him a worthy one.

But the Hardin tradition was short-lived. Mr. Booker's search was completely successful. He found not only the marriage return, signed by Rev. Jesse Head, but he found the marriage bond, signed by Thomas Lincoln and Richard Berry. These documents completely confirm the affirmations of Mr. Thompson and other old residents concerning the marriage of Thomas and Nancy Lincoln. The Hardin tradition died with this discovery. I am reliably informed that it is now completely discredited in the county where it originated.

I should not have considered the Hardin story worth noticing, had I not been attempting a complete survey of the field of these reports. As I have mentioned that, I may add that now and then one hears a name thrown out in utter recklessness as that of a possible father of Abraham Lincoln. I will give a single, and fairly representative instance, which will serve as an example.

From time to time as I made these investigations, I heard the confident assertion that Lincoln was the son of Patrick Henry. I cannot claim to have investigated this statement in any careful fashion. Parick Henry was born May 29, 1736, and died June 6, 1799. As he had been dead nearly ten years before Abraham Lincoln was born, the story that he was Lincoln's father appears to me improbable. I mention it, however, in order that this volume may be complete.

CHAPTER XXII

ABRAHAM ENLOE OF NORTH CAROLINA

AMONG all the seven putative fathers of Abraham Lincoln there are only two who have their claims set forth in cloth-bound volumes. One of these, which traces Lincoln's descent from Chief Justice Marshall, we shall presently consider; the other is Abraham Enloe of North Carolina. I approach the discussion of his claims with some reluctance, not because they are strong, for the contrary is true, but because I have come through correspondence into somewhat close relations with the author of this book, and I do not find it easy to say in terms as courteous as his letters to me, how fallacious I deem his arguments.

The story as Mr. Cathey gives it dates back, as he believes, to the early years of the nineteenth century; but he does not produce any date, or any fact which implies a date, earlier than the last quarter of the same century. The first time any part of this story appeared in print, appears to have been in the article already quoted from the Charlotte *Observer*, September 17, 1893, in the very last decade of that century. All Mr. Cathey's attempts to impart antiquity to the narrative failed signally.

He has not been sufficiently careful in checking up his witnesses. He relates this story on the authority of Colonel Davidson:

"There is a lady now living who, as a girl, was visiting Abram Enloe. This lady says that Nancy Enloe Thompson, having become reconciled with her parents, had returned from Kentucky to North Carolina. They were to start to Kentucky again in a few days, and she remembered hearing a neighbor say, ' I am glad Nancy Hanks and her boy are going to Kentucky with Mrs. Thompson. Mrs. Enloe will be happy again."

Colonel Davidson goes on to say that he himself married into the Enloe family, and settled the estate of Abram Enloe, and has no doubt of the truth of the story.

Colonel Davidson must have been a very credulous man. This lady, who was visiting Abram Enloe, and so presumably an adult, old enough to know and be interested in salacious gossip in 1808 or 1809, was still living in 1913, and was not then a woman of extraordinary age.

John P. Arthur, in that year, was gathering material for his *History of Western North Carolina,* and was seeking proof of the illegitimacy of Lincoln, which he was very willing to believe. I have before me a letter of his, dated, Boone, North Carolina, July 28, 1913, in which he says:

"As to the lady referred to on page 73 of Cathey's book, I have a full account of what it is claimed she saw and heard, but as she was not herself born before 1809, I have sent for further information as to that. I think that instead of seeing and hearing what it is now claimed she saw and heard, she only heard Mrs. Felix Walker say what she, Mrs. Walker, had seen or heard."

Or quite possibly she heard some one tell what some one else had heard that Mrs. Felix Walker heard that some one had told. Arthur found that he had no direct evidence of even the indirect evidence to which Cathey referred.

It is evident that when this story first appeared, the Enloes themselves denied any knowledge of such a tradition. In an article quoted, from the Charlotte *Observer,* Wesley Enloe definitely stated that he had never heard any such story. This was in 1893. By 1909 he had grown proud of being called the half-brother of Abraham Lincoln, and made the statement, quoted in this volume from Cathey's book, directly contradicting his earlier and truthful statement.

Moreover, it is evident from the same article that when the investigation, if such it can be called, began, people were unable to discover the alleged resemblance between the Enloes and Abraham Lincoln; nor do the photographs which Cathey reproduces resemble Mr. Lincoln more than would a group of portraits from almost any family in the Southern moun-

tains. The men are habitually tall and lank; and one need
not ride far into the hills to find along any mountain creek a
reasonably good model for a statue of Abraham Lincoln.

Mr. Cathey's witnesses disagree lamentably as to where
Abraham Lincoln was born. Some of them are sure that
he was born in North Carolina; others that he was born in
Tennessee, though the mischief was done in North Carolina; others affirm that he was born on the way, as Thomas
and Nancy were on their pathetic honeymoon journey; and
still others give them time to get to Kentucky. These are not
variants of the same story. They are, in good part, the odds
and ends and leavings of several separate stories, of different
births, remodeled clumsily to fit the alleged situation of Nancy
Hanks and Thomas Lincoln.

Mr. Cathey is hopelessly lame on dates. He declares that
he obtained his information from people who were primitive
but honest, dealing little in dates, but accustomed to transmitting oral information correctly. I know that kind of people, and they are good people. But they are people among
whom rumors grow incalculably. The " grape-vine telegraph "
of those regions transmits gossip sometimes with amazing
speed, and not by any means is the transmission always
accurate.

In the gathering of information for this volume I endeavored to avoid discussion with my correspondents and the
people whom I interviewed. I represented myself as being
desirous of knowing the truth, and of wishing to hear all
that was to be said in favor of any theory held by honest
people and current in any section of our country. Mr. Cathey,
however, asked me directly for my opinion of his theory, and
I told him frankly what I thought.

I wrote to Mr. Cathey that I thought he had given his
whole case away. He had started out to prove that Abraham
Lincoln was the son of a particular Abraham Enloe, who lived
in North Carolina; and he had reached the point where he
summed up his feeble argument in the very lame belief that
Lincoln was the son of " some Abraham Enlow." I said
to him that that admission completely nullified his argument.

He replied in a lengthy argument, based, not on his local evidence, but on the alleged fact that Herndon's book had been bought up and suppressed by Lincoln's friends on account of the implication which it was supposed to contain that Lincoln was illegitimate.

I answered that it was not certain that the book had thus been suppressed; that it still could be had by any one who really wanted to get it; that if it was suppressed there were other possible reasons; and that it was not certain that Herndon held as a final view the theory that Lincoln was illegitimate.

Mr. Cathey replied as he was about to go to the hospital. He reproached me for thus lightly thrusting aside "the traditions of an honest people for three quarters of a century," but he brought no proof.

Our correspondence grew less regular, as his health was frail, and we had about covered the ground. But I should like to quote the ending of one of his letters:

"So far as my own personal intermeddling with this sacred incident, in the Providence of God, is concerned, I have about made up my mind that I should have let the matter rest where it was born. I am sure if I had it to do over again, I should not touch it. What do you think? Answer me in your accustomed freedom.

" Cordially,

" JAMES H. CATHEY."

It is not necessary for me to quote my answer to Mr. Cathey. His own letter is the best possible ending of this chapter.

CHAPTER XXIII

CHIEF JUSTICE MARSHALL AND ANDREW

We come now to one of the most distinguished of the proposed fathers of Abraham Lincoln, and our inquiry involves a double quest. For this story tells us that Chief Justice Marshall was the grandfather of Abraham Lincoln, and Marshall's foster son Lincoln's father.

The story as it is told by Mrs. Lucinda Boyd, and well fortified with affidavits and appeals to Truth, suggests three questions, which we put in turn:

The first of the three questions we must ask is as to the identity of Lucy Hanks, Hornback or Sparrow, with the maternal grandmother of Abraham Lincoln.

The inquiry need not be a long one. Apart from the facts that we do not know the name of Hornback in connection with the ancestry of Lincoln, and that that appears to have been the real name of the woman whom Mr. Rogers had in mind, with the two names of Hanks and Sparrow added, and Hornback is a familiar name in the heart of Kentucky to which this young woman is alleged to have gone, is the simple fact that Lucy Hanks did not die unmarried at the foot of the Blue Ridge, leaving Nancy to make her way to Kentucky as best she could. Lucy Hanks married Henry Sparrow, bore him eight children, and lived in Kentucky.

Thus readily does Lucy Hanks lose her place in the cast of Mrs. Boyd's drama.

Our second inquiry is as to the foster or adopted son of Chief Justice Marshall, named Andrew, son of an Englishman, killed in border warfare with Chief Justice Marshall's son, after which death of his own son, Judge Marshall is alleged to have adopted Andrew, who removed to Winchester, Kentucky, where he found Nancy Hanks and became the father of Abraham Lincoln.

The author has been unable to discover any such Andrew in the early life of Winchester as recorded in the various county histories of Kentucky or by inquiry of leading citizens in Winchester. He has been unable to find any Englishman of this description, perishing in this manner, and leaving his son to the adoption of Judge Marshall; nor did Judge Marshall need to adopt any sons; he had five sons of his own. Nor did Judge Marshall find bereavement in any such fashion as to require this kind of comfort of Andrew. Judge Marshall lived to the year 1835. His five sons died, respectively, in 1835, 1832, 1833, 1862 and 1873. He was seventy-eight years old when the earliest of his sons died, and was not only a father but the grandfather of many children, and had no need of any such adoption. Nor is any such name as Andrew to be found in the family record as very fully set forth by his genealogical biographer, Paxton.

Thus are we grievously disappointed in our second inquiry, to say nothing about our inability to locate the battle in which Andrew's father died. Wherever he died and whoever he was, he appears in this story as a pure myth.

In order to run no risk of losing " Andrew " if he existed, the author made diligent search in the pages first of Paxton's work on the Marshall family, and then in Senator Beveridge's two volumes on the *Life of John Marshall:* and as these yielded no result, and the Senator was known to be sitting beside the press with the remaining two volumes, the author wrote to him. Senator Beveridge wrote in part as follows:

BEVERLY FARMS, MASSACHUSETTS,
September 17, 1919.

MY DEAR DR. BARTON:

Your letter of September 4 has just been forwarded to me here, where I have been working to complete the last two volumes of my *Life of Chief Justice Marshall,* which will be published by Houghton Mifflin & Co. of Boston next month.

I have not run across any record or intimation that Chief Justice Marshall ever had an adopted son; and I am quite sure that he never did have one.

I have been all over the ground. Not only is there no letter which refers directly or indirectly or gives the smallest intimation of any adopted son, but there is no tradition of any kind in Richmond supporting the idea, and none of his relatives has ever heard of such a thing.

It is just possible that the legend may have taken its rise from the fact that when Charles Marshall, brother of the Chief Justice, died in 1805, he took his brother's son, Martin Pickett Marshall, into his family for a little time. This lad was born between 1794 and 1799.

You can, I think, be fairly sure that there is nothing in Mrs. Boyd's book. It is as certain as anything human can be that if the Chief Justice had had such a young man in his home, there would be some reference to it. Surely Paxton would have referred to it, for he gathered up not only all the facts that he could ferret out, but many traditions and much gossip, some of it being far from fact. I am confident there is nothing in it.

Faithfully yours,

ALBERT J. BEVERIDGE.

So far as Martin Pickett Marshall is concerned, one fact which makes it improbable that he was the father of Nancy Hanks is that she was born eleven years before he was.

This, therefore, answers our second inquiry.

In the matter of Lincoln's resemblance to Chief Justice Marshall, Mrs. Boyd was well within the bounds of truth Any thoughtful person who looks at the statue of the Judge and bears in mind the form and features of Lincoln, must be impressed as she was impressed. The resemblance between the two men was so great as to be startling. Senator Beveridge has given two or three pages to this in his four volume *Life of John Marshall*. Not only were the two men alike in face and form, but their habits of life and their mental and moral characteristics were alike.

They were so much alike that one wonders why Mrs. Boyd did not make better use of her material. The whole Marshall family moved to Kentucky, except Chief Justice John Marshall, and his brother James Marshall himself visited Kentucky twice; and, while it is not certain that Judge Marshall's eldest son ever visited that new state, it is not unlikely that he did so, and he may have been there several times. The possibility of linking the lineage of Abraham Lincoln to that of Justice John Marshall is so apparent to one who knows the history of the Marshall family, that one hesitates to suggest how much better story Mrs. Boyd could have made if she had made a little effort to learn the facts. They are not difficult to obtain. Paxton, in his Genealogy of the Marshall Family, records not only the dry facts of lineage, but innumerable details and much gossip: and there are other sources of information. With a few real facts she could have made a better piece of fiction.

The third inquiry is as to the son of Chief Justice John Marshall who is alleged to have been the father of Nancy Hanks.

This is a more detailed inquiry, for Chief Justice Marshall had six children, of whom five were sons. We will name them in order.

John Marshall, first Chief Justice of the Supreme Court of the United States, was born near Germantown, Va., September 25, 1755, and died in Philadelphia July 6, 1835. He was married at Yorktown, Va., to Mary Willis Ambler, by whom he had issue:

1. Thomas Marshall, was born in Richmond, Va., July 21, 1784, and died in Baltimore, June 29, 1835. He married Margaret W. Lewis, October 19, 1809. He was a graduate of Princeton, and a lawyer. His health failed, and he retired to his farm. He became a zealous member of the Episcopal Church. He was a member of the Constitutional Convention of Virginia, over which his father presided. He was a man of literary taste and culture, a lover of poetry, music and the fine arts.

2. Dr. Jacquelin Ambler Marshall was born December 3, 1787, and died July 7, 1852. He married, January 1, 1812, Eliza E. S. Clarkson. Though a physician, he did not engage in active practice, but was sought in consultation. He was a well-read country gentleman of good reputation.

3. Mary Marshall was born September 7, 1795, married General Jacquelin B. Harrie, and died April 29, 1841.

4. John Marshall was born January 15, 1798, and died November 25, 1833. He married, February 3, 1822, Miss E. M. Alexander. He was a graduate of Harvard, a lawyer, and several times a member of the Virginia Legislature.

5. James Keith Marshall was born February 13, 1800, and died December 2, 1862. He married Clarinda H. Burwell. He was a graduate of Harvard, and led the life of a country gentleman. He was several times elected to the State Senate. He opposed the secession of Virginia, but when she seceded he went, as did all the Marshalls, with his State, but died early in the war. He was highly esteemed as a generous and honorable man.

6. Edward Carrington Marshall was born January 13, 1805, and died February 8, 1872. He married, February 12, 1829, Rebecca C. Peyton. He was a graduate of Harvard, a regular church and Sunday School attendant, fond of good reading. He sympathized with the South but was too old to fight. He had suffered from the fall of a horse which he was riding and whose fall nearly killed the rider, and was for some years an invalid. After the War, which impoverished him, he was offered and accepted a clerkship in the Pension Office, in Washington, and thus earned his daily bread.

These are the five men among whom we are now to look in order to find a father for Nancy Hanks and a grandfather for Abraham Lincoln. There should be no doubt of our success with so many to choose from, and if we do not wholly succeed, we can leave an aroma of scandal attaching to the entire five. We can learn, if we try, which of these boys was a little wild in his youth; which of them had questionable love affairs before he went to college; which of them led too gay a life in college; which of them caused domestic distress by too great frivolity after marriage.

Moreover, among the four hundred living descendants of John Marshall, we shall be able to find some, who, when the matter is suggested to them, will remember to have heard that the wife of one of the sons of John Marshall caught him in the act of kissing the cook; and, with a little further suggestion, we shall doubtless be able to establish the name of the cook as Nancy Hanks. Having done this, we shall find that Thomas Lincoln was sufficiently migratory to admit of our bringing him to the rescue wherever and whenever the exigencies of our story require. We can quite easily evoke a story which no one can disprove, and which will make every one of the four hundred descendants of the first Chief Justice of the United States blush for shame. It is surprisingly easy to do it.

Let us first begin by discovering which of these five sons was " killed in border warfare." That is a sufficiently elastic term to cover any kind of violent death.

But here we meet another disappointment. All five of these men appear to have died at home, each in his own bed, and most of them on the farm, far from the madding crowd and from scenes of violence. We search in vain through Senator Beveridge's *Life of John Marshall* for his adjournment of court to stand by the coffin of a son slain in battle of any kind.

However, it will not do to be discouraged. That is a small and immaterial item. Perhaps he was not so killed, but deserved to have been so killed. Let us find out which of the five sons would have been most likely to seduce Nancy. The whole family were Episcopalians, but some of them did not take their religion very seriously; we can find something if we try hard.

But just as a matter of caution, let us pause and consult that very arbitrary volume, the almanac. It is a volume which scandal-mongers pass by on the other side. This whole body of tradition has in it hardly a single date that is material to the evidence. We will find a few.

As a matter of chronology, which of the five sons of John Marshall would have been most likely to have been the father of Nancy Hanks?

In a painstaking and gossipy volume of more than 400 pages, William M. Paxton, in 1885, published the Genealogy of the family and descendants of John Marshall.   His five sons were born thus:

Thomas in 1784; Jacquelin in 1787; John in 1798; James in 1800, and Edward in 1805.

Nancy Hanks was born in 1783.

Instead of being the daughter, she might have been the elder sister of John Marshall's oldest son, and the mother of the youngest!

Mrs. Lucinda Boyd begins her story with an appeal to Truth.   History, she says, should be painted with Truth on her right hand and Memory on her left.   Truth is her guide and inspiration, Truth with a capital T, Truth emphasized, *the whole truth* italicized.   Nothing but the Truth, *the Truth*, will satisfy Mrs Lucinda Boyd.   To be sure that she has *the Truth* she obtains affidavits, certifying to what the affiants have heard that other people heard of what had been told by nobody knows who to nobody knows whom.   It is perhaps because *the Truth* is so precious to her that she uses it so economically.   Having now run down into its remotest rat-hole her story that would give to Abraham Lincoln as a great-grandfather the first Chief Justice of the Supreme Court of the United States, and having shown that the story thus supported by a stack of affidavits, her own included, is absurdly false, and should have been known to her as false before she ever printed a page of her sloppy and slanderous story, I now renounce Lucinda and all her works.

CHAPTER XXIV

JOHN C. CALHOUN

As compared with most of the stories concerning the paternity of Abraham Lincoln, the theory that he was the son of John C. Calhoun is entitled to thoughtful consideration. Such consideration we have given to all of them; most do not deserve it. Mr. Knotts, the protagonist of this theory, has wrought it out with a care and in a spirit which call for recognition. Among all who have sought to provide Abraham Lincoln with a father other than Thomas Lincoln, he alone has shown some respect for chronology. He only has examined public records of wills, marriages and land transfers. Mr. Cathey has shown diligence in assembling traditions from members of the Enloe family and their neighbors, and assigning to them a conjectural antiquity which the evidence does not sustain, but in all the large volume of his accumulated tradition, there is not a single fixed date. If the calendar had smallpox, his theory would be immune. There is no point in his book where one may begin and reckon in terms of time and distance. It is otherwise with Mr. Knotts and his theory. He has some respect for the almanac. He has shown marked industry in collecting data concerning the Hanks family in several states. I have reproduced it in this book more largely than might otherwise have seemed necessary, partly that he might set forth in full the evidence as he judged it to be important, and partly that others, who may care to go more deeply into the difficult question of the Hanks family, may have full benefit of his material. He has sought out the relations between Thomas Lincoln and his uncle Isaac, thus endeavoring to establish for that convenient gentleman, Thomas Lincoln, who is certain to be needed for the assistance of some lady in distress, a convenient base of operation, nearer to South Carolina than Kentucky is or could have been.

It is to be noted, further, to the credit of this theory, that it provides for Abraham Lincoln a male parent of real ability, a man incontestibly superior to Thomas Lincoln, which some of the substitutes have not been.

Mr. Knotts has a carefully wrought scheme of chronology, and has articulated his theory so well that John C. Arthur took it over bodily, with full credit to Mr. Knotts, in his *History of Western North Carolina.* This was a high compliment, especially as North Carolina had its own aspirant to the paternity of Abraham Lincoln in the person of Mr. Cathey's Abraham Enloe. That Arthur accepted this story and not the other is a hard blow to the Enloe story, which, indeed, is no longer worth considering.

Pursuant to this chronological scheme, John C. Calhoun, who has been studying law at Litchfield, Connecticut, comes back to his native state in 1807, and hangs out his shingle in Abbeville, and travels the circuit to adjacent counties, and stays at a tavern half way between two county seats. The date is correct. Calhoun did all those things, including, probably, stopping occasionally at this particular tavern, which may at that time have been kept by Ann, the widow of Luke Hanks. And there might have been a Nancy Hanks helping about the tavern; and she might have been the kind of girl which all these various Nancy Hankses are supposed to have been, and Calhoun may have been the kind of young man whom this story supposes. So far forth, the story is not without its elements of plausibility.

To this is added the lodge-room gossip to the effect that John C. Calhoun's intimate friends whispered that he had sown certain wild oats in his youth; and the story among the women of what Mrs. Felix Walker told. The story assumes some elements of possibility as it is thus viewed. And that is saying more for it than can be said for most of them.

John Caldwell Calhoun was born in the 96th District South Carolina, March 18, 1782, and died in Washington, March 31, 1850. His grandfather, James Calhoun, emigrated from Donegal County, Ireland, to Pennsylvania, in 1733, when his son Patrick, father of John C., was six years old. Patrick Calhoun was an Irish Presbyterian, energetic, patriotic, and sided with the colonies in the War for Independence. In 1770 he married Martha Caldwell, daughter of an Irish Presbyterian minister. Patrick Calhoun was a public-spirited man, and a member of the Virginia Legislature.

Of such parents John C. Calhoun was born. He was prepared for college by his brother-in-law, Rev. Dr. Waddell, a Presbyterian minister, and went to Yale in 1802. He studied law with local members of the bar, and then finished his course at Litchfield, Connecticut, where he was graduated in 1807, and in the same year admitted to the bar.

His experience as a lawyer was of four years' duration, for in November, 1811, he was elected to Congress.

He was riding the circuit at the time required in Mr. Knotts' theory, and, if the mother of Abraham Lincoln was there at that time, the story is physically possible.

But to show that a thing is possible is not to prove that it is true. And before we go much farther, it will be well to inquire what particular Nancy Hanks, if any, was actually at the tavern kept by Mrs. Ann Hanks in the short period during which Calhoun rode the circuit. For the law did not hold him long; politics soon claimed him; and the period in which he was riding the circuit is just the period when this story requires his presence, and that of some Nancy Hanks, at the tavern at Craytonville.

It is not very easy to follow the generations of the Hanks family through their intermarriages, their migrations and their duplication of names. Fortunately, we are not concerned with the entire problem, but with only so much of it as is necessary to the determination of the question whether one particular Nancy Hanks, and she the mother of President Lincoln, was at the tavern at Craytonville in the spring of 1808. This inquiry warrants a brief survey of the Hanks genealogy.

Mrs. Hitchcock traces the maternal line of Abraham Lincoln from the Hanks family of Plymouth, Massachusetts. The third son of Benjamin Hanks, William by name, is believed by her, though without documentary evidence, to have gone to the Rappahannock County in Virginia, where his sons, Abraham, Richard, James, John and Joseph were born. All except John removed and settled in Amelia County about 1740. Here documentary evidence begins. On January 12, 1747, Joseph sold two hundred and eighty-four acres of land to his brother Abraham, and on July 12, 1754, bought in the same county, the land where his children were born, among them a daughter Nancy, whom she believes to have been the mother of the President.

In the next county to Amelia, Lurenburg, an Englishman named Robert Shipley bought three hundred and fourteen acres of land on September 16, 1765. He and his wife, Sarah Rachel Shipley, had five daughters,—Mary, who married Abraham Lincoln of Rockaway County, Virginia, grandfather of Abraham Lincoln the President, Lucy, who married Richard Berry; Sarah, who married Robert Mitchell; Elizabeth, who married Thomas Sparrow, and Nancy, who married Joseph Hanks.

Joseph and Nancy Shipley Hanks had eight children,— Thomas, Joshua, William, Charles, Joseph, Jr, Elizabeth, Polly and Nancy. This is the Nancy Hanks whom Mrs. Hitchcock believes to have been the mother of President Abraham Lincoln.

Joseph Hanks migrated to Kentucky in 1789, and died four years later. His will, dated January 9, 1793, was probated May 14, 1793. He left a horse to each of his sons and a heifer to each of his daughters. Nancy received a yearling heifer named Piedy. He left to his "beloved wife Nanny" his whole estate during life. She and her son William were the executors.

Mrs. Hitchcock sets forth what is, in fact, one of the chief difficulties of the inquiry, the fact that the Hanks family did not go far afield for family names, and had a special fondness for the name Nancy:

"This little Nancy Hanks had also many cousins named Nancy. . . . Theirs was a large and happy colony of cousins, and merry were the days passed in hunting, hawking and fishing in the great estates of nearly a thousand acres owned by these kind uncles and aunts " (*Nancy Hanks,* p. 26).

Their hunting may have been more merry than the hunt of genealogists for the true Nancy Hanks, but the estate of a thousand acres was small compared with the area over which the latter chase has been extended, with no little fishing for possible clues of identification.   The fact that the marriage bond of Nancy Hanks and Thomas Lincoln was signed by Richard Berry, is supposed to indicate him to have been her uncle and guardian.   Mrs. Richard Berry is stated by Mrs. Hitchcock to have been " her mother's sister."   She says " With this kind Uncle Richard and Aunt Lucy, Nancy Hanks lived until she was married."

There is no Lucy in the list of Joseph Hanks' children as given in his will, and any neighbor could have signed the marriage bond, which for a woman of twenty-three in a land where girls marry at sixteen was a mere formality.   Almost any by-stander around the court house will sign a marriage bond in Kentucky.   The name upon the bond is not conclusive, but it is inferential proof of the relationship, and is probably correct.

The short and simple annals of the Hanks family as given by Lamon, on the basis, of course, of Herndon, who had his information from Dennis and other members of the Hanks family, are these:

Nancy Hanks was the daughter of Lucy Hanks.   Her mother was one of four sisters, Lucy, Betsy, Polly and Nancy. Betsy married Thomas Sparrow; Polly married Thomas Friend; Nancy married Levi Hall, but not until she had given birth to Dennis Hanks.   Lucy became the mother of Nancy Hanks, and subsequently married Henry Sparrow, by whom she had eight children.   The younger Nancy, however, did not live with her mother, Lucy Hanks Sparrow, but with the other Sparrow family, that of Thomas and Betsy Sparrow.

This, it will be noted, brings the place of Nancy Hanks Lincoln one full generation later than the list given by Mrs. Hitchcock, with much uncertainty as to marriages in the two lists.   The difficulty, of course, arises partly from the incom-

pleteness of records, partly from the overlapping of generations, and partly from repetition of names. As there were
many Hanks girls named Nancy, so there were duplicate
Pollys, Betsys and Lucys.

Nicolay and Hay give the same list of sisters and of
their marriages as that given in Lamon:

"Mrs Lincoln's mother was named Lucy Hanks; her
sisters were Betty, Polly and Nancy, who married Thomas
Sparrow, Jesse Friend, and Levi Hall. The childhood of
Nancy was passed with the Sparrows, and she was oftener
called by their name than her own. The whole family connection was composed of people so little given to letters that it
is hard to determine the proper names and relationships amid
the tangle of traditional cousinships."—NICOLAY AND HAY:
Abraham Lincoln, A History, Vol. I, p. 24.

Mr. Knotts begins where Mrs. Hitchcock does, with William, in Rappahannock County, and accepts on her authority her
attempt to connect him with the Plymouth family. He finds
William migrating to Amelia County, just as Mrs. Hitchcock
does, but instead of the five sons whom she gives, Abraham,
Richard, James, John and Joseph, he declares that there were
twelve children. Thus far there may be no conflict. Mr
Knotts' twelve may have included the five of Mrs. Hitchcock;
but the son through whom he traces the paternity of Nancy is
not one of her five, but "the youngest son, Luke" Among his
daughters were Lucy, and Nancy, the very Nancy who became the mother of the President.

Luke, James and John migrated to South Carolina. James
and John went on to Kentucky, but Luke and his wife Ann
lived and died in Anderson County, South Carolina.

The children of Luke and Ann Hanks, as Mr. Knotts
gives them, are five sons and six daughters,—Thomas, Luke,
John, Robert, George, Lucinda, Scilla, Elizabeth, Martha,
Susan and Judith, all of whom remain in South Carolina.

It will be noted that this places Nancy Hanks Lincoln
one generation earlier than Herndon and the Hanks family,
and two full generations earlier than Mrs. Hitchcock.

In his first letter he says:

"My own research is from Amelia County, Virginia, where William Hanks came from the Rappahannock country and raised a family of twelve children. One of the girls married Abraham Lincoln's father, Thomas Lincoln, and settled in Kentucky."

But the children of William Hanks appear to have been grown and doing business on their own account when the family came to Amelia County about 1740.

Nancy Hanks, the mother of the President, was, however, by Mr. Knotts' showing, three years and three or four months old in May, 1799. There is a wide margin and apparent discrepancy here.

If Mr. Knotts really intended to locate Nancy in this generation, as the daughter of William Hanks, and a sister of Luke, she would have been, as I estimate, at the time of her alleged indiscretion, a giddy young thing of somewhere between sixty-four to seventy-two. I could not think Mr. Knotts intended this, particularly as he included her in the list of heirs of Luke Hanks. Neither could I obtain from the county officials a certified list of the heirs of Luke Hanks with a statement of their relationship to him, although I exhausted all known possibilities in this direction.

Here is the first weakness in the argument of Mr. Knotts; his articles are not clear as to the precise Nancy Hanks who flirted with John C. Calhoun. He shows with convincing detail how many women of that name there were, and sets forth the difficulty of accepting the conclusions of Mrs. Hitchcock and Miss Tarbell as to her identification with the heiress of the pied heifer; but he does not give us a clear statement concerning the only Nancy in whom for the purpose of this investigation we are interested.

John C. Calhoun returned to South Carolina from the law school about a year and a half before the birth of Abraham Lincoln. The family of Luke Hanks was in that neighborhood. But the list of Luke Hanks' children, as furnished by Mr. Knotts as from the first court records, contains no daughter of his named Nancy;[1] and if she were a sister of

[1] There was a daughter Nancy, however, as shown by these records, and she completely upsets Mr. Knott's theory as we shall discover.

approximately the age of Luke, the youngest son of William, she was, to say the very least, old enough to have known better. She was nearer seventy-three than twenty-three.

I confided this difficulty to Mr. Knotts who tells me that this is not what he intended, that Nancy was not the sister but the youngest daughter of Luke Hanks. But I could not find Nancy in his own list of Luke Hanks' children. Her name first appears, as he declares, in 1833:

"Nothing more is of record until 1833" when the suit for division was brought, and a list of heirs filed, evidently not all of them children, for there were fifty-six of them, with degree of relationship apparently not stated, and twenty-seven are beyond the State; and "Amongst them appears a new heir to this humble estate, Nancy Hanks."

I made diligent effort to secure from the court officials of Anderson and Abbeville something that would enable me to determine the relationship of this Nancy Hanks to the family in general and to the mother of Abraham Lincoln in particular, but they wrote me that they could give me no assistance.

But in a work of this kind one must never be discouraged. After I had nearly given up the effort to locate this particular Nancy Hanks, I tried once more, and I find that Mr. Knotts is mistaken in a vital point.

The long list of heirs at law of Luke and Ann Hanks as divergently set forth in the two suits for partition, included, of course, grandchildren as well as children. I desired to learn precisely the names and if possible the relative ages of the children of Luke and Ann Hanks, in order to determine, if possible, whether there was, in 1807, a youngest and unmarried daughter Nancy, who might have been the wife of Thomas Lincoln Several attempts to secure this information failed; but a further search, made for me by Mr. G. H. Geiger, attorney at law in Anderson, brings me the following lists as they were presented and approved at the two suits:

The two lists of children of Luke and Ann Hanks as contained in:

Judgment Roll N. 286 in the Judge of Probate's Office For Anderson County, at Anderson, South Carolina.
State of South Carolina
County of Anderson.

Personally appeared David Rupell and Luke Hanie and being in due form of law sworn say that they are well ac-

quainted with the land belonging to the estate of—Anna— Hanks decd for which application is now made for partition by the Court of Ordinary & that it is not worth one thousand dollars. Sworn to and subscribed Jany. 1st, 1838, before me.

A. Evins, Not. Pub. &
   Ex Off. Q.h.

David Rupell
Luke Haynie

The land of Luke Hanks, decd.
The Heirs of
 1. Elizabeth Hanie, formerly E. Hanks (out of the state)
The Heirs of
 2. Nancy South " Nancy " (out Of)
 3. Stephen Hanie by right of his wife Martha H. (in)
 4. Thomas Hanks ....(out)
 5. Luke Hanks ....(in)
 6. Polly Hanks, Wife of George Hanks (in)
 7. Charles Hanie by right of his wife Susan (in)
 8. Louie Pruitt formerly Louie Hanks (out)
 9. Robert Hanks   (out)
 10. Judith Hanie Alias Judith Hall for, Hanks (in)
 11. John Hanks—   (out)

     Luke
Land of—Anna—Hanks D'ecd. 210 acres lying on waters of Rockey River bounded by lands of Luke Hanks John Martin, Wm. Prichard and others

 1. Thomas Hanks
 2. Luke Hanks (in the State)
 3. Robert Hanks
 4. (in) Polly Hanks, wife of George Hanks, deceased.
 5. John Hanks
   The Heirs—

6. Elizabeth Hanie, formerly E. Hanks
7. Martha Hanie, wife of Stephen Hanie
8. (in) Scilla South, wife of Wm. South
9. The heirs of Nancy South, formerly Hanks
10. Judith Hanie, wife of Anthony Hanie
11. Lucretia Pruit.

Sold on a credit of twelve months.

This is the complete record of the judgment roll.

G. H. Geiger,
Attorney at Law.

Anderson, South Carolina.

It is evident that these two lists were prepared independently, and that the latter was not copied from the earlier list. This is shown in the different order in which the names appear, the fact that at least one of the heirs appears to have died between the first and second suits, and that there is a discrepancy as to one of the daughters. As that discrepancy does not concern our inquiry, I have made no effort to reconcile it. I may suggest, however, that Susan and Scylla may have been the same daughter and that she was twice married. That is for our purpose immaterial; and the two lists may be thus compared as to the number and position of the names:

THE TWO LISTS OF HANKS' HEIRS

1. Elizabeth Hanie (out)

2. Nancy South, formerly Hanks (out)

3. Martha, wife of Stephen Hanie (in)

4. Thomas Hanks (out)

5. Luke Hanks (in)

6. Polly, wife of George Hanks (in)

7. Susan, wife of Charles Hanie (in)

8. Lucretia or Louie Pruitt (out)

6. Elizabeth Hanie, formerly Hanks

9. Heirs of Nancy South, formerly Hanks

7. Martha Hanie

1. Thomas Hanks

2. Luke Hanks

4. Polly, wife of George, deceased

11. Lucretia Pruitt

9. Robert Hanks (out)
10. Judith Hanie, alias Hall (in)
11. John Hanks (out)

3. Robert Hanks
10. Judith, wife of Anthony Hanie
5. John Hanks
8. Scilla South, wife of Wm. South.

These two lists are valuable for our purposes. They show that,—

1. There was a Nancy Hanks, daughter of Luke and Ann Hanks.

2. She probably was not the youngest daughter, since her name occurs early in the first list; and it is not likely that she was unmarried and serving in the tavern as late as 1807.

3. She is not unaccounted for. Though living beyond the State, her name is known.

4. She never married Thomas Lincoln. She was married, and her name was South.

Not only was there no missing Nancy, but Nancy had been married to one South, and was dead before the final settlement, but not in 1833.

This completely settles the report that the young woman whom Thomas Lincoln married was a daughter of Luke and Ann Hanks, who had previously been seduced by John C. Calhoun.

We may dismiss with brief scrutiny the lodge-room gossip.

John C. Calhoun died March 31, 1850. He and Lincoln probably met during Lincoln's one term in Congress in 1848-9. General Armistead Burt, who is said to have married a niece of Calhoun, is said to have told in confidence to a few companions in a lodge-room that Calhoun in his young manhood became intimate with a poor girl, whom the tradition, as it came to Mr. Knotts many years afterward, named as Nancy Hanks. This confidential conversation is supposed to have occurred in the seventies, sixty or more years after the event, and another forty years went by before Mr. Knotts learned and published it. In these two periods of oral transmission there was abundant opportunity for such a story to grow out of nothing to any conceivable proportions. As a leak from the confidential gossip of a lodge-room it stands on no basis which entitles it to any more than passing attention.

Mr Knotts thinks he has established a connection between these stories of Calhoun and the paternity of Lincoln, in the alleged interview of James L Orr, a young man from South Carolina, who visited Washington in 1849, where he met Abraham Lincoln, and found him uncommunicative on the subject of his Hanks ancestry. If such an interview occurred, there is no reason to dispute that Mr. Lincoln showed reticence; but that is no proof that he admitted by implication any such story as has now grown up in South Carolina.

The other line of gossip, which is based on what Mrs. Felix Walker is alleged to have said about the young girl whom her husband had arranged to send over the mountains, is of just as little evidential value, excepting for this, that it shows this to be an outgrowth of the North Carolina Enloe story. Even with John C. Calhoun as the principal actor, it is necessary to bring in Abraham Enloe as an accessory. The Calhoun story ought to have been created with sufficient strength of its own to stand upon its own feet, and not limp on the Enloe crutch.

We move rapidly over these details, for they are not worth discussing. They bring us to the real issue, and to a certain result. John C. Calhoun may have stopped at the Craytonville tavern in 1808, but if he did the girl who passed him the corn-bread and long-sweetening was not Nancy Hanks Lincoln. She was not there. She was living temporarily on the Brownfield farm, in Hardin County, Kentucky, and had a baby girl toddling about the cabin where she baked hoe-cake for Thomas Lincoln, and dreamed of the day when she should be living in her own home over by the Rock Spring, and the mother of a son.

Abraham Lincoln was born not quite three miles south from where the village of Hodgenville now stands, in Hardin, then La Rue County, Kentucky, on Sunday, February 12, 1809. Let us fix that date in our mind as one that we shall not need to move. Any credible theory of the paternity of

Lincoln must face the fact that he was born there and on that date.

What Mr. Knotts has proved is this:

That John C. Calhoun rode the circuit after his return from law school in 1807, and may have stopped once or more at the tavern at Craytonville, which for a time, and perhaps at that time, was kept by Ann, the widow of Luke Hanks.

That there were more Hanks girls named Nancy than one, and that there is a reasonable doubt whether Mrs. Hitchcock's conjectural identification is correct.

That there were certain rumors afloat some twenty years after the death of Mr. Calhoun, and sixty or more years after the events narrated, to the effect that Mr. Calhoun, while generally a moral man, looked back on his youth with regret for one mistake, involving a girl whom this belated rumor named after the mother of President Lincoln, Nancy Hanks.

That certain features of the Enloe story of North Carolina, and certain facts concerning the residence of Thomas Lincoln's uncle Isaac, can be wrought into the story.

But this is a house of cards, which a very mild breeze might blow over, and it falls utterly before the tempestuous fact that Thomas Lincoln and Nancy Hanks were married at Beechland, Washington County, Kentucky, by Jesse Head, on June 12, 1806, and that they lived together continuously in Hardin County, Kentucky, until the birth of their second child, Abraham, on February 12, 1809, and that they continued thereafter to live together as husband and wife in that county and in Indiana until the death of Nancy Hanks Lincoln.

In the face of that indubitable fact, there is no use wasting any more time over the charge that Abraham Lincoln was the son of John C. Calhoun.

CHAPTER XXV

DO THESE STORIES SUPPORT EACH OTHER?

IT is important to ask whether these stories support each other, or whether they contradict each other.

A wholly unwarranted inference has been drawn by some writers from the number of forms in which the Enlow story is found.

"Behold," they say, "how widespread is this rumor. Where there is so much smoke, there must be some fire. Each of these stories, though having a different man for its hero, adds its element of cumulative proof that *some* Abraham Enlow was the father of Abraham Lincoln."

Precisely the opposite is the logical inference.

Any proof adduced to show that Abraham Lincoln was the son of Abraham Enloe of North Carolina is adverse proof of his having been the son of any and every other Abraham Enlow. These stories devour each other like the Kilkenny cats.

If we adduce sufficient evidence that Abraham Lincoln was sired by a man in North Carolina, whether his name was Abraham Enloe or John C. Calhoun, or John Doe or Richard Roe, we weaken to that same extent any claim or rumor or suspicion that he was the son of Abraham Inlow, the miller of Thatcher's Mills, or Abraham Enlow, the farmer of Hardin County.

What is more, we are compelled to see that the process of creating these rumors is very simple. Once let it be said that Abraham Lincoln's father was Abraham Enlow, any community that had an Abraham Enlow in 1808 can easily start a story that Lincoln was begotten there. Whether Abraham Enlow was fourteen or eighty makes little difference; some even of his descendants will abet the rumor that links their name to that of Lincoln.

It is not necessary that the Enlow selected shall ever have seen Kentucky. It is always possible to create a Nancy Hanks, a servant girl, who in the space of nine months could have made her journey thither; and if nine months is not long enough, as in some instances it is not, then an extension can be arranged for her journey, though with a baby in her arms.

Not only are innumerable Abraham Enlows produced by the laudable desire to produce a worthy male parent for Abraham Lincoln, but nearly if not quite as many Nancy Hankses have been discovered also, and each of them in dangerous propinquity to an Abraham Enlow. Mary and her little lamb are not more invariably together than the Abraham Enlows and the Nancy Hankses. Everywhere that Abraham went, Nancy was sure to go. Without exception, all the Abraham Enlows were men ready to betray a poor girl, and invariably each and every several Nancy fell a prompt victim to his seductive snare.

And each Nancy ultimately married Thomas Lincoln, the same Thomas Lincoln. Solomon in all his glory had hardly more wives than Thomas Lincoln, if all these stories are true; but Solomon did not have to call them all by the same name. It is impossible to supply a sufficient number of Thomas Lincolns to meet the demand of the numberless Nancys in distress; and it is sad to contemplate his embarrassment who never could adequately support one wife in having thrust upon him a harem of young women who had loved not wisely, but too well, and who depended upon his sole chivalry to save them from disgrace.

It will be noted that whenever the holder of any one of these several theories of the illegitimacy of Lincoln is confronted by an argument which he cannot answer, he replies, in substance, as Cathey does,—

" The very fact that Herndon's and Lamon's lives of Lincoln were suppressed by men of high standing and influence some years ago, and that expurgated parts of those " lives " were the paragraphs which related to Lincoln's Enloe origin, is sufficient proof of the foundation on *fact* of these statements. Neither Col. Lamon nor Mr. Herndon would have recorded a lie about Lincoln's paternity, and these suppressors knew it."—*Cathey's letter to Burton, May* 16, 1919.

This statement is not conclusive.

First, while it is generally believed that influential friends of Lincoln, some of whom are named in the story of the alleged suppression, bought up a considerable portion of the edition of each of these two books and destroyed it, that statement is also denied. Mr. Weik informs me that he personally has been unable to find any proof of it.

In the second place, the portions which suggest that Lincoln was illegitimate are not wholly removed from Herndon's second edition. There was no second edition of Lamon's *"Life."* His *"Recollections"* is a wholly different book, and does not relate at all to Lincoln's birth, but only to some personal reminiscences of Lamon himself.

In the third place, there were other and valid reasons why the relatives of Lincoln should not have enjoyed the books of either Lamon or Herndon. Lamon first published the Browning letter, and his tone throughout is unpleasant, while his representation of Lincoln as cold, unsympathetic, ungrateful and barely honest, as well as utterly destitute of religious faith and willing to deceive people or let them deceive themselves concerning him, was reason enough why it might have been suppressed if suppression had been possible. As for the expurgated portions of Herndon, the principal one is the *"First Chronicles of Reuben,"* and it is a question whether that piece of backwoods vulgarity having once been printed, it would not have been better to let it stand to prevent people who knew that it had been cut out from supposing it to have been worse than it really was. It certainly was nothing for the friends of Lincoln to be proud of; but the worst that can be said about it is that it records a rude practical joke alleged to have been played upon two newly married couples in showing each bridegroom to the bed where the other's bride was. No very serious consequences appear to have resulted before the speedy discovery of the joke; but Lincoln, who is alleged to have had a hand in planning it, wrote it up in his rough boyhood, and the community laughed over the joke and his account of it. It was not a pretty incident, but it has been taken too seriously. It was this, chiefly, which was eliminated in Herndon's second edition.

These stories lend each other no support. On the contrary, each one of them contradicts all the others at some vital point. The more nearly any one of them appears to be true, the more does it become apparent that truth has been outraged in that and in the others. These stories have no cumulative value. They effectually disprove each other, and each is disproved also by independent evidence.

CHAPTER XXVI

A SCHOOL FOR SCANDAL

THE avowed purpose of those who disseminate these various stories is to provide for Abraham Lincoln a worthy and adequate father. God did not make Lincoln out of nothing, as one of them remarks, and to believe that Thomas Lincoln was his father is to hold that view. Some one must have been his father who was capable of transmitting qualities great enough to have developed into Abraham Lincoln.

The question naturally rises, If this necessity exists, why stop with Abraham Enlow? In what respect of body, mind or estate were the Enlows superior to the Lincolns? Sarah Bush and the Johnstons looked down upon them both: what evidence is there that any one of the numerous Abraham Enlows who are credited with the paternity of Lincoln could have transmitted to him anything superior to what was inherent in Thomas Lincoln? The Enlows bred mightily in several Appalachian States: where is their list of additional Lincolns? They are, indeed, a reputable family: the worst thing that is known against them is the readiness of some of them, but not all, to smirch the reputation of their own grandfathers for the sake of establishing a fictitious relationship with Abraham Lincoln.[1] Why have none of them afforded to the world more convincing proof by begetting other Lincolns? They still live, the Enlows, in homes not greatly superior to that in which Abraham Lincoln was born: why did they not transmit their genius and enterprise to some other of their sons?

A family that has so much genius to spare that it can deposit its cuckoo eggs in other nests and hatch eagles should rear brave birds at home, and have no need to claim what does not belong to it in other families.

[1] The Kentucky Enlows I have found free from any complicity in this libel of their ancestor

One is impressed with the poverty of the imagination of those who exploit these opinions. If a worthy father must be had for Abraham Lincoln, why stop with Enlow? Why not select a character really great enough for the purpose?

For instance, there is Benjamin Franklin: why not stir up one of the stories which are not few, of his gallantries while he was in France, and obtain an illegitimate son of high birth, who, returning to Philadelphia, made his way into what was then the western part of Pennsylvania, there to quarter his arms with the Lincolns? That would account for Abraham Lincoln's rare common sense, his native shrewdness, his sound judgment, his wise and benevolent humanity.

Or, why not take Thomas Jefferson, whose reputation would not be greatly damaged by the story, and let the man who wrote the Declaration of Independence be the father of the man who wrote the Emancipation Proclamation, each asserting, and the latter in terms of universal application, that all men are created free and equal, and endowed by their Creator with certain inalienable rights, among which are life, liberty and the pursuit of happiness?

Either of these could be done, and in a very plausible way, and one that would have much to commend it. Moreover, there would be even greater opportunity to appeal to Providence, and show how thus God designed through Abraham Lincoln to accomplish what was inherent in the purpose of the founders of the Republic, and wrought it through the son of the one deemed most appropriate.

And there is always George Washington. When he was a young man he went to the far West—through Western Virginia and Pennsylvania, where the Lincolns foregathered. He was about twenty-two, and being detained by high water, he may have spent a few days in the home of, let us say the Herring family. We do not know that he did so, but no matter about that. Why should not George Washington be the father of Bathsheba Herring, the mother of Thomas Lincoln? To be sure, Bathsheba may have been rather young: her future husband being only about thirteen: but she may have been three or six years older than her Abraham Lincoln, the grandfather of President Lincoln, whom she subsequently married.

And, to make the story complete, why shall not the son of Martha Curtis, who married George Washington, have a more or less innocent flirtation with Lucy Hanks, and so become the father of Nancy?

This would provide for Lincoln a really adequate parentage. It would explain his height—he and Washington were about the same stature, and each with very large hands and feet and relatively small head. And it would show us, too, why Providence left George and Martha Washington without children, that he might become the father and she the mother, by descent, of the greatest of the children of the land that calls him the Father of his Country.

I am trying to make this whole thing as ridiculous as I can,—to reduce the whole affair to an absurdity: but like the hero of Holmes' poem, who did not dare to be as funny as he could, I dare not work out in detail an absurd imagination like this, because I could make it so plausible that some foolish reader would surely believe it.

It is not possible even to suggest a line of reasoning in such matters that shall be sufficiently absurd to be of use as a *reductio ad absurdum*. Nothing is too absurd for scandal-mongers in matters of this character. Wherefore I will not show how plausible this and any of the following suggestions could be made.

But, to show how easily this sort of thing can be done, let me remind the reader that if we were really to decide to propound George and Martha Washington as progenitors of Lincoln, it would not be necessary to stop there. We could embellish Lincoln's ancestry through innumerable collateral lines, and make each one plausible. The farther back we go the easier it becomes.

Every man has two parents, and in the second generation his ancestors number four. In the next there are eight, then sixteen, then thirty-two, and so on. In 1700 Abraham had approximately thirty-two living ancestors, and in 1620 he had 256. The Lincoln line has been traced by Lea and Hutchinson; the Hanks line by Mrs. Hitchcock. There is opportunity, with the assistance of their books, to embellish the record through almost any of its maternal lines.

For instance, take Samuel Lincoln, Abraham's first American ancestor, who was baptized in Hingham, England, August 24, 1622, and, coming to America in 1637, married there a girl named Martha, whose last name is unknown. Why not let Martha be a Plymouth girl, of any of the best families who came over in the Mayflower?

Then, with a little work in the collateral lines of the Hanks family, why not prove that Nancy Hanks was a descendant of John Rolfe and Pocohontas? It could very easily be done. At least, it would be easy to find a plausible possibility, and that without scandal, to fortify it with wills and marriage registers and other old records, and leave a story that could not easily be disproved, and one much more to the point than any of the Enlow stories.

Every female line that breaks off abruptly, as in the old records a majority of them do, is an invitation to the imagination. A few weeks spent in the library of the New England Historic-Genealogical Society would give to any person who liked this sort of thing material to keep the admirers of Lincoln busy for a generation, and it might be so ingeniously done that it could never be disproved.

It might be objected by some lover of scandal that while this would be a very pleasant diversion, it would hardly be nice to dip one's pen in slime and write all over the fair name of Martha Washington and other noble women.

But Truth, it must be remembered, is too sacred to be satisfied with anything less. To those who deal in these scandals, *Truth,* naked and shameless *Truth,* is so holy that we must not hesitate to strip the fig-leaf from the reputation of any woman.

He who slanders the mother of Abraham Lincoln need have no qualms concerning George Washington or his wife or mother. This high and holy quest for Truth, TRUTH, must be pursued though the heavens fall.

Very well, let us note a few of these collateral lines, and see what more we can do for Abraham Lincoln.

We can find among his parental ancestors, Oliver Cromwell, and among his maternal forbears a daughter of Charles II. and naughty Nell Gwyne. That should be easy. While we are about it, we might as well find him another paternal ancestor in Charles VII. of France, and that gay flirt, Agnes Sorrel; and we might wed one of their sons with a daughter of the Huguenots. We might also find among the Quaker friends of the Lincolns in Pennsylvania a descendant of William Penn, and there is no reason why his wife should not be a descendant of stern John Endecott, who did not love Quakers. It would be well, also, to obtain, still in Pennsylvania, one of the Pennsylvania Dutch, descended from William, Prince of Orange: and we could wed him to a Scandinavian daughter some degrees removed from Gustavus Adolphus.

· Having done this, we might find what other body of immigrants to America were most in need of representation in the ancestry of Lincoln, and with a suitable infusion of Mennonite and Scotch-Irish and other blood, we could make him the incarnate spirit of cosmopolitan America.

Let no one suppose this sort of thing to be difficult. If those who have invented the various stories about Lincoln had possessed a little more imagination, and access to a good genealogical library, they could have wrought wonders.

But when this mountain of scandal labors, it brings forth this mouse—Abraham Enlow.

That, positively, is not worth doing. We might as well accept Thomas Lincoln and be done with it.

If I were interested in smirching the name of Abraham Lincoln, and had a few hundred dollars to spare, I could put a good genealogist at work to create for me an ancestral tree for him that would cast its shade over all the feeble and well-watered but rootless saplings that have been industriously set out and named for the various sons of the tribe of Enlow. But I could not make one sufficiently absurd to prevent its being believed. It is an easy thing for Aaron to cast down his rod and produce a serpent that will swallow the serpents of the magicians: I will not do so, for it would be sure to raise up a new serpent cult that would burn incense to my snake.

There is still another and yet more interesting possibility for the makers of Genealogy to order. Abraham Lincoln was born in La Rue County, Kentucky, February 12, 1809. Jefferson Davis is alleged to have been born in Christian County, Kentucky, June 3, 1808. Seven months is the time and sixty miles the distance which is alleged to have separated these two men at birth. It is preposterous that so brief an interval of time and so short a distance should stand in the way of the devotee of Truth. What is more easy than to prove that these two men were twins? As to Jefferson Davis' birth there are as many stories as about that of Lincoln. Both were tall men: both were by nature kind-hearted men. There are resemblances enough for the purposes of the story, and a few more can be invented. Contrasts, also, are abundant.

Now, that would be a story worth while. With these two men born as twins and separated in infancy, meeting in the Black Hawk War, and parting to command opposing armies and governments in the Civil War—what a story that would make!

For two things we cannot bring ourselves to forgive the men and women who have disseminated these stories about Lincoln's birth. The first is that they have ruthlessly defamed the virtuous mother of America's noblest and best loved American. The second is that they are possessed of such poverty-stricken imaginations as to be incapable of inventing a story worth telling. There are, to be sure, the exceptions of Mrs. Boyd with her Marshall story, and Mr. Knotts, who really has put some labor and research into his John C. Calhoun story and believes it. But those who seek to relieve Abraham Lincoln from the disgrace of being a son of Thomas Lincoln and can get no further than Abe Enlow, have weak imaginations.

If we want to unite the name of Abraham Lincoln more closely to Kentucky, let us remember that Henry Clay, who was born in Virginia on April 12, 1777, and came to Lexington, Kentucky, when he was twenty years old, and died in Washington on June 29, 1852, was a member of the Legislature in 1808, and stumped the State in the interests of his campaign for home-made clothes, maintaining that we should always be subject to Europe until we had our own manufactures, and calling upon America to clothe as well as feed itself. In this campaign he may well have visited Hardin County; why should not the great Compromiser have been the father of the great Emancipator? Why shall we not bring compromise to an end in the son of the man who for years invented the compromises?

And, shall we not find in Lincoln's early enthusiasm for Clay, and his cooled ardor later, a discovery on Lincoln's part that Clay had not treated Lincoln's mother honorably?

Henry Clay was tall, raw-boned, awkward, friendly, patient, an orator who appealed to common sense and fair play; what more do we want to prove that he was the father of Abraham Lincoln? And where might Abraham Lincoln have looked for a better father? Why need we go to Bourbon County for Abraham Enlow when Lexington and Henry Clay were nearer?

With a very little cutting and fitting, the events of Henry Clay's life could be shaped to the need; and there must still be old people in Kentucky who, if sufficiently prompted, could remember that he once loved a girl named Nancy Hanks.

If we decide upon Henry Clay as a suitable father for Abraham Lincoln, we shall have no serious difficulty in strengthening our hypothesis by documentary material. It is not necessary to be so shy of the calendar as are most of those who advocate these theories, and to say that things happened in the year 18—; we can do better than that without damage to the theory.

For instance, in 1808, when Henry Clay may have visited Hardin County, we remember that he had recently returned from his first experience in Washington, where he had served a fractional term as United States Senator. He had a gay time in the Nation's Capital. Besides his salary, he had three thousand dollars which his friends made up in a purse to retain him on certain suits that might rise in the Supreme Court, and he got his money's worth in Washington. William Plummer, a Senator from New Hampshire, wrote in his diary:

"December 29, 1806. This day Henry Clay, the successor of John Adair, was qualified, and took his place in the Senate. He is a young lawyer. His stature is tall and slender. I had much conversation with him, and it afforded me much pleasure. He is intelligent and appears frank and candid. His address is good, and his manners easy."

On February 13, 1807, he wrote:

"Henry Clay is a man of pleasure; fond of amusements. He is a great favorite with the ladies; is in all parties of pleasure; out almost every evening; reads very little; indeed, he said he meant this session should be a tour of pleasure"

It is not necessary to make him a grossly immoral man. He was fond of ladies and they were fond of him, and he did not leave all of that fondness in Washington. He returned to Kentucky, happy to be back in his own State, saying, "After all that I have seen, Kentucky is still my favorite country."

John G. Holland tells in his *Life of Lincoln* that subsequently to Mr. Clay's defeat for the Presidency, which was a disappointment to Lincoln, "Mr. Lincoln paid a personal visit to Mr. Clay. . . . On returning home from this visit, he did not attempt to disguise his disappointment." (p. 95.) Lamon denies that Lincoln ever made such a visit; but comments at length on the fact that, on July 1, 1852, Mr. Lincoln was chosen by a public meeting of his fellow-citizens in Springfield to deliver in their hearing an eulogy on Clay, who had recently died; and that Lincoln did so on the 16th of that month, but his address was cold and tame. (p. 339.) Surely, here is material such as we want! Lincoln, an enthusiastic supporter of Clay, making a secret visit to him at Ashland, and his biographers trying to hush it up, and Lincoln, with the honor thrust upon him of delivering an eulogy upon the man whom he was known to have admired, doing it with such constraint that it was noticeable! What material have we not here for scandal! Let us desist from this sort of thing, lest we find ourselves believing the lies we are inventing, and get our minds tangled in the web we spin out of our own bowels!

But if we really were to undertake the task of finding a father for Lincoln, could we not make a story that would cause all the rest to turn green with envy?

But it is all nonsense; and is here introduced to show how easy it is to make better stories than those that very credulous people have so willingly believed.

This school for scandal is about to close its doors, and they will not reopen. But before this is done, let me suggest one more interesting possibility for those who would find another parent than Thomas Lincoln for Abraham, and who are not content with anything so contemptibly weak as the Enloe story.

"In the year 18—," meaning thereby in a very early year of the nineteenth century, a prosperous man in Pennsylvania addressed his son who had completed his legal studies in language something like this:

"I have purchased a large tract of land in Kentucky. It is a land of promise. There will be opportunities there for a rising young lawyer, and in time the land will make him rich. If you are disposed to go there and establish yourself in your profession and grow up with the country, the land shall be yours."

In due course the young man, whose name was James, arrived at Elizabethtown, the county seat of Hardin County. The county then contained all of what is now Hardin and La Rue and much beside. It was a hundred and forty miles in length and had an average width of nearly fifty miles. He rode his good horse to the tavern, and there took up his abode.

On the first court day he met Ben Hardin, attorney at law, for whose family the county had been named, and was shocked to see him enter court in an ill-fitting suit of unbleached tow-linen which hung in unshapely folds about him; but a little later was surprised when this and other lawyers addressed the court in the rough log court house to discover with what rude dignity and forensic skill they did their legal business. This, surely, was the place for an educated lawyer from Pennsylvania.

At the carpenter shop, where he went to see about a table and some shelves for his small office, he met not only the carpenter, Joseph Hanks, but he met also a very attractive girl named Nancy Hanks. Incidentally he met a big, illiterate, but good-natured, apprentice, Tom Lincoln, by name.

The business of procuring the table and book shelves called James to the carpenter shop a number of times, and each time he was more deeply smitten with the charm of Nancy. She, poor girl, was flattered by the attentions of the best dressed man in town, the rising young lawyer and owner of a great domain.

After matters had gone much too far, James considered the social gap between him and this young woman, and thought of the more cultured beauties of his early life.

He had a secret interview with the young apprentice, and said:

"You love Nancy and so do I; but I will not be selfish. You loved her first, and while she seems to like me, I know that her heart is yours. Tomorrow I go to court at Lexington, and I shall not come back. Marry her, and may you both be happy."

He rode away, and soon Nancy received word that he was never to return. Appalled by the situation in which she found herself, she accepted the offer of Tom Lincoln, who then learned why James had been so generous, but determined to make the best of it.

James returned to Pennsylvania and established a lucrative practice. In time he entered politics and became noted. But he never married. Famous beauties attempted to ensnare his heart, but he never was able to love any of them. All that he ever told was that he had loved once and found that he could never love again.

Years went by. The nation was on the brink of civil war. The man in the White House was unable to command the situation. During the last months of his administration his exhibition of weakness was pitiable. The nation and the world awaited the coming of the man whose mastery of the situation was to save the country.

On the fourth day of March, 1861, the retiring President and the President-elect stood together in front of the Capitol, and the new President took the oath of office and delivered his brief inaugural. Why was the retiring President so pale? Why did he tremble as he stood beside the powerful giant who had risen from Kentucky's woods to the White House? Was it because he saw, underneath all the mighty contrasts between himself and this man, a resemblance that could mean but one thing? Had Providence denied him wife and child that he might see his own son come now to honor while he, the father, slunk away into merited oblivion?

The reader will see what an attractive theme the scandal-mongers have missed. It would be very easy to make it so plausible that a goodly number of people would believe it.

Yes, it is true that the father of James Buchanan bought land in Hardin County, and that James went thither and began a law practice, and left suddenly and did not return. And enough more details could easily be discovered or created to make as good or bad a story as any one might desire. It is true that he never married.

But before the reader becomes too greatly fascinated with this interesting story, let him consider the bearing of one or two inconvenient dates. Abraham Lincoln was born February 12, 1809. James Buchanan first came to Elizabethtown in the spring of 1813, four years after Abraham Lincoln was born.

It is a pity to wreck so good a story on so small a fact. But the fact is that Abraham Lincoln was not the son of James Buchanan any more than he was the grandson of Washington or Jefferson or Franklin. But he was as much their son as he was the son of Abraham Enlow.

It is a poor rule that will not work both ways. It is not fair that Thomas Lincoln should be the invariable cuckold, or that every woman named Nancy Hanks and no others should be frail. The worm will turn. Let Thomas Lincoln have his innings. If we are to invent stories of this character as freely as stories have been invented, let at least half of them deal with the notable children of Thomas Lincoln.

Let us send Thomas Lincoln in 1808 on a visit to his uncle,

Isaac Lincoln, in East Tennessee, and on into North Carolina. Was there not born in that period a lad who rose so
far above his own supposed heredity and his early environment as to give rise to serious question of his paternity? We
can explain it very easily if we suppose Thomas Lincoln to
have been the father of Andrew Johnson, who was born December 29, 1808, and who became Vice-President with Lincoln, and succeeded him as President. A great many hitherto
unexplained events will now become clear.

But there is no need to stop here. May not Thomas Lincoln in the spring before his marriage to Nancy Hanks have
made a journey back to his old State, Virginia? Robert E.
Lee was born January 19, 1807. What a dramatic story
could we make out of the half-brotherhood of Lincoln and
Lee! Moreover, the story can be worked out in elaborate
detail, and with much of plausibility, which I forbear to com-
mit to print.

A good many distinguished men were born in Indiana between 1816 and 1830, some of them unaccountably greater
than their fathers. Why may not Thomas Lincoln have been
considering in that period his nation's need of more men like
his son Abraham?

· There have lived and still live in Illinois a considerable
number of statesmen born within the period of Thomas Lincoln's residence in that State who are proud of their resemblance to Abraham Lincoln. They wear their beards like him.
They affect a style of dress that suggests him. They fall into
poses that remind people more or less vividly of Lincoln. Some
of these men are now dead, but a few still are living, and
the author can bear testimony to their pride in their supposed
resemblance to Lincoln. Shall we account for this wholly in
terms of inches of height or of the work of the barber? Why
not accept the conclusion that they are all half-brothers of
Abraham Lincoln, and that Thomas was the father of innumerable sons?

If one begins in this way there is no ending. But a series
of stories of this character would have one marked advantage
over the stories that impugn the virtue of President Lincoln's

mother.   There is a limit to the number of Nancy Hankses who could by any possibility have been the mother of Abraham Lincoln; but there is no corresponding limit to the number of sons who might have been born to Thomas Lincoln.   That which is sauce for the goose is sauce for the gander.   If we are to lend a credulous ear to every foolish story that challenges the paternity of Lincoln, let us remember that if all we have to do is to discover physical possibilities, then for every possible illegitimate son borne by Nancy Hanks, we can produce ten such sons, illustrious and widely distributed, who might possibly have been sired by Thomas Lincoln.

And these stories about Abraham Lincoln's parentage are all lies, and proceed from the father of lies.

This chapter is not as original as I supposed when I wrote it.   Mr. Hugh McLellan informs me that his father, a Confederate officer, often heard in the army that Abraham Lincoln and Jefferson Davis had a common father; and I have found traces of the Henry Clay story also.

This school for scandal is now closed.

But it will have done good educational work if it reminds the students therein that if one cares for stories of this kind he can invent them, a dozen in a day, and support them with dates and details far more plausible than attend any of the stories about the paternity of Abraham Lincoln.

CHAPTER XXVII

A FEW FIXED DATES

IN the process of this inquiry we have fixed a few dates beyond question. There are a few more that should be recorded. For he who undertakes to challenge the record of the parentage of Abraham Lincoln must deal with definite places and times. Indictments are frequently quashed because the crimes alleged are not shown to have occurred within a definite county or on any particular date.

Quaint old Thomas Fuller wrote:

"Chronology is a surly, churlish cur, and hath bit many a man's fingers. Blame me not, therefore, if willing to keep my hands whole."

That little sentiment might well have been adopted by all who have circulated these stories about Abraham Lincoln. At the first whistle for that surly dog, Chronology, they flee in terror; and all of them emerge with bleeding fingers and clothing torn to shreds.

The importance of the date of Abraham Lincoln's birth is so great that we may be justified in assuming that some one will ask on what authority we receive the date of February 12, 1809, as the birthday of Abraham Lincoln.

First of all, we have it on the testimony of the Lincoln family Bible, in which the record was written by Abraham Lincoln himself, while his father was yet living, and long before any of these questions came into controversy, and when there was not the slightest reason on the part of either to deceive. That is in itself ample evidence, and all that in any ordinary case can be produced to establish the date of a man's birth.

Let the reader pause a moment and ask what proof he has of the date of his own birth; and he may find that he has little more than this.

244

But it happens that we have still another proof. As Abraham Lincoln approached his twenty-first year he grew very restless, and wished for his freedom. On this point Mr. Herndon had first-hand evidence from William Wood, the " Uncle Wood " of the Lincoln household in Indiana. On the basis of this and such other information as Herndon had assembled, Lamon says:

In 1828 Abe had become very tired of his home. He was now nineteen years of age, and becoming daily more restive under the restraints of servitude which bound him. He was anxious to try the world for himself, and make his way according to his own notions. " Abe came to my house one day," says Mr. Wood, " and stood round about, timid and shy. I knew he wanted something, and said to him, ' Abe, what's your case?' He replied, ' Uncle, I want you to go to the river, and give me some recommendation to some boat ' I remarked, ' Abe, your age is against you. You are not twenty yet.' ' I know that, but I want a start,' said Abe. ' I concluded not to go for the boy's good " Poor Abe! Tom still had a claim on him, which even Uncle Wood would not help him evade. He must wait a few weary months before he would be of age, and could say that he was his own man, and go his own way. Old Tom was a hard taskmaster to him, and no doubt consumed the greater part, if not all, of his wages.—" *Life of Lincoln,*" pp. 70-71.

" Uncle Wood," who subscribed for two newspapers, which Abraham regularly read, had influence with the boy. Abraham remained with his father until he was of age. He removed to Illinois with the family, assisted his father in erecting his new home, and then hired himself out to other farmers in the vicinity, and did not return to his home to live. Abraham Lincoln knew when his twenty-first birthday occurred, and did not hesitate to take advantage of his freedom when it was legally his.

But beside all this, Abraham's memories of Kentucky as he recalled them in after life were those of a child under ten; and his growth in body and mind in Indiana was the normal growth of such a boy of the age which he should have been and was, reckoning his birth from February 12, 1809.

The birthday of Abraham Lincoln is a fixed date.

The marriage of Thomas and Nancy Lincoln is a fixed date. No one knows this better than Mr. Knotts, or realizes better than he that the marriage record at Springfield, Kentucky, is absolutely fatal to his theory. He, therefore, has recourse to the desperate and futile expedient of attacking the record. According to his theory, the discovery of the marriage bond and record was a fraud. There was no Jesse Head; there was no marriage of Thomas and Nancy Lincoln at Beechland, Washington County, Kentucky, on June 12, 1806. To prove this, he submits the fact that he has written to the authorities of the Southern Methodist Church in Nashville and Louisville, a denomination which had no existence in 1806, or until the Civil War, and that that denomination has no official record of Rev. Jesse Head!

There is record, however, of Rev. Jesse Head.

Jesse Head was a resident of Springfield before 1800, and in that year was a Justice of the Peace in and for Washington County. At that time there was a bounty for wolves' scalps, and there are several certificates by Justices authorizing the bounty for those scalps. One of these reads thus:

"This day came Leroy Smith before me, a Justice for Washington County, and produced a wolf head above six months old, and took the oath prescribed by law in that case. Given under my hand this 8th July, 1800. Jesse Head."

JESSE HEAD'S COURT MARTIAL

A remarkably interesting record has been found for me by Mr. L. S. Pence, attorney, of Lebanon, Kentucky. It is contained in an aged book entitled "Record of Court Martials in Washington County." The records begin under date of July 15, 1791, and come down to the year 1812. The record concerning Jesse Head is as follows:

"May 25, 1793. Jesse Head, returned as a delinquent is cleared of [off?] muster roll, he having a license to preach according to the rules of the sect to which he belongs."

Here is a clear official record of Jesse Head absolved from militia duty in 1793, because he was a licensed preacher; and we have records of him from that date until 1842.

In 1802 he was a trustee of the town of Springfield. Among the persons voting for him was Felix Grundy, a jurist of considerable distinction, whose biography can be found in the annals of the Kentucky bar. On March 6 of that year, Felix Grundy was made President of the Board, and on April 3 of the same year Jesse Head was appointed Commissioner " to contract with some proper person to erect posts and rails around the well and public spring of this town and all necessary repairs to same."

In the following year, 1803, Jesse Head was again elected a Trustee of the incorporated town of Springfield, and succeeded Felix Grundy as President of the Board.

Although he was a Justice of the Peace, his marriages in Washington County appear all to have been performed by him as a Deacon in the Methodist Church.

Between February 19, 1803, and December 25 of the same year, he married thirteen couples, making a single return for them on January 2, 1804, thus: " Witness my hand, January 2, 1804. Jesse Head."

Some of the old records are lost, or at least have not been located.

The list immediately preceding that which contains the names of Thomas Lincoln and Nancy Hanks was returned by him April 28, 1806, and contains the names of sixteen couples married by him in the months preceding that date.

Hon. Joseph Polin, County Attorney of Washington County, who made for me a more exhaustive search of records than has ever been made before in that county with respect to the Lincoln family, writes:

" All these records are signed, ' Jesse Head, D M E C.' It is to be observed that he uses the old style letter ' s ', making the name appear as though it were ' Jefse.' His signature to the orders as Justice is identical in form with that on the Lincoln marriage certificate, and demonstrates to a certainty that it was the same man."

He who would prove Jesse Head a myth and his signed return of the marriage of Thomas and Nancy Lincoln a forgery confronts the cheerful task of attacking a series of continuous records in Washington County from 1793 until some years after the marriage of Thomas Lincoln, these records being official and of varied character, and relating, in the matter of marriages, to some scores of families known to have been resident in Washington County; and after that another series of records in Harrodsburg and vicinity down to the probation of his estate in 1842. Mr. Knotts would never have suggested the forgery theory if he had known what body of evidence he must confront.

This is the place to mention also the affidavit of Dr. Christopher Columbus Graham and the affidavit of William Hardesty, both of them unimpeached witnesses, who declare that they were actually present at the wedding, and the declaration of Judge Richard J. Browne of Louisville, who was born in Springfield:

"Old Mr. James Thompson and William Hardesty told me many years ago that they were at the marriage of Thomas Lincoln and Nancy Hanks at old Dick Berry's, the grandfather of Nancy Hanks, on the banks of the Beech Fork."

The occasion for the search for the documents in Washington County, where it had not been supposed worth while to look for them, was the fact that people were still living whose parents had told them that they were present at the wedding and that it occurred in Washington County and not in Hardin. The man who made this discovery, Mr. W. F. Booker, is described by all who knew him as a man of the highest integrity.

The forgery theory is squarely contradicted by the whole appearance of the documents, which I have handled and examined, and which bear on their face the marks of their genuineness, which is attested also by every detail in the circumstances of their discovery. Only the most desperate necessity would have driven Mr. Knotts to the hypothesis of forgery, and it will not avail to save his theory from utter wreck.

It now becomes our duty to account for Thomas Lincoln,

so far as this may be done from records available and indisputable, during the period when according to these various
stories he was ranging the country from South Carolina
through North Carolina, East Tennessee and Clark and Bourbon Counties, Kentucky, helping various rascals out of the
troubles into which they had gotten themselves and divers
young women. These several stories present him to us as
a fugitive and a vagabond, wandering from State to State,
going about like a roaring lion, seeking whom he might marry
who should have married some one else.

The early records of the several counties in Kentucky are
incomplete. The tax lists were made out on sheets of paper
ruled by hand, sewn together with covers of the same, and
made into very insubstantial and easily mislaid books.

In 1796 Thomas Lincoln was listed as resident in Washington County as a male over sixteen years of age and under
twenty-one. His age then was just sixteen and this is doubtless his first record on the public documents.

His name does not appear in the list for 1797, and the
lists for the next two years have not been found, but his name
appears in the lists for 1800 and 1801.

In 1802 and 1803 his name is not found there. The reason appears to be that he was at that time in Hardin County,
for there we find him in the latter year purchasing land, and
there is where he was living at the time of his marriage Hardin County does not lie eastward from Washington toward
the old States of Virginia and Carolinas.

Abraham Lincoln, in the sketch which he prepared for
John Locke Scripps, stated that his father, Thomas Lincoln,
passed one year, before reaching his majority, in the farm of
his uncle, Isaac Lincoln, in East Tennessee. He said:

" Thomas, the youngest son, and father of the present subject, by the early death of his father, and very narrow circumstances of his mother, even in childhood was a wandering laboring-boy and grew up literally without education. He
never did more in the way of writing than to bunglingly
write his own name. Before he was grown he passed one
year as a hired hand with his uncle Isaac on Watauga, a

branch of the Holston River. Getting back into Kentucky, and having reached his twenty-eighth year, he married Nancy Hanks, mother of the present subject, in 1806. She also was born in Virginia."

In what year did Thomas Lincoln work for his uncle Isaac? In one of the years, certainly, when he was not listed on the tax book of Washington County, Kentucky. And also it was " before he was grown." It was, therefore, in some year between 1795 and 1800. Possibly his residence there covered parts of two years, and was longer than twelve actual months; which might account for two missing years.

It was probably in 1797, when he was seventeen years old, that he went to the farm of his uncle Isaac in East Tennessee. He returned to Washington County presumably in 1798 or 1799, for which years the tax lists have not been found, and was there, as we have seen, in 1800 and 1801, then moving farther west to Hardin County, with which thereafter he is chiefly identified.

It is unlikely that Thomas Lincoln made any journeys back to the Eastern States from his home in Hardin County. That county lies farther west. It was more remote, not less so, from the temptation to go back along the Wilderness Road through Cumberland Gap to assist young women in the Eastern States. The farther we go into the records the less likely does it become that Thomas Lincoln ever made any such journey as would have been necessary for him to participate in any of these adventures.

At any rate, he was in Washington County in 1796 and 1800 and 1801. He was there in one other year, which cannot certainly be identified at present, because the cover of the book is worn away and the year cannot be positively determined until some other books are found which may identify it by the number of taxpayers and of negroes in the county.

He was not living there in 1802 and 1803, but was then purchasing a farm of 230 acres in Hardin County, and was probably there continuously after that time.

He was in Hardin County in June, 1806, and went to

Washington County to marry Nancy Hanks, which he did on June 12, 1806.

He was not wandering abroad in the next few months, but living in Elizabethtown, where, on February 10, 1807, his eldest child, Sarah, was born.

We may pause just a moment to consider the baseless declaration that there was no such child; that the Sarah whom Abraham Lincoln called sister was his step-sister, Sarah, a daughter of Sarah Bush Lincoln. There was such a step-sister, but she did not die in Indiana, as did Lincoln's sister Sarah, but lived and married Dennis Hanks, her sister Matilda marrying Squire Hall. Furthermore, William H. Herndon interviewed Dennis Hanks and his family, and they told him much about this sister Sarah, who in 1826 married Aaron Grigsby, and died in childbirth while yet a very young woman. And, if it were necessary to make the testimony stronger, we have it in Abraham Lincoln's own letters, as in one written to his friend Johnson on April 18, 1846, inclosing some verses which he had written after his visit to his old home in Indiana:

"In the fall of 1844, thinking I might aid some to carry the State of Indiana for Mr. Clay, I went into the neighborhood in that State in which I was raised, where my mother and only sister were buried, and from which I had been absent about fifteen years."

He could not have written thus of a step-sister, for Sarah Johnston was not his only step-sister, and she was not buried in Indiana in 1844, but living in Illinois with her husband Dennis Hanks.

Let us then dismiss all this nonsense about Thomas Lincoln's daughter Sarah having been a step-daughter. Sarah was born to Thomas and Nancy Hanks Lincoln on February 10, 1807, and Thomas Lincoln had little time to roam abroad. He had to work for a living for his wife and baby. That gives us another fixed date.

We are very fortunate in knowing one important piece of work in which he was engaged in the latter part of that year.

Denton Geoghegan, a prominent man in that part of the

county which still is Hardin, engaged Thomas Lincoln to hew timbers for a mill. The job was a long one, and a dispute arose concerning the settlement of it. Geoghegan is a well-known character and was in his day a man of standing in the county.

Denton Geoghegan was in later years a Justice of the Peace He and his family lived in that part of Hardin which is still Hardin, and never in that part which is now La Rue. He sued Thomas Lincoln in 1808, when Lincoln was living in Elizabethtown.

Mr. O. M. Mather, of Hodgenville, to whom I am indebted for many kindnesses, was searching for me the records of Hardin County, when he discovered the record of this suit, hitherto unpublished. The suit was not finished until March, 1809, when Thomas Lincoln had removed to that part of the county which is now La Rue, and had become the father of Abraham In the months preceding the birth of Abraham Lincoln, Thomas Lincoln was not moving around the country assisting young women in distress. He was attending to business at home, a part of which was defending himself in this law-suit. Mr Mather was unable to find the whole record, but the remainder of it was discovered for me by Mr. George Holbert of Elizabethtown, Kentucky.

Thomas Lincoln was not wandering about the country in the latter part of 1807 and the early part of 1808; he was hewing timbers for Geoghegan's mill, and assisting in the erection of that structure. It was no small task It involved the manufacture of a great overshot wheel; the construction of a wooden aqueduct raised to the level of the top of the wheel and carried back sufficiently far to meet the water at its higher level. It occupied several months. The dispute lasted no one knows how long before it came into court, but we know, what no previous volume about Lincoln has known, the fact and the date and character of this suit.

This suit of *Geoghegan vs. Lincoln* was filed June 1, 1808. The petition alleged that Denton Geoghegan, the plaintiff, had employed Thomas Lincoln, the defendant, to hew certain timbers for a saw-mill, and to do the work " in good workman-

like manner " at 1½ penny per square foot; that the work
was not done in workmanlike manner, the timbers not being of
such workmanship as to answer the purpose; that they were
not square and not true and some were too short; that Geoghegan had paid Lincoln $10 more than the work actually
came to at the agreed price, and by the alleged bad workmanship had been damaged in the sum of $100.00

Mr. Holbert writes, " From the judgment in this case it
would appear that Lincoln was vindicated. Geoghegan was
my wife's great-grandfather, and I am interested in the case."

Thomas Lincoln's contract with Geoghegan was the last
important piece of work he did before removal from Elizabethtown, and fixes the approximate date of the removal   In
the spring of 1808 he was working for Geoghegan near Elizabethtown; in the summer he was working for Brownfield near
Hodgen's Mill. It is not necessary to suppose that he did not
move until after the suit was brought; I am inclined to believe
that he moved in May.

The suit continued for several months, and in the end
Thomas Lincoln won it, and recovered the costs of his defense.
The significance of this lawsuit for us is in the dates which it
fixes, and which never before have been published.

Just as I was reading the first proofs of this book, Mr.
Holbert, on July 27, 1920, discovered another record in the
judgments, not of the Circuit, but of the County Court, of
Hardin County. It is of a judgment rendered May 9, 1808.
It shows that Thomas Lincoln, at some earlier date not
recorded, had sued Denton Geoghegan in a magistrate's court,
for the unpaid balance due him on account of his work upon
the mill aforementioned, and had recovered judgment against
him in the sum of four pounds and nine shillings. Geoghegan
took an appeal to the County Court, which at its next monthly
sitting rendered the following judgment, recorded in Order
Book C, page 230, Hardin County Court:

" At a court begun and held for Hardin County at the
Courthouse in Elizabeth Town on Monday, the 9th day of
May, 1808: Present Adin Coombs and Dudley Rountree,
Esquires:

"Denton Geoghegan against Thomas Lincoln on an appeal from a Magistrate's judgment. The Court being fully advised of and concerning the premises, do consider and order that the said appeal be dismissed, and the Magistrate's judgment be and hereby is confirmed; and that the defendant recover against the said plaintiff the sum of four pounds and nine shillings & 4/6 costs and also the costs of this appeal."

Twice beaten, Geoghegan came back at Lincoln in the Circuit Court with a complaint that the work had not been properly done and that Lincoln had been overpaid. This suit, as we have seen, continued until the following March, when Lincoln again, and for the third and last time, was successful.

The following court order is in Record Book C, Hardin Circuit Court Records, under date of March 17, 1809:
"Denton Geoghegan, Plaintiff,
         against
Thomas Lincoln, Defendant.

"This case being agreed and settled by and between the parties herein, it is therefore considered by the Court that it be and the same is hereby Dismissed, and that the Defendant recover against the Plaintiff his cost by him about his defense expended."

These tax and court records are of great interest and importance Fragmentary as they are, they do not permit of the wandering of Thomas Lincoln to fill the rôle assigned to him in any of the stories that are told to the discredit of his wife. The carefully arranged scheme of dates which Mr. Knotts has presented to us, the only one worth a moment's attention so far as chronology is concerned, falls utterly before this list of certain records concerning Thomas Lincoln.

From the time he was sixteen until he was twenty-five we find him in public records, and where there are gaps, we are able to fill them with reasonable probability.

From the time of his marriage until the birth of his daughter, and from then until the birth of his son, he is well accounted for. The suit of Denton Geoghegan, and the contract out of which it grew, cover the period from the autumn of 1807 until after the birth of Abraham Lincoln on February

12, 1809. Thomas Lincoln left Nancy with the baby in her arms, and went to Elizabethtown to court on March 17, 1809 He returned that evening with the good news that the suit was settled out of court, and that the court in entering the record adjudged that the man who had prosecuted him should not only pay the costs of the suit, but make payment also to Thomas Lincoln for the damage he had suffered in defending the suit. So he came home that night either with money in his pocket, or with something which he had purchased with money at Helm's store for Nancy and the baby and little Sarah.

Researches made for this volume give us another fixed date, September 2, 1803. On that date John Tom Slater, or as it is recorded in another place, Stator, conveyed to Thomas Lincoln "of Hardin County" 238 acres of land on Mill Creek. This locates Thomas Lincoln in the period in which his name disappears from the Washington County tax lists. He had left Washington County to work for his uncle Isaac Lincoln on Watauga River in the hill country of Tennessee; had returned to Kentucky and taken up his residence in Hardin County. The deed definitely states Hardin County as his residence. Hardin County tax lists for the period have not been discovered at this writing; but no entry is found concerning him in any other county until June 12, 1806, when he was married to Nancy Hanks in Washington County, and returned to Hardin County to live.

The period between his marriage and his removal to that part of Hardin County which is now La Rue is fairly well covered by his large contract to furnish timbers for Geoghegan's mill, and by the resulting lawsuit.

These dates appear to indicate that after his return from Tennessee, Thomas Lincoln lived in Washington County for two or three years, paying taxes there in 1800 and 1801; that he then removed to Hardin County, where he purchased a farm in 1803, the deed mentioning Hardin County as his place of residence; that he remained upon this farm on Mill Creek in Hardin County until perhaps 1805, when he gave up farming and moved to Elizabethtown, working as an apprentice in the shop of Joseph Hanks, where he met and wooed Nancy; that he was married to Nancy Hanks on June 12, 1806, and immediately set up his home in Elizabethtown; that he thenceforth worked for himself at the carpenter's trade, having at least one contract of importance, which occupied a considerable part of the year 1807; that this contract resulted in a lawsuit which began in a magistrate's court, presumably in April, 1808, where he won his case, and again on appeal in the County Court, Monday, May 9, 1808, where he was again successful, and still again in the Circuit Court, beginning June 1, 1808, and continuing until March 17, 1809.

This record covers all the years in which Thomas Lincoln might have been wandering in other States in adventures such as the stories we have been considering imply, and they are remarkably interesting in all their implications, wholly creditable to him, and in themselves a sufficient alibi against the charges that locate him in any other State or in any other portion of the State of Kentucky in any of the years between 1800 and 1809

And that is all we have to say about the whereabouts of Thomas Lincoln in the period concerning which he has been falsely accused.

CHAPTER XXVIII

WHAT WE KNOW ABOUT THOMAS LINCOLN

THE first American ancestor of Abraham Lincoln was Samuel Lincoln, who came to Salem, Mass., in 1637, and died at Hingham, May 26, 1690, aged 71. He was a son of Edward Lincoln of Hingham, Norfolk County, England, and had an honorable lineage which has been traced for several generations. Samuel married in America, before 1650, Martha, whose surname is unknown, and who died April 10, 1693.

The fourth son of Samuel and Martha Lincoln was Mordecai, who was born at Hingham, Mass., June 14, 1657 and removed to Scituate He was an iron founder. He died November 8, 1727, aged 70. He married Sarah Jones, daughter of Abraham Jones of Hull, through whom the name Abraham may have come into the Lincoln family She died before 1708

The eldest child of Mordecai and Sarah was Mordecai Lincoln, who was born April 24, 1686, removed before 1710 to Monmouth County, New Jersey, where he followed his father's vocation of iron founder. He died May 12, 1736. He married before 1711, Hannah, daughter of Richard and Sarah Salter of Freehold, N. J. She died about 1720.

The eldest child of Mordecai and Sarah was John Lincoln, born May 3, 1711. He was a weaver, and lived in Caernarvon, Uniontown and other places in Pennsylvania; removed to Virginia about 1768, and died probably about 1790. He married Rebecca, whose surname is believed to have been Moore.

The third son of John and Rebecca was Abraham Lincoln, grandfather of the President, who was born July 16, 1739 He was Captain of Virginia Militia in 1776; removed to Kentucky in 1781-2, and was killed by Indians about 1785 His first wife was Mary Shipley, daughter of Robert Shipley of

Lunenburg County, Virginia, who bore him two sons and two daughters and died before 1779.

The children of Abraham and Mary (Shipley) Lincoln were:

(1) Mordecai Lincoln, born 1764; Sheriff of Washington County, Kentucky; removed to Illinois, and died in 1830. His three sons were Abraham, James and Mordecai.

(2) Josiah Lincoln, born July 10, 1766; removed to Indiana and died in 1836, leaving one son, Thomas Lincoln of Corydon, Indiana.

(3) Mary Lincoln, married Ralph Krume or Crume of Kentucky.

(4) Nancy Lincoln, married William Brumfield of Kentucky.

The second wife of Abraham Lincoln was Bathsheba Herring, daughter of Leonard Herring, of Heronford, Rockingham County, Virginia.

The only child of Abraham and Bathsheba Lincoln was Thomas Lincoln, father of the President.

In this volume I have followed the data given by Lea and Hutchinson as to the date of the birth of Thomas Lincoln. That book is so imposing in its appearance and in many respects so valuable that I adopted it in the beginning, and have here and there departed from it with reluctance. But the date given on the tombstone of Thomas Lincoln at Farmington, Coles County, Illinois,—" Thomas Lincoln, Born January 6, 1778; died January 15, 1851," is in several respects the more probably correct. The date of his birth was given by Lea and Hutchinson as January 20, 1780. The place of his birth was Rockingham County, Virginia. He was little more than an infant when his parents, Abraham Lincoln, and Bathsheba, his second wife and the mother of Thomas, removed to Kentucky. Abraham, father of Thomas, and grandfather of the President, was killed by Indians when Thomas was a child of five.

Thomas Lincoln married at the age of twenty-eight, at Beechland, Washington County, Kentucky, Nancy Hanks,

June 12, 1806. They had three children, all born in Hardin County, Kentucky, as follows:

(1) Sarah Lincoln, often incorrectly called Nancy, born February 10, 1807, married, August, 1826, Aaron Grigsby, and died in childbed, May 20, 1828.

(2) Abraham Lincoln, born February 12, 1809, sixteenth President of the United States, died April 15, 1865, He married, November 4, 1862, Mary Todd, by whom he had four sons.

(3) Thomas Lincoln, born in 1811, and died in infancy before the family left Kentucky.

Nancy Hanks Lincoln, mother of the President, died in Indiana, October 5, 1818. Her husband married as his second wife, Sarah Bush Johnston. She had three children by her first husband, John D. Johnston; Sarah, who married Dennis Hanks; and Matilda, who married Squire Hall.

Thomas Lincoln spent the greater part of his youth in Washington County, Kentucky. One year of his late boyhood was spent with his uncle Isaac Lincoln on the Watauga River in East Tennessee. He was then a day laborer on other people's farms, and became a carpenter of no great skill.

In 1803 he purchased an improved farm with buildings on Mill Creek in Hardin County, paying for the same in cash, and presumably worked his own farm until an unknown date which may have been 1805.

After his marriage on June 12, 1806, he settled in Elizabethtown, county seat of Hardin County, Kentucky, where he resided about two years, and where his first child, a daughter, Sarah, was born February 10, 1807.

He then removed, probably in May or early June, 1806, to that part of Hardin County which is now La Rue, living for the first few months on the farm of George Brownfield, whence, in the following autumn, he removed to the farm which he occupied as his own, though without recorded title, and which is known as the Lincoln Farm. It is located on Nolin Creek, two and one half miles south from the present site of Hodgenville, and about as far in the other direction from a settlement called Buffalo. Here his son Abraham was born.

A few years later he lived upon the Knob Creek Farm, about fifteen miles distant, and across Muldraugh's Hill, and, though living in the same county, he was in quite another neighborhood.

There is some reason to believe that between his residence on the Lincoln Farm and that on the Knob Creek Farm he spent at least one year among his wife's relations in Washington County, the chief documentary evidence of this being a tax book in Washington County bearing his name, and apparently of the year 1811. This year, however, is not quite certain.

I had earnestly hoped that the uncertainty concerning the date of this book would have been cleared up by the time the present volume went to press. The early tax records of Washington County were prepared by the clerk upon sheets of paper $15\frac{7}{8}$ inches long and $12\frac{1}{2}$ inches wide, written on both sides and afterwards bound together by stitching at the end. The cover was a sheet of the same kind of paper, with the date and clerk's certificate on the outside. In the case of the book whose date is uncertain, the cover is worn away, but a cover accompanies it, and is supposed to belong to it, giving the year 1811, which I still incline to think is the year. Unfortunately, that is the only place in the book where the year appears. The dates in the book are those of the month and day on which the assessment is made. The last leaf, also, is missing, which would have contained the total number of white male inhabitants and the number of white males above 16 and the number of blacks above 16. These are totaled at the foot of each page, and are complete to about the middle of the list of names beginning with W. If the books could be found for years showing a few more or a few less of each of these classes, it would be easy to fix the year to which this book belonged. But unfortunately, the books for these years are not found. Mr, Joseph Polin, County Attorney, who at first was sure that this book belonged to 1811, now thinks he was mistaken, and that it belongs either to 1809 or 1810. In my judgment his previous opinion is the correct one; and if that is not correct, it certainly does not belong to the year 1809, but either to 1810 or 1812. In either case, it confirms what on other grounds I have come to believe, that the residence of Thomas and Nancy Lincoln in the Nolin Creek home, where Abraham Lincoln was born, was a very brief one, and that between that residence and the one on Knob Creek, from which in 1816 the family of Thomas Lincoln migrated to Indiana, he lived for a year in Washington County, among the relatives of his wife.

This is an unrecorded migration of the Lincoln family, and one concerning which no assistance is to be gained from other books. Even so good a book as Lea and Hutchinson's *Ancestry of Abraham Lincoln* is hopelessly at sea on these migrations. Its chapter on "Thomas Lincoln the Man," contains many errors. Other and less painstaking works are wholly unreliable on these and related matters.

Thomas Lincoln was assessed in Washington County, May 11, 1796, as a white male above sixteen. He was assessed as Thomas Linchorn, in the same county, on February 14, 1800, as a white male above twenty-one; and he owned one horse. He was assessed again in the same county on August 5, 1801, and owned a horse. Between the first assessment in 1796 and the second in 1800 occurs, as I have shown elsewhere, his year or more of residence with his uncle, Isaac Lincoln, in East Tennessee; for the list for 1797 is found and his name is not in it. Also the lists for 1802 and 1803 are found, and his name is not in them; but that was the time he was acquiring his Mill Creek farm, in Hardin County, where he continued to live until some year, which I still think to have been 1811, when he returned and lived for a year in Washington County; whence he went back part way, but stopped east of Muldraugh's Hill, and lived for a few years on the Knob Creek farm This was the first home Abraham remembered, and the place where he first went to school

The cover of the tax book for 1811 gave a total of 1,827 white males above 21, and 974 negroes above the age of 16. The list of white males down to the middle of the initial letter W seemed to me to give totals both of whites and negroes just about in proper proportion to have made up those totals if the lists had been complete. Mr. Polin, however, is of opinion that they would not reach quite to the necessary aggregates, and thus he is inclined to think that the date may have been one or possibly two years earlier. Possibly he is correct and the date should be 1810; but the cover appears to me to belong with the book. It certainly is not of 1809; and if it be 1810, it only proves that the migration of Thomas and Nancy from the birthplace of Abraham occurred a few months earlier than I have supposed.

While Thomas Lincoln was living on the Knob Creek farm he attained his one political appointment. The records for Hardin County contain this entry:

"Monday, 18th May, 1816

"Ordered that Thomas Lincoln be and he is hereby appointed Surveyor of that part of the road leading from Nolin to Bardstown which lies between the Bigg Hill and the rolling fork, in place of George Rodman and that all the hands that assisted Rodman do assist said Lincoln in keeping said road in repair."

I have ridden over this road, all the way from the Bigg Hill to Rolling Fork, and my sympathies are with Thomas Lincoln. Muldraugh's Hill is a Bigg Hill with at least two g's in Bigg; and the wash of the spring rains is heavy. This was afterward a section of the Louisville and Nashville turnpike, and has always been an important strip of road. The emoluments of Thomas Lincoln's one office cannot have been large, but the work of keeping that road in any kind of repair was no sinecure.

In the brief sketch of his own life prepared in 1860 by Abraham Lincoln he intimates that some trouble concerning a land title had a shade in the reasons for his father's leaving Kentucky in 1816, and establishing his home in Indiana. An intimation of the nature of this trouble would appear to be furnished in the record of a suit for whose discovery I am indebted to Mr. George Holbert, attorney, of Elizabethtown, Kentucky.

This was a suit in ejectment, instituted on January 1, 1815, in the Hardin Circuit Court, by " John Doe on demise of Hannah Rhoades, Thomas Stout and Abraham Sheridan, plaintiffs, vs Richard Roe, defendant " The old English form of bringing suit in the name of John Doe against Richard Roe was extensively used in Kentucky courts in the early days, especially in ejectment suits During the progress of the suits all persons in possession of portions of the premises were ascertained, and their names substituted as defendants. However, in this case Thomas Lincoln did not wait to be substituted, but on June 13, 1816, on Thomas Lincoln's own motion by attorney, his name was substituted as defendant. One George Lindsey also had his name substituted. This suit was over the Knob Creek farm Evidently Thomas Lincoln believed that he was right, and was ready to have the court determine the matter.

Had the case come promptly to trial, it is possible that Thomas Lincoln would not have removed from Kentucky, in which event a large volume of history would have been written otherwise than as it subsequently occurred. The trial was, however, postponed for two years and occurred on June 9, 1818. The trial was before a jury whose verdict is of record. The jury " sworn the truth to speak upon the issue joined, upon their oaths do say that the defendants are not guilty of the trespass, ejectment and detention of the premises in the declaration mentioned." Judgment follows " that the defendants recover of the plaintiff their costs." The records of this suit are found in Civil Order Books E and F, Hardin Circuit Court.

This suit for ejectment shows that the Knob Creek farm was part of a tract of ten thousand acres surveyed in 1784, and patented in 1786 by Thomas Middleton, father of the Hannah Rhoades who was one of the parties to the suit. She lived in Philadelphia, as did Abraham Sheridan, Inn Keeper, another plaintiff.

The jury found for the defendants; and the order of the Court was " that the plaintiff take nothing for his bill, but for his false claimour be in mercy, &c., and that the defendants go hence without a day, and recover against the lessors of the plaintiff their costs by them about their defense herein expended, and may have executors, etc."

In this, as in his earlier lawsuit, Thomas Lincoln was victorious

In 1816 Thomas Lincoln and his family migrated to Indiana, where his wife, Nancy Hanks, died, October 5, 1818. A year later he returned to Hardin County, Kentucky, and married Sarah Bush Johnston, who proved an excellent wife and a remarkably good step-mother to his children. She had previously married, March 13, 1806, Daniel Johnston, who died April, 1814. She died April 10, 1869.

A further record of Thomas Lincoln is found in Hardin County, Kentucky, in the marriage register, Book A, folio 96. There his marriage is entered in due form to Sarah Johnson. This is the spelling of her name as it is found in the Kentucky records, but her son John D. signed his name Johnston, and was so addressed by his step-brother Abraham Lincoln

Sarah Johnson, or Johnston, was a Miss Bush, and came of an excellent family. She was a great-aunt of W. P. D. Bush, reporter of the Court of Appeals of Kentucky from 1866 to 1879. There are fourteen volumes of the Kentucky reports edited by him, and familiarly known to Kentucky lawyers as the Bush Reports. Another great-nephew, F. H. Bush, still lives in Elizabethtown, an honored and venerable member of the local bar, and an old Confederate soldier. By her first marriage Sarah Bush was united to Daniel Johnson, jailer of Hardin County. The marriage occurred March 13, 1806, three months before Thomas Lincoln's marriage to Nancy Hanks. The marriage is recorded in Marriage Register A, folio 23. An undisputed tradition and one entirely credible, is that Thomas Lincoln made love to Sarah Bush before he sued for the hand of Nancy Hanks. It is wholly creditable to Thomas Lincoln that he returned for his second wife to where he was so well known as at Elizabethtown. His suit is said to have been favored by Sarah's male relatives who had accompanied Thomas Lincoln on a voyage down the river to New Orleans. Thomas Lincoln's marriage to Sarah Bush Johnson, or Johnston, occurred, December 2, 1819.

In March, 1830, Thomas Lincoln and his family, accompanied by John D. Johnston and his two sisters and their husbands, Dennis Hanks and Squire Hall, migrated to Macon County, Illinois, and settled on land near to that owned by John Hanks. Later, and after one or two experiments in location, he removed to Goosenest Prairie, near Farmington, Illinois, where he died, January 17, 1851.

Thomas Lincoln was about five feet nine or ten inches tall, and weighed about a hundred and eighty to a hundred and ninety-five pounds. He had a well-rounded face, dark hazel eyes, coarse black hair, and was somewhat round-shouldered. He was compactly built, so that Dennis Hanks said that he had never been able to find the point of separation between his ribs, though he often felt for it. He was slow of movement, slow of thought. Herndon describes him as careless, inert and dull. He was sinewy and of great strength He was disinclined to constant hard labor, but was capable of performing it when he chose. He was inoffensive, quiet and peaceable, but capable of strong anger and of fierce fighting. He was fond of jokes and stories, as was his illustrious son. While not a total abstainer, he was temperate in his use of liquor. He was neither a drunkard nor a gambler, nor is he known to have possessed any vicious habit. He was naturally indolent, and was lacking in ambition. He did not care for great physical comfort, and preferred to get on with few conveniences rather than exert himself unduly to obtain things which he did not greatly need. When John Hanks said of him that "pleasure was the end of life for him," he did not mean that Thomas Lincoln had any inclination toward sensuality, but that with sufficient hoe-cake and bacon he was reasonably content.

Thomas Lincoln was a religious man. In another book [1] I have shown the error of Herndon in his declaration that Thomas Lincoln was a Free Baptist in Kentucky, a Presbyterian in Indiana and a Disciple in Illinois. He was a Baptist, and not a Free Baptist, in Kentucky, Indiana and Illinois. Near the end of his life he became a New Light. But that was,

[1] *The Soul of Abraham Lincoln,* by William E. Barton, pp. 36-45.

from his point of view, no great change. He joined the Little
Pigeon Baptist Church in 1823, and was a consistent member
of it

In the tax lists of Washington County, Thomas Lincoln
first appears on May 11, 1796, as a white male above sixteen.
His name is not in the list for 1797, in which year he was
probably in East Tennessee. He appears in the list of 1800,
the date when listed being February 14. His name in this one
list is spelled " Thomas Lincorn," but in the others it is Lincoln. He owned one horse, and no other taxable property.
Again he appears, and with his name correctly spelled,
in 1800 and 1801, and was listed on August 5. He still owned
one horse.

It is interesting to note that in only one of these lists
is his name spelled other than " Lincoln." The report that
the name was uniformly known as Linkhorn, and that Abraham Lincoln changed it, is incorrect. Thomas was called Lincoln when a lad, he was married as Lincoln, and he signed his
name, as early as 1806, the date of the first known signature
and uniformly thereafter, as Lincoln.

It cannot fail to surprise us when we learn that Thomas
Lincoln at the age of twenty-three had ready cash to the
amount of 118 pounds with which to purchase a farm, which
appears to have been improved, but that thereafter he lived
upon farms in Kentucky to which he had no recorded title,
and that whatever land he occupied in other states in subsequent years he held precariously and lost it by abandonment,
mortgage or other such misfortune as came commonly to
the shiftless and improvident. It cannot fail to suggest the
question where he obtained the money for these initial purchases before his marriage.

I am not able to answer this question. The hypothesis
which I suggest is, that, on his return from East Tennessee,
when he was twenty-one or twenty-two, he secured a settlement of his father's estate which his eldest brother, Mordecai,
had held in trust until Thomas should reach his majority, and
that Thomas took his share of the estate in cash.

I have read in several books how his hard-hearted eldest

brother, Mordecai, taking full advantage of his legal rights under the old English law of primogeniture, defrauded this little lad out of his honest share in his father's estate, and how Thomas, by sheer force of character and resolute industry, earned money with which to buy the farm which he owned at twenty-three. That pretty tale may be true, but I doubt it. A man so industrious at twenty-three would not have been likely to part with so much of his industry thereafter, nor abandon a farm which he had earned by his own toil It is much more probable that he bought the Mill Creek farm when he was twenty-three, with money paid him by his older brothers on the settlement of his father's estate, a few months after Thomas attained his majority; and that he had more money then than he ever possessed at one time afterward so long as he lived.

John D. Johnston doubtless lied in the letter which he sent to Abraham Lincoln in the name of Thomas, when Abraham was in Congress, pleading for a gift of twenty dollars to save the Illinois farm from being sold under judgment: but he would not have told a lie of that character if he had not known that Abraham knew that only Abraham's generosity could be relied upon to keep a roof over the head of his father, or to prevent his incurring debts that would have robbed him of his home, except for the timely and repeated assistance of Abraham.

It is affirmed in many books that Thomas Lincoln and Nancy Hanks were first cousins. This statement is made on the assumption that Thomas Lincoln was the son of the first wife, Mary Shipley, of his father Abraham Lincoln Thomas Lincoln was the son and only child of Abraham Lincoln's second wife, Bathsheba Herring. The statement also assumes that Nancy Hanks was the daughter of Joseph Hanks and his wife Nancy Shipley. Mrs. Richard Berry, at whose home Nancy Hanks was married to Thomas Lincoln, was also a Lucy Shipley.

Lawyers in Hardin County assure me that the name of Thomas Lincoln is found on the records of the several courts in Hardin County as doing jury duty; but, as the jury lists are not indexed, such search as they have been able to make for me has not yet yielded results, and I must leave this to others or to my own future investigation. The tax-lists of Hardin County for the years of Thomas Lincoln's residence are lost; but there is in the Sheriff's office a book of Tax Delinquents which covers the years from 1798 to 1824, and the name of Thomas Lincoln is not contained in it. Even if he had owned no property his name would have been there had he not paid taxes; for there are hundreds of names of men delinquent on poll-tax who had no taxable property. But Thomas Lincoln had real estate in 1803, and always, so far as we know, a horse.

Thomas Lincoln's name, so far as official records go, is an honorable one. He paid his taxes; he had four lawsuits and won them all. The records contain nothing, so far as my researches have shown, that is not to his credit

To the credit of Thomas Lincoln, let it be remembered that he did not restrain Abraham from his securing of an education. Sarah Bush doubtless told Herndon truthfully of her part in the process:

"I induced my husband to permit Abe to read and study at home as well as at school. At first he was not easily reconciled to it, but finally he too seemed willing to encourage him to a certain extent."—Mrs. Thomas Lincoln, September 8, 1865; in *Herndon*, I, p. 33.

But it should be remembered that before the migration to Indiana Abe had had three brief terms of school in Kentucky, before Sarah Bush appeared on the scene. For this, doubtless, we have to thank Nancy Hanks, in good part. But Thomas Lincoln, who, after he had reached manhood, cared enough for education to learn " bunglingly to write his name," must have had some little interest in his son's progress in book-learning. It need not be assumed that he cared as much for it as either Nancy Hanks or Sarah Bush; but it is due him to remember that he did not oppose Abe's learning more than his father knew.

The interior wall of the Memorial erected over the Lincoln cabin contains an interesting inscription in honor of Thomas Lincoln. It is incorrect in some of its dates; Thomas Lincoln was not born in 1770, and he was twenty-nine and not twenty-five when he became "possessor of this cabin home and its neighboring acres." It is not known that he built any one of the houses which he occupied in Kentucky. The inscription reads:

THOMAS LINCOLN

January 20, 1770   January 17, 1851
Fifth in descent from Samuel Lincoln, weaver, who landed at Hingham, Massachusetts, May 26, 1637. Orphaned at six years of age by an Indian bullet, he grew up homeless in the wild woods of Kentucky. At twenty-five he was the possessor of this cabin and its neighboring acres. In 1818 he moved to Indiana, then a territory. Five years later he followed the tide of emigration to Illinois, where he lived a peaceable, industrious, respected citizen, a genial, honest and contented pioneer. With courage and energy he built with his hands five homes, each better than the preceding one. He won and held the love and confidence of two noble women, and he was the father of Abraham Lincoln.

"My father insisted that none of his children should suffer for the want of education as he had."—*Abraham Lincoln*

"He was a good carpenter for the times. He had the best set of tools in Washington County. The Lincolns had a cow and a calf, milk and butter, a good feather bed, for I have slept on it. They had a home-woven and single 'kilerlid' big and little pots, a loom and wheel. Tom Lincoln was a man, and took care of his wife. Reverend Jesse Head, the minister who married Tom Lincoln and Nancy Hanks, talked boldly against slavery, and Tom and Nancy Lincoln and Sarah Bush were just steeped full of Jesse Head's notions about the wrong of slavery and the rights of man as explained by Thomas Jefferson and Thomas Payne."—Professor T. C. Graham[2] of Louisville, Kentucky.

I am sure that the foregoing was written by Jenkin Lloyd Jones. Its language is very similar to that which he used in his address at the Lincoln Home. In that address I find another reference to the five houses, or possibly six, which Thomas Lin-

[2] Dr. Graham's name was Christopher Columbus Graham, not "T. C."

coln is supposed to have built with his own hands. In that he speaks of Thomas Lincoln as, " A man who built, with his own hands, three homes as I figure it, in Kentucky, and one in Indiana and perhaps two in Illinois, each one better than the last " It must not detract from our high appreciation of the excellence of this inscription if we remind ourselves that while Thomas Lincoln built for himself a home in Indiana, beside the " half-faced " camp whch sheltered him and his family during their first few months in that state, we have no reason to believe that he built any home for himself in Kentucky.

A distinguished authority has said,—
" Abraham Lincoln came of the most unpromising stock on the continent, ' the poor white trash ' of the South. His shiftless father moved from place to place in the western country, failing where everybody else was successful in making a living; and the boy had spent the most susceptible years of his life under no discipline but that of degrading poverty."— WOODROW WILSON, *Division and Reunion*, p. 216.

There is some truth in this, but it is not unqualifiedly true. Lincoln's parents were poor and they were white; but it does not follow that they were of the " poor white trash." Thomas Lincoln did, indeed, fail repeatedly, and fail where other men were succeeding; and none of the apologists for him have succeeded in proving him an industrious or thrifty man But it is not certain that the poverty upon which Abraham Lincoln looked back with such morbid sorrow was really degrading.

The author of this volume was born in the North; but he lived for seven years among people like the Lincolns and Hankses in Kentucky and Tennessee, and he does not like to hear them called " poor whites " or " mountain whites." He has eaten and slept on many a night in a cabin of one room, much like the cabin in which the Lincolns lived, and both as schoolmaster and as preacher he has shared the life of the kin of the Lincolns and the Hankses The Lincoln blood was good blood; and the Hanks blood had in it no vicious or criminal tendency.

Nicolay and Hay say of Thomas Lincoln:

" Thomas, to whom were reserved the honors of an illustrious paternity, learned the trade of a carpenter. He was an easy-going man, entirely without ambition, but not without self-respect. Though the friendliest and most jovial of gossips, he was not insensible to affronts· and when his slow anger was roused, he was a formidable adversary Several border bullies, at different times, crowded him indiscreetly, and were promptly and thoroughly whipped. He was strong, well-knit, and sinewy; but little over the medium height, though in other respects he seems to have resembled his son in appearance. . . .

" Thomas Lincoln joined the Baptist Church of Little Pigeon in 1823; his oldest child, Sarah, followed his example three years later. They were known as active and consistent members of that communion. Lincoln was himself a good carpenter when he chose to work at his trade. a walnut table made by him is still preserved as part of the furniture of the church to which he belonged."—NICOLAY AND HAY: *Abraham Lincoln; A History*, I, pp. 23, 32-33.

Perhaps the best tribute we have to the character of Thomas Lincoln is that of the minister of whose church he was a member in his last years, and who preached his funeral sermon on his death in 1851. Of him, in 1887, Rev Thomas Goodwin of Charleston, Illinois, wrote:

" In his case I could not say aught but good . . . He was a consistent member through life of the Church of my choice—the Christian Church or Church of Christ—and was, as far as I know—and I was a very intimate friend—illiterate, yet always truthful, conscientious and religious "—Quoted by HON. JOSEPH H. BARRETT, in *The New England Historical and Genealogical Register* for July, 1894; volume 48, p. 328.

CHAPTER XXIX

WHAT WE KNOW ABOUT NANCY HANKS

THE log cabin in which Abraham Lincoln was born stands now very near to its original site. It has been carted over the country to one exposition after another, and shown to the curious at twenty-five cents a head. While it was away, its supposed original site was marked by a post, which still is visible in the middle of the cabin floor, attesting that it stands where it stood immediately before its migrations began. Older persons, however, who remember the cabin before its occupant became President, inform me that it was built lower down and nearer the spring; and this I think probable. But it stands in a very fit and sightly place, a long line of polished stone steps leading up to it from the level of the spring, and reminding us that the way to such eminence involves a long climb. Inside the marble temple that enshrines the log cabin where Abraham Lincoln was born, are tablets to his parents. I copy that to Nancy Hanks, which I think must be from the facile pen of my friend, now dead, Jenkin Lloyd Jones.

NANCY HANKS LINCOLN
FEBRUARY 4, 1784—OCTOBER 5, 1818
Born in Virginia. When three years old, her parents, Joseph and Nancy (Shipley) Hanks, crossed the mountains into Kentucky. Orphaned at nine, she was adopted and reared by Richard and Lucy Shipley Berry, at whose home in Beechland, Washington County, Kentucky, she was married to Thomas Lincoln, June 12, 1806 [1] Of this union were born Sarah, Abraham and Thomas. The first married Aaron Grigsby and died in Indiana in 1828 The last died in infancy. The second lived to write the Emancipation Proclamation. The days of the distaff, the skillet, the Dutch oven, the open fireplace, with its iron crane, are no longer, but home-

[1] The tablet erroneously says "June 17, 1806"

making is still the finest of the fine arts. Nancy Hanks was touched with the divine aptitudes of the fireside. Loved and honored for her wit, geniality and intelligence, she justified an ancestry reaching beyond seas, represented by the notable names of Hanks, Shipley, Boone, Evans and Morris. To her was entrusted the task of training a giant, in whose childhood's memories she was hallowed. Of her he said, " My earliest recollection of my mother is sitting at her feet with my sister, drinking in the tales and legends that were read and related to us." To him on her deathbed she said, " I am going away from you Abraham, and I shall not return. I know you will be a good boy, that you will be kind to Sarah and your father. I want you to live as I have taught you, and love your heavenly Father."

 " All that I am or hope to be I owe to my angel mother."

Of Nancy Hanks William H. Herndon wrote:

Nancy Hanks, the mother of the President, at a very early age, was taken from her mother Lucy—afterward married to Henry Sparrow—and sent to live with her aunt and uncle, Thomas and Betsy Sparrow. Under this same roof the irrepressible and cheerful waif, Dennis Hanks, whose name will be frequently seen in these pages, also found a shelter. Dennis Hanks, still [1889] living at the age of ninety years in Illinois, was the son of another Nancy Hanks, the aunt of the President's mother. I have his written statement that he came into the world through nature's back door. He never stated, if he knew it, who his father was. At the time of her marriage to Thomas Lincoln, Nancy was in her twenty-third year. She was above the ordinary height in stature, weighed about 130 pounds, was slenderly built, and had much the appearance of one inclined to consumption. Her skin was dark; hair dark brown; eyes gray and small; forehead prominent; face sharp and angular, with a marked expression for melancholy which fixed itself in the memory of all who ever saw or knew her. Though her life was clouded by a spirit of sadness, she was in disposition amiable and generally cheerful. Mr. Lincoln himself said to me in 1851, on receiving news of his father's death, that whatever might be said of his parents, and however unpromising the early surroundings of his mother may have been, she was highly intellectual by nature, had a strong memory, acute judgment, and was cool and heroic. From a mental standpoint she no doubt rose above her surroundings, and had she lived, the stimulus of her nature would have accelerated her son's success, and she would have been a much more ambitious prompter than his father ever was.—*Life of Lincoln,* Vol. I, pp. 13-14.

Lamon describes her as:

A slender, symmetrical woman, of medium stature, a brunette, with dark hair, regular features, and soft, sparkling hazel eyes. Tenderly bred, she might have been beautiful; but hard labor and hard usage bent her handsome form, and imparted an unusual coarseness to her features long before the period of her death. Toward the close, her life and her face were equally sad; and the latter habitually wore the woeful expression which afterwards distinguished the countenance of her son in repose. By her family, her understanding was considered something wonderful. John Hanks spoke reverently of her "high intellectual forehead," which he considered but the proper seat of faculties like hers. Compared with the mental poverty of her husband and relatives, her accomplishments were certainly very great; for it is related by them with pride and delight that she could actually read and write. The possession of these arts placed her far above her associates, and after a little while even Tom began to meditate upon the importance of acquiring them. He set to work, accordingly, in real earnest, having a competent instructor so near at hand; and with much effort she taught him what letters composed his name, and how to put them together in a stiff and clumsy fashion. Henceforth he signed no more by making his mark; but it is nowhere stated that he ever learned to write anything else, or to read either written or printed letters.—LAMON: *Life of Lincoln,* p. 11.

Mrs. Hitchcock gives this picture of her appearance:
"Traditions of Nancy Hanks' appearance at this time (the time of her marriage) all agree in calling her a beautiful girl. She is said to have been of a medium height, weighing about 130 pounds, light hair, beautiful eyes, a sensitive mouth,

and a kindly gentle manner " (p. 51). " Bright, scintillating, noted for her keen wit and repartee, she had withal a loving heart " (p. 51). When she went to live with the Berrys, " Her cheerful disposition and active habits were a dower to those pioneers."—HITCHCOCK: *Nancy Hanks*, p 73.

These two traditions agree as to her weight. Herndon is more likely to be accurate than Mrs. Hitchcock where the accounts vary. He talked earlier with people who had known her personally. His authorities were John and Dennis Hanks and Sarah Bush Lincoln. But we do not have a very clear picture of her personality, though what we know commends her to our interest and regard.

The earlier descriptions agree that Nancy Hanks was dark, but recent sentimental literature tends to make her a blonde, and not to be content with her possession of all the womanly arts, enabling her to " spin the longest threads " as members of the Hanks family affirmed, but also, as in one recent book, *The Matrix,* by Maria Thompson Daviess, endowing her with masculine strength, so that she was famous as a champion at corn huskings, a breaker of colts, a driver of wild horses, and a woman of wonderful wit, vivacity and intellectual power.

The *Atlantic Monthly* for February, 1920, contained an article by Mr. Arthur E. Morgan, of Dayton, Ohio, who, in travels through the Ozark mountains came upon a branch of the Hanks family descended from Polly Hanks, the sister of Nancy, through her daughter Sophie. Sophie Hanks was just a month younger than President Lincoln. She is the sister who, according to Lamon, married Thomas Friend, and according to others married Jesse Friend. According to " The Doctor " a son of this Sophie Hanks, from whom Mr. Morgan obtained most of his information,—

" Sophie Hanks's mother, Sarah or Polly Hanks, was a sister of Lincoln's mother. Though she never married, she had six children, all of whom lived to maturity, bearing their mother's name Sophie Hanks died in November, 1895, but her three children, living in different parts of the Ozarks, retained a part of the information they received from her."

The name of " The Doctor " is not given; and the article

is reticent on a number of important points. It leaves upon the mind of the reader the question whether illegitimacy stopped with Polly Hanks. It is evident from the article that the children of Sophie Hanks were the children of more than one father; and whether she was married to these two or more men in turn is not stated. The Doctor, however, gives this very interesting information:

"Those stories about Abraham Linkhorn being an illegitimate child are untrue. Aunt Nancy and Uncle Tom were married regular. But his mother was an illegitimate child. I have always understood this from what my mother said about it. But my cousin said that our grandmother Hanks and Linkhorn's mother were half-sisters and also cousins. My mother never told me that, but I have often heard her say that we were badly mixed."

I was, of course, eager to know if Mr. Morgan had additional information, and I have troubled him with many letters. He has searched his notes for me, and he has given me all the additional information which he can obtain. I have incorporated it in the Appendix. Let me here call attention to the fact that while "The Doctor," whose name Mr. Morgan gives me as James Legrand,[2] states positively that Nancy Hanks was the illegitimate daughter of Lucy Hanks, John T. Hanks, son of Dennis Hanks and Elizabeth Johnston, and daughter of Abraham Lincoln's step-mother, affirms that she was a daughter of Joseph and Nancy Hanks.

Although the plan of this book does not contemplate investigation of the maternal line of Abraham Lincoln's ancestry, I desired to inform myself as accurately as possible on all questions of the family of Nancy Hanks which had or might have relation to the special field of this present inquiry. Mrs Hitchcock announced in 1909 that her *Nancy Hanks* would be followed soon by the publication of a complete Hanks genealogy. This would have been of considerable service, and I sought for it, but could not find that it had been published. I therefore wrote to the New England Historic Genealogical

---

[2] As this book goes to press, a letter informs me of the probably fatal illness of Dr Legrand

Society, as Mrs. Hitchcock was a New England woman and traced the Hanks family from a New England line, and I received this reply:

BOSTON, MASS., April 23, 1920.
DEAR SIR:

In reply to your letter of April 21 seeking information about a Mrs. Hitchcock who published a book on " Nancy Hanks" in 1909, I beg to say that we are unable to tell you whether Mrs. Hitchcock is still living or not; nor do we know where her manuscript relating to the Hanks family is at the present time.

Very truly yours,
THORNTON KIRKLAND LOTHROP, JR.,
Corresponding Secretary.

This ends my hope of securing in time for this volume any added light on the Hanks family from Mrs. Hitchcock or her manuscript For my purpose it does not greatly matter; but I think that authors who are hereafter to go into that side of the question should go more thoroughly into the inquiry than does her little book. I am not expressing the opinion that in this particular her book is inaccurate; I simply have not been able to confirm all of her affirmations, and I do not know where the data may be obtained.

Lea and Hutchinson, in their invaluable work on *The Ancestry of Abraham Lincoln,* have placed all students of this subject under permanent obligations to them, especially for their researches into the English ancestry. They have not always been discriminating in their research in American records, and I have discovered not a few errors in their book. In the matter of the Hanks genealogy, they accept almost without question the results of Mrs. Hitchcock's investigations; but this has not carried them out of the region of perplexity. They say:

While the indefatigable researches of a member of the Hanks family, Mrs. Caroline Hanks Hitchcock, have forever silenced by overwhelming and cumulative proofs the vicious and unclean fabrications and slanders which cast doubt on the parentage of the mother of the President, it is greatly to be deplored that the ascending line of her ancestry, beyond her parents, still remains without positive proof.   Two theories have been propounded of which both will be given here as worthy of respectful attention, but of which neither can be accepted by the writers as demonstrated beyond the reasonable doubt caused by lack of complete proof.   In other words, we still lack legal demonstration of the paternity of Joseph Hanks, husband of Nancy Shipley and father of Nancy Hanks, the mother of the President.—*The Ancestry of Abraham Lincoln,* p. 112.

The question of the identity of Joseph Hanks is, indeed, one of difficulty, and Lea and Hutchinson are not the only ones who have encountered it.   It is the same difficulty which confronts us at every turn in the annals of this family, with its meager records, its conflicting traditions, its overlapping generations and its reduplication of names.

The case of Joseph Hanks will serve to illustrate what meets us in other inquiries.   We need one Joseph Hanks, and we have three.   One of them appears as the father and two of them as the uncles of the mother of the President.   Surely there were not in the family three sons named Joseph.   Yet we have Joseph Hanks of Nelson County, dying in 1793, leaving to each of his five sons a horse and to each of his three daughters a heifer, of which the spotted one named " Piedy " was inherited by Nancy, the youngest daughter, and the rest of the estate to his wife, Nancy.   We also have Joseph Hanks, uncle of Nancy, living in Elizabethtown in 1808, in whose shop Thomas Lincoln was an apprentice.   And we have Joseph Hanks, uncle of Nancy, who was a shoemaker, and not a carpenter, and who married Sarah Freeman.   These are not all the Josephs, but they are more than enough to bewilder the genealogist.

I venture a suggestion which, if it should be found correct, would remove from this tangle one of the Josephs.   It is that Joseph Hanks, the carpenter, of Elizabethtown, was not the uncle, but the brother, of Nancy Hanks, the mother of the

President. Lamon, on information derived from Herndon, said, in 1872,—

"It was in the shop of her uncle, Joseph Hanks, of Elizabethtown, that he [Thomas Lincoln] essayed to learn the trade. We have no record of the courtship, but any one can readily imagine the numberless occasions that would bring together the niece and the apprentice."—*Life of Lincoln,* p. 10.

Later authorities have followed this without question, and so has the present author. But in one record in Elizabethtown I find a suggestion that this Joseph was not her uncle but her older brother. I have not investigated; but record the suggestion for what it may be worth.

Joseph owned rather large tracts of land in Hardin County, and did jury-duty there, as shown by the court records.

In the case of Nancy Hanks the situation is far more perplexing. I did not at any time intend to explore it, for at the outset I relied with entire confidence on Mrs Hitchcock.

She tells us of Nancy Hanks as born in Virginia, February 4, 1784, the daughter of Joseph and Nancy (Shipley) Hanks, the same Joseph who died in 1793, and left to his youngest daughter, Nancy, the spotted heifer calf. This Nancy was adopted and reared by Richard Berry and his wife, Lucy Shipley Berry, the latter being the sister of Nancy Shipley Hanks, and so the aunt of Nancy. From this home she was married, her uncle and guardian, Richard Berry, signing her marriage bond with the bridegroom, Thomas Lincoln. The will and the marriage bond are incontestable records, and the place of the marriage is as certain as human testimony can fix it at a date so remote, yet within the memory of living and credible witnesses who have left their signed and sworn and indisputable testimony. Although in other matters I have found Mrs Hitchcock's judgment subject to revision, she has in this particular too much of irrefutable fact to be disputed except on evidence much stronger than any that I have found. The age of this Nancy is essentially correct for her requirements as the wife of Thomas Lincoln, and if she did not marry him, we do not know what became of her. The will, the marriage bond, the place and date of marriage, all agree. More-

over, I have found in Washington County large groups of relatives and descendants of the Berrys and Shipleys and related
families, who all accept this theory, and who find that it fits
into their local traditions.   Mrs. Hitchcock is not, therefore,
to be lightly flouted when she identifies the mother of the
President with the little nine-year-old heiress of the Peid heifer.
In spite of all the inherent difficulties in the theory, I find
myself unable to escape from the logic of it   I still hold it
as on the whole the best theory of the paternity of Nancy
Hanks.   I had hoped that in the course of this inquiry into
a closely related question, I should have been able to clear up
the difficulties in a manner that would satisfy myself completely; I regret that I have not been able to do so.

What we encounter on the opposite side is the almost unanimous tradition of the Hanks family.   To be sure, they kept
few records, and their memories do not wholly agree   But
this is what they tell us about the mother of the President,
and it is what he himself apparently believed:

There were four Hanks sisters, Betsy, Polly, Nancy and
Lucy.   Betsy married Thomas Sparrow; Polly married Jesse
Friend; Nancy married Levi Hall and Lucy married Henry
Sparrow.   Before her marriage to Levi Hall, Nancy became
the mother of Dennis Hanks.   Before her marriage to Henry
Sparrow, Lucy became, in 1783, the mother of Nancy Hanks.
The two bridegrooms accepted their respective brides as they
were, but did not accept their illegitimate children, both of
whom were brought up by their maternal aunt, Betsy Hanks,
wife of Thomas Sparrow.   Nancy Hanks was called by the
name of Sparrow, not from the man who subsequent to her
birth married her mother, Lucy, but from her aunt Betsy and
her husband, Thomas Sparrow.   These were the only parents
she ever knew.   She called them father and mother.   They
journeyed to Indiana after her, lived and died with her, and
all their Indiana neighbors understood that they were her
parents.   All her Hanks cousins called Nancy, not Nancy
Hanks, but Nancy Sparrow   They knew nothing about her
relation to the Shipleys, or of her being the daughter of Joseph
Hanks.

They may have been mistaken. The President may have been mistaken, as he was mistaken about certain other matters concerning his relations. He was too sensitive about it to make many inquiries, and those which he made did not reassure him We cannot accept his immature opinions on a matter where he may so easily have been misled. But we may not throw out of court this whole body of Hanks tradition, tangled and difficult as it is.

There are certain facts on each side. The truth must be inclusive of all these facts and of such others as will explain their relation to each other. The unifying and clarifying truth has not yet been produced, and it will be very difficult to obtain it, for the reasons indicated.

I am writing thus concerning the question of the parentage of Nancy Hanks, partly because I wish to record all that is certainly known about her, and partly lest my silence, if I were to be silent, should be construed to mean that I have formed an adverse judgment. Such judgment I have not formed. The materials for a final judgment are not available. Moreover, this is not the question which I set out to answer; though I would gladly answer this in passing if I could do so.

The two dates given for the birth of Nancy Hanks, one an undesignated day in 1783, and the other, February 4, 1784, present no serious discrepancy; and both traditions place her birth as in Virginia. It is possible that some one will take the materials gathered by Mrs. Hitchcock, and those assembled by Mr. Knotts, which largely for this reason I am printing in this volume, and those that had previously been collected by Mr. Herndon, and after further, and I fear extended, investigation, present to us the true story of the parentage of Nancy Hanks. Until then, we have as our best documentary proof the will of Joseph Hanks, the marriage bond with his signature, a significant even if not a certain piece of evidence of guardianship, and in addition to these the clearly established fact that she was married under his roof, and that her relatives resident in that vicinity believe her to have been the legitimate daughter of Joseph Hanks, an honorable man, who died in 1793. There, until conclusive evidence is presented, my own mind is constrained to rest.

Miss Tarbell gives account of the parents, particularly of the mother, of Abraham Lincoln as follows:

The father, Thomas Lincoln, far from being a " poor white," was the son of a prosperous Kentucky pioneer, a man of honorable and well established lineage, who had come from Virginia as a friend of Daniel Boone, and had there bought large tracts of land and begun to grow up with the country, where he was killed by the Indians. He left a large family. By the law of Kentucky the estate went mainly to the oldest son, and the youngest, Thomas Lincoln, was left to shift for himself. This youngest son grew to manhood, and on June 10, 1806, was married, at Beechland, Kentucky, to a young woman of a family well known in the vicinity, Nancy Hanks. There is no doubt whatever about the time and the place of this marriage. All the legal documents required in Kentucky at that period for a marriage are in existence. Not only have we the bond and the certificate, but the marriage is duly entered in a list of marriage returns made by Jesse Head, one of the best-known early Methodist ministers of Kentucky. It is now to be seen in the records of Washington County, Kentucky. There is even in existence a very full and amusing account of the wedding and the fan-fare which followed by a guest who was present, and who for years after was accustomed to visit Thomas and Nancy. This guest, Christopher Columbus Graham, a unique and perfectly trustworthy man, a prominent citizen of Louisville, died only a few years ago.

But while these documents dispose effectually of the question of the parentage of Lincoln, they do not, of course, clear up the shadow which hangs over the parentage of his mother. Is there anything to show that Nancy Hanks herself was of clear and clean lineage as her husband? There had been nothing whatever until, a few years ago, through the efforts of Mrs. Caroline Hanks Hitchcock of Cambridge, Mass., who had in preparation the genealogy of the Hanks family in America, a little volume was published, showing what she had established in regard to Nancy Hanks. Mrs. Hitchcock had begun at the far end of the line—the arrival of one Benjamin Hanks in Massachusetts in 1699.

She discovered that one of his sons, William, moved to Virginia, and that in the latter part of the eighteenth century his children formed, in Amelia County of that State, a large settlement. All the records of these families she found in the Hall of Records in Richmond. When the migration into Kentucky began, late in the century, it was joined by many members of the Hanks settlement in Amelia County. Among others to go was Joseph Hanks with his wife, Nancy Shipley Hanks, and their children. Mrs. Hitchcock traced this Joseph Hanks, by means of land records, to Nelson County, Kentucky, where she found that he died in 1793, leaving behind a will, which she discovered in the records of Bardstown, Kentucky. This will shows that at the time of his death Joseph Hanks had eight living children, to whom he bequeathed property. The youngest of these was "My daughter Nancy," as the will puts it.

Mrs. Hitchcock's first query, on reading this will, was: "Can it be that this little girl—she was but nine years old when her father died—is the Nancy Hanks who sixteen years later became the mother of Abraham Lincoln?" She determined to find out. She learned from relations and friends of the family of Joseph Hanks still living that, soon after her father's death, Nancy went to live with an uncle, Richard Berry, who, the records showed, had come from Virginia to Kentucky at the same time that Joseph Hanks came. A little further research, and Mrs. Hitchcock found that there had been brought to light through the efforts of friends of Abraham Lincoln all the documents to show that in 1806 Nancy Hanks and Thomas Lincoln were married at Beechland, Kentucky. Now, one of these documents was a marriage bond. It was signed by Richard Berry, the uncle of the little girl recognized in the will of Joseph Hanks. Here, then, was the chain complete. The marriage bond and marriage returns not only showed that Nancy Hanks and Thomas Lincoln were married regularly three years before the birth of Abraham Lincoln, thus forever settling any question as to the parentage of Lincoln, but they showed that this Nancy Hanks was the one named in the will The suspicion in regard to the origin of Lincoln's mother was removed by this discovery of the will, for the recognition of any one as his child by a man in his will is considered by the law as sufficient proof of paternity.

Now what sort of people were Thomas Lincoln and Nancy Hanks? It has been inferred by those who have made no investigation of Thomas Lincoln's life that Nancy Hanks made a very poor choice of a husband. The facts do not entirely warrant this theory. Thomas Lincoln had been forced from his boyhood to shift for himself in a young and undeveloped country. He is known to have been a man who in spite of this wandering life contracted no bad habits. He was temperate and honest, and his name is recorded in more than one place in the records of Kentucky. He was a church-goer, and, if tradition may be believed, a stout defender of his peculiar religious views. He held advanced ideas of what was already an important public question in Kentucky, the right to hold negroes as slaves. One of his old friends has said of him and his wife, Nancy Hanks, that they were " just steeped full of notions about the wrongs of slavery and the rights of men, as explained by Thomas Jefferson and Thomas Paine." These facts show that he must have been a man of some natural intelligence. He had a trade and owned a farm.

As for Nancy Hanks, less that is definite is known of her. In nature, in education, and in ambition she was, if tradition is to be believed, far above her husband. She was famous for her spinning and her household accomplishments, it is said.

It was to these two people, then, that Abraham Lincoln was born on February 12, 1809. His birthplace was a farm Thomas Lincoln owned, and near Elizabethtown, Kentucky. The home into which the little chap came was the ordinary one of the poorer Western pioneer—a one-roomed cabin with a huge outside chimney. Although in many ways it was no doubt uncomfortable, there is no reason to believe it was an unhappy or a squalid one. The log house, with its great fire-place and heavy walls, is not such a bad place to live in—some of us are thankful to get away into the country to one now and then even in winter. Its furniture was simple, and no doubt much of it home-made. The very utensils were of home manufacture. The feathers in the beds were plucked from the geese Nancy Lincoln raised. She patched her own quilts, spun her own linsey-woolsey. No doubt Thomas Lincoln made Abraham's cradle and Nancy Lincoln spun the cloth for his first garments. They raised their own corn, dried their own fruit, hunted their own game, raised their own pork and beef. It was the hard life of the pioneer where every man provides for his own needs. It had discomforts, but it had, too, that splendid independence and resourcefulness which comes only from being sufficient to your own needs.

That the two people who endured its hardships and made in spite of them a home where a boy could conceive and nourish such ideals and enthusiasms as inspired Abraham Lincoln from his early years should have their names darkened by unfounded suspicions is a cruel injustice against which every honest and patriotic American ought to set his face.

In all the twenty-eight years of her life Nancy Hanks never was permitted to spend a year or even a day under a roof that she could legally have called her own. In her first twenty-two years she lived among her relatives. The humble cabin to which Thomas Lincoln took her on her marriage, and where she lived until her first child Sarah was a little more than a year old, was not his own; the lot in Elizabethtown which many years afterward he sold, came to him from his second wife. On the Brownfield farm he lived for a few months as a tenant. The Rock Spring farm on Nolin Creek where Lincoln was born was occupied by Thomas and Nancy Lincoln without any deed of record, and the title, or at least the equitable title, rested during his occupancy in a man with whom Thomas Lincoln is not known to have had any dealings. If after this he lived for a year in Washington County, as appears to have been the case, his home was presumably among his wife's relations, or possibly his own relations; he paid no taxes there on real estate. The Knob Creek farm, by far the most picturesque and fertile of his Kentucky holdings, he occupied without title so far as known, and removed from it without making a deed. He settled on government land in Indiana, and in the course of years entered it and received a patent from the government for half of that which he originally entered; but before he received his patent Nancy had died. She could have sung with some of the old time camp-meeting preachers:

> No foot of land do I possess,
> No cabin in this wilderness,
>   Till I my Canaan gain.

Like her husband, Nancy Hanks was a Baptist. So far as we know, their association with Rev. Jesse Head, who was a local Methodist deacon at Springfield, was casual; but Dr. Christopher Columbus Graham affirms that Mr. Head was a strong abolitionist, and that Thomas and Nancy were well saturated with abolition principles which they learned from him. This may be true, but we have no other witness to this. Dr. Graham was a truthful man, but was a very old man when he made this statement. The minds of old men tend to elaborate such themes. The statement that Jesse Head was an abolitionist is not at all improbable. But I have not found other evidence than this that Thomas Lincoln was an abolitionist. However, his son, Abraham, could say that he could not remember a time when he did not believe slavery to be wrong; and it is easily possible that Thomas Lincoln held to this same opinion, and that he may have learned it, or been strengthened in it, by Jesse Head. It is easy to believe that Nancy would have shared this opinion, and there is no good reason to contradict Dr. Graham; though we could wish we had confirmatory proof.

The name Nancy became such a general favorite in the Hanks family, it would be interesting to discover, if possible, who was the original Nancy Hanks. Apparently that name came into the Hanks list of family names with the marriage of James Hanks of Virginia, son of William. The name of his wife was Nancy. James, it will be remembered, removed to South Carolina with his brothers John, Joseph and Luke. We know nothing about the personality of Mrs James Hanks, but it is not going far into the realm of imagination to conjecture that this daughter-in-law of the family must have been attractive and good, since all branches of the family appear to have begun at once the practice of naming their daughters after her; and thus the name came into immediate and permanent prominence in that family.

CHAPTER XXX

DID LINCOLN HONOR HIS FATHER?

THOMAS and Abraham Lincoln had some traits in common, such as their coarse black hair, their deep-set gray eyes, their ability to tell, and their enjoyment in the telling of, a good story, and their disinclination to perform needless manual labor. Neither of them ever demanded too much in the way of physical comfort; Abraham to the end of his life never was fastidious about his bed or his food, or knew or seemed to care whether the sheets were clean or the food was well cooked. Thomas, as Lamon says, "was satisfied with indifferent shelter, and a diet of corn-bread and milk was all he asked. John Hanks naively observes that 'happiness was the end of life with him'" (*Life of Lincoln,* p. 15). Abraham was much like Thomas in this, preferring meager physical comfort to too great physical exertion, and being quite indifferent to the refinements of living.

Beyond this, they were not very congenial. If Thomas Lincoln did not like to work, he wanted Abe to work; and Abe was given to joking, to mounting a stump and orating, not only to the total interruption of his own labor in the field, but the labor also of Dennis Hanks and John Johnston, who were very willing to stop work and sit down while Abe delivered stump speeches or sermons. There is good reason to believe that this more than once vexed the righteous soul of Thomas Lincoln, who was vicariously industrious, and that some incidents of reproof and perhaps physical castigation lie behind Colonel Chapman's statement, derived doubtless from his wife, and by her from her father Dennis Hanks, and so with abundant opportunity for exaggeration, that " Abe's father treated him with habitual cruelty."—LAMON, *Life of Lincoln,* p 40.

The only specific instance, however, that has come down

to us, of the cruelty of Thomas Lincoln, is that he is alleged by Dennis to have knocked Abe off the fence for answering a traveler's questions about the road. (LAMON, *Life of Lincoln,* pp. 40 and 77.) But it is evident, first, that this incident was exceptional, and secondly, that we do not have the whole story. If we knew all the facts, we probably should learn that Abe sat on the fence for a good while and chatted with the passing stranger while Thomas waited for him to return and hoe out his row. If all that Abe did was to answer a civil question, it was not necessary for him to climb the fence and sit upon the top rail. He could have answered from the field. Thomas may have been unduly harsh, but he probably had provocation. The top of a rail fence was an attractive place for Abraham Lincoln, who had more than one reason to think highly of fence rails.

We are justified in moderating somewhat Colonel Chapman's statement which is to be taken with some abatement. The most that we need believe is Dennis Hanks' direct answer to Herndon's question, "Did Thomas Lincoln treat Abe cruelly?"

"He (Tom) loved him. I never could tell whether Abe loved his father very well or not. I don't think he did, for he was one of those forward boys. I have seen his father knock him down off the fence when a stranger would ask the way to a neighbor's house. Abe always would have the first word. The old man loved his children."—LAMON: *Life of Lincoln,* p. 77.

This is definite as to Thomas Lincoln's love for Abe, spite of his rough discipline; and it is about what we might expect as to Abe's love for his father. Abe was "forward," always wanted the first word with a passing stranger, and in no haste to say the last word, and how much he loved the man whom he rather quickly outgrew in intellectual attainment and in ambition, we are not sure. He does not appear to have had an affection rooted in mutual interests and common sympathies, but he loved him as much, apparently, as such a son would have been likely to love such a father; and to say that is not to speak very ill of either of them.

Sarah Bush Lincoln told Herndon that she was interested in Abe's love of books, and obtained for him leisure to read and study. Thomas Lincoln appears to have acceded to her request as cheerfully as, under all the conditions, might have been expected. But it is not to be supposed that he entered into all the hopes and vague longings of this lazy, moody, dreamer.

If half the marriages can be said to be of persons perfectly adapted to be each other's life companions, there remain the other half more or less imperfectly matched. Of these, it may be presumed, the wife is the husband's superior in at least half the cases. Certainly Sarah Bush was, in education and social standing and ambition, the superior of Thomas Lincoln, and there are cases of this sort, not a few.

Every one who will look around him can discover without difficulty families in which a mother cherishes higher ambitions for her son than that he shall follow in the footsteps of his father. In many cases the father shares the ambition of his wife and son, feeling painfully his own lack of youthful advantages and making large sacrifice that his son may rise higher in the world than he has been able to rise. But it is not always so. Sometimes such a father, even though willing to do all that seems to him necessary for his son's welfare, sees no necessity for educating him above his father's station and his own probable station in life.

In such a home there is no question of legitimacy; but the mother, and not the father, becomes the interpreter of the boy's best impulses. Father is good, but he does not understand. The boy shares his hopes with his mother, and she keeps all these things in her heart, as mothers do, and ponders them.

It is the ambition of the average American man to create for his wife a leisure which he does not share, and for his an opportunity greater than his own. American fathers not ungenerous as a rule. Nevertheless, cases are not in which the wife has received the better education, has up her reading, and encourages her son in ambitions to wh the father is almost a stranger.

It is easy to understand that in the home of Thomas L.

coln, situated as it was declared by Lincoln to have been, in a region in which " There was absolutely nothing to excite ambition for education," as he wrote to Jesse W. Fell, it was hardly to have been expected that Thomas and Abraham Lincoln would have lived together for twenty-one years in complete sympathy.

On the other hand, it is not known that they quarreled, and Abraham does not appear to have cherished toward his father any deep resentment or personal hatred. On the contrary, what evidence we have of his feeling toward his father, indicates that he cared for him as much as could reasonably have been expected under all conditions.

After Abraham Lincoln was of age, and might have claimed his own time, and was eager for his freedom, he remained with his father long enough to see him established in his new home in Illinois, and thereafter he sent him money as long as he lived. Lamon, who does his best to make his readers think that Abe cared little for his father, says that the remittances were sent to his step-mother. This probably is true. She was the more literary of the two, and money sent to her should have been safer than if sent to Thomas, for she was likely to spend it for necessities; but it is doubtful whether her son John did not coax the most of it away from her. Lamon says:

" As soon as Abraham got up a little in the world, he began to send his step-mother money, and continued to do so until his own death; but it is said to have ' done her no good,' for it only served to tempt certain persons about her, and with whom she shared it, to continue in a life of idleness."— LAMON: *Life of Lincoln*, p. 76.

Abraham did, however, give and send money direct to his father. When Lincoln was on his circuit he repeatedly visited his father's home, and left money, and he was importuned by his father from time to time to send him more. So far as is known, he invariably did so.

The most damaging answer to the question whether Abraham Lincoln honored his father, has been given by Lamon in his *Life of Lincoln*, in a letter of Abraham Lincoln, dated

Washington, December 24, 1848, in which he appears to question his father's veracity; and Lamon does not hesitate to call attention to the fact. The letter is as follows:

WASHINGTON, Dec. 24th, 1848.

MY DEAR FATHER:

Your letter of the 7th was received night before last. I very cheerfully send you the twenty dollars, which sum you say is necessary to save your land from sale. It is singular that you should have forgotten a judgment against you; and it is more singular that the plaintiff should have let you forget it so long, particularly as I suppose you have always had property enough to satisfy a judgment of that amount. Before you pay it, it would be well to be sure that you have not paid it; or, at least, that you cannot prove you have paid it. Give my love to Mother, and all the connections.

Affectionately your son,

A. LINCOLN.

The implication appears a fair one. Abraham Lincoln, in receipt of a piteous appeal from his father to send him twenty dollars to save his land from being sold under judgment, sent the money, but did not believe that the land was in danger of being sold under judgment. Did Abraham Lincoln believe Thomas Lincoln a liar?

I did not know the answer to this question until Mr. W. K. Bixby of St. Louis who had owned the original letter presented me a photographic fac-simile of it.

This letter occupies the first fifteen lines on the first page of a four-page letter sheet, and below it and on the following pages is Abraham Lincoln's letter to his step-brother, John D. Johnston. Lamon had both these letters, or copies of them, and printed them both, but not together. Their significance is in the fact that they were written on the same sheet. The letter to Johnston as Lamon says, makes Johnston an intimate acquaintance of the reader; but the acquaintance is made more intimate by the knowledge, which Lamon withheld, if indeed he knew it, that the two letters are virtually one. The second letter, without separate date or post-office, begins on the line below the first signature of Abraham Lincoln:

DEAR JOHNSTON:

Your request for eighty dollars I do not think it best to comply with now. At the various times when I have helped you a little you have said to me, " We can get along very well now," but in a very short time I find you in the same difficulty again. Now this can only happen by some defect in your conduct. What that defect is, I think I know. You are not *lazy*, but you *are* an *idler*. I doubt whether since I saw you you have done a good whole day's work in any one day. You do not very much like to work, and still you do not work much, merely because it does not seem to you that you could get very much for it. This habit of uselessly wasting time, is the whole difficulty; and it is vastly important to you, and still more so to your children, that you should break this habit. It is more important to them, because they have longer to live, and can keep out of an idle habit before they are in it easier than they can get out after they are in.

You are now in need of some ready money; and what I propose is, that you shall go to work " tooth and nail " for somebody who will give you money for it. Let father and your boys take charge of things at home—prepare for a crop and make the crop; and you go to work for the best money wages, or in discharge of any debt you owe, that you can get. And to secure you a fair reward for your labor, I now promise you that for every dollar you will, between this and the first of next May, get for your own labor either in money or in your own indebtedness, I will then give you one other dollar. By this, if you hire yourself at ten dollars a month, from me you will get ten more, making twenty dollars a month for your work. In this I do not mean that you shall go off to St. Louis or the lead mines, or to the gold mines, in California, but I mean for you to go at it for the best wages you can get close at home, in Coles County. Now if you will do this, you will soon be out of debt, and what is better, you will have a habit that will keep you from getting in debt again. But if I should now clear you out, next year you will be just as deep as ever. You say you would almost give your place in Heaven for $70 or $80. Then you value your place in Heaven very cheaply, for I am sure you can with the offer I make you get the seventy or eighty dollars for four or five months' work. You say if I furnish you the money you will deed me the land, and

if you don't pay the money back, you will deliver possession—
Nonsense! If you can't now live *with* the land how will you
then live without it? You have always been kind to me, and I
do not mean to be unkind to you. On the contrary, if you will
but follow my advice, you will find it worth more than eight
times eighty dollars to you.

Affectionately your brother,

A. LINCOLN.

Now we know the whole story. Abraham Lincoln knew
that Johnston was the author of both requests, the eighty
dollars for himself and the twenty dollars for Thomas Lincoln. Abraham sent the latter sum, though showing plainly
that he was not deceived by the hard-luck story which accompanied the request, a story doubtless written by Johnston, to
which Thomas Lincoln may have "bunglingly signed his
name."

I am not aware that any writer has discovered the fact,
or in any event the significance of the fact, that Abraham Lincoln's letter of December 24, 1848, to his father, was on the
same sheet with a letter to Johnston, and was virtually a part
of the same letter. Certainly Nicolay and Hay had no sense
of this relation. They printed the two letters separated by a
considerable space in time and in book pagination, and as this
leaves the Johnston letter without a date, they supplied the
conjectural date, January 2, 1851, which is a very bad guess,
as will be seen by their *Abraham Lincoln: Complete Works*,
two volume edition; volume I, pages 147, 164-5; and the
Gettysburg edition, twelve volumes, volume II, pages 96, 144-
146. This date, which Nicolay and Hay supplied as conjectural, other compilations took over from them without question, as in the Putnam Edition, volume II, and also in the
Current Literature edition of the Life and Works of Abraham Lincoln; Letters, volume II.

So far as the letter to Johnston is concerned, the date is not
very important; but as affording the basis of an interpretation
of the spirit of Lincoln's letter to his father, and his alleged
belief that his father was not telling him the truth, the date is
of very great importance; and the fact that the two letters were

written on one sheet shows that Lincoln knew who was lying, and that he wanted Johnston to know that he knew.

Lincoln's letter to his father was all that under the circumstances it ought to be, and he was generous in sending the money, which, as we know from other sources, Abraham more than suspected Johnston would be likely to share. His offer to Johnston was more than generous, and his letter was in every way admirable.

We must remember that at this period Lincoln himself was under a heavy strain. He was just paying the last of his "national debt" that had been a millstone about his neck ever since the days of his disastrous merchandizing at New Salem. He already knew that he was not to return to Congress, and he needed all his money, but he was generous with it.

My impression is that at this time members of Congress were paid a per diem, and that it then was, or later was increased to be, eight dollars a day. In my boyhood, which was long after the time of this correspondence, I heard a song like this:

> "In Washington full once a year
> Do politicians throng,
> Contriving there by various arts
> To make their session long;
> And many a reason do they give
> Why there obliged to stay,
> But the clearest reason yet adduced
> Is eight dollars a day"

To John D. Johnston eight dollars a day seemed the zenith of affluence, and its possessor a plutocrat to be plucked and plundered, and he was more skilled in devising ways of making Abraham divide his wealth than he was in producing an honest living for himself and his children. These letters appear to have been both wise and generous. They afford no reason for the conclusion that Abraham Lincoln did not honor his father, but they show that he was magnanimous and at the same time discriminating toward his indolent step-brother.

A family that has always lived upon a farm in conditions far from market, where very nearly everything eaten and worn is produced upon the land, handles very little money, and has a distorted notion of the value of money. Thomas Lincoln probably seldom handled two hundred dollars of actual cash in a year. When Abraham moved to Springfield, and received fees of twenty dollars for a day's work in court, and sometimes took in as much as an hundred dollars in a single month, his relatives could have no real measure of his prosperity. How could they understand that that very year, 1848, in which this twenty dollars was requested, was that to whose close Abraham was looking forward with hope long deferred, of paying the last of his "national debt" incurred while he sold goods at New Salem?

It appears to be true that Lincoln neglected the graves of both his father and his mother; that the grave of Nancy Hanks was not marked until 1879, when Mr. P. E. Studebaker of South Bend, Indiana, erected a suitable marble slab above it; and that the grave of his father was visited by him in February of 1861, at which time he made, and promptly forgot, a promise to erect a stone above it.

With reference to this it must be said that the grave of Nancy Hanks shared the fate of all graves in that part of the wilderness at that time. There probably was no marble slab within many miles of Gentryville. As to his father's grave, it must be admitted that Lincoln lacked appreciation of situations which were out of sight, and when he was away from his father's grave it was easy for him to forget it. On the other hand, it must be remembered that while Mr. Lincoln had accumulated some money prior to the campaign of 1860, he had to borrow money to go to Washington for his inauguration, and that the extravagance of Mrs. Lincoln and other causes kept him constantly in debt, so that he died in arrears. He may have hoped from month to month that next month he would have a little spare money, and so have neglected it till it passed from mind as a duty requiring immediate attention. He ought not to have forgotten; but the fact that he did so does not of necessity imply that he did not honor his father.

It is true that Abraham Lincoln did not go to see his father when the latter was dying. There was sickness in his own home, and he also said frankly that it was doubtful whether if he could go it would be more pleasant than painful. But it is also true that he wrote insisting that his father should have every attention, and that no medical or other care should be lacking; and the tone in which he wrote concerning faith and the life to come implies not only that he had a sincere religious faith of his own, but that he honored his father's religion. This is not the kind of letter Abraham Lincoln would have written to a man whom he believed to be a hypocrite. The letter is addressed to John D. Johnston:

SPRINGFIELD, Jan. 12, 1851.

DEAR BROTHER: On the day before yesterday I received a letter from Harriet, written at Greenup. She says she has just returned from your house, and that father is very low and will hardly recover. She also says that you have written me two letters, and that, although you do not expect me to come now, you wonder that I do not write. I received both your letters; and although I have not answered them, it is not because I have forgotten them, or not been interested about them, but because it appeared to me that I could write nothing which could do any good. You already know I desire that neither father nor mother shall be in want of any comfort, either in health or sickness, while they live; and I feel sure you have not failed to use my name, if necessary, to procure a doctor or anything else for father in his present sickness. My business is such that I could hardly leave home now, if it were not, as it is, that my wife is sick abed. (It is a case of baby-sickness, and I suppose is not dangerous.) I sincerely hope father may yet recover his health; but, at all events, tell him to remember and call upon and confide in our great and good and merciful Maker, who will not turn from him in any extremity. He notes the fall of a sparrow, and numbers the hairs of our heads; and He will not forget the dying man who puts his trust in Him. Say to him, that if we could meet now, it is doubtful whether it would not be more painful than pleasant; but that, if it be his lot to go now, he will soon have a joyous meeting with loved ones gone before, and where the rest of us, through the help of God, hope ere long to join him.

Write me again when you receive this.

Affectionately,

A. LINCOLN.

Such evidence as is before us justifies the conclusion that, while Abraham in his youth smarted under the restraints of a lazy and spasmodically exacting and more or less unsympathetic father, he did not fail either then or afterward to yield to him a large measure of sincere respect. There is no evidence of hostility or hatred or contempt, but on the contrary, a large degree of thoughtful consideration which continued to the end of his father's life. A more ardent love could be imagined, but filial duty and honor were not lacking.

We have no reason to suppose that Thomas Lincoln was ever despised in any community in which he lived. Far back in Kentucky, when he was very poor, Miss Tarbell found, and recorded in her *Early Life of Lincoln* book accounts which showed that he had local credit, and that he paid his debts. His reputation there cannot have been bad, for he went directly back in quest of his second wife, who knew all about him. Lamon records, on the authority of Dennis Hanks, that her own judgment and heart were assisted by the advice of her male relatives, with some of whom Thomas Lincoln had made journeys to New Orleans. If Sarah Bush who knew what the women said about him. and her male friends who " all liked Lincoln " were in accord, the fact speaks well for Thomas Lincoln.

In a word, there is no reason to credit an otherwise unproved story of bastardy to account for whatever we know of lack of sympathy between Thomas and Abraham Lincoln. We understand the situation well enough to be rather well satisfied with what we learn of the relations between them. If they were not those of ardent affection, they were those of mutual regard; on the side of Thomas it is to be remembered that, though at the instance of Sarah, his wife, he did not forbid Abraham to study; on the side of Abraham it is to be remembered that he did a son's duty to the end.

CHAPTER XXXI

DID LINCOLN HONOR HIS MOTHER?

SOME of Lincoln's references to his mother appear to have been intended for Sarah Bush. Between him and her existed a strong bond of sympathy which lasted on his side during his life and on her part after he had gone. Herndon did valuable service in giving to posterity his interview with her in 1866. It showed an affection on her part for Abraham and on Abraham's for her which is worthy of all admiration

But some of Lincoln's references to his mother cannot refer to Sarah Bush. When Lincoln said to Herndon, " God bless my mother; all that I am, or ever hope to be, I owe to her," he certainly did not refer to Sarah Bush; for that was the conversation in which he confided to Herndon his belief that his mother was the illegitimate daughter of a Virginia planter of good family, and that he had inherited through this unnamed grandfather the qualities that distinguished him.

So far forth, therefore, we know that Lincoln held the memory of his mother in honor. And there are other references to his mother which may, at least, refer to her. All his allusions to his " mother," whether intended for Nancy Hanks or Sarah Bush, are affectionate. He remembered both mothers with tender regard.

The story has been told that the boy Abraham, sad to think that his mother should have been buried without religious service, procured the attendance of Rev David Elkin to preach her funeral sermon some months after the burial. In another book the author has dealt with this story.[1] The truth is that it was not the custom among the people to whom

---

[1] See *The Soul of Abraham Lincoln*, by William E. Barton. George H Doran Company, New York

the Lincolns belonged to have the funeral at the time of burial. There was nothing unusual about the funeral of Nancy Hanks Lincoln

In the state of society in which Lincoln was born and spent his youth, there was little pride of family. In the backwoods of Kentucky and Indiana "kin and kin in law did not count a cuss." If there was a stain on the family escutcheon, it did not carry the disgrace which attached to the bar sinister in some conditions of life. It was recognized that "Accidents will happen, in the best regulated families," and when they happened, the best possible was made of them. If one or more of the Hanks sisters gave birth to a baby before she was married, that was recognized as an undesirable situation. But there was no hiding of it She had no opportunity to go away to a hospital, under pretense of visiting relations in the city, and having her child cared for by a foundlings' home. In the backwoods, the babies which the family "sorter fell heir to" were taken in and kept and brought up with the other children. They knew and felt a difference between them and other children, but they were not disinherited. The mother felt the disgrace, but it was not always a hopeless disgrace. Dennis Hanks was born before his mother was married; but she married, and behaved herself, and had other children, and Dennis grew up happy and by no means crushed by the misfortune of his birth. He married, and his children married well, and are not ashamed of their name.

Whether there is more or less immorality in primitive settlements than in more refined society, the author does not care to discuss; he has seen and knows both sorts. But that in primitive society is the more frank and honest. It is often unmoral rather than deliberately immoral.

We know more or less about the relatives of Nancy Hanks,—her half-sisters and her cousins and her aunts. They were women of a primitive type, nor lacking in fine qualities; and if they were any of them weak and primitive in their passion, they were not degenerate.

The Lincolns and Hankses were not abnormal people. They were fair specimens of a large part of the population flowing in the early part of the nineteenth century from Kentucky into Indiana and Southern Illinois.

But if Gentryville had little place or occasion for pride of family, the same was not true of New Salem, where the Rutledges felt themselves to be representatives of the finest families of South Carolina. Lincoln could not contemplate marrying Ann Rutledge without considering the relative standing of the Rutledges with their record stretching back to colonial days, and always with honor, and the Lincolns and Hankses. When he arrived in Springfield the situation was worse. There he met men whose ancestors came over on the *Mayflower,* and others who claimed descent from the First Families of Virginia. When he wrote his little biography for campaign purposes, and told how he came of Virginia's " second families," he knew the difference between the patricians of Virginia and the poor whites.

When he began to think of marrying Mary Todd, he met the same contrast. He had occasion to remember, as he had not had occasion in his earlier years, about the privations of his boyhood, and the low estate of his family. He grew morbid about it. He felt more sensitive than an entirely normal man should have felt. The memories of his childhood, which had not been intolerable at the time, grew painful in the retrospect.

But there is no occasion to believe that he ever despised his mother or thought of her otherwise than with affection.

What would Lincoln have said or thought if he had believed himself to have been the son of another and a better man than Thomas Lincoln? How greatly would he have blamed his mother for giving to the world a greater man than Thomas Lincoln could have begotten? He read Shakespeare, not entire, but with interest, and he probably at one time or another read King John. Would he have said to Nancy Hanks what Bastard said to his mother, Lady Falconbridge?

Bastard. Madam, I was not old Sir Robert's son;
Sir Robert could not do it; we know his handiwork:
Therefore, good mother, to whom am I beholden for these
limbs?
Sir Robert never holp to make this leg.

Lady Falconbridge. King Richard Coeur de Lion was thy father

Bastard. With all my heart I thank thee for my father,
Who lives and dares to say thou did'st not well,
When I was got, I'll send his soul to hell

It would neither be safe nor fair to accept the judgment of Dennis Hanks at its face value on the attitude of Abraham Lincoln toward his relatives. It is evident in the material which he furnished Herndon that Dennis was no violet blushing to a mossy stone. He charged Herndon to remember that his book would not be a success unless it had much in it about Dennis:

"I will say this much to you: if you don't have my name very frequently in your book, it will not go."—LAMON: *Life of Lincoln,* p. 41

John Hanks has more that commends him to our high regard than Dennis, but even he had quite a sufficiently exalted idea of his own importance. Many years ago, an American actor then in Great Britain, endeavored to write a play about him. It does not appear to have been a great success, though the same thing has been done of late by John Drinkwater, and the public has received the play with enthusiasm. In this earlier attempt, the playwright obtained his material from John Hanks. It is interesting for many reasons, one of which is that it is difficult to tell who is the real hero, John or Abraham.[2]

We need not be surprised that Dennis was somewhat disappointed that Abraham did not distribute offices more freely among the Hankses, and that Johnston thought he did not do enough for his parents. On the whole, even these witnesses give Abraham a very good record.

In recalling the attitude of Abraham Lincoln toward his relations, one thing is to be remembered, and that is that we know of these relations almost wholly through people who were disappointed that Lincoln did not give them office. Abraham Lincoln, himself a persistent office-seeker, did not like to be bothered by office-seekers, especially by those who pleaded

[2] *The Tragedy of Abraham Lincoln,* in five acts. By an American artist Glasgow: Published by James Brown & Son There is no date on the title page, but the copyright is of 1876. The author, unnamed, was Hiram D Torrie It is said that only twenty-six copies of this pamphlet are in existence, most of them with scorched edges.

favors they had done him, or kinship with him, and whom he knew to be incompetent. Lamon was made Marshal of the District of Columbia by Lincoln, and was kept in that position by him in spite of protest in high places, but there is reason to believe that Lamon was none too grateful. Herndon is alleged to have wanted an office, and would not take the one which Lincoln offered him. John D. Johnston, Lincoln's worthless half-brother, was ready for anything, and finally got a concession to make daguerreotypes in the army, but was not satisfied with that. Old John Hanks, who could not read, was an eager applicant for office. Dennis was ready for anything from the postoffice at Farmington to a place in the Cabinet.

These people could not very well discuss Lincoln's relations to his family without some prejudice. Yet they agree in such statements as are here recorded, and they are, on the whole, highly creditable to Lincoln.

When Dennis was asked about this matter, he said that in his judgment Lincoln "done more for John Johnston than he deserved." He also recorded that John did not think Abe did enough for the old people, which is not surprising, considering who got the money that Abe sent to them.

CHAPTER XXXII

A FINAL WORD ABOUT HERNDON

WILLIAM H. HERNDON was born in Greensburg, Kentucky, on December 28, 1816. Two years later, his father, Archer G. Herndon, moved to Troy, Madison County, Illinois; and thence, in 1821, to Sangamon County, to a farm five miles northeast from Springfield. This was nine years before the Lincolns came to Illinois, and while Chicago was a microscopic village. Archer Herndon was active in efforts to make Illinois a slave-state; but his son, William, imbibed anti-slavery views at Illinois College, for which reason his father removed him from that school before the completion of his course. In 1825 Archer Herndon moved to Springfield, and erected a tavern, which was not good for his son.

Young Herndon first saw Lincoln in 1832, when Lincoln was engaged as assistant to Rowan Herndon, a cousin of William, as pilot of the *Talisman,* the famous little steamer on the Sangamon River. Many years later he became Lincoln's partner, and continued in that relation until Lincoln's election; the partnership was never formally dissolved, and the sign "Lincoln and Herndon" continued to adorn their office in Springfield until the death of Lincoln.

Herndon served as Mayor of Springfield, a position in which Lincoln had no interest; for local politics never troubled him. Herndon, though a victim of alcohol, was an advocate of temperance, the earliest directory of Springfield showing his name as an officer in a temperance lodge; one of his early publications, like one of the earliest of Lincoln, being a temperance address. Herndon was counted an infidel, and sometimes accepted the term; but his three daughters, separately, have testified to me that their father constantly taught them reverence for God. He wrote to Theodore Parker:

" I love and reverence religion with all my whole soul; it is as deep in me as my being."

Herndon's study of Lincoln may be said to have begun with his acquaintance with the future President, and it continued until the death of Herndon. A few days before he died he wrote to Horace White:

I am still diligently gathering well-authenticated facts about Lincoln. Many I reject, because they are not in harmony with the fundamental elements in his nature, and because they came to me in unauthentic shape. I expect to continue gathering facts about Lincoln as long as I live, and when I go hence, the reading world shall have the manuscripts, unchanged and un-altered, just as I took them down. I think they will be of value to mankind some time. I have been at this business since 1865. Every day I think of some fact, and it suggests other facts. The human mind is a curious thing. I have been sick all winter.

On March 14, 1891, he died on his farm five miles from Springfield, his invalid son dying earlier on the same day. His last words were:

" I have received my summons. I am an over-ripe sheaf; but I will take the weaker one with me."

His life possessed many contradictions. He was an ardent temperance man, and a drunkard. He was an early and sincere Republican, but in his later years affiliated with the Democrats. He believed in God, and had a reverent regard for much that was high and noble in religion, but was called and called himself an infidel. He loved Lincoln with passionate admiration, and is remembered as the chief of sinners among Lincoln's detractors.

Among all the charges against him, none is more bitterly alleged, nor with more color of justice, than this, that he caused the world to doubt the honorable birth of Abraham Lincoln.

In an earlier chapter I have given the views of William H. Herndon on the paternity of Lincoln, including not only what he published, but also a short tract hitherto unpublished, which appears clearly to indicate that at the time it was written

Herndon believed Mr. Lincoln to have been an illegitimate child. That Herndon held this view is the opinion of his biographer, Dr. Joseph Fort Newton, who says:

> After a diligent search at Elizabethtown, the county seat of Hardin County, no record of the marriage [of Thomas Lincoln and Nancy Hanks] was found; and no one need be told that such a discrepancy would occasion all sorts of campaign gossip, especially at a time when the swarm of lies was blacker than usual. When, in 1865, Mr. Herndon went to look into the matter for himself he found no record, and was assured that there had been no marriage at all; so he concluded that Lincoln, like Alexander Hamilton, had been born out of wedlock. Nor is it easy to see, with such a state of facts before him, how he was much at fault; though, upon the advice of Horace White, he removed all hint of it from the second edition of his biography. That is the sum of the matter so far as Mr. Herndon had anything to do with it.—*Lincoln and Herndon,* pp. 320, 321.

I am convinced that there were times when Herndon was inclined to this view of Lincoln's parentage. Mr. Jesse W Weik assured me that such was not the final opinion of Herndon; and I was not sure for a time that Mr. Weik was correct in this affirmation, though he had better opportunity to know than any other man.

I have, however, complete assurance that Mr. Weik is correct in this declaration; and that on quite independent authority. There exists an important collection of Herndon manuscripts which, so far as I am aware, Mr. Weik has never seen, and which, as I have reason to believe, no biographer of Lincoln except myself has ever examined, which goes into this matter in detail much more minute and particular than Herndon ever went into it in print. I am not at liberty to disclose the ownership of those documents, nor will I answer inquiries by mail concerning them; but to any serious student who for a worthy purpose desires to know their content I will show copies which I made with my own hand, and will inform him where the originals are and give him satisfactory proof of their genuineness. They are where they are not likely to be lost or burned, and where they cannot be seen by the prurient or the curious, but where they are available for the verification of the statements in this chapter, and for such serious use as this volume makes of them.

Let me now be as specific as I deem it right to be, in order that I may make a clear and incontestable statement. Mr. Herndon at one time had, or believed he had, one more reason than he ever published for believing that Abraham Lincoln was not the son of Thomas Lincoln. This reason was based upon what he believed to be a fact, and which, in the very confidential letters and manuscript notes alluded to, he affirms with the greatest confidence. He does not give the source of his information, and I infer that it was Dennis Hanks. For myself, I should not count this conclusive evidence, and I do not think that Dennis gave it to Herndon with any supposition that it would be used as the basis of Herndon's inference, as I do not know that Dennis Hanks was the source of Herndon's information: I am of that opinion because I do not think that Herndon could have learned of this particular fact, if it was a fact, from any other source. Certainly he did not learn it from Abraham Lincoln.

I learn from Herndon's manuscript that when Dennis began to suspect, from the nature of Herndon's questions, the inference which Herndon was drawing, he became uncommunicative. This interview with Dennis occurred in Chicago in 1866, and Herndon at intervals afterwards endeavored to get Dennis to add to what he there said. His reticence increased Herndon's suspicion. In his notes covering these interviews, and the other rumors and suspicions which he had gathered up to that time, Herndon wrote: " From all this evidence, Abraham's legitimacy may be doubted." This was Herndon's state of mind in 1866 and subsequent years. He later revised this judgment, as the quotations in this chapter clearly show.

This fact, if it was a fact, was circumscribed by certain limitations; if it occurred outside of certain geographical or time limits, it weighed heavily against the legitimacy of Abraham Lincoln; if, on the other hand, it occurred within certain other limits, its implication was the exact opposite. This fact in itself was not derogatory to the moral character of either Thomas or Nancy.

I trust I am making clear the logical implications of this alleged fact, without betraying any indication of its nature. Its nature was somewhat remote, but its implication, in the one event or the other, was important, provided Herndon was correctly informed.

I do not wish to tell what this fact was, because it has never been printed, and I have no desire to be the first to print it; indeed, I know of no good reason why it should ever be printed. But if Dennis told it to Herndon, I am confident that Dennis did it without himself drawing any such inference from it as Herndon drew or supposing such an inference from it to have been possible; and I am not convinced that Dennis, if it was Dennis who told it, was correct. For these sufficiently good reasons I do not state, nor mean to suggest, the nature of this fact, or alleged fact.

There was a time when this alleged fact, in addition to such other facts as Herndon knew or thought he knew, inclined him to the belief that Abraham Lincoln was a bastard. *I am able to state unqualifiedly that this was not his final view.* By a process of reasoning which I cannot here reproduce, but which lies before me in the copy which I made from his own handwriting, he came to believe that the preponderance of evidence was in favor of that interpretation of this alleged fact which supported the legitimacy of Abraham Lincoln instead of disproving it. He wrote thus as his deliberate opinion, and I have reason to believe that he never altered it:

" It was—it is still charged that Abm. Lincoln was the son of one Enlow. My own opinion after a searching examination is that Mrs. Lincoln (Nancy Hanks) was not a bad woman, was by nature a noble woman. My own opinion is that Abraham Lincoln is the son and heir of Thomas Lincoln and Nancy Hanks Lincoln   I admit all things are not perfectly clear to me, and yet I think that the weight of the testimony is in my favor on both these grounds."

By " both these grounds " he meant the grounds of the

argument on which, by two converging lines of investigation, he had arrived at this conclusion.

This conclusion was written subsequent to the little tract which is quoted in the earlier chapter.

Those persons, therefore, who have been disposed to believe that Lincoln was illegitimate because they believed his partner Herndon to have believed it, are at liberty to revise their judgment as Herndon did. During the last seven or eight years of his life, whatever he may have thought before, Herndon believed Abraham Lincoln to have been the legitimate child of Thomas and Nancy Hanks Lincoln. There is no possible escape from this view unless there be in existence somewhere documentary proof that Herndon again revised his opinion, and this I do not only not believe, but am confident that I have proof that there was no such change of opinion by Herndon. The discovery of the marriage return was an important element in the changed view of Herndon, and there was at least one other reason. The mature and final opinion of William H. Herndon, "after a searching investigation," was that Abraham Lincoln was the child of Thomas Lincoln and Nancy Hanks Lincoln, born in lawful wedlock; and that all previous opinions to the contrary, either his own or Mr. Lincoln's, were erroneous. I am in position to substantiate this affirmation concerning the opinion of Mr. Herndon. He is henceforth not to be quoted among those who denied, but among those who believed, in the legitimacy of Abraham Lincoln.

I am able to state also that Herndon's literary associate, Mr. Jesse W. Weik, is unqualified in his affirmation that he believes Abraham Lincoln to have been the legitimate son of Thomas and Nancy Lincoln.

Incidentally I may mention that I have found evidence in Mr. Herndon's unpublished manuscripts that he encountered the report that some man or men living at the time of his investigations declared that he or they had had intercourse with Nancy Hanks. So far as I am able to judge he did not personally meet this man or these men, for he does not name the man or men or give such details as he was accustomed to record in such instances He did not credit the report. He remembered that there was another Nancy Hanks, mother of Dennis, and thought if there was any truth in these statements, it was more likely to have been true of the other Nancy than of the mother of the President. The report as a whole did not appear to him to be worthy of credence. It deserves only such attention as belongs to the allegation of a senile and unclean imagination. The unnamed old blackguard who recalled from his misspent youth the alleged memory of such an incident may without any great risk be assumed to have been a liar as well as the doer of other ill deeds.

One story which Herndon heard in Kentucky from men whom he thought he could believe, and whom he did believe, was that, " Old Abe Enlow always claimed that Abe Lincoln was his child." This was stated with complete confidence, and Herndon felt that he must accept it as true that Enlow made that claim. That did not in itself prove that the claim was true, but it was a thing that Herndon recorded in his private notes, and it had weight with him.

I am able to state with confidence that Herndon was misinformed. Abraham Enlow never claimed that Abraham Lincoln was his child. He claimed that the boy was named for him on account of his going for the midwife or granny-woman, and because of the kindness of his family to the Lincolns at the time of the boy's birth. The rest of the story is a lie.

Further, I have learned definitely that it was Herndon who heard, and told Lamon, about the fight between Abe Enlow and Thomas Lincoln. As Herndon did not print this in his own book, I thought that Lamon obtained his information from another source. I now know that this was a mistake. Herndon heard the story and told it to Lamon; and Herndon was misinformed. There was no such fight between those two men.

In my own investigations I have not discovered any such testimony that seemed worthy of a moment's attention; and Herndon held much the same opinion.

I have talked this matter over in full with Hon Hardin W. Masters of Springfield, who knew Herndon intimately, who talked with him innumerable times about Lincoln, and who was chosen by the Herndon family to deliver the oration at the dedication of the monument to Herndon. I have talked with Hon. G. W. Murray, who was Herndon's law-partner in Herndon's last years. These men assure me most positively that Herndon never receded from this opinion. He died believing that Abraham Lincoln was the legitimate son of Thomas and Nancy Lincoln.

I greatly desire that the full significance of this disclosure of the final opinion of Herndon shall have its full force in the mind of the reader. The first man to suggest in print that Lincoln was illegitimate was Lamon, and his authority was Herndon. I am confident that I am correct in my opinion that what Herndon furnished to Lamon was virtually, and probably exactly, a copy of the four-paged tract which I have quoted. I have found to a certainty that it was Lamon's book that started the discussion at the Atherton distillery that led to the discovery of the marriage record of Thomas and Nancy Lincoln. Lamon's book, and Herndon's, are the basis of the Coleman pamphlet, and, except for its North Carolina local color, of Cathey's book.

Here, then, is the deliberate and final opinion of the man on the basis of whose mistaken and immature judgment, these reports got into print, and grew to such volume:

"MY OWN OPINION, AFTER A SEARCHING EXAMI-
NATION, IS THAT MRS. LINCOLN (NANCY HANKS)
WAS NOT A BAD WOMAN—WAS BY NATURE A NOBLE
WOMAN—FREE, EASY AND UNSUSPECTING. MY OWN
OPINION IS THAT ABRAHAM LINCOLN IS THE SON AND
HEIR OF THOMAS AND NANCY HANKS LINCOLN."

Did Herndon ever change this opinion? I have shown that his friends did not believe that he changed it. I have further evidence in the unpublished manuscripts, which I have copied, and which continue until a few days before his death, some of them written while he was sick and making mention of his illness. These manuscripts in places show that he did not forget the evidence, or apparent evidence, on the basis of which he had at one time doubted whether Lincoln was legitimate. In several places I find him writing in language that shows how serious he had at one time considered these charges, and by what a careful weighing of the evidence he had come to his conclusion, in which still he encountered some difficulties. But I find him re-affirming his conviction in unmistakable terms, and in an assurance which, after he had arrived at his conviction, never left him. In another place I find this unqualified declaration, which expresses the faith in which he died:

"I AM SATISFIED THAT ABRAHAM LINCOLN WAS THE LAWFUL CHILD OF THOMAS LINCOLN AND NANCY HANKS AND THAT SHE WAS A VIRTUOUS WOMAN."

CHAPTER XXXIII

THE ORIGIN AND DESTINY OF THESE STORIES

I HAD little hope when I began this study that I should reach a settled conviction as to the precise origin of these stories; all that I thought to discover was their truth or falsehood; but I have succeeded beyond my expectation. How easy it is for a lie to begin—in a question, a shrug of the shoulder, a circumflex accent, a suggestion that some one has suggested that it may be so! And how nearly impossible it is thereafter to keep up with the lie itself in its many transformations, its protean changes, its adaptation to circumstances! How unlikely that any one, even if he could assure himself of the falsity of rumors that had their origin a half century ago, and traveled long underground before they appeared in print, could reach their actual beginning! And yet, I think that I have accomplished this, which at the outset I did not anticipate. I have followed the sluggish estuary of these rumors with their seven clogged and befouled mouths back to where they begin in a single muddy stream, and I am confident that I have reached its fountain head.

Let us remember first that the earliest biographers of Lincoln did not make swift journeys to Hodgenville to learn all they could about Lincoln on the ground. They were correct in their opinion that there was not very much to be learned there that would meet their requirements. The number of men living there who had known Abraham Lincoln as a small child was very few, and their testimony had in it nothing of value for a campaign biography. None of them were prepared to write such a biography. D. W. Bartlett had just published a book of 360 pages on the Presidential Candidates of 1860, containing twenty-one biographies, beginning with William H. Seward and ending with John C. Fremont, and the name of Abraham Lincoln was not included in his list of presidential possibilities. Bartlett had to hurry around and pick up what material he could for a campaign Life of Lincoln and Hamlin, and get his material where he could, which was from the sketch which Lincoln furnished Scripps; this he was able to work up into a cloth-bound book of 354 pages, which was doing well with his material, but it involved no journey to Kentucky. Nor did any of the 1860 biographers go there for material: they rushed to the press as quickly as they could.

The campaign of 1864 produced no necessity for local investigation; people then were chiefly interested in the events of the War. Moreover, La Rue County was not then a friendly place in its attitude toward Lincoln. Hodgenville was difficult of access and there was little to be learned by going there. So there was little to stimulate the people on the ground to invent stories of this character.

The rumor began with the knowledge that Samuel Haycraft, clerk of the County Court at Elizabethtown, had written to Abraham Lincoln, just after his nomination by the Chicago convention in 1860, asking whether he was not born in Elizabethtown, and whether he was not the son of Thomas Lincoln and Sarah Bush. Lincoln wrote to him under date of May 28, 1860:

In the main you are right about my history. My father was Thomas Lincoln, and Mrs. Sally Johnston was his second wife. You are mistaken about my mother Her maiden name was Nancy Hanks. I was not born at Elizabethtown, but my mother's first child, a daughter, two years older than myself, and now long since deceased, was. I was born February 12, 1809, near where Hodginsville [Lincoln misspelled the name] now is, then in Hardin County. I do not think I ever saw you, though I know very well who you are—so well that I recognized your handwriting, on opening your letter, before I saw the signature. My recollection is that Ben Helm was first clerk, that you succeeded him, that Jack Thomas and William Farleigh graduated in the same office. Am I right? My father has been dead near ten years; but my step-mother (Mrs. Johnston) is still living.

Mr. Haycraft had already found what he first supposed was the record of the marriage of the parents of Abraham Lincoln, Thomas Lincoln and Sarah Bush Johnston, and he thought that Abraham was born in Elizabethtown. On receipt of Lincoln's letter he made diligent search for the record of the marriage of Lincoln's own parents, and was unable to find it. This failure gradually became known; and as the search was pursued in the counties immediately adjacent and did not yield results, the suspicion gradually took shape, at first in political circles, that Lincoln's parents were not married, a suspicion that found some approach to confirmation in Lincoln's own reticence and the reserve of his biographers. But this at first was not construed to mean that any other man than Thomas Lincoln was Abraham's father.

Only gradually did Hodgenville awake to the fact that Lincoln was born in the county of which by division it had become the shire town. Elizabethtown had claimed that honor, and for that matter is still disposed to claim it, and Hodgenville displayed no great alacrity in setting up claim to the birth of Lincoln. Yet there were a very few old people who knew that while Tom Lincoln had a daughter when he came to the Rock Spring Farm, on Nolin Creek, a son was born to him there.

One of those very few men, in all not more than a half dozen living in 1860 and named as remembering him, was Abraham Enlow. He had a personal recollection which he told in 1860 and until his death in 1861. Not yet, however, did Hodgenville know of the rumor that Lincoln was illegitimate; Mr. Haycraft was still pursuing his search. It was some months before he gave it up, and the news of his failure spread slowly, and at first was quietly discussed by politicians. There was no immediate attempt to learn anything by gathering local gossip; the quest was for the records. When that stopped, the gossip began. Gradually it reached Hodgenville. By that time Abraham Enlow was dead. He died in 1861.

As this rumor spread, it took on an uglier form. It was not enough to say that Thomas and Nancy Lincoln, being poor white trash, lived together without the formality of marriage.

It was easy to go a step farther, and that step was taken, in the inquiry, which soon grew to a rumor and the rumor into an affirmation, as to the responsibility of some other man than Thomas Lincoln for the birth of the boy At first this story was told without any attempt to name the man, but by the time it got fairly well noised abroad in La Rue County, a name became almost necessary.

When La Rue County fully woke to the realization that Lincoln was born within its bounds, it took its honor without due elation.   Lincoln was no favorite there, as shown by the three votes which the county gave him in 1860 But by 1864 the political pot was boiling, and the ugly rumor was current in the country, and finally its backwater came seeping through the sluggish soil of La Rue County that Abraham Lincoln who was born there was of illegitimate birth.

To its honor, let it be recorded that La Rue County's first response was an emphatic denial.   Men who are still living, and are of the highest character, remember the effect of the rumor upon the old people, the few then living, who had known the Lincolns.   They denied it.   They declared that no such rumor had been current there at the time of the birth of Lincoln, and that Mrs. Lincoln bore a good reputation during the short period of her sojourn in that community

But these people were few in number, and their voices did not reach the outer world.   One by one these old people died; and the lie lived on.

But if Abraham Lincoln was conceived and born in La Rue County, and was not the son of Thomas Lincoln, a father must be found for him; who could he be?

We can trace the actual process by which the myth was built up, and almost the hour of its birth.

Abraham Enlow was one of the nearest neighbors of the Lincolns, living only a matter of two miles away, and one of the few living in 1860 who had even the faintest memory of him.   He had this one recollection:

On a day which must have been Saturday, February 11, 1809, he was on his way to the Kirkpatrick mill.   He was riding his horse, having on his saddle under him a sack of corn

which the dull stones of the mill would reduce to meal. As
he passed the house of Thomas Lincoln, he was hailed by
that gentleman with a request that he return home and bring
his mother, who was locally famous as a " granny-woman."
He and Thomas lifted the sack down, and he rode back home,
and soon returned with his mother, Mary La Rue Enlow,
seated on the horse behind him. His half-sister, Peggy La
Rue, who was twenty years old, and married to Conrad Walters, was there, also; and there were other women.

Abraham let his mother down at the cabin, replaced the
sack of corn with the help of Thomas Lincoln, and rode on
to the mill, returning late in the afternoon. The granny-
woman and her assistants were still occupied, and he went
home with his sack of meal. Some time after midnight, on
the morning of Sunday, February 12, 1809, a little boy was
born.

Either then or later Abraham Enlow got the idea that the
child was named for him in recognition of his kindness in
going after the granny-woman. He did not know that the
boy's name was already chosen, being that of Thomas Lincoln's
own father.

It pleased his fancy when he was an old man, in 1860, to
tell, and he did tell, that he had the impression that Tom Lincoln named little Abe for him as a reward for assisting in the
bringing of the granny-woman. If that innocent illusion
did Abraham Enlow any good, no one should begrudge him
that measure of satisfaction. But we know for whom
Abraham Lincoln was named; and Abraham Enlow had small
consideration in the choice of the name.

Abraham Enlow died in 1861, and the rumor that Abraham
Lincoln was an illegitimate child reached Hodgenville during
the campaign of 1864. Not before that time is there one
vestige of record of any such rumor in La Rue County.

When that rumor got afloat, and began to find willing and
credulous listeners, it became the manifest duty of La Rue
County to furnish a father for Abraham Lincoln. The choice
was limited. There were no living candidates for the honor.
There were few dead men who were known to have known

Abraham Lincoln. Knowledge of the family as having ever lived on the Rock Spring farm had almost totally vanished. There was not a shred of record of the birth in the county offices Everything depended upon the declaration of Abraham Lincoln that he was born there, and on the dim recollections of a very few elderly people who could recall hardly any incidents.

But people began to remember that Abraham Enlow, who had died three or four years before, had boasted that Abe Lincoln was named for him, and that he was hanging around the cabin when Abe was born. Why should he have been there unless he had reason to be interested? Why should the child have been named for him unless it was his?

Necessity is the mother of invention. La Rue County, faced with the necessity of finding a father for Abraham Lincoln, did the best it knew with the very scanty materials at its disposal, and about 1865 the story was in full tide of currency, that Abe Lincoln was named Abraham for his real and Lincoln for his putative father.

And this is the way it began. I have traced it from this beginning, through all its multitudinous forms, and they all come back to this.

By 1872, when Lamon's book was published, these stories were at high tide. One had no need to go to Hodgenville to learn them. Indeed, by keeping away from there one could learn more than any one in Hodgenville knew, as for instance, the story about the fight between Tom Lincoln and Abe Enlow, which was the story of another fight, in another county, that came to embellish the Lincoln story as lawyers retold it and amplified in the telling.

Did not Hodgenville know the age of Abraham Enlow, and that he was only a boy when Lincoln was born? For the most part, no. Abraham Enlow died an old man, and in that region an old man is an old man, and that without overmuch concern about his precise age. But that part of Hodgenville that gave much real thought to the matter knew at once that the story was untrue; less because of any computation of Abraham Enlow's age than because the Lincolns were not yet resident of his neighborhood until several months after Abraham Lincoln was on the way. That was why the Brownfield story was invented. People who said that the Enlow story was impossible would sometimes add that if such a story were true at all, there was only one man of whom it could well be true, and that was George Brownfield; Tom Lincoln worked for him that summer and fall, and George Brownfield's sons were tall men; and there might possibly be something in that suggestion. But the Brownfield story, though it had at least the fact of physical possibility in its favor, never found any favor outside the immediate neighborhood, and not very much there. And the Abe Enlow story spread.

It is not necessary to show in detail how the story took on a new form wherever there was or had been a man named Abraham Enlow. There had been a man in Bourbon County, near the border of Clark, named Abe Inlow, a miller; and there once was a young woman named Nancy Hornback, who, though the mother of an illegitimate child, found a husband and went with him and her child to one of the western counties of Kentucky. There was a girl in North Carolina who had worked as a servant and was sent over the mountains into Kentucky or Tennessee, and there was an Abraham Enlow there, of whom, a half century afterward, it was possible to relate the story with suitable local adaptations. And so the story grew.

The discovery of the marriage record of Thomas and Nancy Lincoln in Washington County had no effect upon the story as it was told in La Rue County; for there it had always been assumed that Thomas and Nancy were married; and if theirs was only a common law marriage, that did not greatly alter the situation as it related to Enlow. No one there cared whether the certificate was found or not. The discovery of the certificate was indeed a hightly important event as establishing the conjugal relations of Thomas and Nancy Lincoln, but if Nancy was untrue to Thomas, as the La Rue County story assumed, the certificate was not of any considerable importance. And the story, once rooted, persisted. But it never would have started if the marriage return had been found before Abraham Lincoln became a candidate for the Presidency, and if he could have told Jesse Fell and John Locke Scripps the date of his parents' marriage   It would not have started if Abraham Lincoln had not displayed that " significant reserve " of which so many of his biographers speak, and which he would not have displayed had he been sure of that fact and date.   As it was, the failure of Samuel Haycraft to find the record started a story that locally had little to do with the record, and which proved the root of all the other stories.

Now this is the way it began, and the conditions were ripe for its dissemination.   But it was false from beginning to end, and the time has come to say so with an emphasis that shall forever forbid its repetition even as a conjecture or a peradventure.

Thus far we deal with the story as oral tradition   When and how did it get into print?   How did it evolve from local gossip into general publicity?

The story that Lincoln had reason to be ashamed of his birth began in a vague rumor to the effect that Thomas and Nancy Lincoln were " white trash " who lived together without the formality of marriage; but when this rumor began, about 1861, it was without the slightest intimation that any other man than Thomas Lincoln was Abraham Lincoln's father.   When, about 1864, the rumor reached Hodgenville, it had enlarged into the report that another man than Thomas Lincoln was Abraham's father, but no other man was named. Hodgenville itself supplied the name, choosing from among the few neighbors of Thomas Lincoln one who was remembered to have told that he was interested in the birth of Abraham Lincoln to the extent of loaning a horse to bring the midwife, and that Abraham Lincoln was named after him. The name of Abraham Enlow having once been spoken, it gave occasion for a new form of the story wherever there was a branch of the Enlow family.

But not in 1861 nor yet in 1864 was there a word in print that hinted that Abraham Lincoln was not born in lawful wedlock.

I have been very desirous of learning where the first suggestion appeared in print, and to this end I wrote to several authorities. The first of these was Jesse W. Weik, Herndon's associate in the preparation of his *Life of Lincoln.* Mr. Weik, who has studied this question for many years, replied at once that the first appearance of this story in print was in Lamon's *Life of Lincoln,* issued in 1872.

Hon. Daniel Fish is the foremost authority on Lincoln literature, and the compiler of the standard Bibliography of Lincolniana. He replied:

" Lamon's biography, so far as I know, was the first publication in book or pamphlet form to suggest a query about the legitimacy of Lincoln; and that, as you know, is very indefinite."

Judd Stewart, besides being the owner of the largest Lincoln collection in existence, is a discriminating student of Lincoln literature. He wrote:

" I think Lamon's *Life of Lincoln,* published in 1872 (preface dated May, 1872) is the earliest publication that in any way suggests the illegitimacy of Abraham Lincoln."

Mr. Appleton P. C. Griffin, Chief Assistant Librarian of the Library of Congress, made search for me, and gave the same answer.

I could think of only one other way of learning. The Senators of the United States are permitted to ask for assistance in the Library of Congress to an almost unlimited extent in the gathering of literary material that may be of value to them for their speeches. I have found occasion to avail myself of the courtesy of Senators in this and other matters, and I wrote to Senator Medill McCormick, asking him to have thorough search of periodical literature in the Library of Congress to find whether in any newspaper or magazine this rumor appeared prior to the publication of Lamon's book. The answer is:

" With reference to the attached letter of Dr. Barton, we have made a careful search and have been unable to find any reference to Lincoln's alleged illegitimacy before 1872."

Some men are said to be born great, others to achieve greatness, and others to have greatness thrust upon them. To the last class belonged Abraham Enlow; and he died before he knew it.

He was a life-long Democrat, and with all his family he sympathized with the South when the Civil War broke out. La Rue County cast three votes for Abraham Lincoln, and Abraham Enlow's was not one of them. He had been sick in 1859, and knew, as he said in his will, that his years at most could not be many; and he had no mind to imperil his immortal soul by voting for a Republican on the chance that posterity might assign him a paternal interest in the candidate. He voted in the autumn of 1860, casting a good old-fashioned Democratic ticket as was his wont, and died a year later with the consciousness that he had done his duty. But when he knew that Abraham Lincoln was elected, he was as little displeased as he could well have been with a candidate whose political views he did not approve; and he told his friends, as he stood in front of the Hodgenville drug-store, that when Abe Lincoln was born, he loaned his horse to fetch the granny-woman, and he rather thought they named the boy Abe in his honor. With this pleased reminiscence, he spent his last few months, and died, never suspecting what use would be made of his boyish act of generosity.

It was meager material for the manufacture of so great a lie, and for the propagation of so large a family of lies; but it sufficed.

It no longer suffices. It is weighed in the balance and found wanting. Let Abraham Enlow have full credit for having lived an upright and honest life, and for a name which he did nothing to dishonor; but among the good or bad deeds that he did there is one that is not to be included. Neither he nor any other man than Thomas Lincoln was the father of Abraham Lincoln.

The hills of Kentucky have their own stolid type of mirth, and their sententious sayings are sometimes informed with a quizzical humor. There is a saying current there, and Abraham Lincoln would have heard it had he lived there longer, when a story or a political issue or candidate is completely and effectually disposed of. They say, as I have heard them say in stump speeches, that that story or issue or candidate is now buried so deeply that if he or it ever scratches out, it will be less laborious "to keep on a-scratchin' downwards, and come out face to the fire."

That is the depth at which I have now buried the story that Abraham Lincoln was an illegitimate child. Let any man who proposes to exhume that putrid reminiscence go prepared to dig deep and stay long, for he will not find it on this side of the place prepared for every one that loveth and maketh a lie.

APPENDICES

APPENDIX I

REV. JESSE HEAD

After the publication of the discovery of the marriage record of Thomas and Nancy Lincoln, Rev. Dr. J. M Buckley, of the *New York Christian Advocate,* conducted a correspondence to secure information about Rev. Jesse Head, who solemnized the marriage. A number of letters were received from men who had known him, the most important being from Jesse Head's grandson, Rev E. B Head, Presiding Elder of the Lawrenceburg Conference in Kentucky:

LAWRENCEBURG, KENTUCKY,
ANDERSON COUNTY, May 3, 1882.
To THE REV. J. M. BUCKLEY, D D

Dear Sir and Brother —Your favor reached me on the eve of my leaving Harrodsburg for this place, hence the delay in responding to your request. The Rev. Jesse Head referred to was my grandfather. He was born in Maryland, near Baltimore: was married to Miss Jane Ramsey, of (what is now) Bedford County, Pennsylvania. He removed to Kentucky, and settled at Springfield, Washington County. He was an ordained minister of the Methodist Episcopal Church, but was never connected with the itinerancy in Kentucky, on account of feeble health He held several prominent civil offices while living in Springfield, and was actively engaged preaching the gospel of God's grace. He celebrated the rites of matrimony between Thomas Lincoln and Miss Nancy Hanks, father and mother of President Lincoln, in 1806, near Springfield. He afterwards moved to Harrodsburg, Mercer County, where he lived until his death, which occurred in March, 1842. At Harrodsburg he engaged in merchandizing, also owned and edited the county paper for a term of years. He was largely instrumental, if not wholly, in building the first church ever erected in Harrodsburg; also organized and conducted the first prayer-meeting In gospel labors he was always abundant. His house was the home for several years of Rev. H. B. Bascom, afterwards Bishop; also

325

of Bishop McKendree especially, as they were bosom friends. Some time before his death he left the Methodist Episcopal Church, and connected himself with the Radical Methodists, on account of *slavery*, and also some dissatisfaction with the Episcopacy. He then had charge of and preached for a church for years at Lexington, Kentucky. His name at Harrodsburg and through the surrounding country is as ointment poured forth. He was a man of decided and positive character, bold and aggressive, and died loved and honored by all. He died as he lived, in the triumph of the faith of the Gospel of God's Son.

Fraternally yours,

E. B. HEAD, P.E.,

Lawrenceburg Circuit, Kentucky Conference.

2. THE RETURN OF MARRIAGES, INCLUDING THAT OF THOMAS
   LINCOLN AND NANCY HANKS BY REV. JESSE HEAD

Copied from the Original in the Office of the County Clerk in Springfield, Washington County, Kentucky, by William E. Barton.

I do hereby certify that the following is a true list of the Marriages Solemnized by me the subscriber from the 28th of April 1806 untill the date hereof.

June 26th 1806 Joined together in the Holy Estate of Matrimony agreeable to the rules of the M.E.C. Morris Berry & Peggy Simms
Nov 27th 1806 David Mige(?) & Hannah Xten(?)
March 5th 1807 Charles Ridge & Anna Davis
March 24th 1807 John Head & Sally Clark
March 27th Benjamin Clark & Dolly Head
Jany 14th Edward Pyle & Rosanah McMahon
Decr 22nd 1806 Silas Chamberlin & Betsey West
June 17th 1806 John Springer & Elizabeth Ingram
June 12th 1806 Thomas Lincoln & Nancy Hanks
September 23rd 1806. John Cambion & Hanah White
October 2nd 1806 Anthony Lykey & Keziah Putte
October 23rd Aaron Harding & Hannah Rottet
April 5th 1807 Daniel Payne & Christiana Pierre
July 26th 1806 Benjamin Clark & Polly Clark
May — 1806 Hugh Haskin & Betsy Dyer
September 25th 1806 John Graham & Catherine Jones
Given under my hand this 22nd day of April 1807

JESSE HEAD, D. M.E.C.

3. MARRIAGE BOND OF THOMAS LINCOLN AND NANCY HANKS AT SPRINGFIELD, KENTUCKY

Copied from the Original by William E. Barton.

Know all men by these presents that we Thomas Lincoln and Richard Berry are held and firmly bound unto his Excellency the governor of Kentucky for the Just and full sum of fifty pounds current money to the payment of which well and truly to be made to the said governor and his successors we bind ourselves and our heirs &c Jointly and severally firmly by these presents sealed with our seals and dated this 10th day of June, 1806. The Condition of the above Obligation is such that whereas there is a marriage shortly intended between the above bound Thomas Lincoln and Nancy Hanks for which a license has issued now if there be no lawful cause to obstruct the said marriage then this obligation to be Void or else to remain in full force & virtue in law.

THOMAS LINCOLN (Seal)
RICHARD BERRY   (Seal)

Witness, John H. Parrott.

John H. Parrott, the witness, was also the clerk of court. The writing shows that it was the custom of the clerk to write out the text of marriage bonds in blank, filling in the names as occasion demanded. The names and dates show spaces larger than required, and give evidence that the clerk found it convenient to keep one or two bonds in readiness.

Miss Tarbell credits the discovery of the marriage return correctly as by W. F. Booker, Clerk of the Court of Washington County, Kentucky, but sets the date of discovery as 1885. Unfortunately the exact date is not known; but it was discovered at least as early as 1878.

4. ALLEGED MARRIAGE CERTIFICATE OF THOMAS LINCOLN AND NANCY HANKS

From tracing by Henry Whitney Cleveland, of Louisville, in Miss Tarbell's "Early Life of Lincoln."

I do hereby Certify that by authority of License Issued by the Clerks Office of Washington Co. I have solemnized the rites of Matrimony between Thomas Lincoln and Nancy Hanks, June 12th 1806 A.D. agreeable to the rites and ceremonies of the Methodist Episcopal Church witness my hand

JESSE HEAD Dn.M.E.C.

I do not know from what source this document emanated, and I propound no theory as to who, if any one, forged it. But in my judgment Miss Tarbell was imposed upon. This does not appear to me, as shown in the tracing, to be a genuine document.

5. THE FIRST ANNOUNCEMENT OF THE MARRIAGE RECORD

So many and such contradictory accounts have been published concerning the discovery of the marriage bond, and the minister's return for the marriage of Thomas Lincoln and Nancy Hanks I was very desirous of learning not only how but if possible exactly when the discovery was made. I have interviewed Mr. Booker's successor, who has made for me a signed statement, with the seal of the court affixed. I have also been able to procure a very small pamphlet which Mr. Booker issued, and which is now practically impossible to obtain, relating how these documents were found. The essential facts of the story are given in this volume, and are based upon first-hand testimony. They do not, however, give the date of the discovery. The county officers of Washington County are agreed that it was in the early eighties,—1881 or 1882. I had found definitely that it was earlier than 1882, and had accepted 1881 as the probable date, when by rare good fortune, I found, in the Massachusetts Historic Genealogical Society. in Boston, an editorial clipping from the *Boston Journal* of Monday, January 27, 1879, referring to an article in the *New York Tribune* of the preceding Saturday, and containing the following statements:

It has long been a disputed point whether the parents of Abraham Lincoln were ever married; and in a *Life of Lincoln,* published by Ward H. Lamon in 1872, it was intended to show that, owing to their extreme poverty, the parents of Lincoln never were legally married, as, according to the laws of the State of Kentucky, it would have been necessary to file a bond to guard the State against an over-supply of paupers. Much other matter bearing on the same part was also intended to be included in the book, and the Lincoln family desired to have it suppressed. The family and its most intimate friends were positive that there was not the least ground for a charge of illegitimacy against Lincoln Accordingly, Judge David Davis and Leonard Swett, a prominent lawyer living in Illinois, who had been a firm friend of Lincoln, exerted themselves successfully to have much of this matter suppressed. Lamon, however, stated in the book that no record of the marriage could be found, and represented Lincoln as very reluctant to talk about his parents and their early life. The *New York Tribune* of Saturday says, however, that while in Kentucky last fall ex-Secretary Bristow met a lawyer of high reputation, R. J. Browne. Mr. Browne lives in Springfield, Washington County, Kentucky, is a man of wealth, a Republican, and one who takes great pride in guarding the memory of the dead President. He heard of the reports referred to above, and caused a diligent search to be made for the record of the marriage of Lincoln's parents. The search was successful, and Mr. Browne mentioned the fact to Mr Bristow, who urged him to make the result public in order to remove the doubt in the minds of many on the subject. Mr. Browne promised to send copies of the bond and certificate to General Bristow, and recently he did so.

The letter of Mr. Browne to General Bristow follows under date of December 16, 1878. With it is an accurate copy of the marriage bond, certified by W F. Booker, clerk; and also a condensed copy of the return of Jesse Head, abbreviated so by the omission of the names of all the couples except Thomas Lincoln and Nancy Hanks. In making the copy, Mr. Booker inadvertently copied the date belonging to the next couple, and that is why some of the Lives of Lincoln give the marriage date as September 23, 1806, instead of June 12, 1806

This form, also, as I suspect, suggested to some one clever with the pen that he could create a certificate that would have commercial value But this I suspect only: I do not know the origin of the so-called certificate

The reference to the marriage bond is incorrect. The purpose of the bond is not to guarantee the State against the birth of paupers; nor is it certain that a bond that makes marriage difficult would have that result. The bond is issued to protect the officer who issues the license against the possibility that the persons may be under age or already married. The bond is usually a mere formality. In the case of a man of 28 and a woman of 23, there would have been no difficulty in securing bondsmen.

Nicolay and Hay derive the interest of the Berrys in the marriage of Thomas and Nancy, not from their supposed relation to the bride, but through their relation to the Lincoln family, through the first wife of the father of Thomas:

Richard Berry was a connection of Lincoln; his wife was a Shipley.—*Abraham Lincoln: A History*, I, p. 24.

I think General Bristow was mistaken in his impression that Mr. Browne caused the record to be discovered. Mr. Browne had probably learned of the recent discovery of the document by Mr. Booker, and his conversation with General Bristow led to its publication, first of all, as I suppose, in the *New York Tribune*, January 25, 1878.

This seemed to me so important that I went at once to New York, and found the original article. I am able now definitely to fix, not the date of discovery but the date of publication of the discovery; and it is several years earlier than is usually claimed for it. I give this article in full:

(*From the New York Daily Tribune, Saturday, January 25, 1879*)

LINCOLN'S PARENTAGE

NEW FACTS ABOUT HIS FAMILY

Letters and documents now first published, which prove the legal marriage of Lincoln's father and mother. Flat contradiction of the story told in Lamon's " Life of Lincoln."

Recent developments promise to settle the long disputed question whether the father and mother of Abraham Lincoln ever were legally married. Shortly before Ward H. Lamon published his *Life of Lincoln* in 1872, it became known to some of those who had been the warmest friends of the dead President that Lamon intended to publish the statement that on account of their extreme poverty the parents of Lincoln never were legally married, as, according to the laws of the State of Kentucky, it would have been necessary to file a bond to guard the State against an over-supply of paupers. Much other matter bearing on the same point was also intended to be included in the book, and the Lincoln family desired to have it suppressed. The family and its most intimate friends were positive that there was not the least ground for a charge of illegitimacy against Lincoln. Accordingly, Judge David Davis and Leonard Sweet, a prominent lawyer, living in Illinois, exerted themselves successfully to have much of this matter suppressed.

It appears, however, from Lamon's book, that in his own mind the author had grave doubts as to whether Lincoln's parents ever were married, and he seems to wish to render the home of Lincoln's parents as unattractive as possible in order to make the contrast between Lincoln's early and later surroundings as strong as possible Lamon speaks of Thomas, Abraham's father, as " wanting in character " and says that this was one of the reasons why " Sally " Bush, " a modest and pious girl and all things pure and decent" refused to marry him Lamon refers to the marriage of Thomas Lincoln and Nancy Hanks as follows:

" Sometime in the year 1806 he married Nancy Hanks. It was in the shop of her uncle, Joseph Hanks of Elizabethtown, Hardin County, that he had essayed to learn his trade. . . . It is admitted by all the old residents of the place that they were honestly married, but precisely when and how, no one can tell. Diligent and thorough searches by the most competent persons have failed to disclose any trace of the fact in the public records of Hardin and the adjoining counties The license and the minister's return in the case of Thomas Lincoln and Sarah Johnston his second wife, were easily found in the place where the law required them to be; but in the Nancy Hanks marriage there exists no evidence but that a mutual acknowledgment and cohabitation. At the time of their union Thomas was twenty-eight years of age and Nancy about twenty-three."

Again, on page 17 is found the following:

" The lives of his (Abraham's) father and mother, and their history and character of the family before their settlement in Indiana, were topics upon which Mr. Lincoln never spoke but with great reluctance and significant reserve. In his family Bible he kept the register of births, marriages and deaths, every entry being carefully made in his own handwriting. . . . It has not a word about the Hankses or Sparrows. It shows the marriage of Sarah Bush first with Daniel Johnston and then with Thomas Lincoln, but it is entirely silent as to the marriage of his own mother. It does not even give the date of her birth but barely recognizes her existence and demise to make the vacancy which was speedily filled by Sarah Johnston."

To show Mr. Lincoln's reticence about his parentage, Lamon gives several extremely brief replies which were sent to applicants for biographical sketches " Mr. Lincoln," writes one of these applicants, " communicated some facts to me about his ancestry which he did not wish published, and which I have never spoken of or alluded to before "

While in Kentucky last fall, ex-Secretary Bristow met a law-

yer of high reputation, R. J. Browne. Mr. Browne lives in Springfield, Washington County, is a man of wealth, a Republican, and
one who takes great pride in guarding the memory of the dead
President. He heard of the reports referred to above and caused
a diligent search to be made for the record of the marriage of
Lincoln's parents. The search was successful, and Mr. Browne
mentioned the fact to General Bristow who urged him to make
the result public, in order to remove the doubt in the minds of
many upon the subject. Mr. Browne promised to send copies
of the bond and certificate to General Bristow, and recently he
did so. Mr. Browne's letter and the accompanying copies of
documents were as follows:

" Springfield, Ky., Dec. 16, 1878.

Dear Sir:—
When I saw you last in Louisville I promised to send you a
copy of the record of President Lincoln's father's marriage. I
now send it to you. The record ought forever to silence the
charge of the President's illegitimacy. I have talked with men of
the highest veracity who have told me that they attended the
wedding. With a sincere wish, etc., I am,

" Truly yours,
" R. J. Browne."

" To Genl. B. H. Bristow,
   New York City.
   The following is a copy of the bond:
   Know all men by these presents that we Thomas Lincoln and
Richard Berry are held and firmly bound unto his Excellency the
Governor of Kentucky for the Just and full sum of fifty pounds
Current money to the payment of which well and truly to be made
to the said governor and his successors we bind ourselves our
heirs &c., Jointly and Severally firmly by these presents sealed
with our seals and dated this 10th day of June 1806. The Condition of the above obligation is such that whereas there is a marriage shortly intended between the above bound Thomas Lincoln
and Nancy Hanks for which a license has issued now if there be
no lawful cause to obstruct the said marriage then this obligation
to be Void or else to remain in full force & Virtue in Law.

THOMAS LINCOLN   (Seal)

Witness JOHN H. PARROTT.   RICHARD BERRY   (Seal)

The certificate is as follows:
Washington County ss.
   I do certify that on the 22nd day of September 1806 I
solemnized the rites of matrimony between Thomas Lincoln and

Nancy Hanks according to the rites of the Methodist Episcopal church.

JESSE HEAD, D. M. E. C.

The above are sworn to be true copies as follows·
STATE OF KENTUCKY
WASHINGTON COUNY

I, W. F. Booker, Clerk of the Washington County Court, do certify that the within is a true copy of the marriage bond, as well as of the marriage certificate of the minister of the marriage of Thomas Lincoln and Nancy Hanks, as shown from the records on file in my office.

Given under my hand and seal of office as Springfield, Ky., this 17th day of December, 1878.

W F BOOKER, Clerk.

By this certificate which is now published for the first time, it appears that the marriage of Lincoln's parents occurred on September 23, 1806. Lamon, however, states that the first child of the family was born February 10, 1807—a girl at first called Nancy, and subsequently, on the death of her mother, Sarah. Search for this certificate was made in La Rue County some time ago by a man named Samuel Haycraft, but without success, for the obvious reason that when the certificate was issued Washington County included La Rue County.

NOTE ON THE FOREGOING ARTICLE

The article above is of remarkable interest and appears to have escaped notice of all previous authors. We are not yet informed concerning the precise date of the discovery of this record. It is safe to assume a slight error in the article and to be reasonably certain that Mr. Browne knew of the discovery of the bond and return of the minister at the time of his conference with General Bristow in Louisville in the autumn of 1878 He could hardly have been so confident of his ability to furnish a copy of these documents if he had not known that the documents had been found. Knowledge of their existence must have been common property in Springfield at that time, but neither Mr. Browne nor Mr. Booker had thought of giving this information to the press.

The publication must certainly be credited to General Bristow.

Benjamin Helm Bristow was born in Elkton, Todd County, Kentucky, June 20, 1832, and was graduated from Jefferson College, Pennsylvania, in 1851. He was admitted to the bar in 1853 and practiced law in Kentucky. On the outbreak of the Civil War he entered the Union Army as Lieutenant-Colonel of the 25th Kentucky Infantry, and distinguished himself on the battlefield, where he won the rank of Brigadier-General. At the close of the war he removed to Louisville, where in 1870 he became law partner of General John M. Harlan. In 1871 President Grant appointed him Solicitor-General, and in 1874 Secretary of the Treasury. At the Republican National Convention in 1876 he received on the first ballot 123 votes, the largest number cast for any candidate on that ballot for President of the United States. He removed to New York City where he practiced law until his death June 22, 1896.

Attention must certainly be called to the fact that in attempting to issue a certificate which would include the record of the Lincoln-Hanks marriage without the necessity of copying all the others in Jesse Head's return, Mr. Booker made the very serious mistake of taking the date September 22, 1806 from the marriage next recorded, instead of June 12, 1806, which belonged to this marriage.

It may also be added that if Samuel Haycraft's failure to find the certificate could have been attributed to so obvious a reason as that " when the certificate was issued, Washington County included La Rue County," Samuel Haycraft, County Clerk of Hardin County, would have been of all men on earth most likely to remember it. Washington County at that time did not include La Rue; Hardin County included La Rue, and it was in Hardin County he looked for the record of the marriage. Thomas Lincoln was listed as a tax-payer in Hardin County before his marriage, and Nancy Hanks was supposed to have lived in the home of her uncle, Joseph Hanks, of Elizabethtown where Thomas Lincoln learned his trade. The explanation of the failure to find the record is entirely intelligible; but if it had been quite so " obvious " the effort would not have failed.

This article affirms that Lamon intended to have told more than he did, but was restrained by the Lincoln family, and by David Davis and Leonard Swett. This raises the question what Lamon would have told had he not been restrained? He might have elaborated more than he did, and said a little more plainly what he evidently thought; but I am confident he told all he knew, and somewhat more. In this my opinion is fully sustained by Mr. Weik, who answers my inquiry on this point:

Greencastle, Ind., July 16, 1920.

DEAR DR. BARTON:

Your letter is just received. Yes, I have heard the story that David Davis and Leonard Swett kept Ward Lamon from reflecting on Lincoln's legitimacy. Horace White and Henry C Whitney both told me something about it; but the truth is (and I joined them in the belief) neither thought Lamon knew very much beyond what Herndon had told him. He never visited Kentucky or Indiana in pursuit of information—in fact, never dug into the subject. When he conceived the project of a Life of Lincoln, he simply bought and copied what Herndon had so carefully gathered, and he essayed to write the book; and even then he did not write the book, but turned the material over to Chauncey F. Black of Pennsylvania, who did the required work.

I have never seen the article alluded to by you and published in the N. Y. *Tribune*, January 25, 1879, but would be delighted if you could furnish me a copy.

My understanding has been that inasmuch as, at the time Lamon entered upon the preparation of his book, he was unable to locate the record of the marriage of Thomas Lincoln and Nancy Hanks, and fell into the error of concluding that they were not married at all. He drank a good deal, and his reckless talk doubtless stirred David Davis and Leonard Swett into believing that he was in possession of some vital and possibly damaging evidence. Hence their so-called attempt to bottle him up.

Hastily,

JESSE W. WEIK.

My own opinion is in complete agreement with that of Mr. Weik, that Lamon had no evidence on the basis of which he could have added anything of importance to what he actually wrote. I am confident I have seen all that Herndon gave to Lamon touching this matter, and much that he wrote subsequently which Lamon never saw; and Mr. Weik has wider experience with regard to the Herndon manuscripts than any one else.

APPENDIX II

WITNESSES TO THE MARRIAGE OF THOMAS LINCOLN AND NANCY HANKS

I. AFFIDAVIT AND STATEMENT OF DR CHRISTOPHER COLUMBUS GRAHAM

The following affidavit by Dr. Graham was procured by Captain J. W. Wartman, Deputy Clerk of the United States Circuit Court at Evansville, Indiana, in whose home Dr. Graham was visiting at the time:

I, Christopher C. Graham, now of Louisville, Kentucky, aged ninety-eight years, on my oath say: That I was present at the marriage of Thomas Lincoln and Nancy Hanks, in Washington County, near the town of Springfield, Kentucky; that one Jesse Head, a Methodist preacher of Springfield, Kentucky, performed the ceremony. I knew the said Thomas Lincoln and Nancy Hanks well, and know the said Nancy Hanks to have been virtuous and respectable, and of good parentage. I do not remember the exact date of the marriage, but was present at the marriage aforesaid, and I make this affidavit freely, and at the request of J. W. Wartmann, to whom, for the first time, I have this day incidentally stated the fact of my presence at the said wedding of President Lincoln's father and mother. I make this affidavit to vindicate the character of Thomas Lincoln and Nancy Hanks, and to put to rest forever the legitimacy of Abraham Lincoln's birth I was formerly proprietor of Harrodsburgh Springs; I am a retired physician, and am now a resident of Louisville, Kentucky. I think Felix Grundy was also present at the marriage of said Thomas Lincoln and Nancy Hanks, the father and mother of Abraham Lincoln. The said Jesse Head, the officiating minister at the marriage aforesaid, afterward removed to Harrodsburgh, Kentucky, and edited a paper there, and died at that place.

CHRISTOPHER COLUMBUS GRAHAM.

Subscribed and sworn to before me, this March 20, A.D. 1882. N. C. Butler, Clerk United States Circuit Court, First District, Indiana. By J. W. Wartmann, Deputy Clerk.

2. DETAILED STATEMENT OF CHRISTOPHER COLUMBUS GRAHAM.

The foregoing was published, and led to a further statement which Dr Graham made two years later to Mr Henry Whitney Cleveland by Dr Graham, written by Mr Cleveland, and signed by Dr Graham. It was published in the *Louisville Courier-Journal* and in other papers, and has appeared in Miss Tarbell's *Life of Lincoln* and in other books:

DR GRAHAM'S STATEMENT

I, Christopher Columbus Graham, now in my hundredth year, and visiting the Southern Exposition in Louisville, where I live, tell this to please my young friend Henry Cleveland, who is nearly half my age. He was often at the Springs Hotel in Harrodsburg, Kentucky, then owned and kept by me for invalids and pleasure-seekers   I am one of the two living men who can prove that Abraham Lincoln, or Linkhorn, as the family was miscalled, was born in lawful wedlock, for I saw Thomas Lincoln marry Nancy Hanks on the twelfth day of June, 1806   He was born at what was then known as the Rock Spring Farm—it is now called the Creal Place—three miles south of Hodgensville, in Larue County, Kentucky.

Kentucky was first a county of Virginia after its settlement, and then was divided into three counties; and these, again divided, are pretty much the present State.   The first historian was Filson, who made and published the first map of the separate territory, with the names of streams and stations as given by Daniel Boone and Squire Boone, James Harrod, and others.   I knew all of these, as well as President Lincoln's parents.

I think they lived on the farm four years after he was born. Another boy was born in Hodgensville, or, I should say, buried there.   The sister, Sally, was older than Abe, I think.   I think the paper now owned by Henry Cleveland is the "marriage lines" written by Rev. Jesse Head, a well-known Methodist preacher.   I do not think the old Bible it was found in was that of Tom Lincoln.   It would cost too much for him.   All of the records in it were those of the father's family—the John M Hewetts—of the wife of Dr Theodore S. Bell.   Dr. Bell was only about twenty years younger than I am, and probably got the certificate in 1858 or 1860, when assertions were made that Tom Lincoln and Nancy Hanks were not married when Abe was born.

He was reputed to have been born February 12, 1809, and I see no good reason to dispute it. Sally, I am sure, was the first child, and Nancy was a fresh and good-looking girl—I should say past twenty. Nancy lived with the Sparrow family a good bit. It was likely Tom had the family Bible from Virginia, through his father, called Abraham Linkhorn. His brothers, however, were older—if they were brothers, and not uncles, as some say. I was hunting roots for my medicines, and just went to the wedding to get a good supper, and got it.

Bibles cost as much as the spinning-wheel, or loom, or rifle, and were imported in the main. A favorite with the Methodists was Fletcher's, or one he wrote a preface for. Preachers used it, and had no commentaries. A book dedicated to King James or any other king did not take well in Revolutionary times. The Bibles I used to see had no printed records or blanks, but a lot of fine linen hand-made paper would be bound in front or back. On this, family history and land matters were written out fully like a book. Some had fifty pages. The court-houses even were made of logs, and the meeting-houses too, if they had any. No registers were kept as in English parish churches, and are not yet. Before a license could be had, a bond and security was taken of the bridegroom, and the preacher had to return to the court all marriages of the year. This was often a long list, and at times papers were lost or forgotten, but not often. The "marriage lines" given by the preacher to the parties were very important in case the records were burned up by accident. Such is the paper that Henry Cleveland has shown to me. The ring was not often used, as so few had one to use. The Methodist Church discipline forbid "the putting on of gold or costly apparel," and I think a preacher with a gold watch—if not an inherited one—would have been dismissed. A preacher that married was "located," and that ended his itinerancy in the Methodist Church. The Presbyterians were educated and married; Baptists not educated.

Tom Lincoln was a carpenter, and a good one for those days, when a cabin was built mainly with the ax, and not a nail or bolt or hinge in it, only leathers and pins to the door, and no glass, except in watches and spectacles and bottles. Tom had the best set of tools in what was then and now Washington County. LaRue County, where the farm was settled, was then Hardin.

Jesse Head, the good Methodist preacher that married them, was also a carpenter or cabinet-maker by trade, and as he was then a neighbor, they were good friends. He had a quarrel with the bishops, and was not an itinerant for several years, but an editor, and county judge afterwards, in Harrodsburg. Mr. Henry Cleveland has his commission from Governor Isaac Shelby.

Many great men of the South and North were then opposed to slavery, mainly because the new negroes were as wild as the Indians, and might prove as dangerous. Few of the whites could read, and yet Pope and Dryden and Shakespeare were as well known as Bunyan's *Pilgrim's Progress* and Baxter's *Saints' Rest*. Some were educated in Virginia and North Carolina before they came, and these, when they became teachers, wrote out their school-books entirely by hand.

Thomas Lincoln, like his son after him, had a notion that fortunes could be made by trips to New Orleans by flatboat This was dangerous, from snags and whirlpools in the rivers, from Indians, and even worse—pirates of the French, Canadians, and half-breeds. Steam was unknown, and the flats had to be sold in New Orleans, as they could not be rowed back against the currents. The neighbors joked Tom for building his boat too high and narrow, from an idea he had about speed, that has since been adopted by ocean steamships But he lacked in ballast He loaded her up with deer and bear hams and buffalo, which last was then not so plenty for meat or hides as when the Boone brothers came in. Besides, he had wax, for bees seemed to follow the white people, and he had wolf and coon and mink and beaver skins, gentian root (that folks then called "gensang" or "'sang"), nuts, honey, peach-brandy and whisky, and jeans woven by his wife and Sally Bush, that he married after Nancy died. Some said she died of heart trouble, from slanders about her and old Abe Enloe, called Innlow, while her Abe, named for the pioneer Abraham Linkhorn, was still little. But I am ahead of my story, for Nancy had just got married where I was telling it, and the flatboat and Sally Bush Lincoln come in before he goes over to what people called "Indiany." I will finish that, and then go back.

He started down Knob Creek when it was flush with rains; but the leaves held water like a sponge, and the ground was shaded with big trees and papaw and sassafras thickets and "cain," as Bible-read folks spelt the cane, and streams didn't dry up in summer like they do now. When he got to the Ohio it was flush, too, and full of whirlpools and snags. He had his tool-chest along, intending to stop and work in Indiana and take down another boat. But he never got to the Mississippi with that, for it upset, and he only saved his chest and part of his load because he was near to the Indiana shore. He stored what he saved under bark, and came home a-foot, and in debt to neighbors who had helped him. But people never pressed a man that lost by Indians or water.

Now I go back for a spell. Thomas and Nancy both could read and write, and little Abe went to school about a year. He was eight years old at the time of the accident to Tom Lincoln's down-the-river venture. Thomas and Nancy were good common people, not above nor below their neighbors, and I did not take much notice of them, because there was no likelihood that their wedding would mean more than other people's did.

The preacher Jesse Head often talked to me on religion and politics, for I always liked the Methodists. I have thought it might have been as much from his free-spoken opinions as from Henry Clay's American-African colonization scheme in 1817, that I lost a likely negro man, who was leader of my musicians. It is said that Tom Corwin met him in Ohio on his way to Canada, and asked if I was along. The boy said no, he was going for his freedom. Governor Corwin said he was a fool; he had never been whipped or abused, but dressed like a white man, with the best to eat, and that hundreds of white people would be glad of such a good place, with no care, but cared for.

The boy drew himself up and said: " Marse Tom, that situation with all its advantages is open to you, if you want ter go an' fill it."

But Judge Head never encouraged any runaway, nor had any "underground railroad." He only talked freely and boldly, and had plenty of true Southern men with him, such as Clay. The Eli Whitney cotton-gin had now made slavery so valuable that preachers looked in Hebrew and Greek Testaments for scripture for it.

Tom Lincoln and Nancy, and Sally Bush were just steeped full of Jesse Head's notions about the wrong of slavery and the rights of man as explained by Thomas Jefferson and Thomas Paine. Abe Lincoln the Liberator was made in his mother's womb and father's brain and in the prayers of Sally Bush; by the talks and sermons of Jesse Head, the Methodist circuit rider, assistant county judge, printer-editor, and cabinet-maker. Little Abe grew up to serve as a cabinet-maker himself two Presidential terms.

It was in my trip to Canada after my negro that I met the younger brother of the great chief Tecumseh. A mob wanted to kill me because I was after my property that had legs and a level head. The Indian was one of the finest-looking men I ever saw, and in the full uniform of a British officer. He protected me, and we had a talk after the danger was over. He said that history was right about the death of his great brother

Tecumseh at the battle of the Thames in 1813. But the story of his skin being taken off by soldiers to make razor-straps was all a lie, as they never had the chance He was not even slain at the point in the battle indicated by Colonel Richard M. Johnson, whose accession to the Vice-Presidency in 1836 was largely due to the credit which he gained for this supposed exploit. My Indian protector said he was a lad at the time, but [was] there, and that the red men never abandoned their chiefs, dead nor alive

I come back again to the Lincoln-Hanks wedding of 1806 Rev. or Judge Jesse Head was one of the most prominent men there, as he was able to own slaves, but did not on principle Next, I reckon, came Mordecai Lincoln, at one time member of the Kentucky legislature. He was a good Indian fighter; and although some say he was the elder brother of Tom Lincoln, I understood he was his uncle, or father's brother. The story of his killing the Indian who killed old Abraham Linkhorn is all "my eye and Betty Martin."

My acceptance of this whole pedigree is on hearsay, and none of it from the locality of Tom Lincoln's home. There is a Virginia land warrant, No 3,334, of March 4, 1780, for four hundred acres of land, cost one hundred and sixty pounds, located in Jefferson County, Kentucky, on Long Run, and signed by William Shanon, D. S. J. C., and William May, S J C, witnessed by Ananiah Lincoln and Josiah Lincoln, C. C. (chain-carriers), and Abraham Linkhorn, Marker, dated May 7, 1785, five years later. "Mordecai Lincoln, Gentleman," is the title given one who died in Berks County, Pennsylvania, in 1735, and his will is recorded in the Register's office in Philadelphia. New Jersey, Virginia, and Tennessee also have the name correctly, in the last century. The fame of General Benjamin Lincoln of the Revolution was on every tongue at that time. In the field-book of Daniel Boone, owned by Lyman C Draper, five hundred acres of land was entered for Abraham Lincoln on treasury warrant No. 5,994, December 11, 1782 The officers of the land-office of Virginia could spell, and so could the surveyor and deputy surveyor (Record "B," p 60 of Jefferson County in 1785). The two chain-carriers spelled the name correctly Why not also think that the third man spelled his correctly? A very illiterate man could pronounce what he could not spell, and Abraham Linkhorn, who had money and could write, knew his own name. President Lincoln told James Speed: "I don't know who my grandfather was, and am more concerned to know what his grandson will be." I am not sure that we know, either, perfectly yet

While you pin me down to facts I will say that I saw Nancy

Hanks Lincoln at her wedding, a fresh-looking girl, I should say over twenty. Tom was a respectable mechanic and could choose, and she was treated with respect. . . .

I was at the infare, too, given by John H. Parrott, her guardian, and only girls with money had guardians appointed by the court. We had bear-meat (that you can eat the grease of, and it not rise like other fats); venison; wild turkey and ducks; eggs, wild and tame (so common that you could buy them at two bits a bushel); maple sugar, swung on a string, to bite off for coffee or whisky; syrup in big gourds; peach-and-honey; a sheep that the two families barbecued whole over coals of wood burned in a pit, and covered with green boughs to keep the juices in; and a race for the whisky bottle. The sheep cost the most, and corn was early raised in what is now Boyle County, at the Isaac Shelby place. I don't know who stamped in the first peach-seed, but they grew before the apples. Our table was of the puncheons cut from solid logs, and on the next day they were the floor of the new cabin.

It is all stuff about Tom Lincoln keeping his wife in an open shed in a winter when the wild animals left the woods and stood in the corners next the stick-and-clay chimneys, so as not to freeze to death; or, if climbers, got on the roof. The Lincolns had a cow and calf, milk and butter, a good feather bed, for I have slept in it (while they took the buffalo robes on the floor, because I was a doctor). They had home-woven " kiverlids," big and little pots, a loom and wheel; and William Hardesty, who was there too, can say with me that Tom Lincoln was a man and took care of his wife.

I have been in bark camps with Daniel and Squire Boone and James Harrod. We have had to wade in the " crick," as Daniel spelt it, to get our scent lost in the water, and the Indian dogs off our trail. When trailed and there was no water handy, I have seen Daniel cut a big grapevine loose at the bottom, with his tomahawk, from the ground. Then, with a run and swing from the tree it hung to, swing and jump forty feet clear, to break the scent on the ground. I have done it too, but not so far. He could beat any man on the run and jump, but it took more than two Indians or one bear to make him do it. If no dog barked in the silent woods, we could run backward very fast, and make Mr. Indian think we had gone the way we came. They went that way, and we the other for deer scalps and hair, Squirrels barking or chattering at Indians, or dogs, often told us of our danger. I wanted to have a pioneer exhibit at the great Louisville Southern Expositions of 1883 and 1884. I wanted the dense laurel and the pawpaw thickets planted in rich soil; the bear climbing the bee-tree, and beaten by the swinging log hung by the hunter in his way; the creeping Indian with his tomahawk, and the hunter with the old flint-and-steel rifle, just as I had seen them. Then I wanted to have women from the mountains and the counties that railroads and turnpikes have not opened, and have them in real life, to spin and weave, or bead and fringe the moccasin and hunting-shirt and leggings as they did when I was a boy. This, by the side of the industries and arts of the new era, and the wool and cotton machinery in its present perfection, would indeed tell to the eyes of the changes seen by an old man who has lived a hundred years. As they did not listen to me, I have asked Henry Cleveland, who was a boy and played with my little children at the Harrodsburg Springs in the forties, to write it as I talked to him. I am very deaf, but can see and talk, and will now write my autograph to what he has written and copied off, and will take up James Harrod at another time.

CHRISTOPHER COLUMBUS GRAHAM
in my 100drth year.

3. STATEMENT OF MRS. C. S. H. VAWTER

An important independent witness to the marriage of Thomas and Nancy Lincoln is revealed in the testimony of Mrs C. S. H. Vawter, who published a communication in the Louisville *Courier* of April 18, 1874, saying:

In the year 1859 I went to Springfield, Ky., to teach, and was in the same neighborhood when Lincoln received the nomination for President On the announcement of the news of the candidate all were on the *qui vive* to know who the stranger was, so unexpectedly launched on a perilous sea A farmer remarked that he should not be surprised if this was the son of Thomas Lincoln and Nancy Hanks, who were married at the home of Uncle Frank Berry. In a short time this supposition of the farmer was confirmed by the announcement of the father's name.

She then gives details of the wedding as she gathered them from neighbors.

It will be noted that this publication, as early as 1874, definitely located the marriage in Washington County. Mrs Hitchcock attributes the discovery of the marriage bond to the publication. Miss Tarbell rather credits it to the discussion that followed the publication of the affidavit of Dr. Graham.

In this Miss Tarbell is mistaken. The affidavit of Dr. Graham did not lead to the discovery of the marriage record; for the discovery was made not later than 1878, and published January 25, 1879, and Dr. Graham's affidavit is dated March 20, 1882, more than three years after the record was in print.

The testimony of Dr. Graham is not without value; but it would have been worth ten times as much if it had been published, as Miss Tarbell supposed that it had been published, prior to the publication of the discovery of the record. We cannot help asking why, if Dr. Graham knew all this, he did not tell it sooner. The fact that he waited does not discredit his evidence, but it makes it impossible for us to recognize him as a wholly independent witness.

Mrs. Vawter, however, brings to us testimony which possesses that distinct value. Her letter was published April 18, 1874, more than four years before the publication of the finding of the marriage bond and return. It bears irrefutable witness that there existed, in Washington County, a tradition, supported by the testimony of truthful people who claimed to have been eyewitnesses, that Thomas Lincoln and Nancy Hanks were legally married, and that in Washington County. These old people made that statement before any one knew that there was any record of the fact; and they agreed that the marriage occurred in the house of Richard Berry, the very man whose name subsequently appeared with that of Thomas Lincoln on the bond. Mrs. Vawter is a much more important witness than Dr. Graham. But his testimony is in full accord with hers, and, while it is evidently inaccurate in certain minor details, it is in its essential content in accord with truth.

APPENDIX III

THOMAS LINCOLN AS A LANDHOLDER

I. DID HE INHERIT LAND FROM HIS FATHER?

The grandfather of President Abraham Lincoln, whose name also was Abraham, was killed by an Indian, at a date which Lea and Hutchinson fix conjecturally as in the early summer of 1785. Lincoln, from family tradition, gave it as 1784. He appears to have been alive and to have acted as a marker in the survey of his tract of 400 acres in Jefferson County, May 7, 1785

Thomas Lincoln was five years old when his father, Abraham, was murdered.

Concerning his inheritance in his father's estate, Lea and Hutchinson, who do not appear to have given much original investigation to that part of their otherwise excellent book, say:

Taking advantage of the old English law of primogeniture then in force in Kentucky, the two elder brothers ousted their infant half-brother from all his rights of inheritance in his father's estate, his own mother, Bathsheba, being then almost certainly dead, or we may be sure that she would have protected him at least to the limit of her own dower rights, and the unhappy child was left to the tender mercies of strangers in a wilderness swarming with savage beasts and still more savage men —(pp. 83-4.)

The three sons of Abraham Lincoln were:

1. Mordecai Lincoln, born probably in 1764; a prosperous farmer and large landed proprietor; sometime sheriff of Washington County; removed to Howard County, Indiana, and about 1828 to Hancock County, Illinois, where he died in 1830. He was married, and had three sons, Abraham, James and Mordecai.

2. Josiah Lincoln, born July 10, 1766; removed to Harrison County, Indiana, where he died in 1836. He was married and left one son, Thomas Lincoln, late of Corydon, Harrison County, Indiana.

3. Thomas Lincoln, born in Rockingham County, Virginia,

January 28, 1780; married, June 12, 1806, Nancy Hanks; and died near Charleston, Illinois, December 2, 1849. His first wife died October 5, 1818, and he married Sarah Bush Johnston (December 2, 1819), who survived him and died April 10, 1869.

The Field Book of Daniel Boone shows an entry of 500 acres of land by Abraham Lincoln, on Treasury Warrant Number 5994, on December 11, 1782. The land was located on Licking River. A facsimile of the entry is in *Abraham Lincoln: A History*, by Nicolay and Hay, I, p.12.

On May 7, 1785, a survey was made of 400 acres of land for Abraham Lincoln, located in Jefferson County, on Treasury Warrant Number 3334. He himself served as marker at this survey, which fixes a possible limit on the date of his death. A facsimile of the surveyor's certificate is given in Nicolay and Hay, *supra*, I, p. 14.

As yet I have been unable to determine what disposition Mordecai Lincoln made of all his large landed estate, a portion of which was in Hardin County, or whether he inherited it all from his father, and whether he took it all under the right of primogeniture, or whether he acted as guardian of his minor brother Thomas and as custodian of his interests. One naturally conjectures that the land which Thomas Lincoln appears to have owned in Hardin County in 1803 may have been some part of his father's domain; but his deed to Milton, given eleven years later, gives the name of John Tom Stator as the man from whom he acquired it. No record appears to show why Thomas Lincoln lived around on other men's farms when he had one of his own. The old records in these Kentucky counties were not filed systematically and many of them are hopelessly lost. I suppose myself to have made a much more diligent search than has ever been made before, and have, of course, the advantage of all that has previously been discovered; but questions remain unanswered The men who have kindly assisted me in these researches in several Kentucky counties hold out little hope of the discovery of more papers. It is possible, however, that growing interest and some fortunate accident may later lead to the discovery of some document which thus far has eluded me. I give what I have been able to find.

2. THOMAS LINCOLN'S LAND AS MRS. HITCHCOCK IMAGINED IT

Mrs. Hitchcock says:

Considering the disadvantages under which he labored, he had a very good start in life when he became engaged to Nancy Hanks. He had a trade and owned a farm which he had bought in 1803 in Buffalo, and also land in Elizabethtown. If all the conditions of his life be taken into consideration, it is not true, as has been said, that Thomas Lincoln was at this time a shiftless or purposeless man.—*Nancy Hanks*, pp. 57-8.

The farm which Thomas Lincoln is supposed to have bought in 1803 was not the farm at Buffalo, which is the farm on Nolin Creek, where Abraham was born. Nor did he own any land in Elizabethtown. We did not know how he obtained money to buy his land on Mill Creek in 1803, but he abandoned it long before he occupied the land near Buffalo in 1808.

The tax lists of Washington County contain the names of the three Lincoln brothers, Mordecai, Josiah and Thomas. Both Mordecai and Josiah owned land. Josiah had 100 acres, Mordecai had 275 acres in Washington, 940 in Madison and 1130 acres in Hardin Counties. Mordecai continued to acquire land. Deed Book A, of Washington County, shows the transfer from Terah Templin to Mordecai "Linkhorn" of 600 acres of land on "Beech Fork River." Terah Templin was brother of Rev. Moses Templin, an early Presbyterian minister, who appears to have written the deed. It is a deed quite unusual in its language.

But while the two older brothers had land in abundance and added to their acreage, Thomas Lincoln is known to have owned the only land which appears to have been the farm on Mill Creek which he acquired five years before his marriage, and abandoned

He may have been wronged out of his inheritance by his older and designing brothers, but any one who really wanted land in that day could obtain it.

3 THE TITLE TO THE LINCOLN FARM

The ownership of the farm where Abraham Lincoln was born from the time of its original patent to the present is given me by Mr. Charles F. Creal of Hodgenville, Kentucky, as follows:

The chain of title from the Commonwealth to the present owner, so far as I have been able to trace it, is as follows:

1. *The Commonwealth of Virginia to William Greenough.* At a date unknown to me, but prior to July 29, 1786, William Greenough patented 30,000 acres, that is to say he was granted a patent or land grant, from the Commonwealth of Virginia.

2. *William Greenough to Joseph James.* By deed of July 29, 1786, Greenough conveyed one half of said grant, or 15,000 acres, to Joseph James of New York City.

3. *Joseph James to Richard Mather.* On June 11, 1798, Joseph James by endorsement on the deed of Greenough transferred his right and title to Richard Mather. In a legal proceeding of some character Charles Helm and Samuel Haycraft, Commissioners, by deed of date February, 1817, and of record in the office of the County Court of Hardin County, Kentucky, in Deed Book F, page 172, conveyed the 15,000 acres to Richard Mather.

4. *Richard Mather to William Duckworth.* By a title bond dated March 19, 1814, Richard Mather conveyed 100 acres of land to William Duckworth.

5. *E. Duckworth to Micajah Middleton.* By a bond still preserved, E. Duckworth conveyed to Micapah Middleton 300 acres " on which William Duckworth, deceased, formerly lived."

6. *Micajah Middleton to Richard Creal.* By endorsement on the above bond, dated July 21, 1828, Micajah Middleton transferred the 300 acres to my grandfather, Richard Creal, who held that portion of the land now known as the Lincoln farm down to the time of his death, when it passed by inheritance to his heirs.

7. *Creal Heirs to 'A. W. Dennett.* My father, J. C. Creal, and the other heirs of Richard Creal, conveyed the Lincoln Farm to Alfred W. Dennett of New York on February 12, 1895.

8. *Decretal Sale to Robert Collier and the Lincoln Farm Association.* Mr. Dennett attempted to convey the farm to the Christian Missionary Alliance, but his trustee in bankruptcy attacked the conveyance as fraudulent; and in a proceeding in the Circuit Court of this County the conveyance was set aside and a decree entered for the sale of the farm. At the decretal sale, in 1904, Robert J. Collier was the purchaser. He conveyed it to the Lincoln Farm Association, which was organized to take over the property; and it has since been transferred to the Government.

It will be seen from the foregoing that Thomas Lincoln had

no title to the farm, unless it may have been a verbal contract or written land bond which he forfeited by non-payment. It is evident from the above that Richard Mather had at least the equitable title to the Lincoln Farm when Thomas Lincoln lived here.

4. THE MILL CREEK FARM

The only land which Thomas Lincoln is known to have owned in Kentucky was located on Mill Creek in Hardin County, and title was obtained from John Tom Stator, September 2, 1803. This farm so far as known was not identified until the researches made for this book. Previous writers have made errors with reference to it. Lamon and Herndon supposed it to have been the Knob Creek farm   Others have thought it the farm where Abraham was born. Others have suggested that it might have been land adjacent to Elizabethtown, and that Thomas Lincoln's home in that town was on a corner of it. All are wrong   Mill Creek is well known, and the farm was none of those above suggested.

This land was deeded by Thomas and Nancy Lincoln to Charles Milton, October 27, 1814. The family continued to live upon the farm for one or two generations, and was known as " Melton."

The County Court Clerk of Hardin County, Mr. J. L Irwin, was copying for me the deed of Thomas and Nancy Lincoln, when a well-known surveyor of the county came in, and by comparison of the boundaries with others which he had run, identified the Lincoln farm. I am informed that **Mr. Morgan** is a thoroughly reliable surveyor. Mr. Irwin writes:

While I was copying this deed, Mr. William Morgan, who was sitting in here and who has done a great deal of surveying over the county, said that this description just fits the boundaries of the Melton land on Mill Creek   He knew the land and the family, but the family are now all dead or have moved away.

5. DEED OF THOMAS AND NANCY LINCOLN TO CHARLES MILTON

This Indenture made this twenty seventh day of October in the year of our Lord One Thousand eight hundred and fourteen, between Thos Lincoln and Nancy his wife of the County of Hardin and State of Kentucky, of the one part and Charles

Milton of the county and state aforesaid of the other part, Witnesseth:

That the said Thomas Lincoln and Nancy his wife, hath this day granted, bargained, sold and by these presents doth grant, bargain, sell, alien and confirm unto the said Charles Milton a certain tract or parcel of land containing two hundred acres, for and in consideration of One hundred pounds to the said Lincoln and Nancy, his wife, in hand paid by the said Milton, the receipt whereof is acknowledged, which land was patented in the name of William May and is conveyed from John Tom Stator to said Lincoln by deed bearing date the 2nd day of September 1803, lying and being in the said County of Hardin on Mill Creek and bounded as follows, to wit:

Beginning at a hickory corner to Robert Huston's survey, part of a sixteen hundred acre survey, thence south thirty degrees west one hundred and eighty three poles to a stake, corner to Huston, thence north forty five degrees west one hundred and fifty five poles to a black oak, corner to the original survey, north twenty four degrees west one hundred and forty poles to a white oak in Shepherd's line, corner to the original, thence north thirty one degrees west sixty poles to a dogwood, white oak and gum corner to Thomas Williams in the original line, thence with Williams' line south sixty seven east two hundred and fifty poles to a white oak and hickory, south thirty one degrees west twenty two poles to the beginning which courses contains two hundred and thirty eight acres, and the said Milton is at liberty to take two hundred acres out of the said two hundred and thirty eight acres where he thinks proper and the said Lincoln and Nancy his wife does forever warrant and defend the said two hundred acres of land from themselves and their heirs executors, administrators or assigns forever, to the said Milton, but not from the claim or claims of any other person. But if the said land should be lost by any better or prior claim, then the said Lincoln is to pay to the said Milton the sum of one hundred pounds. In witness whereof the Said Thomas Lincoln and Nancy, his wife, hath hereunto set their hands and affixed their seal the day and date before written. Interlined before signing

THOMAS LINCOLN (seal)
her
NANCY X LINCOLN
mark

HARDIN COUNTY sct.

I Samuel Haycraft, Jr, Deputy Clerk of the county court for the county aforesaid, do hereby certify that on the day of the date hereof, Thomas Lincoln and Nancy his wife, personally appeared before me and acknowledged the within indenture or deed of bargain and sale to Charles Milton as and for their voluntary act and deed, she the said Nancy being at the same time examined by me separate and voluntarily relinquished her right of dower which she has or may have in and to the land hereby conveyed, and that she was willing the same should be recorded and that I have truly recorded the same this 27th day of October 1814.

SAMUEL HAYCRAFT, JR. D.C., H.C.C.

Recorded Deed Book E, page 193.

A copy attest,

J. L. IRWIN, Clerk H.C.C.

It will be noted in the above deed that the thirty-eight acres was apparently abandoned. Probably Milton had another deed with the same boundaries calling for two hundred acres, and Thomas Lincoln's was virtually a quit claim No attempt was made to draw any boundary line between the two hundred acres conveyed and the thirty-eight acres supposed to have been left over.

6. THE DEED OF SLATER TO LINCOLN

The deed of John Tom Slater, or Stator, to Thomas Lincoln shows a transfer of 238 acres of land to Thomas Lincoln of Hardin County, Kentucky, in consideration of 118 pounds, paid in cash. The deed was signed and sealed, and left with the Clerk of the court to be delivered, and it remained with him for nearly eleven years. Apparently Lincoln abandoned the farm, and did not trouble to take the deed until he was approached by Milton with an offer for his equity in the farm. The record shows in the margin the following entry:

1814—Apr. 23rd. Delivered to Thomas Lincoln.

This was shortly before his sale to Milton, who paid two hundred pounds, or made some payment which was acknowl-edged as the equivalent of that amount, and took title October 27, 1812, to a tract of land with the same general boundaries, but whose acreage was stated as two hundred. The deed of Lincoln to Milton stated that the courses called for two hundred and thirty-eight acres, and he was at liberty to take the two hundred where he chose; which meant that Thomas Lincoln sold to Milton the whole tract, but did not guarantee that it contained more than two hundred acres. The original deed is in Deed Book B, page 253, Hardin County Deeds.

This indenture made this 2nd day of September one thousand eight hundred and three, between Dr. John F. Slator of Green County and state of Kentucky, of the one part and Thomas Lincoln of Hardin County, state aforesaid of the other part WITNESSETH: That for and in consideration of the sum of one hundred and eighteen pounds in hand paid, the receipt of which before the signing and sealing of these presents, he the said Dr. John F. Slator doth hereby acknowledge have bargained and sold and by these presents doth grant, bargain and sell unto the said Thomas Lincoln a certain tract or parcel of land containing two hundred and thirty-eight acres, part of the 1600 acre survey patented to William May, bought by said Slator of Joseph Fenwick and bounded as follows, to wit: Beginning at a hickory corner to Robert Huston survey, part of said 1600 acre survey, thence South thirty degrees west one hundred and eighty three poles to a stake corner to Huston, thence North forty five degrees West one hundred and fifty five poles to a black oak corner to the original survey North twenty four degrees West one hundred and forty poles to a white oak in Shepherds line corner to the original, thence North thirty one degrees West fifty poles to a dogwood white oak and gum corner to Thomas Williams in the original line, thence with Williams line South sixty seven East two hundred and fifty poles to a white oak and hickory South 31 degrees West twenty two poles to the beginning.

To have and to hold the above mentioned two hundred and thirty eight acres of land with all its appurtenances barns, stable, ways, houses, water and conveniences, to the above mentioned Thomas Lincoln his heirs executors and administrators forever against him, the said Dr. John T. Slator, his heirs executors or administrators forever, and he the said Dr. John F. Slator as well for his heirs as for himself doth further covenant and agree to and with the said Thomas Lincoln and his heirs that he will warrant and forever defend the above mentioned two hundred and thirty eight acres of land with all its appurtenances to the said Thomas Lincoln his heirs executors and administrators forever to their only proper use and behoof, against him the said Dr. John T. Slator and his heirs executors, etc. forever, but not against the claim or claims of any other person or persons whatever, but be it plainly understood should said land be taken by any prior or legal claim, then the above bound Dr. John T. Slator his heirs executors &c., to pay to the said Thomas Lincoln his heirs, executors etc, the above mentioned sum of one hundred and eighteen pounds In witness of the above bound Dr. John T. Slator doth hereunto set his hand and affix his seal the day and date above written.

JOHN TOM SLATOR (Seal)

Hardin County:

      Sct. s.s.

    I hereby certify that on the second day of September last this indenture.. from John Tom Slator to Thomas Lincoln was acknowledged by the said Slator to be his act and deed and the same was admitted to record on this 26th day of November 1803.

BENJAMIN HELM, H C.C.

A copy attest:—

J. L. IRWIN,
Clerk H C C.

Recorded in Deed Book " B," page 253

7. THE KNOB CREEK FARM

Of this farm, Lamon, relying upon Herndon's researches, said:

The land he now lived upon (two hundred and thirty eight acres) he had pretended to buy from a Mr Slater[1] The deed mentions a consideration of one hundred and eighteen pounds The purchase must have been a mere speculation, with all payments deferred, for the title remained in Lincoln but a single year. The deed was made to him, September 2, 1813; and October 27, 1814, he conveyed two hundred acres to Charles Milton for two hundred pounds, leaving thirty eight acres of the tract unsold. No public record discloses what he did with the remainder. If he retained any interest in it for the time, it was probably permitted to be sold for taxes. The last of his voluntary transactions, in regard to this land, took place two years before his removal to Indiana; after which, he seems to have continued in possession as the tenant of Milton.—LAMON, *Life of Lincoln*, p. 15.

Lamon is completely mistaken about this farm. Thomas Lincoln had no title to the Knob Creek farm, so far as records

---

[1] The name is given in the deed of Thomas and Nancy Lincoln as Stator. But the earlier deed to Lincoln gives the name as Slater, which I judge to be correct. But the deed was not to the Knob Creek Farm.

show. The farm which he "pretended to buy" from Slater, was bought in 1803, and that was the farm which he and Nancy sold on October 27, 1814. It was located on Mill Creek, in that part of Hardin which is still Hardin County. There is no evidence that Thomas Lincoln ever lived upon it after his marriage. He may have lived there alone or with some fellow pioneer when he first secured title in 1803, when he was twenty-three years old.

The record of ejectment suit on the Knob Creek Farm is cited in the chapter on Thomas Lincoln.

8. THE ELIZABETHTOWN LOT

On September 8, 1829, in consideration of $123, Thomas Lincoln and his wife, of Spencer County, Indiana, conveyed to T. J. Wathen a lot in Elizabethtown, sometimes alleged to have been the lot on which stood the log cabin to which Thomas Lincoln took his bride after their marriage, June 12, 1806.

Perhaps the money, $123, received by Thomas and Sarah Lincoln from the sale of this lot, assisted in paying the balance due on the eighty acres that remained of his Indiana farm before he sold it to Charles Grigsby; or he may have invested it in oxen for the removal into Illinois. The date of the sale would indicate that the money came most opportunely.

This deed is recorded at Elizabethtown, Kentucky, in Deed Book L, page 219.

When the author discovered that Thomas Lincoln on September 8, 1829, sold to Thomas J. Wathen of Hardin County, Kentucky, at lot in Elizabethtown, the county seat of Hardin County, he was happy in what he hoped might prove an indication that Thomas Lincoln took Nancy Hanks to spend her honeymoon with him in a house which though primitive, was certainly his own. That hope was doomed to disappointment. So far as any records thus far discovered show Thomas Lincoln never had or gave title to any land in Elizabethtown. The lot which he and Sarah sold for $123.00 in 1829, was one-half of a lot containing one and a quarter acres, and had never belonged to Thomas Lincoln. It was the property of Sarah Johnston after the death of her first husband. The lot was well located, and adjoined the Haycraft residence. It was sold to her at an unknown date by Samuel Haycraft, Sr. Her first husband had been the jailer, and during his lifetime they probably lived either in a residence adjacent to the jail and owned by the county, or as sometimes happens in Kentucky county seats, in a hotel. Some early Kentucky jailers found it profitable to operate a hotel as well as a jail. To this deed both Thomas and Sarah Lincoln made their mark.

Samuel Haycraft, Sr., was one of the oldest and most reputable citizens of Elizabethtown. The deed was acknowledged before Samuel Haycraft, Jr., for many years clerk of the County and Circuit courts. He was the man with whom Abraham Lincoln corresponded in 1860 with reference to the record of his parents' marriage. Mr. Haycraft lived to a ripe old age. He wrote a history of early times in Hardin County which was published in the Elizabethtown *News* but the articles have never been issued in book form.

This indenture made this 8th day of September in the year of our Lord one thousand eight hundred twenty nine, between Thomas Lincoln and Sarah, his wife, of the county of Spencer, and state of Indiana, of the one part and Thomas J. Wathen of the county of Hardin and state of Kentucky, of the other part, witnesseth; That the said Thomas Lincoln and Sarah his wife for and in consideration of the sum of one hundred and twenty three dollars to them in hand paid before the signing and sealing and delivery of these presents the receipt whereof in hereby acknowledged, have this day granted, bargained and sold, and by these presents do grant, bargain and sell to the said Thomas J. Wathen his heirs and assigns forever one undivided *moiety* or half part of a certain lot or piece of ground containing one acre and one-quarter lying near Elizabethtown, adjoining Samuel Haycraft, or the lot on which said Haycraft now lives, which lot is bounded as follows, to wit: Beginning about four feet northeast of the southeast corner of said Haycraft lot running thence South seventy degrees East twenty poles to a stake thence North thirty one degrees West twenty two poles to a stake in a line of said Haycrafts lot, thence west the same to the beginning. The *moiety* hereby conveyed to be taken off the end adjoining said Haycraft.

To have and to hold the said undivided *moiety* or half part of the aforesaid lot together with all and singular the appurtenances thereunto belonging or in any wise appertaining thereto to the said Thomas J. Wathen his heirs and assigns forever. And the said Thomas Lincoln and Sarah his wife, do further covenant and agree to and with the said Thomas J. Wathen that they will forever warrant and defend the aforesaid undivided half part of the said lot with its appurtenances from the claim of themselves their heirs and every other person or persons whomsoever claims the same. The said lot above described being the same conveyed by Samuel Haycraft, Sr., and wife to said Sarah Lincoln late Sarah Johnson. In testimony whereof, the said Thomas Lincoln and Sarah his wife have hereunto set their hands and seals the day and year above written.

his
Thomas (x) Lincoln   (Seal)
mark

Attest:

    G. A. F. George

her
Sarah (x) Lincoln   (Seal)
mark

Commonwealth of Kentucky.
    Hardin County s.s.

I, Samuel Haycraft, clerk of the county court, for the county court for the county aforesaid, do hereby certify that the foregoing deed from Thomas Lincoln and Sarah his wife, to Thomas J. Wathen, was on the 8th day of September 1829 produced to me in my office and acknowledged by the said Thomas Lincoln as and for his act and deed.

And the said Sarah being at the same time examined by me privately and apart from her said husband, declared that she did freely and willingly seal and deliver said writing and wishes not to retract it, and acknowledged said writing again shown and explained to her to be her act and deed and consented that the same may be recorded.

Whereupon the same is duly admitted to record in my office.

Given under my hand this 18th day of November 1829.

Samuel Haycraft, clerk.

A copy attent:
..   J. L. Irwin,
..   Clerk H.C.C.
Recorded in Deed Book " L," page 219.

9. THOMAS LINCOLN'S LAND IN INDIANA

William H. Herndon made inquiry concerning Thomas Lincoln's title to land in Indiana and obtained from the Commissioner of the General Land Office information concerning the patent that was issued " Thomas Lincoln, alias Linckhern." The letter contained the following information:

In reply to the letter of Mr. W. H. Herndon, who is writing the biography of the late President, dated June 19, 1865, herewith returned, I have the honor to state, pursuant to the Secretary's reference, that on the fifteenth of October, 1817, Mr. Thomas Lincoln, then of Perry County, Indiana, entered under the old credit system,—

1 The South-west Quarter of Section 32, in Township 4, South of Range 5 West, lying in Spencer County, Indiana.

2. Afterwards the said Thomas Lincoln relinquished to the United States the east half of the said South-west Quarter; and the amount paid thereon was passed to his credit to complete payment of the West half of the South-west Quarter of Section 32, in Township 4, South of Range 5 West; and accordingly a patent was issued to Thomas Lincoln for the latter tract. The patent was dated June 6, 1827, and was signed by John Quincy Adams, then President of the United States, and countersigned by George Graham, then Commissioner of the General Land Office.

Commenting on the transaction, Lamon says:

It will be observed, that, although Lincoln squatted upon the land in the fall of 1816, he did not enter it until October of the next year. And that the patent was not issued to him until June, 1827, but a little more than a year before he left it altogether. Beginning by entering a full quarter section, he was afterwards content with 80 acres, and took eleven years to make the necessary payments upon that. It is very probable that the money which finally secured the patent was furnished by Gentry or Aaron Grigsby, and the title passed out of Lincoln in the course of the transaction. Dennis Hanks says:

"He settled on a piece of government land,—eighty acres This land he afterwards bought under the two dollar act, was to pay for it in installments; one-half he paid, the other half he never paid, and finally lost the whole of the land."—LAMON: *Life of Lincoln,* pp 25-26.

10. THOMAS LINCOLN'S LAND NEAR DECATUR

Lamon says:

On the first day of March, 1830, after fifteen days' tedious and heavy travel, they arrived at John Hanks' house, four miles north-west of Decatur. Here John Hanks had cut some logs in 1829, which he now gave to Lincoln to build a house with With the aid of John, Dennis, Abe, and Hall, a house was erected on a small bluff, on the north bank of the north fork of

the Sangamon   Abe and John took the four yoke of oxen and
" broke up " fifteen hundred acres of land, and then split rails
enough to fence it in —LAMON: *Life of Lincoln*, p 75.

Concerning the land near Decatur the Circuit Clerk says:

We have made a pretty thorough search of the records of
this office from 1829, the beginning of the County, down to 1840,
during which time we do not find anywhere the title of any
property vested in Thomas Lincoln or Dennis Hanks. We do,
however, find numerous conveyances made to John Hanks, and
to various other people by the name of Hanks. For instance
we find upon September 2, 1834, John Hanks received a deed
from John Tuttle for the West ½ of the N.W. ¼ of Section 33,
Township 17 North, Range 2, East of the Third Principal
Meridian. I also find where the heirs of Joseph Hanks received
a deed from William Hanks, Senior, for the East ¹½ of the
West ½ of the N E. ¼ of Section 22, Township 16 North,
Range 1 East of the Third Principal Meridian. This is a small
tract of land very close to the place where Thomas Lincoln
erected a log house and lived during his stay in Macon County

Thomas Lincoln and Abraham Lincoln occupied a piece of
land in the S W. ¼ of Section 28, Township 16 North, Range 1
East of the Third Principal Meridian, which is about two and a
half miles south of the site of the present village of Harristown;
but neither Thomas nor Abraham Lincoln ever held title to
the land. At that time it belonged to the government.

JOHN ALLEN, Clerk Circuit Court, Decatur, Ill.

10. THOMAS LINCOLN'S FINAL HOME IN ILLINOIS

Lamon says:

It is with great pleasure that we dismiss Tom Lincoln, with
his family and fortunes, from further consideration in these
pages. After Abraham left him, he moved at least three times
in search of a " healthy " location, and finally got himself fixed
near Goose Nest Prairie, in Coles County, where he died of a
disease of the kidneys, at the ripe old age of seventy-three. The
little farm (forty acres) upon which his days were ended, he
had, with his usual improvidence, mortgaged to the School Commissioners for two hundred dollars,—its full value. Induced by
love for his step-mother, Abraham had paid the debt and taken
a deed for the land, " with a reservation of a life-estate therein,
to them, or the survivor of them." At the same time (1841)
he gave a helping hand to John Johnston, binding himself to

convey the land to him, or his heirs, "after the death of Thomas Lincoln and his wife," upon payment of the two hundred dollars, which was really advanced to save John's mother from utter penury. No matter how much the land might appreciate in value, John was to have it upon these terms, and no interest was to be paid by him, "except after the death of the survivor as aforesaid." This, to be sure, was a great bargain for John, but he made haste to assign his bond to another person for "fifty dollars paid in hand."—LAMON: *Life of Lincoln*, pp. 76-7.

APPENDIX IV

HERNDON'S ATTITUDE TOWARD LINCOLN

I have asked every one known to me in Springfield who knew William H. Herndon such questions as these:

Beyond the sale to Lamon of copies of his manuscripts, and his public defense of Lamon after the publication of his book, how far was Herndon responsible for what Lamon published? How do you account for some things which Herndon published about Lincoln, particularly after he had witnessed the reception of Lamon's book? Was Herndon jealous of Lincoln? Did he wish to bring Lincoln down to his own level? Was it a case in which no man is a hero to his valet? Was Herndon resentful because Lincoln did not give him office?

To these questions I obtained a very wide variety of answer. One of the best examples of the reply unfavorable to Herndon was furnished me in a recently discovered letter of Hon. Milton Hay, who knew both men well, and who wrote while the Herndon book was undergoing active discussion in Springfield.

Hon. Logan Hay, former State Senator of Springfield, gives me this information about his father:

My father, Milton Hay, was born in Kentucky in 1817, and died in 1893. He came to Springfield in 1832. He was the uncle of John Hay, the secretary of President Lincoln; my father's brother, Dr. Charles Hay, was John Hay's father. My father was in Lincoln's office as a student and young lawyer. His contact with Lincoln was at the beginning the contact of a boy with a man, but he came to know Lincoln intimately. There was a break of some years in their close association. My father practiced law in Pittsfield from 1843 to 1857, but his father's family lived here, and he met Lincoln frequently. From 1857 to 1861 he was very close to Lincoln.

I. LETTER OF HON. MILTON HAY

SPRINGFIELD, ILL., Jan. 26, 1892.

HON. THOS. VENNUM:

Your letter of the 24th instant in regard to that queer produc-

360

tion, Herndon's *Life of Lincoln,* came duly to hand, and but for a spell of the grip would have been answered sooner.

Herndon was a peculiar kind of crank, and his work is regarded as deserving of but little credit by those who were acquainted with both Lincoln and Herndon Although professing to have been gotten up with friendly intentions toward Lincoln, such professed good intentions are not credited. Herndon had a sort of loose connection with Lincoln as a partner in local business of this county, and after Lincoln's election, as the understanding is here, he went to Washington, as an applicant for some place and was disappointed. He returned home soured and sore-headed, and thereafter was active with the Democrats.

Immediately upon Lincoln's death, he proclaimed himself as the only living man who knew all about Lincoln, assumed that he had been Lincoln's conscience-keeper, that he was the man who had made Lincoln what he was, and particularly that Lincoln confided to him secrets known to nobody else.

It is not believed here that any such confidence had existed Much of the narrative contained in the book is known to be erroneous here. Herndon states the matter as though he was personally acquainted with the facts, and it has impaired credence in whatever he has stated as being only within his own knowledge.

The general opinion of the book seems to have been to magnify disproportionately those acts of Mr. Lincoln's life which Mr. Lincoln himself outgrew and would have wished his friends to forget. As illustration of this, we may take the undue prominence given to his rather ridiculous love scrapes as told by Herndon, but of which much is known to be misstated and exaggerated; also the Shields dual affair. About this latter affair, Mr. Lincoln in after life was rather sore. I was present on one occasion when one of the participants in the affair was in Mr. Lincoln's office, trying to rehearse the particulars of that affair, to which Mr. Lincoln seemed much disinclined. After that person left Mr. Lincoln remarked to me, " That man is trying to revive his memory of a matter that I am trying to forget "

The story of Lincoln's having told Herndon that his mother was a bastard is wholly discredited by everybody who knew Lincoln, as well as much other matter in the book alleged to have been derived from conversations with Lincoln.

I think I have fairly given you the criticism made here by those best acquainted with both Lincoln and Herndon.

Yours truly,

M. HAY.

The above letter by Hon. Milton Hay, uncle of John Hay, and a close friend of Lincoln, at one time in the office with him, was found in the papers of the law firm of McAnulty, Allen & Humphrey, who were successors to the firm of Green & Humphrey, who were in turn successors to the firm of Hay, Green & Littler. It was furnished and certified, April 4, 1919, by the senior member of the firm, Mr. R. H. McAnulty.

2. MORE FAVORABLE OPINIONS

On the other hand, Hon. Hardin W. Masters, who knew Herndon intimately, assured me that in innumerable conversations with Herndon, he never detected any indication of resentment, but that Herndon always spoke of Lincoln with deepest reverence. I went with Mr. Masters to Petersburg, where he spent many years of his life, and where for a time he was district attorney. During the period of Masters' activity there, Herndon habitually attended court at Petersburg His brother-in-law lived there, and Herndon, reduced in circumstances, could obtain free board during the term of court, and pick up a few dollars in fees as associate or senior counsel with younger lawyers. When Herndon was not thus employed, he would sit on one of the settees on the court-house lawn, glad to have any one sit down beside him, and listen to him while he talked about Lincoln. Mr. Masters tells me that he saw Herndon in all moods, and under varying conditions, for I regret to say that Herndon was not always a sober man, and Mr. Masters tells me that Herndon never spoke the name of Lincoln without reverence His feeling reached the level, as he declares, of adoration; and he is confident that gross injustice is done Herndon in attributing to him spite or resentment.

I called on Hon. G. W. Murray, who for one year was Herndon's law-partner. He tells a pathetic story of the close of Herndon's public career. Herndon struggled on against poverty, against his temptation, against failing sight and hearing. One day he slammed his book shut, lifted his hand, and, rising, cried out in agony of spirit: " My God! I can't see; I can't hear! I'm going to quit." He put on his hat, left the office, and did not return. Judge Murray gave to me a formal statement and signed it. It deserves to be printed, and I give it herewith:

LINCOLN AND HERNDON

By Honorable G. W. Murray of Springfield

The following statement was made by Hon. G. W Murray, of Springfield, Illinois, to Rev. William E. Barton, D D , April 21, 1920:

I was partner of William H Herndon in this city in the year 1878. I had come in 1876 from Ohio, my native State, in 1876. I was born near Troy, Ohio, in July, 1839, and shall be 81 on my next birthday. I was elected Judge in 1890, and served continuously, excepting between 1894 and 1898, when I was not on the bench. My whole term of service as judge was sixteen years.

I came to Illinois with great admiration for Abraham Lincoln, and was glad to be associated with a man who had known him intimately as Mr. Herndon had known him. Mr. Herndon was as willing to talk about Lincoln as I was to listen.

Continuously, when we were not busy, and perhaps at some times when we should have been at work, he talked to me of Lincoln. There was hardly any period of Lincoln's life or phase of his character that we did not discuss.

It has been charged that Mr Herndon was embittered against Mr. Lincoln, and a reason has been assigned in Mr. Lincoln's alleged refusal to give Mr. Herndon an office which Herndon is alleged to have coveted. I believe this to be untrue, both as to the fact and the motive.

So far from Mr Herndon's cherishing resentment against Mr. Lincoln, the whole character of his conversations, which were many, discredits that statement. I can remember no single word spoken by him concerning Mr. Lincoln in which there appeared to be any such animus. He held Lincoln in the highest admiration. He had no regrets for anything that had ever occurred between them.

Mr. Herndon told me that Mr. Lincoln offered him office. My impression is that there was more than one such offer. One that I remember was of a judicial character, a position in what I think was called the Court of Claims, a court established to consider claims of Southern people against the Government for damages alleged to have been suffered by them during the war. He spoke of other positions which he believed he might have had. He said that he did not desire office.

There is absolutely nothing in the charge that Mr. Herndon cherished any spirit of unfriendliness toward Mr. Lincoln, or any feeling of disappointment because of his failure to secure through Mr Lincoln political appointment.

Toward Mrs. Lincoln, Herndon had no kindly feelings. He did not denounce her, nor refer to her in terms which a gentleman might not with propriety use toward a lady, but he did not like her and she did not like him, and he believed that she made Mr. Lincoln's home life unhappy   He believed that Mr. Lincoln had loved Ann Rutledge, and that her memory was very dear to Lincoln.

Mr. Herndon continually spoke of Mr. Lincoln's greatness and goodness   He told me of traveling over the State from one county seat to another with the meager law-library in saddlebags.   Often Lincoln went to a session of court without any client, but he almost always secured clients on the ground, through his association with local attorneys.   Herndon spoke of Lincoln's ability as a lawyer and statesman. He also admired greatly Lincoln's kindness of heart, his forgiving disposition. He was greatly impressed by Mr. Lincoln's attitude of kindness toward young men in the army who were found guilty of transgression of military regulations.

His habitual attitude toward the memory of Lincoln was one of admiration.

In short, I cannot remember a single instance in which he spoke unkindly of Lincoln, but invariably the reverse.

I was a warm admirer of Abraham Lincoln before I became Herndon's partner; but under the influence of Herndon that admiration grew to a sincere affection and devotion.

Largely through what Mr. Herndon related to me, I have spoken from time to time about Mr. Lincoln, in public addresses, one of which I delivered at the Lincoln monument in this city in 1903, and another before the Authors' Club in 1913.   The sincere admiration which in these and other addresses I have invariably expressed for Abraham Lincoln is in full accord with the spirit in which Mr. Herndon always spoke of him.

It has been charged that Mr. Herndon believed and charged that Abraham Lincoln was an illegitimate child.   I know what Herndon wrote which has been thus construed, and in my judgment Mr. Herndon did not intend to convey that impression. I believe that Herndon believed that Lincoln was of legitimate birth, and would have resented a charge to the contrary.

I knew Mr Herndon too intimately and talked with him too freely to be mistaken about his real feeling toward Mr. Lincoln.   He honored Lincoln, and I learned in association with

Herndon, to honor more and more the character of Abraham Lincoln.   G. W. MURRAY.
    April 21st, 1920.

3. STATEMENTS BY HERNDON'S DAUGHTERS

Mrs Fleury, Mr. Herndon's eldest daughter, said to me:

"It is a serious wrong to the memory of my father to speak of him as an infidel. He was not orthodox in his belief, and he was driven into controversies which caused him to emphasize what he did not believe rather than what he did believe. But the inscription on his monument, copied from his own signed statement, refutes completely the claim that he was an infidel. I know that people called him so, and he did not always take the trouble to deny it, but he was a reverent man.

"His reverence, however, was not so much for the God of the Bible, whom he identified with the God of certain creeds that he could not accept, as for the God of nature. He did not believe in miracles, nor in supernatural revelation. He held that nature and the human mind are the vehicles of God's revelation He loved nature, and he studied it constantly. In this respect he was very unlike Mr. Lincoln, who did not care for such studies.

"It was his custom on Sunday to send to the livery stable for a slow horse and carriage, and take his children out into the country He studied botany and geology and the habits of birds. Nothing escaped his attention, and he did not permit it to escape us. He pointed out to us the beauty of the earth and sky, and said, 'Remember, a great Power made all this.' He plucked flowers and showed them to us, and pointed out their parts and their functions, and the wonder of them, and spoke reverently of the God who made them, and the birds and ourselves.

"He was an habitual teaser. He joked with his children. He was always teasing his daughters. When he came home from the office, he would ask me, 'Who was that dirty-faced little boy I saw kissing you through the fence?' He was delighted with my indignant denials, and would catch me up and laugh heartily at my loudly proclaimed innocence. When he was through with his teasing, he would romp with us, and instruct us. He was a loving father. He was not orthodox, and was much opposed to the theology of his time. I think if he were living now he would not be thought of as an infidel. He had his faults and his weaknesses; and his children have some memories that are not happy ones. But he was an honest man, an intelligent man, a man who loved freedom and God and his children and Mr Lincoln"

Similar testimony comes to me from his other daughters, both those by his first wife and one by his second wife, and I am confident they are essentially correct.

APPENDIX V

THE SUPPRESSED PAGES OF THE REED LECTURE

The first publication that suggested the illegitimacy of Abraham Lincoln was the *Life of Abraham Lincoln* by Ward Hill Lamon, published in 1872. It was based upon manuscripts sold to Lamon by William H. Herndon, who had been for many years the law-partner of Lincoln It would be difficult to exaggerate the indignation which the publication of this book roused against Lamon, Herndon, and Chauncey F. Black, who was known to have some share in the authorship and whom Herndon afterward declared to have " written quite every word of it." The Rev. James A. Reed, pastor of the First Presbyterian Church in Springfield, prepared and delivered, there and elsewhere, a lecture which was published in *Scribner's Monthly* in 1873 and is now difficult to obtain.[2] Mr. H. E Barker, bookseller and collector in Springfield, obtained the original manuscript of certain portions of this address which were eliminated before publication They appear, however, to have been used in the delivery of the lecture. They contain very hot shot for those who were understood to have been responsible for this slander against Lincoln and his mother These sentiments, as expressed by Dr. Reed, met the hearty approval of the major part of his audiences, while some thought them needlessly severe in their castigation of Herndon, who was still living in the city where this vehement denunciation was uttered. These suppressed pages may now be published without any harm to any one, and will serve to show what Lincoln's Springfield neighbors heard with approval when this address was given by the minister of the church which he attended. The largest section of this manuscript begins without a heading, at page 1 of the lecture, and contains twelve consecutive pages. There are three other pages, detached and less important:

[2] The text of this lecture, as published in *Scribners' Magazine*, is reprinted in the appendix to *The Soul of Abraham Lincoln*

THE SUPPRESSED PAGES

THAT INJUSTICE has been done the life and sentiments of Mr. Lincoln, is not simply the judgment of my own mind. Judge Advocate General Holt, has expressed sentiment that no pains have been spared, to collect materials with which to defame the character of Mr. Lincoln. And while he is now so loved as to render what has been published in a measure harmless, yet he fears it is calculated to do him great injury in another generation.

A prominent and influential Journal of the country also makes an appeal to the old friends and neighbors of Mr. Lincoln at Springfield to defend his good name against the attacks of those who, while claiming to be his friends, seek to blacken and defame his character. "We arraign them all," says this journal, "in the name of the dead, who cannot be heard again; in the name of the Nation; in the name of religion and morality, for the crime of remaining silent while one of their own citizens, pretending to speak for them, persists in blackening the reputation of him they love.

"By common consent of this country the body of Abraham Lincoln was borne from the scene of his martyrdom to his home in the city of Springfield, and by loving hands laid to rest at Oak Ridge. Shall it be said that those who of old knew him and loved him, and take to themselves something of the honor that clings to his name, and who are to keep watch and ward by his grave, shall sit in dumb self-complacency while birds of evil omen croak and mousing owls peck at his laurels?"

Whether the public is generally aware of it or not, it is very evident from this appeal that Mr. Lincoln's character has been unfairly dealt with from some quarter. And the first question that is asked is, Who are the persons and what are their motives?

This is the question I am first of all compelled to answer. And these gentlemen cannot complain of me if I am as frank as they have been in telling who Mr. Lincoln was

The first man who attempted to blacken the reputation of Mr. Lincoln after his death was a low, drunken, infidel by the name of William H. Herndon; a man of such disreputable character and sentiments that nobody about Springfield cared to give the notoriety even of a passing kick. This man, soon after Mr. Lincoln's death, collected what he considered sufficient materials with which to immortalize himself as the historian of Mr. Lincoln. But not having the means to publish it, as it seems, he deposited the manuscript for safe-keeping in the First National Bank of Springfield, where it remained in durance vile as a sort of collateral security for a small claim which the distinguished author was not able to discharge, and where it would most likely have remained in its merited obscurity but for the assistance of his distinguished friend and associate, Colonel Ward H. Lamon, who brought the precious document to light by purchasing it, paying $2,000 for it, as I am reliably informed, and incorporating it in a book of his own. These gatherings of Mr. Herndon, thus coming before the public, endorsed by Mr. Lamon, and published in a large and expensive volume, and circulated all over the country, claiming to be the only real and fair and reliable history of Mr. Lincoln and his sentiments, it does seem fitting that some notice should be taken of these gentlemen and their infamous publication

In all that has been written and published of the life and services of Abraham Lincoln, these two men are the only ones who have had the complacency like Joab of old to come forward and take their hero by the beard with the right hand, and to kiss him and then gallantly stab him under the fifth rib

While the voice of calumny was silent, speaking no evil of the dead, these two men, professing to be his familiar friends, and who did eat at his table, and whom like the little ewe lamb that did sleep in the poor man's bosom, and brought up; Mr. Herndon as an indifferent and second-rate lawyer, enjoying for a time the advantages of a connection with him, the vanity of which caused him to force himself upon the notice of the public; and Mr Lamon, reaping the emoluments of an office, as martial of the District of Columbia, worth from $10,000 to $15,000 a year; these two worthy friends of the President, with the assistance of a third, whose name does not appear in the book, but who is known to be the son of Jeremiah S. Black of this state, by a singular combination of their wits and meager talents, form a tri-partite mountain of authorship, and this mountain labors, and there comes forth this *ridiculus mus*—Lamon's *Life of Lincoln*—a volume that will disgrace its author as long as it will disgrace the character and do injustice to the memory of Abraham Lincoln.

The motives of these men, in contributing to this work, vary with their individuality. No one can read this book without making the discovery that it is written only in the pretense of friendship. The chagrin of an unrecognized and disappointed aspirant for political favors appears on all that Mr. Herndon writes And Mr. Lamon writes as one who has heard the voice of his master saying, " Give an account of thy stewardship, for thou mayest no longer be steward." Mr. Lincoln had evidently read the character of both these men, and had given them to understand that he did not need their services. They were weights he cared no longer to carry. And for this they undertake the grateful task of writing his biography, and make him out a bastard and an infidel. The patriarch Job once exclaimed in the midst of a persistent attempt of his distinguished friends to defame his integrity, "Oh, that mine enemy had written a book!" Mr. Lincoln has been spared that wish. His distinguished friends have written a book, and a book that proclaims them and justifies him as clearly as it did Job in calling them his enemies. For never was there cooler or meaner detraction if not malignancy, concealed beneath the mask of apparent friendship than we have in this book.

It has been said that the celebrated Dr. Johnson once made the remark that he thought a man might be justified in taking the life of another to estop the biographical taking of his own. It is not to be supposed that Dr. Johnson seriously meant to justify the killing of a man short of self-defense. But if there was a clear case in which a man could be justified, for biographical reasons, in killing off a few of his anticipated and ambitious historians before he died, I don't know a clearer case than that of Mr. Lincoln.

Mr. Herndon's earnest and zealous effort to prove that Mr. Lincoln was an infidel to the day of his death is simply the last service to which he can put his hero to his own advantage. It is well known that the infidelity which he attributes to Mr. Lincoln is simply the reflection of his own infidel sentiments. He would fain give them character by palming them off as the dying sentiments of a man whose shoe latchets he is not worthy to stoop down and unloose. He so shapes his detraction of the President as that he may have the prestige of his name to bolster up and give currency to his own miserable infidelity.

It is easy to detect the underlying motive in this bold and unscrupulous effort to fasten this charge of final scepticism upon Mr. Lincoln. The very pains and persistency of the effort of these men to make the allegation good, bears on its face the confession that the public impression of a change in Mr. Lincoln's sentiments previous to his death was well founded, and betrays the fear that unless the evidence which sustains this impression be annihilated, Mr Lincoln's name will go down to posterity bearing its testimony to the truth of Christianity rather than to the lie of infidelity. There would have been no necessity for such a labored effort of friendship to keep Mr. Lincoln's name in the rank and file of infidelity had there not been a strong

and general impression that Mr. Lincoln had changed his sentiments and was not an infidel when he died.

.   .   .   .

I wonder not that a distinguished gentleman writing me
from Washington expresses his indignation by saying, "I am
amazed at Lamon's book. It is the compound fruit of a serpent
and a jackal."

APPENDIX VI

WASHINGTON COUNTY AFFIDAVITS

It is firmly believed in Washington County, Kentucky, that Abraham Lincoln was born there and not in Hardin. These affidavits, excepting that of County Attorney Polin, which was made for this book, were procured for the purpose of establishing that claim In another place that opinion is discussed. These depositions are here recorded because, apart from the question of the birth of Lincoln, they show a body of consistent recollection concerning the marriage of his parents.

I. AFFIDAVIT OF WILLIAM THOMAS HARDESTY

The deposition of William Thomas Hardesty, taken before me at the Law Office of Polin & Polin, in Springfield, Kentucky, and in the presence of the County Judge, W. A. Waters, and the County Attorney, Joseph Polin, for the purpose of preserving his testimony as a historical record for Washington County. Witness after being duly sworn and examined by Joseph Polin, testified as follows:

Q—State your name, age, residence and occupation?

A—William Thomas Hardesty, born April 30th, 1837, reside near Walton's Lick, in Washington County and am a farmer.

Q—Please state your father's name and your mother's maiden name?

A—William Hardesty, who married Annie Moody. William Hardesty was born on the....day of........17...

Q—Please give us a short sketch of your father.

A—My father came from Maryland about the year ...., in company with his father, Charles Hardesty, and settled near Walton's Lick, where Edward Smothers now lives. This Walton's Lick is named for General Matthew Walton, who manufactured salt at this place in the days of the early settlement of the county and the old salt well is on the north bank of Lick Creek just east of the ford. I still have in my possession one of the old kettles which were used by Walton in the manufacture of salt. It is rather peculiar looking, the vessel having no legs and only one ear, and holding 40 gallons. People came to this place for miles and carried away salt on horseback. My father died

372

about the......day of........18... There lived in the same neighborhood the Moodys, the Berrys, the Reddings, the Haydens, and the Lincolns and quite a number of others

Q—Please state what you know about the history of the Lincoln family in Washington County from having heard your father talk about them.

A—I have often heard my father say that he knew Thomas Lincoln and Nancy Hanks· that he remembered distinctly when as a small boy he slipped away from home and went to their wedding in the year 1806 when they were married by Jesse Head in the small log cabin which formerly stood on the east side of the Litsey and Valley Hill pike at a point just north of the Mill Race near Poortown. They afterwards lived in this cabin and it was there that Abraham Lincoln, the President of the United States, was born. The spring near the roadside has been called the Lincoln Spring since my earliest recollection I have heard my father talk of Abraham Lincoln, the grandfather of the President, being killed by the Indians a short distance from his home in this county. This older Abraham Lincoln lived on the farm now owned by James L. Moran and at a point near the forks of the Litsey and Valley Hill pike with the pike leading to Springfield and on the stream known as Lincoln's Run At this place there is a small branch emptying into Lincoln's Run and the house was located on the north side of the Litsey and Valley Hill pike and on a point between this branch and Lincoln's Run. I recollect that there is a small mound and formerly there were some rocks where the house stood. I remember of seeing many times and of having used many times in hunting the old powder horn which was taken from around the neck of Abraham Lincoln after he was killed by the Indians. This horn had on it the Masonic emblem of a compass and a square. There was also carved on it the image of an eagle beneath which were the words, "Liberty or Death," and the name, "A. Lincoln." This horn remained in our family for quite a number of years. I don't know how my father came into possession of it but have often heard him say in speaking of it what I have related above. He finally gave this horn to the late attorney, Richard J. Brown, and that is the last trace I have of it. I have frequently heard my father say that he knew Abraham Lincoln, the President, when he was a small boy living with his parents in this county. My father was always quite positive of the fact that the President was born in this county, being born a few years before the family moved to that portion of Hardin County which is now Larue.

W. T. HARDESTY.

STATE OF KENTUCKY.

WASHINGTON COUNTY.

I, Olive Walker, Examiner for and within the county and state aforesaid, certify that the foregoing deposition of William Thomas Hardesty, was taken before me at the time and place and for the purpose stated in the captian; that said witness was duly sworn before giving it; that it was written by me in short-hand and afterwards transcribed by me on the typewriter and that it was signed by the witness: that there were present County Judge, W. A. Waters, and County Attorney, Joseph Polin.

Given under my hand, this 7th day of November, 1919.

OLIVE WALKER,

Examiner for Washington Co. Ky.

2. AFFIDAVIT OF R. M. THOMPSON

This affiant, R. M. Thompson, says that he is native of Washington County, Ky., 79 years of age. He was raised in said county, and has lived therein all of his life except eight years, when he resided at Indianapolis, State of Indiana. His present address is Springfield, County and State aforesaid. The mother of Nancy (Hanks) Lincoln, who was the mother of Abraham Lincoln, was an own cousin of affiant's mother. Affiant knew well Richard Berry, Jr., who was a grandson of Richard Berry, Sr., who was the guardian of said Nancy (Hanks) Lincoln, wife of Thomas Lincoln. Said Richard Berry, Jr., lived with his father, Frank Berry, a son of Richard Berry, Sr. The marriage of Thomas Lincoln and Nancy Hanks, parents of President Abraham Lincoln, occurred in the same house or premises recently sold and conveyed by Mrs. Sallie Reed, wife of Henry F. Reed, to Maj. D. W. Sanders, of Louisville, Ky. Said Richard Berry, Jr., told affiant as he now recollects, and his memory serves him well, about the close of the late Civil War, that President Abraham Lincoln was born in said house in Washington County, Ky., the same in which his parents were married. Affiant was well acquainted with William Hardesty, who lived to an extreme old age, and whose residence was always in the neighborhood of said premises.

Said William Hardesty was an honorable, reputable and creditable citizen, and every way worthy of belief. He has made affidavit (that is said William Hardesty) and sworn that he was present, and witnessed the marriage of Thomas Lincoln and Nancy Hanks in said house, by the Rev. Jesse Head, deacon of the Methodist Episcopal Church. Said William Hardesty has frequently told affiant that there was born to Thomas Lincoln and his said wife a daughter older than President Abraham Lincoln, said daughter being the first child and born in said house. She died at an early age. Said Richard Berry, Jr., was a good citizen, reputable and worthy to be believed

R. M. THOMPSON.

STATE OF KENTUCKY, WASHINGTON COUNTY, ss.

I, James L. Wharton, Clerk of the Circuit Court for the State and county written above, certify that R. M. Thompson, who is a most reputable citizen, subscribed and made oath and was sworn to the foregoing affidavit this day   He is entitled to be believed, and reputable, upright, moral, and creditable in every way.   Before he executed said affidavit, I read it over to him and explained its contents to him and he understood the same, and did, in my presence freely and voluntarily execute said affidavit.   Said affidavit was dictated for said R. M. Thompson

Witness my hand and seal of office this 13th day of April, 1891.

J L WHARTON (Seal)
Clerk of Washington Circuit Court.

3. AFFIDAVIT OF MR. JOSEPH POLIN, COUNTY ATTORNEY OF WASHINGTON COUNTY, SPRINGFIELD, KENTUCKY

Affiant, Joseph Polin, states that he was born in Washington County, Kentucky, April 28th, 1883; that he has made diligent search for record evidence and evidence traditional concerning all matters relating to Abraham Lincoln and his antecedents, so far as they belong to the history of this county. He is familiar with the rumors that gained currency at one time in Larue County, concerning the alleged illegitimacy of Abraham Lincoln. The affiant states that to the best of his knowledge and belief these rumors were never credited in this county among the people who had known the Lincoln family. The record of the Lincoln family in this county, as shown by records both published and unpublished, is an honorable one. The Berrys and the collateral families also were reputable people and their descendants are still living in this county and are highly esteemed. Before the discovery of the marriage return for Thomas and Nancy Lincoln, the reliable people of this county, indignantly denied, as I have been reliably informed, the charges which they deemed slanderous, affecting the character of the mother of Abraham

Lincoln. The discovery of that document is a complete confirmation of their confidence in the chastity of Nancy Hanks Lincoln.

JOSEPH POLIN.

Subscribed and sworn to before me by Joseph Polin, this 16th day of March, 1920.

JNO. A. POLIN.
Notary Public.

My commission expires May 22, 1923.

APPENDIX VII

LA RUE COUNTY AFFIDAVITS

I. THE AFFIDAVIT OF HON. RICHARD W. CREAL

STATE OF KENTUCKY ss.
COUNTY OF LARUE

The affiant, Richard W. Creal, states as follows, after being duly sworn—

My name is Richard W. Creal. I was born in Larue County Kentucky 1853 and I am a son of Richard Creal who formerly owned the farm in Larue County upon which Abraham Lincoln was born, the same now owned by the Lincoln Farm Association. Upon one occasion when with my father, " Aunt " Peggy Walters, who was an old woman, pointed out to us the place where Abraham Lincoln was born. The cabin which she said Abraham Lincoln was born in was situated a short distance from the Cave Spring (now known as the Lincoln Spring). I was about twelve years old at the time I heard Mrs. Walters make this statement. She stated further that she knew the Lincoln family well, both before and after the date of the birth of Abraham Lincoln; that she was living hardly a mile away from the Lincolns at the time of the birth of Abraham

Affiant further states that shortly after this conversation he and his father were passing the home of one of the early settlers Jack McDougal who lived on the Bardstown and Green River Turnpike, about four miles from the Lincoln farm. That he heard a conversation between his father and McDougal in which McDougal stated that he knew the Lincoln family, that they were living in this county at the time Abraham Lincoln was born; that they lived in a cabin about two and one half miles south of Hodgenville, on the Hodgen's Mill and Aetna Furnace road.

(Signed) RICHARD W CREAL.

Subscribed and sworn to before me by Richard W. Creal this July 6th 1906.
CHARLES WILLIAMS
N P L C

2. THE AFFIDAVIT OF W. D. KIETH

STATE OF KENTUCKY SS.
COUNTY OF LARUE

The affiant, W. D. Kieth, after being duly sworn deposes and says—

My name is W. D. Kieth, and I live at Buffalo, Larue County, Ky., and I am 62 years of age. I was born in the state of Indiana. I am a son of Nehemiah Kieth who was born in Hardin County, Ky. (now Larue County) the 14th day of February 1807, on a farm about three fourths of a mile from the farm now owned by the Lincoln Farm Association, the birthplace of Abraham Lincoln.

When Lincoln was making his first race for the presidency, and while we were living in Indiana, I heard my father say that he remembered Lincoln when they were boys together down in Larue County, and that they had played together many a day. My father told me further that his mother, my grandmother, was present at the birth of Abraham Lincoln, in Feby 1809; that he was born near the Cave Spring about two and one half miles south of the Hodgen's Mill and Aetna Furnace road, on the farm now owned by said Lincoln Farm Association in Larue County, Ky. My grandmother was a Larue, a daughter of one of the early pioneers in this section of the country.

And further the affiant sayest not.

W. D. KIETH.

Subscribed and sworn to before me by W. D. Kieth this July 6, 1906.

CHARLES WILLIAMS,
Notary Public Larue Co. Ky.

3. THE AFFIDAVIT OF ROBERT ENLOW

STATE OF KENTUCKY Sct.
COUNTY OF LARUE

The affiant, Robert Enlow, after being duly sworn, upon his oath states that he is 45 years old, was born and reared in LaRue County, Kentucky, on the North Fork of Nolin, about 2½ miles east of the town of Hodgenville. Affiant further says, I am a farmer, have resided on a farm all my life. I taught in the public schools of LaRue County fourteen years, and have for the last two sessions represented LaRue County in the legislature.

My Grandmother Kirkpatrick stated in my presence that at the time of Abraham Lincoln's birth she was living on the South Fork of Nolin, about two miles west of Hodgenville; that she knew of her own personal knowledge that he was born on the farm ever since known as the Lincoln Farm, and now owned by the Lincoln Memorial Association.   She further stated that the affiant's great-grandmother, and the mother of Abraham Enlow, was sent for and taken to the Lincoln home on this event and attended on Mr. Lincoln's mother, she being a practicing physician at the time.

At the time my grandmother made this statement there was a conversation going on as to the exact spot of Lincoln's birthplace and my grandmother detailed these facts as facts that she knew of her own personal knowledge

(Signed) ROBERT ENLOW.

Subscribed and sworn to before me by Robert Enlow, this the 10th day of July 1906.

CHARLES WILLIAMS
Notary Public LaRue County Ky.

4. THE AFFIDAVIT OF JOHN BROWNFIELD

STATE OF KENTUCKY
COUNTY OF LARUE

The affiant, John Brownfield, after being duly sworn upon his oath states that he was born in Hardin County Ky. (now Larue Co.) and is now 86 years old.   He says " I have heard my father George Brownfield, who came to what is now Larue County and located at Buffalo, about 2½ miles from the Lincoln farm, in 1790, say that Abraham Lincoln was born in this county on the farm known as the Lincoln Farm.

I have also heard Wm. Cessna, another very old citizen and father of Judge Jonathan Cessna of Larue Co., say that he knew it to be a fact that Lincoln was born on said farm in Larue County.   I have lived all my life in the vicinity of this farm.

JOHN BROWNFIELD, SR.

Subscribed and sworn to before me by John Brownfield this the 6 day of July 1906.   I further certify that this affiant's memory was clear at the giving of this statement and he read this affidavit and signed it without the aid of his eye glasses, which he had forgotten and left at home.

CHARLES WILLIAMS
Notary Public Larue Co. Ky.

5. THE AFFIDAVIT OF THOMAS C. WALTERS

STATE OF KENTUCKY ss.
COUNTY OF LARUE

The affiant, Thomas C. Walters, after being duly sworn deposes and says:

I was born in Larue County, Ky., in 1855, and I now live in said county, and my post office address is Sonora, Ky. I am a grandson of " Peggy " Walters, one of the early pioneers in this section of the country. Upon an occasion I heard her speaking to one Mr Helm in which she said that she knew the Lincoln family well; knew them while they were living about two and one half miles from Hodgenville, Ky., on the farm now owned by the Lincoln Memorial Association; that she knew this family well both before and after the birth of Mr. Lincoln (Abraham); that Abraham Lincoln was born at this place; that she frequently went to see the Lincoln family, who were in poor circumstances, and that she assisted the mother with the infant child (Abraham Lincoln). ·Affiant further says that the mind and memory of grandmother was perfectly clear at the time of this conversation.

Affiant further says that he knew Abraham Enlow, another old settler; that he heard Enlow say that Abraham Lincoln was born out at the Lincoln farm in Larue County. That he rendered the Lincoln family many little acts of kindness and that he believed they named their infant son for him " Abraham " because of the kind treatment he had given the family.

THOMAS C. WALTERS.

Subscribed and sworn to before me by Thomas C. Walters this July 4th, 1906.

CHARLES WILLIAMS,
Notary Public.

6 THE AFFIDAVIT OF AMOS WALTERS

My name is Amos Walters. I live in Larue County about two miles from the town of Hodgenville and am a farmer. I was born in this county (Larue) in 1841 and I have made this my home all my life I had an aunt by the name of " Peggy " Walters who was present at the Lincoln home the night Abraham Lincoln was born. She, together with my uncle, Conrad Walters, lived in that vicinity about one mile from the Lincoln place.

Some time before the death of my aunt, and about the time Mr. Lincoln was coming into prominence, I heard my old aunt make this statement: That she recollected very well the birth of Mr. Lincoln; that she was present at the time of his birth; that she knew the father and mother of Mr. Lincoln; that he was born in the cabin near the old spring on the farm now owned and controlled by the Lincoln Memorial Association in Larue County, Ky.

Affiant states further that his aunt at the time of this conversation was quite an old woman, but her mind was bright and her memory was clear on this.

AMOS WALTERS.

Subscribed and sworn to before me by Amos Walters this the 30th day of June, 1906.

CHARLES WILLIAMS,
Notary Public.

7. THE AFFIDAVIT OF DAVID T. BROWNFIELD

STATE OF KENTUCKY
COUNTY OF LARUE   ss.

The affiant, David T. Brownfield, after being duly sworn deposes and says:

My name is David T. Brownfield. I was born in Larue County, Kentucky, in 1837. I was born about two miles from the birthplace of Abraham Lincoln. My father, George Brownfield, came to this county in about 1790 and moved to the site of my birthplace. He knew the Lincoln family and I have heard him speak of them. He knew they were living in Larue County at the time of the birth of Abraham Lincoln. I have heard him say that Abraham Lincoln was born in this county. Affiant further says that he knew Abe Enlow and Charles Friend, two early pioneers of this section of the country; that they were each living in this county at the time Abraham Lincoln was born here and they each said that the old Creal farm, about two and one half miles south of Hodgenville, was the place where Abraham Lincoln was born.

The affiant further says: "I was in Washington City July 1861 and visited the president. I asked Mr. Lincoln the direct question where he was born as I wanted to hear this from his own lips. He told me that he was born at the Cave Spring about 2½ miles south of the town of Hodgenville, that this farm was situate on the road known in the early days as the Hodgen's Mill and Aetna Furnace road. In this conversation Mr. Lincoln asked me about his boyhood friend and playmate Austin Gollaher, and appeared to be very much interested in the old settlers of Larue County.

The affiant further states that he lives in Louisville, Ky., and that his street address is 620 West Chestnut.

DAVID T. BROWNFIELD.

Subscribed and sworn to before me by David T. Brownfield this the 5th day of July 1906.

CHARLES WILLIAMS
Notary Public for Larue Co.

8. THE AFFIDAVIT OF JOHN C. FRIEND

STATE OF KENTUCKY
COUNTY OF LARUE } ss.

My name is John C. Friend and I live in Hodgenville, Ky., and I have been in the active practice of law for over fifteen years. Many years ago I heard a conversation in front of the old drug store building on the site of which now stands the business house of G. O. Kirkpatrick in Hodgenville, Ky., in which Mr. Abraham Enlow, who at the time was a very old man and who has been dead for a number of years, made the following statement:

That he was on the way to the old Kirkpatrick mill with a "turn" of corn, and Thomas Lincoln, the father of Abraham Lincoln, halted him and asked that he loan him the horse that he (Enlow) was riding, explaining that he wanted to go after a midwife or "granny-woman" as he denominated her. Mr. Enlow said that Mr. Lincoln assisted him in removing the sack of corn from the horse and that he (Enlow) remained by the roadside until Mr. Lincoln returned with the old woman riding behind him. In a few days thereafter, Mr. Enlow continued, he heard that a boy baby was born into the Lincoln family and that it had been given the name of Abraham. Mr. Enlow thought that possibly this little act of kindness on his part had something to do with the new baby being named Abraham, not knowing quite likely that the name was a family name. Mr. Enlow in this conversation explained that Thomas Lincoln lived at the time the child "Abe" was born on what has since been known as the Richard Creal farm, and that it was necessary for him to pass by it in going from where he (Enlow) lived to the old Kirkpatrick mill aforesaid.

JOHN C. FRIEND.

Subscribed and sworn to before me by John C. Friend this June 30th 1906.

CHARLES WILLIAMS
Notary Public for Larue Co.

9. THE AFFIDAVIT OF CHARLES WILLIAMS

STATE OF KENTUCKY
COUNTY OF LARUE } Sct.

I, Charles Williams, Notary Public in and for the County of Larue and State of Kentucky, hereby certify that I am personally acquainted with each and every witness who has testified to the several foregoing affidavits, as to the birthplace of Abraham Lincoln; that I know the families of all save one, Jack McDougal, and considerable of the family history of all, and certify to the fact that each of these affiants is personally known to me to be worthy of credit on oath, that their families, to wit: the Walters, Brownfields, Friends, Enlows, Kieths, McDougals and Creals are now and have been since the early days of Hardin and Larue counties among the best and leading families of this section. A short time ago I, in company with my law partner, Mr. L. B. Handley, visited the old graveyard near South Fork Church, on the south bank of Nolynn, and being shown the gravestone of "Aunt Peggy Walters" referred to in the accompanying affidavits, by her grandson, we found that she was born on December 11th 1789 and died on the 26th day of Oct. 1864, which becomes an important fact in connection with the statement of her oldest son, the date of her marriage, and her statement that she was present at the birth of Abraham Lincoln.

Given under my hand the 10th day of July 1906.

CHARLES WILLIAMS
Notary Public for Larue Co.

APPENDIX VIII

WHERE WAS ABRAHAM LINCOLN BORN?

These appendices contain affidavits and other documents from Washington County, Kentucky, tending to show that Abraham Lincoln was not born in what is now La Rue County, but in Washington County, and in the home of Richard Berry, where his parents were married. It is commonly, if not universally, held in that county that Thomas and Nancy Lincoln lived for three or more years with the Berrys, and later removed to Hardin County. This affirmation is based on the testimony of old men after the Civil War that they had seen Abraham Lincoln as a little child, playing at the Berry home, and also on a tax return, believed to be of the year 1811, and which contains the name of Thomas Lincoln as a resident of Washington County.

I am rather sorry that Hon. Joseph Polin, County Attorney of Washington County, to whom I am much indebted for assistance, has come to question whether the tax list referred to, and which I have examined carefully, is really of the year 1811, and he has not yet determined in what year it belongs. I am still hoping that it will be found to belong to 1811, as it will then confirm an opinion which I hold tentatively that Thomas and Nancy Lincoln lived only two winters in the cabin on Nolin Creek, where Abraham Lincoln was born, and that before they made their new home on the Knob Creek farm, from which, in 1816, they removed to Indiana, they returned for at least a year to Washington County, and lived with Nancy Hanks' relatives.

The claim of Washington County to have furnished the birthplace of Abraham Lincoln is inadmissible. It is honor enough that his parents should have been married there, and that that county should have preserved the record of the marriage. The house, too, was preserved, and now, much remodeled, it is standing at Harrodsburg, Kentucky, and is used as a sort of historical museum.

Some of the early biographers of Lincoln, apparently learning that he was not born in the Elizabethtown cabin, confused it with the Knob Creek farmhouse, and thus added to the con-

384

fusion. Henry J. Raymond, of the *New York Tribune,* in his octavo volume of more than 800 pages, issued in 1865, printed a good steel engraving, with this title, sub-title and note·

THE EARLY HOME OF ABRAHAM LINCOLN AS IT NOW STANDS IN
ELIZABETHTOWN, HARDIN COUNTY, KY.

His father built this Cabin, and moved into it when Abraham was an infant, and resided there until he was seven years of age when he removed to Indiana.

Thomas Lincoln did not build it, and Abraham never lived in it.
Abraham Lincoln was born in the log cabin, now standing inclosed in a marble temple, above the Rock Spring, on the Lincoln farm, about two and one-half miles south of Hodgenville, in what was then Hardin and now is La Rue County, Kentucky. The farm now is owned by the Government, and is a national park. The purchase of the farm, and the preservation of the cabin, is due to the good work of the Lincoln Farm Association. Of the birth of this Association, and of its successful work in preserving this important building, the president, Mr. Richard Lloyd Jones, said on February 12, 1907:

The most valuable assets of any nation are the traditions, the sacred associations, and shrines made holy by the accumulatory love with which successive generations bedeck them. George Eliot said: "No nation has ever become great without holidays and processions dedicated to the noble." The United States as yet is notoriously poor in this direction. This is not wholly on account of its youth, but on account also of the indifference to spiritual welfare which has characterized a youth enamored of material plenty and drunk with the prosperity that comes from the easy conquest of fertile acres and exhaustless mines American youths have turned longing eyes toward the holy places of Europe, and visited the birthplaces of Robert Burns and Schiller, the tombs of Walter Scott and Victor Hugo, and the millennial monument of King Alfred at Winchester; while the birthplace of our matchless American—the strong-handed, clear-headed, and great-hearted Lincoln—has been left, after its acres have been impoverished by careless tillage, to become a humiliation to the poet and the historian, and the butt of ridicule to the irreverent.
Since that strong yeoman pioneer, Thomas Lincoln, moved

his family across the Ohio into the almost unbroken wilderness of Indiana, this historic ground has been transferred by title but three times. A year ago last August this " little model farm that raised a Man," as Mark Twain has happily called it, was placed on sale at public auction on the court-house steps at Hodgenville, Kentucky, the neighboring town, to free it from the entanglement of a protracted litigation between a private estate and that of a religious society that had tried to acquire it. At the time the Commonwealth of Kentucky directed this public sale it was discovered that this historic spot was coveted by at least two large mercantile establishments, both of which were planning to exploit it for commercial ends. To prevent this, and believing that this birthplace of the " First American " should forever belong to the American people, one of the present officers of The Lincoln Farm Association bought the farm, and at once interested a group of representative American citizens in forming a national association for the preservation of this ground.

This group of citizens, acting as a self-appointed board of trustees, organized the Lincoln Farm Association, which was promptly incorporated under the laws of the State of New York. The title of the Lincoln birthplace farm was transferred to this association, and the program for enlarging the membership of the society was at once begun.

Rather than make it possible for a few men of great wealth to contribute large sums to the development of this national shrine it was decided to receive into membership in the society any one who contributed to the general fund of the association as small a sum as twenty-five cents, and to limit all contributions to twenty-five dollars—thus making the great memorial to Lincoln represent the tributes of all the people, whom he loved and served, and not those of a privileged few.

The purpose and plans of this new patriotic society that was to make this Kentucky farm, almost in the center of population of the United States, a worthy companion of Mt. Vernon in the affections of our countrymen were placed before the President of the United States and his Cabinet, one of whom was one of the organizers of the society. All gave it most enthusiastic and hearty support. The scheme was then laid before members of the United States Senate and House of Representatives, Governors of States, men of letters everywhere, and educators of national fame. With their unqualified endorsement, a year ago this week the Lincoln Farm Association, through the pages of some of the most prominent weekly and monthly publications and the newspapers throughout the country, appealed to the American public for members. The response was immediate and generous.

Subscriptions came in from every State in the Union—North and South, East and West To every subscriber the Association issued a handsomely steel-engraved certificate of membership, bearing a portrait of Lincoln, a picture of the log cabin in which he was born, the White House as it appeared when he occupied it, the autographs of all the officers and trustees, and the seal of the Association The names of these members are filed in card catalogues and classified by States. When the list of members has been completed and the constructive work of the Association has culminated in the centenary of February 12, 1909, this list will be preserved and guarded in the Historical Museum, which will have been erected on the farm, as the honor roll that built the Lincoln Farm Memorial.

The Lincoln Farm Association to-day represents about twenty thousand members. The average subscription has been a little less than a dollar and forty cents to a member, and both the average of the subscriptions and the issue of certificates of membership have increased with each succeeding month.

During the year the trustees of the Association have placed the farm under the personal charge of a competent caretaker, who lives on the ground. They have sent Mr Jules Guérin and Mr. Guy Lowell, two of America's foremost landscape architects, to survey the ground and plan its development, and they have purchased the cabin in which Lincoln was born from the speculators who took it from the little knoll where it originally stood and exploited it as a side-show at various fairs and international expositions. This cabin was found stored in a cellar at College Point, on Long Island, New York. The Pennsylvania Railroad provided a special car, which Mr. John Wanamaker decorated with flags and the national colors. The Governor of Kentucky sent to New York a special squad of State militiamen to escort the old weather-worn logs, Lincoln's old Kentucky home, back to its native soil. Its ride to Louisville is historic. It rested a day under military guard at Philadelphia, Baltimore, Harrisburg, Altoona, Pittsburg, Columbus, and Indianapolis. Thousands of citizens came to see and begged the privilege of touching the sacred pile. Mayors of cities and Governors of States paid eloquent tribute to the rude timbers that first sheltered the sad humorist of the Sangamon. And when at last the special train that bore it, brilliant in red, white, and blue, crossed the Ohio into its native border State it was met at the Louisville depot with martial music and military honors. It was carted through the city's streets and placed in the city's park, where Colonel Henry Watterson, one of the trustees of the Association, and Adlai E. Stevenson, former Vice-President of the United States, himself a Kentuckian, made the formal orations welcoming back to its native soil the cabin in which Abraham Lincoln was born.

The most cordial cooperation has been pledged by many of the surviving commanding generals of the Confederate Army, and the Grand Army of the Republic has officially endorsed the work of the Association, and empowered its commander-in-chief to call upon its upwards of six thousand posts and to enlisting all patriotic citizens as members of the Association.

On the 12th day of February, 1909, the nation will celebrate the one hundredth anniversary of Lincoln's birth. On that day the Lincoln Farm Association will dedicate the birthplace farm to the American people. The principal address will be made by President Roosevelt, and the nation's most distinguished representatives, North and South, will take part in this dedication and centennial celebration. No national park within our vast domain can emphasize our national ideals and our abiding union as will this birthplace farm.

Ninety-eight years have passed since these rough rolling acres made claim to the affections of coming generations. The soil which cradled the man of tender strength, and the air which first fed the heart that suffered for a whole distracted people, and not for a single section, can serve a nobler end than ripening corn and squashes. The inspiration of high citizenship must ever emanate from such a spot. In these years, so crammed with eager life and so possessed with appetite for gain, the lesson of the Lincoln Farm becomes the nation's imperative need. Democracy is ever humble. The full-grown souls made at simple shrines are worth our emulation. The light of history is with each succeeding year revealing with greater clearness the rare beauty of Lincoln's strong spirit. He harmonized his high ideals of speech with conduct; and back of the black clouds of passion through which this uncouth figure led his divided people there always shone the soft radiance of a love unsoiled by a single touch of hate. The country not only reveres the memory of Abraham Lincoln, but it loves the man. To his people—the " plain people "—shall ever be entrusted the care of his first home, and there they shall, as he himself said he always tried to do, " pluck a thistle and plant a flower wherever a flower will grow."

The past half century's unparalleled development of material riches and prosperity has not given our nation the supremacy of the commercial world without cost. Our keener patriotic sensibilities have been dulled in the strenuous competition for individual success. It is a pathetic truth which supports Colonel

Henry Watterson's assertion that to-day we love the dollar as once we loved liberty. Though we are a virile people we are not without need of these things that remind us of times when cheeks blushed for the sorrows of men.

To Lincoln's people to-day is given the rare privilege of revealing to all generations to come that high strain of patriotism known to Lincoln's men of nearly fifty years ago. If laws safeguard nations less than songs, and sentiment alone inspires the souls of men, how better can we ensure the perpetuation of our country's glory than by keeping alive and before us the heroic and unselfish achievements of those who made firm our foundations in the past?

This birthplace farm will symbolize to our posterity the strong heroism that left the New England hills and the fertile valleys of Virginia, self-sufficient in their needs, to hew a nation out of a wilderness. It lies in the neutral State that in our great crisis was torn by its loyalty to all the stars in the flag. It will forever be a monument to our union rather than to our lamentable differences—and it will be the most signal tribute ever paid by the American people to the nation's greatest servant.

Richard Lloyd Jones, who represented *Collier's Weekly* in the purchase of the Lincoln Farm, and was made President of Lincoln Farm Association, was at the time managing editor of *Collier's Weekly*. It was through his influence, in good part, that Mr. Collier became interested. Back of the interest of Mr. Jones lay the interest of his father, Rev. Jenkin Lloyd Jones, Pastor of All Soul's Church, Chicago, editor of *Unity*, veteran of the Civil War, and fearless champion of a hundred good causes. Jenkin Lloyd Jones, more than any other man, deserves to be remembered as the rescuer of the Lincoln Birthplace.

He visited the place in February, 1904, and found it neglected and held in no high local regard. He wrote an article which was published in *Unity* March 24, 1904, calling on Congress to purchase the farm and on the people to contribute memorial buildings, museum, and so on. His whole plan has not been followed, and need not here be reprinted, but the substance of his article and plea was this:

A slow, chilly drive through a drizzling rain over a pasty red clay road of three miles from the little village of Hodgenville, Kentucky, brought me to the cradle spot of the greatest American, the sole American who shares with Washington the love and admiration of the civilized world. Washington and Lincoln are the two names that have been lifted above all sectional, party and social prejudices. They have ceased even to be American—they belong to Humanity. King and Peasant, Monarchy and Republic, rich and poor, foreign and native, North and South, unite in honoring them.

It is a touching tribute to both that their names are so often connected and are fast becoming indissoluble. In the estimation of the competent as well as in the admiration of the young it is not Washington *or* Lincoln, but it is Washington *and* Lincoln. There is no occasion for invidious comparison. So different are they there is no chance for rival interests, for local or other jealousies. So removed are they in time and temperament, so different were their tasks, that they can never be considered as antagonists or rivals. Washington created, Lincoln perpetuated. Washington directed the crude forces of a primitive country, Lincoln directed and controlled the same forces grown turbulent and for a mad space of time defiant and antagonistic

Proud is the Nation that has produced both a Washington and a Lincoln, so different and yet so near akin. Washington was noble; so was Lincoln, but he was loving too Washington was just; so was Lincoln, but he added to justice, gentleness. Washington was sagacious; so was Lincoln, and he was also witty. Washington was pre-eminently guided by the head, he was the judgment of his people and his cause; Lincoln, not wanting in judgment, was dominated by the heart; he was the providence of his people, the friend of his foes, and in the light of time his foes have become his appreciative friends and loyal champions.

And still the birthplace of this great American is the picture of desolation and neglect. The humble cabin wherein he was born has been carried away as a curious show; there remain to mark the spot only a crude pole set in the ground and a few flagstones left there by Nature or by chance. Even the famous spring of water is desecrated and neglected accessible to pigs, cattle and horses. This spring still flows with delicious water, but the pilgrim who drinks from it must drink as I was glad to do without the help of cup or goblet. It still pours its wealth of water from under the overhanging cliffs, as it did when it attracted Thomas Lincoln, the carpenter, and led him to preempt his homestead, to cut the logs and to build the hut into which he brought his bride, Nancy Hanks, and where the three children were born to them.

The great trees are gone, but the ride of sixty-four miles from Louisville enables the tourist to judge even yet what the great forest must have been in its pristine glory. The solitary sycamores, the stately elms, the great oaks and the vigilant pines that still remain, suggest the impressive surroundings of the little cabin into which, on the twelfth day of February, 1809, Abraham Lincoln was born. The farm of 110 acres, the title of which is only two or three removes from the land warrant of Thomas Lincoln, is now worse than an abandoned field The title is in litigation, and the local estimate holds the land well nigh valueless. Fifteen hundred dollars was mentioned as an extravagant price for it. An old house in a state of advanced dilapidation remains on the place and is occupied by an intelligent man of the mountain type, who seems to act as an unauthorized, at least as an unremunerated custodian. A bill was introduced into the Kentucky Legislature a few weeks ago for the purchase by the State of this farm and providing for setting it apart as a memorial park, forever dedicated to the public; but the fate of this bill seemed to be a matter of supreme indifference to the residents of Hodgenville; indeed, its very existence appeared to be unknown to many of them The attitude of this otherwise thrifty little village seems to be that of indifference, not of ignorance. My driver expressed the public sentiment when he said, "We people here think it mighty common, but folks what come from north of the Ohio river make a great to-do about it, and fuss around cutting sas'fras sticks and the like" Surely this ought not to be The intelligence of our own country, our obligation to the future and our respect for the "consensus of the competent" of the world over ought to lift this neglected shrine into the dignity and respect that become the birthplace of a great historical character.

This cannot be done by local enthusiasm, nor does it seem to me to be a State problem or obligation. It is a national lesson, a national opportunity which rises into a national obligation. Surely the government that is expending millions of dollars on the historic parks of Arlington, Gettysburg, Chickamauga, Missionary Ridge and Vicksburg, could spend a few thousands in preserving this shrine as a pacific memorial to the civilian whose splendor outshines all the epauleted heroes of all our wars.

How is this to be done? First let the Lincoln farm be bought by the Government, then all else will follow easily Once the title is secured, a sense of permanence and of adequate maintenance will be assured. Then something like the following should speedily follow:

A word as to the general treatment of the farm. It should be all fenced with a good honest rail fence, worm pattern, six rails high, properly blocked, staked and ridered—"such a fence as father used to build" Such a fence could be made picturesque, for there is the possibility of art in a rail fence as there is in a marble statue

The farm is divided by a public road On the spring side it should be brought to as high a stage of park cultivation as possible; lawn treatment with a few sheep, a lot of chickens and one or two old-fashioned little red cows, not the new-fashioned Jerseys. The opposite section of the farm, on the other side of the road, should be restored as soon as possible to forest glory. Let all the old trees be planted back, the necessary walks arranged for, and then let Nature do her work, and a hundred years from now there will be a forest indeed, dense and majestic, such as the botanist will delight to visit. Near the entrance on the spring side let the Government put the noblest statue of Abraham Lincoln that art ever produced. Awaiting something better, this might well be a replica of St. Gaudens' noble statue, now situated in Lincoln Park, Chicago, the most worthy representation of the great emancipator yet modeled by sculptor's hand.

Has the time not come? Abraham Lincoln can wait; his fame is sure, but the American children and coming generations cannot afford to lose the passing opportunity. The old settlers are dying, the back woods are nearly all cleared, the type of American life represented by Thomas and Nancy Lincoln is fast passing away. Even the relics of that life are becoming scarce, and that life is too valuable, too full of spiritual potency, to pregnant with divine grace and power to be forgotten and lost. For this reason there is occasion for haste. Let the legislators at Washington cease for awhile their clamorings and their clashings in the interests of parties, sections and the enginery of destruction, and apply themselves to this constructive task, so easily accomplished, so filled with pacific potencies, so benignant a contribution to history.

Theodore Roosevelt, then President of the United States, was the principal speaker on the day when the Lincoln Memorial was dedicated; but on Sunday, February 11, 1917, not many months before his own death, a service of remembrance was held at the farm near Hodgenville, and Jenkin Lloyd Jones was the chief orator. He was permitted to see of the fruit of his own toil. The author of this volume met him a few days afterward at Cumberland Gap, and the glow of that memory was still upon the heroic old soldier.

The early illustrated biographies of Lincoln contain a steel engraving showing what purports to have been his birthplace. Even in the Lincoln home in Springfield, this engraving is shown as "the house where Mr. Lincoln was born and where he lived the first seven years of his life." Even the Chicago Historical

Society displayed the engraving with the same information until it was recently corrected. That picture is not of the house where Lincoln was born, but of the house where Thomas and Nancy lived in Elizabethtown when they were first married, and which the early biographers assumed to have been also his birthplace. A number of reputable works have easily, and pardonably, fallen into the same error.

Even among such cabins as abounded in primitive Kentucky, the Lincoln home was humble. Many log houses had two rooms, with an open porch between and a stone fireplace at each end. Not so the Lincoln house, which was small and with a stick chimney.

The farm which Thomas Lincoln occupied was as sterile as any in the region. It was nearly destitute of timber and its growth was low bushes and " barren grass." The land was pleasantly rolling, and nearly all of it tillable. But the soil was a stubborn clay, which even now is only meagerly productive. If Thomas Lincoln had been a very enterprising man he would have bought a better farm, for land was the cheapest thing in sight in those days and no one possessed of enterprise had difficulty in buying a really good tract.

What title, if any, Thomas Lincoln ever had to this farm is not known. Recorded deeds were few. Land transfers were commonly made on what was called a land bond. The bond by which a portion of this same farm, including the site of the birthplace, came into the possession of the Creal family is in existence. It is signed by E. Duckworth, who had inherited it from William Duckworth, deceased, and is made to Micajah Middleton under date of August 17, 1827. A year later, on July 21, 1828, Micajah Middleton endorsed this contract to Richard Creal, whose name in the contract is spelled Crail. The maker of such a bond was theoretically required at any time to change a warranty deed for it, but in a majority of cases this formality was dispensed with.

It is not known that Thomas Lincoln had even this kind of title. Land was sometimes taken over by verbal contract and boundaries were established by piling a little brush at each of the corners. Exact boundaries were seldom attempted, excepting where a stream or other natural object gave a fixed line. Technically, Thomas Lincoln's title to the place where his son Abraham was born may have been nothing more than that of a squatter;

but even squatters' titles had a value in that day and they were generally respected. Whatever the character of Thomas Lincoln's claim upon this land, it afforded him all the protection he needed during the brief period of his occupancy. This is supposed to have been about four years, but there is good reason to doubt his living there for even so long a period as this.

APPENDIX IX

DOCUMENTS OF THE LINCOLN FAMILY

1. THE WILL OF ISAAC LINCOLN

In the name of God, Amen. I, Isaac Lincoln, of the County of Carter and State of Tennessee, being sick and weak of body, but of sound mind and disposing memory (for which I thank God) and calling to mind the uncertainty of human life, and being desirous to dispose of all such worldly substance as it has pleased God to bless me with, I give, devise, and bequeath the same in manner following, that is to say:

Ist. I desire that all my just debts and funeral expenses be paid out of my perishable property, by my executrix hereinafter named.

2ndly. After the payment of my debts and funeral expenses, I give, devise and bequeath to my wife, Mary Lincoln, all my real and personal estate to dispose of as she may think proper.

3rdly and lastly. I do hereby constitute and appoint my beloved wife, Mary Lincoln, my sole executrix of this my last will and testament, hereby revoking all others or former wills or testaments, by me heretofore made. In witness whereof I have hereunto set my hand and seal this the 22nd day of April in the Year of our Lord, 1816.

Signed, Sealed, Published and Declared to be the last will and testament of the above named Isaac Lincoln, in the presence of us, who at his request and in his presence have hereunto subscribed our names as witnesses to same.

(Signed) ISAAC LINCOLN.

GEORGE W. CARTER.
GODFREY CARRIGER.
DANIEL STOVER.
CHRISTIAN CARRIGER.

2. THE WILL OF MARY LINCOLN

I, Mary Lincoln, of the County of Carter in the State of Tennessee, being of sound mind and memory, though weak of body, and being anxious to dispose of all such worldly property as my Creator has left me with, do hereby make, ordain and establish this as my last will and testament. I give my soul to God who created it, hoping that He will receive and bless me in a world of happiness hereafter; and when I shall have departed this life, I desire that my executor hereinafter named shall give my body a decent and Christian burial.

First. I will, give, devise and bequeath to Campbell Crow, the lower plantation, it being the one on which he now lives, adjoining the lands of Alfred M. Carter on the West and South, and of John Carriger on the East.

Second. I will, give, and bequeath to Phoebe Crow, wife of Campbell Crow, my negro girl, Margaret and her four children, to wit, Lucy, Mina, Martin and Mahalla.

Third. I will, give, devise and bequeath to William Stover, the plantation on which I now live, with all the hereditaments appurtenances to the same belonging, the said plantation supposed to be composed of two different parcels and adjoining John Carriger's home plantation and believed also to adjoin the land of Alfred M. Carter on the South and bounded on the East and North by Watauga River.

I give the said plantation to the said William Stover, to have, hold and enjoy during his life and at his death to descend to his heirs.

Fourth I will, give, and bequeath to William Stover, the following negroes, to wit, Patsy (a negro girl) and her two children, Cynthia and Landon; also negro woman, Jane and her two children Sam and Tom; also negro woman Mary and her six children, to wit, Elizabeth, Campbell, Margaret, Charlotte, Delphy and Bill; also Cæsar and Lucy, to whom I desire the said William Stover to permit to remain during their lives on the plantation which I have hereinbefore bequeathed to him. It is my will that the said Stover, so long as the said Cæsar and Lucy continue to live, shall clothe and support them. I also give and bequeath to the said William Stover, to wit, George, Phoebe, Eliza, children of Lucy, whom I wish the said William Stover to remain on the home plantation that they may take care of the aforesaid negroes, Cæsar and Lucy during their lives.

I also give and bequeath the following other negroes to the said William Stover, to wit, Esther, and her seven children, that is to say, Lavisa, Violet, Juba, Lucinda, Mary, Lewis, and Phoeba. I also give and bequeath to the said William Stover, two other negroes, to wit, William and Isaac, children of Lucy.

Fifth. I also give, devise and bequeath to the said William Stover, all my horses, cattle, hogs and sheep, my wagon, all my farming utensils, my household and kitchen furniture and all the debts, dues and demands which may be owing to me at the time of my decease.

Sixth. I also will, give and bequeath to Campbell Crow my interest in any crop which he may have attended for himself upon my land, or which he may be attending for himself upon my land at the time of my decease.

Seventh. I also will, give and bequeath to William Stover all the grain of every description which I own at the time of my death.

Eighth. I will, give and devise and bequeath to Christian Carriger, Senior, the following negroes, to wit: Negro woman Letty and five of her children, to wit, Christy, Tennessee, Mordecai, Nathaniel, and also said Letty's youngest child.

Ninth. I will, give and devise to Mary Lincoln Carriger, daughter of Christian Carriger, Senior, two negro girls, children of Letty, to wit, Sarah, Seraphina and Ann.

Tenth. I will, devise, give and bequeath to William Stover all the other real and personal estate, not hereinbefore specifically named of which I may be possessed, or the owner at the time of my decease.

Eleventh. I require the said William Stover out of the estate herein bequeathed to him to pay and discharge all the honest debts or claims which I may be owing or which may be against me at the time of my death.

Lastly. I do hereby constitute, nominate and appoint the said William Stover the executor of this my last will and testament, and it is my will that the said William Stover be not required to give any security for the discharge of his duties as executor of this my last will and testament.

In testimony whereof I have hereunto set my hand and seal this the 27th day of April in the Year of our Lord, one thousand eight hundred and thirty four.

her

Mary   X   Lincoln (Seal).

mark

Signed, sealed and acknowledged in the presence of

Thos. A. R. Nelson

A. M. Carter

A. W. Taylor.

3. THE FAMILY OF ISAAC LINCOLN

Memoranda of James G. Jenkins, Elizabethton, Tenn., from letters in 1914 and 1915, to D. J. Knotts.

I went to see L. W. Hampton, a grandson of Johnson Hampton, the horse-trader you spoke of. He says he had always understood that his grandfather, Johnson (not John) Hampton was a horse-trader and visited North Carolina, West Virginia and South Carolina in his travels. At the time of my call Mrs. Hampton had become a spiritualist and Mr. Hampton was getting into the business also In a short time he lost his mind over spiritualism and is now in the insane asylum. He came to me and told me that he had called up the spirit of his grandfather and his grandfather refused to talk on the subject very much. He came to the conclusion that his grandfather was the father of Abraham Lincoln.

Isaac Lincoln married Mary Ward, and my great grandfather, Daniel Stover, married also a Ward, a sister of Mary. Isaac had one child and it was drowned when very young. They took my great uncle, William Stover and raised him, and at Mrs. Lincoln's death he inherited most of their estate. They were wealthy for their day. William Stover married Miss Sarah Drake, who claimed to be a descendant of Sir Francis Drake. The Stovers came to Tennessee from Pennsylvania and were of German descent. They were Baptists.

There is a tradition that Abraham Lincoln was born here and his parents took him to Kentucky when a babe in their arms. There was a cabin on the side of Lynn Mountain, near Isaac's residence, where Tom lived. Dr. Nat Hyder, who has been dead many years, gathered up much history and he contended that Abe was born here and was taken to Kentucky, when a babe.

This valley was settled by God-fearing people. At first the Presbyterians predominated, but the Baptists, being more evangelical, grew faster. Now the Baptists predominate, with Methodists second in numbers.

No family stood higher here than the Stovers. I never heard of one of their women going astray. They were noted for their purity. Colonel Daniel Stover married Miss Mary Johnson, daughter of President Andrew Johnson. My grandfather was Solomon Hendrix Stover, son of Daniel Stover and brother of William Stover.

I am under the impression that Abraham Lincoln was born here, but of course have no way to prove it. Of course Kentucky claims him.

4 ABRAHAM LINCOLN'S ACCOUNT OF HIS GRANDFATHER
AND UNCLES

In a letter addressed to David Lincoln, of Virginia, and written from Washington, April 2, 1848, and included in his works edited by Nicolay and Hay, Vol. I., page 117, Abraham Lincoln said, among other things:

There is no longer any doubt that your Uncle Abraham and my grandfather was the same man. His family did reside in Washington County, Kentucky, just as you say you found them, in 1801 or 1802 The oldest son, Uncle Mordecai, near twenty years ago, removed from Kentucky to Hancock County, Illinois, where within a year or two afterward he died, and where his surviving children now live His two sons there now are Abraham and Mordecai, and their postoffice is La Harp

Uncle Josiah, farther back than my recollection, went from Kentucky to Blue River, Indiana. . . .

My father, Thomas, is still living in Coles County, Illinois, being in the seventy-first year of his age. His postoffice is Charleston, Coles County, Illinois I am his only child. I am in my fortieth year and live in Springfield, Sangamon County, Illinois.

I think my father has told me that his grandfather had four brothers, Isaac, Jacob, John and Thomas. Is this correct? And which of them was your father? Are any of them alive? I am quite sure that Isaac resided on Watauga, near a point where Tennessee and Virginia join, and that he has been dead more than twenty, perhaps thirty years Also that Thomas removed to Kentucky, near Lexington, where he died a good many years ago.

APPENDIX X

HANKS MEMORANDA

I. THE WILL OF LUKE HANKS

In the name of God, Amen, I Luke Hanks of South Carolina, Pendleton County, being now in a weake and low state of health but sound of memory do make this my last will and testament this twenty first day of May seventeen hundred and eighty nine in maner and for following viz.

Imperimus I bequeath my sole to allmighty God in hopes of a blessed and glorious reserrection thro the merits of Jesus Christ my savior and my body to the Earth to have a decent and Christian Burial at the charge of my executors and as touching and concerning such worldly goods as it hath pleased God to bestow upon me I give bequeath dispose them in the maner and form following in the first place I will that my just debts and funeral charges be pade.

Item I give and bequeath to my dear and well beloved wife Ann Hanks all my hole estate real and personal during her natural life and at her death to be equally divide among all my children and if any of my children should marry I will that my wife may dispose of any of my estate to them toward their sustenance but shall be accounted for at her death to rest of the children and lastly I constitute and ordain my loving wife, Anne Hanks executrix and my friend John Haynie executor of this my last will and testament sind with my hand and sealed with my seal the day and year within written.

his
LUKE X HANKS.
mark

In presence of
BLAKE MAULDIN
JOHN REAVES.

Note apparently by Clerk of Court:

There is no papers with the will showing what disposition was made of the land.

2. INVENTORY AND APPRAISEMENT OF ESTATE OF LUKE HANKS,
DECEASED

Recorded in Book No 1, page 106, Records of Probate Court of Abbeville County, South Carolina; furnished by J F Miller, Judge of Probate, January 17, 1911, and certified with seal of the Court.

I. *Inventory.*

We the underscribers in obedience to our order of the Court of Abbeville County to us directed, do make the following inventory and appraisment of the estate of Luke Hanks, deceased, to wit:

	L	S	d
2 Cows and Calves—74/—One Steer—35/—One Heifer 20/	6	9	8
1 Mare and Colt—150/—One Bay Filly—80/. .	11	10	0
2 Bells—5/6—6 Hogs—at 10/ each 60/—4 Shoats—12/	3	17	6
1 Feather Bed & Furniture—120/—1 do do—160—do—do—60	17	0	0
1 Chest—12/6—1 Table 3/—1 Churn—3/—1 Tub 2/—	1	0	6
2 Sad Irons—4/—2 Hammers—3/—1 Pr—Nippers—1/—	0	8	0
Table Utencils—12/—Parcel of plantation tools —39/	2	11	0
2 Iron—& Hooks & other kitchen furniture	2	9	0
A Parcel of Pewter & Tin—45/—1 Muskett Gun —17/6	3	2	6
A Parcel of Leather—57/—1 Cotton Wheel—2/ Cards 17/4	3¹	14	4
2 Water Pails—& 2 Piggon—7/	0	7	0
1 Tract of land—210 acres—	42	0	0
2 Razor Hones & Strap	0	10	0

Given under our hands and seals this 6 day of August, 1792—

STEPHEN WILLIS
JOHN READ LONG
JAMES NASH

South Carolina,
Stephen Willis, James Nash and John Read Long appeared before me and being duly sworn to appraise the estate Real and

personal, of Luke Hanks, deceased, that shall be shown them by Ann Hanks, executrix, and John Haynie, executor.

Sworn to this 6th day of September, 1792.

ELIJAH BROWNE, P-J

II. *Probation of Will, Luke Hanks, deceased.*

STATE OF CAROLINA, }
ABBEVILLE COUNTY, to wit. }

In open Court this seventh day of October One thousand seven hundred and eighty nine Personally came Blake Mauldin, one of the witnesses to the above will, and made oath that he saw Luke Hanks, deceased, sign, seal, publish, pronounce and declare the same to be his last will and testament, and that he was then of sound and perfect mind, memory and understanding to the best of Deponents knowledge and belief and that John Reaves together with this deponent did subscribe their names thereto as witnesses, in the present of the testator and at his request, and in the presence of each other—Certified by order of Court the day and date above written.

JOHN BROWN, C.C

Ann Hanks, the executrix, and John Hainey, the executor, named in the above will took the oath of executors of said will in open Court of Abbeville County the seventh of October, 1789

(Seal of Probate Court.)

III. *Extract from Letter, J. F. Miller, Probate Judge* December 30, 1910.

I find among the papers pertaining to the said estate the following papers; to wit; the will of testator, the Appraise Warrant, the Appraise Bill.

The testator does not give the name of his children

The personal property was appraised at 100 pounds—$500. Real Estate—210 acres—42 pounds—$210 Date of appraisements August 6, 1792.   J. F. MILLER.

Note.—It is important to notice that Judge Miller says, and these documents show, that Luke Hanks does not name his children —W. E. B.

3. THE WILL OF JOSEPH HANKS

In the name of God Amen. I Joseph Hanks of Nelson County, State of Kentucky, being of sound mind and memory, but weak in body, and calling to mind the frailty of all human nature, do make and devise this my last will and testament in the manner and form following, to wit:

Item   I give and bequeath unto my son Thomas one sorrel horse called " Major ".

Item   I give and bequeath unto my son Joshua one gray mare called " Bonny ".

Item   I give and bequeath unto my son William one gray horse called " Gilbert ".

Item.   I give and bequeath unto my son Charles one roan horse called " Dove ".

Item.   I give and bequeath unto my son Joseph one sorrel horse called " Bald " Also the land whereon I now live containing one hundred and fifty acres

Item.   I give and bequeath unto my daughter Elizabeth one heifer yearling called " Gentle."

Item.   I give and bequeath to my daughter Polly one heifer yearling called " Lady."

Item.   I give and bequeath unto my daughter Nancy one heifer yearling called " Piedy "

Item.   I give and bequeath unto my wife Nancy all and singular my whole estate during her life Afterwards to be equally divided between all my children.

It is also my will and desire that the whole of the property above bequeathed should be the property of my wife during her life.

And lastly I constitute ordain and appoint my wife Nancy as Executrix of and Executrix to this my last will and testament.

Signed, sealed and delivered in presence of us this eighth day of January, One thousand seven hundred and ninety three

his

JOSEPH   X   HANKS (seal)

mark

ISSAC LANSDALE
JOHN DAVIS
PETER ATHERTON.

At a court begun and held for Nelson County on Tuesday the fourteenth day of May, 1793 This last will and testament of Joseph Hanks dec'd was produced in court and sworn to by William Hanks, one of the executors therein named and was proved by the oaths of Isaac Lansdale and John Davis, subscribing witnesses thereto, and ordered to be recorded.

Attest   BEN GRAYSON, Clerk.

A Copy

Attest   MORGAN GILKEY, Clerk

Nelson County Court, November 10, 1913

4. NOTES ON THE HANKS FAMILY

From Letters of Mrs. J. T. Manon (Mary Ellen Hanks, daughter of John Hanks), with some assistance from her cousin Mrs. M. E. Jordan, in letters to D. J. Knotts, February and March, 1913, and July 11 and October 27, 1913.

SUMMARY OF INFORMATION.

I am a daughter of John Hanks, who split rails with Abraham Lincoln and carried the rails into the Republican Convention in 1860.

I was born in Illinois in 1844, married Dec. 31, 1868, to J. T. Manon, and removed to Humbolt County, California, November 1875.

My father's father lived near the Falls of Rough Creek, Kentucky. His name was William Hanks.

My father, John Hanks, was born near the Falls of Rough, Ky., February 9, 1802; married Susan Malindy Wilson. He moved to Illinois in 1826, and died July 1, 1889, near Decatur.

My mother, Susan Malindy Hanks, was born Feb. 14, 1804, and died March 11, 1865, in Macon County, Illinois.

John and Susan Hanks were parents of the following children:
William, married
Louis
Jane
Phelix
Emily Grayson
Mary Ellen
Levi

The children of William(?) and   Hanks were:
Sons: Charles married a Miss Morehead
John (my father) married Susan Malindy Wilson
James
William married Polly Young
Joseph married Sarah Freeman
Jackson
Daughters: Nancy married a Mr. Miller
Celia married a Mr. Dunham
Lucy or Lucinda married a Mr. Douglas
Elizabeth or Betsy married a Mr. Ray and afterward a Mr. Dillen.

I remember hearing Father speak of the Sparrows and Shipleys, but know nothing definite about them.

My grandfather was a shoemaker and a farmer. He died in Sangamon Co , Ill.

I knew Dennis Hanks very well. He was a shoemaker, and a first(?) cousin of my father. I think his mother was a sister of Lincoln's mother.

I know nothing definite about the Friend family

Dennis was one of those stray boys who often come into the world with no known father. He took the name of Hanks from his mother. His mother was a cousin of John Hanks

John Hanks was a Universalist until a few years before his death when he joined the Disciples Some of my brothers belonged to the Baptist Church; one sister to the Congregational; one to the United Brethren. I belong to the Methodists.

I know nothing about our distant relatives

My uncles were rather above the medium height; so was my father, who weighed about 200 pounds

My cousin, Mrs. M. E. Jordan, is a daughter of my father's sister Lucy or Lucinda. Her maiden name was Douglas.

Mr Knotts has made a pencil note on Mrs. Manon's letter with reference to her grandfather's name. At first she was not sure if it was Joseph or Thomas. Later, after conferring with Mrs. Jordan, they agreed that it was William Mr Knotts says that records show that William's wife was Betty, and the Historical Society says it was Elizabeth Hall

Mrs. Manon's statement that her father was first cousin to Dennis Hanks appears to be contradicted by the statement that his mother was a cousin of John Hanks. John and Dennis were not first cousins; Mrs. Manon is mistaken about this, and appears to be correct in saying that Nancy, the mother of Dennis, was John's first cousin. However, the question is difficult, and I have not been able, with the information now available, to reach a conclusion in these matters. I give these memoranda for whatever they are worth

The article in *The Atlantic Monthly* for February, 1920, by Mr. Arthur E. Morgan, a prominent civil engineer of Dayton, Ohio, told a very interesting story of Mr Morgan's travels in the Ozarks and of his meeting with certain representatives of the Hanks family; and also of his securing additional information through a friend, who, as I now learn from Mr. Morgan, was then Miss Lucy Griscom, and is now Mrs. Arthur E Morgan, on a journey to Oregon, where she met other representatives of the Hanks family. The following is my own summary of the genealogical part of Mr. Morgan's article:

THE HANKS FAMILY.
As disclosed by Mr Arthur E. Morgan in *Atlantic* for February, 1920.

SARAH, or POLLY HANKS, sister of Lincoln's mother, never married, but had six children, *inter alia,* SOPHIE, who died in November, 1895. Her three children were living in different parts of the Ozarks in 1909.

These three children of SOPHIE HANKS were children of at least two different fathers, one of whom was named Lynch. The other's name is not given. It is not stated whether she was married to either or both of these men.

Of only one of SOPHIE HANKS' children is much detail given, and his surname is not stated.

These three children are:

1. JOHN LYNCH, who lived east of Iron Mountain, Mo. Very old, memory failing. He was a voter in 1861, and voted against Lincoln, and is thus older than the son who was Mr. Morgan's chief source of information

2. Mrs. NANCY DAVIDSON, maiden name not given, living in 1909 with her husband at Limestone Valley, Ark.

3 "THE DOCTOR" born in Dubois County, Indiana, December 26, 1843; his name withheld. In spring of 1847 he moved from Indiana to St. Francis County, Mo. Taught school, served in Civil War, and "practiced physic" living in Jasper, Ark., 1874-1909 since when he has lived in Harrison, Ark., having given up his practice. The Doctor is Mr. Morgan's chief source of information concerning Lincoln's school days in Indiana, and his information is in essential accord with such as we already have, and confirms that of Dennis Hanks, our best witness on the youth of Lincoln, though he is none too good. The Doctor's information is through his mother, Sophie Hanks.

The Doctor said his grandmother, Sarah or Polly Hanks, and Nancy Hanks, Lincoln's mother, were half-sisters, and also cousins. This means that one man, President Lincoln's grandfather, had relations with the two Hanks sisters, Polly and Nancy. If so much as that was known in the Hanks family, more must have been known. What was the name of this man?

The article interested me much, and raised more questions than it answered.

Mr. Morgan has generously given me all the information which he has been able to secure. I regret that it does not answer the more important of my questions. He gives the name of "The Doctor" as James Legrand, and says that on the question of the father of Nancy Hanks he could obtain no additional information:

Referring to the Doctor's remark that Nancy Hanks, and Sarah, or Polly, were half-sisters, also cousins, I have no information beyond that contained in the *Atlantic* article and the notes inclosed In many cases interesting facts were lost. Sometimes the Doctor or his wife were willing to fill in the gaps, but when I questioned them closely, I found they were uncertain I last heard from the Doctor indirectly in January, 1920, at which time he was very sick with pneumonia. Letters to his wife have not been answered I am at present making an effort to get in touch with the family, and hope to be able to supply this information soon.

The Doctor had 18 half-sisters and brothers, and one whole sister, nineteen in all

The information obtained by Miss Griscom, now Mrs. Morgan, is from John T Hanks, son of Dennis Hanks, and grandson of Mrs. Sarah Bush Lincoln. He said to her

"Abe Lincoln's step-mother was my grandmother," which was true. John was born in Indiana in 1828, and was one of the sixteen people who went to Illinois in 1830. He was sure that Abraham Lincoln's mother died, not in Indiana, but in Kentucky. He was sure the poverty of Abe in his boyhood had been exaggerated; Abe did not need to read by the light of pine-knots, since there were candles abundant from the family's own hogs.[1]

In the same place in Oregon lived James Lewis Hanks, a son of John Hanks. He and John T. were rivals in their stories about their intimacy with Abraham Lincoln.

Miss Griscom compiled in a family tree their joint knowledge of their lineage. Mr Morgan calls attention to manifest errors in it, and they lie plain on the face of it It is very well worth reproducing here, however, for it shows that in the memory of these two old men, one the son of John Hanks and the other the son of Dennis, Nancy Hanks was legitimate.

The family, as these two men gave the data to Miss Griscom,

---

[1] Did people make candles from the lard of hogs? The author does not remember candles of that character

was descended from Joseph and Nancy Hanks. They gave the names of five children of this couple:

1. *William Hanks*, father of John Hanks, who split rails with Lincoln; who had, at the time of this interview, two living children, James Lewis Hanks, of Canyonville, Oregon, and Mrs. Mary Ellen Hanon, of Eureka, California

2. *Nancy Hanks*, who married Thomas Lincoln and became the mother of Abraham.

3. *Sarah Hanks*, who married M. M Broun, and who had a living daughter, Mrs. Billy Carrol, of Portland, Oregon.

4. *Lucy Hanks*, mother of Dennis. Dennis married Sarah Johnston, daughter of the step-mother of President Lincoln; and had four living children when this interview was had,—Mrs. Harriet Chapman, of Charleston, Illinois; Mrs. Amanda Porman, of Matoon, Illinois; John T. Hanks, of Day's Creek, Oregon, who had eleven children, all scattered; and Theophilus Hanks, of Denver, Colorado.

5. *"Mrs. Sparrow."* John T. Hanks said that Mr. Sparrow brought Dennis up as his own son, and left him his property; which is doubtless correct.

This is all the information which Mr. Morgan could procure for me up to July 2, 1920. It is not all reliable, but it is valuable to any one who is to work on the Hanks family, and is given here, with thanks to Mr. Morgan, for whatever it may be worth.

As this book goes to press, I have a letter from Mrs. Legrand, wife of " The Doctor." He is seriously ill, probably with tuberculosis, and not expected to recover. Mr. Morgan did well to obtain the information when he did. Mrs. Legrand makes one correction. " My husband is not first cousin, but second cousin, of Abe Lincoln. Abe and the Doctor's mother were not sisters, but first cousins."

APPENDIX XI

WAS ABRAHAM LINCOLN A GERMAN?

In 1901 a paper was read before the Fifteenth Annual Meeting of the Society of Germans in Maryland, by Louis Paul Hennighausen, in which he endeavored to prove that Abraham Lincoln was of German descent. The argument was based largely on the fact that the name Lincoln is found in several documents spelled "Linkhorn," which, the writer claimed, is a German name. He held, with considerable skill of argument, that this name had been Anglicized into Lincoln and a false pedigree manufactured to fit the change. The ancestors of the President, as he set forth, came from Pennsylvania into Virginia, and he maintained that they were originally Pennsylvania Germans.

This paper was published in the proceedings of the German Society and it attracted wide attention. The Germans claim Shakespeare; why not Lincoln?

Ingenious as was the argument of Herr Hennighausen, it was utterly fallacious. The name Lincoln is a good, old English name, and it has been traced back, generation by generation, through Kentucky, Virginia, Pennsylvania, and New Jersey, to Massachusetts and thence to England, and President Lincoln's right to use it in its original spelling is incontestable.

Moreover, no German name Linkhorn has been found in Pennsylvania, nor has any family connection been traced whereby a German family of any like name could have quartered arms with the family of Abraham Lincoln

The Hennighausen argument is fully answered in a book entitled *Abraham Lincoln An American Migration*, published, 1909, by William J. Campbell, of Philadelphia The author is Marion Dexter Learned, Professor of the Germanic Languages and Literature in the University of Pennsylvania.

The typical American is often represented as necessarily of mixed nationality; Abraham Lincoln's claim to be fairly representatitve of the life of his nation cannot be based upon any such admixture. While we are not able to trace with complete

certainty the ancestral line of Nancy Hanks, we have no reason
to believe that she was on either side of other than Virginia blood.
The Hanks line is Anglo-Saxon, unmixed so far as we know,
through its generations in the colonies, with families other than
those of English descent. Thomas Lincoln was on both sides, of
pure Anglo-Saxon blood. Both families came originally from
New England through Virginia into the western country. In
coming down through Pennsylvania either family might have
intermarried with the Pennsylvania Germans, but so far as we
know neither family did. The hardy Scotch-Irish stock which
contributed so worthily to the conquest of the wilderness and to
the population of the hill country of Kentucky, yielded so far as
we are informed no single drop of its warm red blood to the life
of Abraham Lincoln Few American families have been traced
with greater care than his, and so far as we know he was in every
line of his ancestry American of pure Anglo-Saxon descent.

INDEX

411

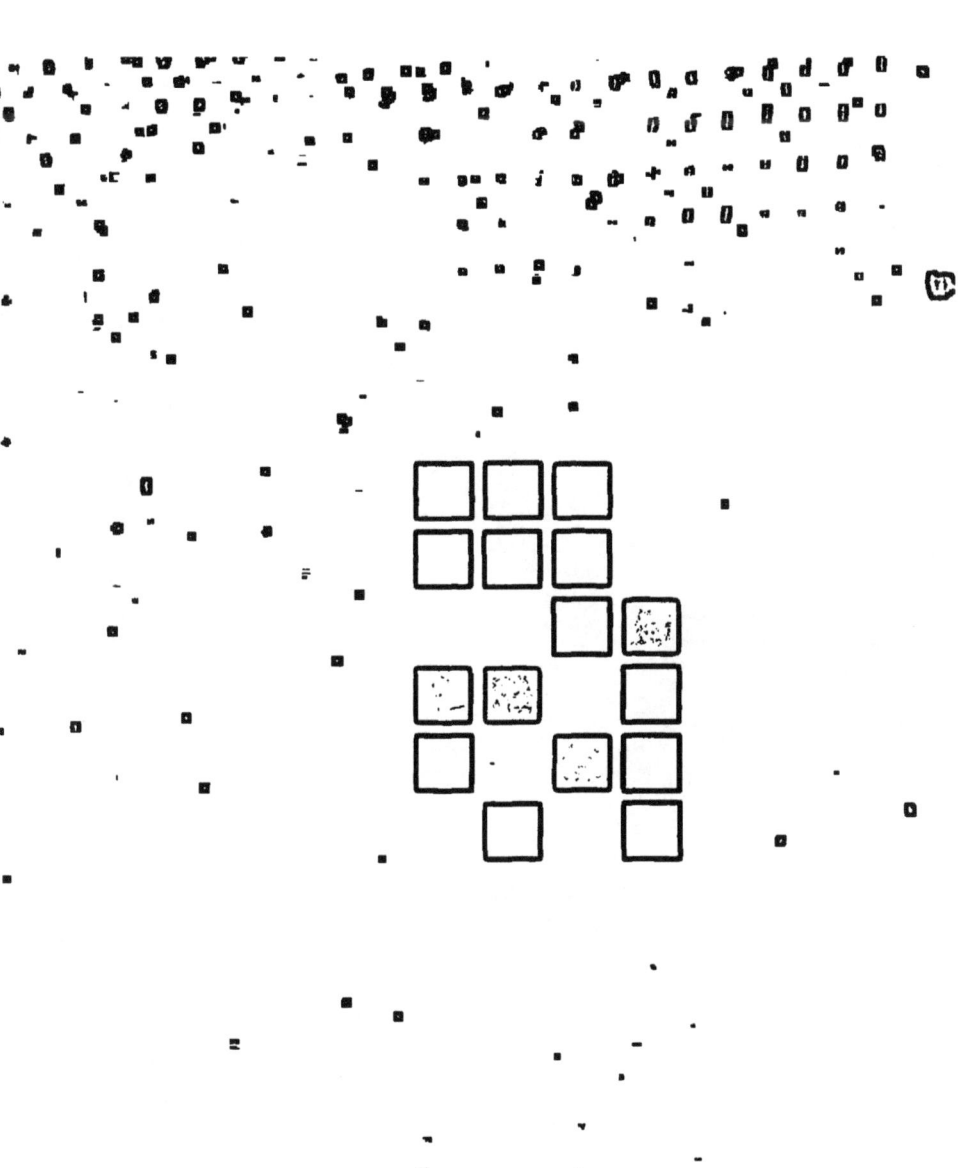

CPSIA information can be obtained
at www.ICGtesting.com
Printed in the USA
LVHW021243070620
657607LV00008B/859